WILLIAM GOLDMAN:
FOUR SCREENPLAYS

WILLIAM GOLDMAN:

FOUR SCREENPLAYS

With Essays

MARATHON MAN • BUTCH CASSIDY
AND THE SUNDANCE KID •
THE PRINCESS BRIDE • MISERY

An Applause Original
WILLIAM GOLDMAN: FOUR SCREENPLAYS

New Material Copyright © 1995 by William Goldman

Butch Cassidy and The Sundance Kid - Copyright © 1969 by William Goldman. Distributed by Twentieth Century Fox Film Corporation.

Marathon Man – Copyright © 1976 by Paramount Pictures. Based on the novel copyright ©1974 by William Goldman. Used by permission of Paramount Pictures Corporation and of Dell Books, a division of Bantam Doubleday Dell Publishing Group Inc.

The Princess Bride – Copyright © 1987 by The Princess Bride Limited, released by Twentieth Century Fox Film Corporation. Based on the novel copyright © 1973 by William Goldman published by Harcourt Brace Jovanovich. Used by permission.

Misery – Copyright © 1990 by Castle Rock Entertainment. Based on the novel by Stephen King. Copyright © 1987 by Stephen King, Tabitha King and Arthur B. Greene Trustee. Published by Viking Penguin Inc. Used by permission.

ISBN: 1-55783-265-X

Library of Congress Cataloging-in-Publication Data

Goldman, William, 1931-
    William Goldman : Four Screenplays
            p.   cm.
    Contents: Marathon Man — Butch Cassidy — The Princess Bride — Misery.
    ISBN 1-55783-265-X
    I. Motion picture plays — United States. I. Title.
PS3557.0384A6   1994
791.43'75'0973—dc20
                                                                                        94-39988
                                                                                        CIP

British Library Cataloging-in-Publication

A catalogue record for this book is available from the British Library.

First Applause Paperback Printing 1997

Applause Theatre & Cinema Books
19 West 21st Street, Suite 201
New York, NY 10010
Phone: (212) 575-9265
Fax: (212) 575-9270
Email: info@applausepub.com
Internet: www.applausepub.com

Applause books are available through your local bookstore, or you may order at www.applausepub.com or call Music Dispatch at 800-637-2852

Sales & Distribution:
North America:
    Hal Leonard Corp.
    7777 West Bluemound Road
    P.O. Box 13819
    Milwaukee, WI 53213
    Phone: (414) 774-3630
    Fax: (414) 774-3259
    Email: halinfo@halleonard.com
    Internet: www.halleonard.com

Europe:
Roundhouse Publishing Ltd.
Millstone, Limers Lane
Northam, North Devon
EX 39 2RG
Phone: 01237-474474
Fax: 01237-474774
Email: roundhouse.group@ukgateway.net

CONTENTS

INTRODUCTION

Butch Cassidy changed my life.

I don't believe I had ever so much as seen a screenplay until I was thirty-three years old. I had been a professional writer by that time for close to ten years. I had written a bunch of short stories (my rejection slip collection was well over a hundred). I had been involved with three plays (all three reached Broadway, all flopped). I had written five novels (all of them published, three sold over a million each in paperback).

Whatever the quality, that's the start of a career.

My connection with the movie business amounted to this: two of the books, *Soldier in the Rain* and *No Way to Treat a Lady* had been made into films. I had written the screenplay of neither, hadn't been asked to, never dreamt of doing otherwise.

Then, in 1964, Cliff Robertson asked me to write a screenplay. I did, sent it to him, was fired. That was it for my movie career. An interesting experience if not an altogether satisfying one. I certainly had no intention of trying it again. Why would I? It was not what I did and the whole experience was nothing but an aberration.

Then a producer who had read *Boys and Girls Together* met with me, said that he wanted to produce a movie with balls. I suggested he read some Ross Macdonald, the author of the brilliant Lew Archer series of detective novels. He did, said he liked them, so I said I would find one and turn it into a movie on spec (meaning speculation, meaning not getting paid until after the work was done. I was not being altruistic. I always worked that way then, did for the first twenty years of my career as a novelist). The script eventually was named *Harper*, became a movie starring Paul Newman, was a hit.

Good for the Jews, of course, but just another aberration, though a happier one.

Another producer asked me to try a screenplay of a wonderful World War II novel, *In the Spring the War Ended*, by Stephen Linakis. The producer liked the script, gave it to a top director, Martin Ritt. He liked it too. So did the studio that owned the property, Fox. The book was very anti-war and anti-military and dealt with a bunch of deserters trying to survive in Europe just after the end of the Second World War. We wanted Steve McQueen for the main deserter and Bridgitte Bardot for the prostitute he got involved with.

Neither of them said no.

Neither of them said yes, either.

Neither of them saw it. Fox buried the project because they were about to embark on a giant World War II epic, *Patton*, and they told us they needed all the military help they could get to make it work. The Pentagon's enthusiasm, they felt, might have been damaged had they also proceeded with the Linakis film. I had spent two years of my life in the Pentagon (by mistake), but I still had no way of knowing if Fox was right in their decision or not. What I did know for certain was this: they were, every one of them, fucking *nuts* in Hollywood.

I went back to being what I was, a novelist.

But in my head was this story I'd read about years before, maybe in the late Fifties, about these two outlaws in the Old West. Throughout the Sixties, I read whatever I could about them. (There wasn't a whole lot then. The cottage industry surrounding Butch and Sundance didn't get started until the movie was released in the Fall of '69, after which their story went across the world.)

Why didn't I write a novel instead of a screenplay? First, I had no idea early on I would ever write it at all. It was just this haunting story. But I knew even then I would never make a novel of it. Why? Easy answer: I don't like horses.

I don't much like anything dealing with the reality of that world. And the notion of spending months doing research so I'd be dead accurate on just what a man could really do with a six-gun, how you cooked what you ate when you were on the run, how the Superposse was formed, outfitted and trained—inconceivable, as Vizzini was wont to say.

Why not write a screenplay, I thought?

So I did. In Princeton, New Jersey, where I was teaching (by accident) over Christmas vacation of 1965/66. And there is no question in my mind that if I had liked horses, if I had written a novel, the movie never happens. Because when the screenplay first went out, every studio turned it down. The book would have been similarly received.

But I wrote the screenplay, and as I said, it changed everything. Because after *Butch*, for the first time, I knew that writing for the screen was going to be a part of my life. The experience had been so remarkable. I had no idea then that George Roy Hill would be the most brilliant director I would ever work with. I had no idea then that casts like that don't happen every Tuesday. I had no idea then it would be the greatest commercial success of my career. I assumed it was normal to meet for two months on a daily basis with the director. I thought two weeks of rehearsal was s.o.p. I figured each movie I wrote would have the screenplay treated with care, would have stars who worked hard to make what I had written work, before pitching it .

I have just had a memory. (Truly.) I am maybe nine or ten and at camp and I am coming back from my first all-day horseback ride. I remember I hurt so much that, at the end of the trip, I clambered down from the horse and ran the last fifty yards to the tack house. All I can say now is that almost my entire career was because of a pain in the ass.

Make of that what you will...

*

One of the problems inherent in any screenplay book is this: which draft do you publish? With a novel or a piece of non-fiction, what happens is I write the book, then I meet with the editor, talk, make changes. My stuff is pretty close to the published version when it comes out of the typewriter, because I can't write until I know what I'm doing, so it's often in my head before I can put it down.

I make the changes and then I fiddle. That can take weeks, months, whatever. But the second draft is pretty much it. When the book comes in galleys, I fiddle some more. But nothing major. Over and out.

Totally different with a movie. And not only because of the group nature of the enterprise. Things just evolve. I don't know why—maybe because so much time passes during the setting up of a production. I think it is safe to say that after the first draft, which belongs to the writer, any other name given to any other version of the screenplay until serious pre-production is totally a matter of contract.

When a screenwriter is hired, he has a contract, and in that contract is a payment schedule. This much for commencement of work, that much for first draft delivery. And these contracts also have payment schedules for the rest of the required second and third drafts. Studio has four weeks in which to request changes, writer has four weeks to expedite said changes, blah de blah.

But the screenplay itself, understand, is always fluid.

When you start into actual pre-production, that's when things get crazy. The work is still totally fluid, and the reason a version is run off and titled is so all the technicians can know they are working on exactly the same material. For example, I happen to have a reasonably complete set of *Misery*. Remember what follows may seem like madness, and of course, it is. But it is not unusual.

First Draft	November	1988
Second Draft	January	1989
Third Draft		
(First Pass)	June	1989
Third Draft	July	1989
Fourth Draft	October 13	1989
Fifth Draft	October 18	1989
(Revised)	October 20 (pink)	1989
(Revised)	October 24 (yellow)	1989
(Revised)	October 31 (blue)	1989
(Revised)	November 2 (salmon)	1989
(Revised)	November 3 (green)	1989
(Revised)	November 6 (grey)	1989
(Revised)	November 17	1989
(Revised)	December 4 (pink)	1989
(Revised)	December 8 (yellow)	1989
(Revised)	December 21 (blue)	1989
(Revised)	January 12 (green)	1990
(Revised)	February 13 (salmon)	1990
(Revised)	February 15 (pink)	1990
(Revised)	February 16 (yellow)	1990
(Revised)	April 5 (green)	1990

This is all I have. There may have been a few more. But this should give you the idea. Twenty-one drafts over eighteen months. To answer a few questions: Each new draft is not an entirely new screenplay. More than likely a scene has been added or deleted. These new pages use different colors so they can be referred to quickly. When they run out of colors they do an all white one again, as they did on November 17th.

Think of all movies as being like a Broadway musical in trouble on the road. Bad jokes are cut one night. That's one version. Hopefully better jokes are put in the next. Still another. The goddam lazy composer finally comes up with a catchier song opening. Yet again. So it goes until the show opens and even then there is often tampering.

Movies are constantly tampered with too. Every day in editing it changes and, if it was frozen at the end of each night, that would be what might be called the 104th draft.

So please do not expect to gain either knowledge or insight from whatever draft number that you may read. *The Princess Bride* is pretty close to the finished film. *Butch Cassidy and the Sundance Kid* has some scenes included that were shot and cut. *Marathon Man* is the second draft, the first with a director's input—all the stuff dealing with cities in crisis was a notion of the director, John Schlesinger. Almost none of it made the finished film. I included the early scenes for the Roy Scheider part because they are the reason he took the role. They were cut and I suspect—I never saw them—but I suspect the film was not helped by their excision.

Misery, for a simple story, went through a remarkable number of changes. We kept delaying the revelation of Kathy Bates' madness. (Rob Reiner felt that, the minute we know she is bonkers, it becomes a different movie. In the novel you know she is a nutcase from the outset.) And we kept trying to close the loopholes in the story. All material of this kind has them, and I don't know that we got them all, but we spent over a year trying. The version here is one of the fifteen revisions of the fifth draft.

You'll have to guess the color...

BUTCH CASSIDY
AND
THE SUNDANCE KID

DIRECTOR	GEORGE ROY HILL
PRODUCERS	JOHN FOREMAN
	PAUL MONASH
CINEMATOGRAPHER	CONRAD L. HALL
EDITORS	JOHN C. HOWARD
	RICHARD C. MEYER
ART DIRECTORS	JACK MARTIN SMITH
	PHILIP JEFFERIES
MUSIC	BURT BACHARACH
ORIGINAL SCREENPLAY	WILLIAM GOLDMAN

For me it was always their story.

These two guys, travelling together for years and decades over countries and continents finally going down, wildly outnumbered, in Bolivia, but they had done what F. Scott said you couldn't do, be American and have a second act in life, because when they fell they were legends again, as famous in South America in 1911 as they had been in their great days in the Old West nearing the turn of the century.

I was moved when I first read about them, always will be. Have no idea really why. (That may sound odd but it happens to be true. Today, their journey is familiar. When I began, maybe ten people left alive had the least idea who they were.) When a great success happens—and this was certainly that—the most gratifying aspect of it for me turned out to be that what I thought was a glorious piece of narrative turned out to be the same for people around the world. It was, if you will, a validation of my sense of story.

Movies are finally, centrally, crucially, primarily *only* about story.

This is not to say I prefer *Die Hard* to *The Seventh Seal*, but you had better give a shit about that Knight's adventures, his chess battle with Death, had better want him to win, had better be locked into his travels, or the movie is just another exercise in style that we can't remember if we saw or not. Sure, Welles did amazing work with the Kane material, but *Citizen Kane* tells a fabulous story.

Movies must tell a compelling story or they stop existing in our minds. Stanley Kubrick once said this: "a good story is a miracle." By good story he meant, oh, maybe something with an interesting premise that develops logically and builds to a satisfying and surprising climax.

Do you know how hard that is?

It just kills us, people who try and storytell to survive. Maybe once, maybe two or three times in a lifetime we get away with it, have the experience of riding confidently atop our material, not praying we can skill our way clear of the falseness, the tricks we hope work so you won't turn away from us with the writer's equivalent of scorn, which is boredom.

For me, I got away with it twice, *Butch* and *Princess Bride*. I'm not saying I'm right, understand. I'm not attributing quality to either of them—I would never do that to anything I've written—but I can look at those two and say, I don't give a fuck what you think, these are mine.

One of the great true Cassidy stories was when he was young and in jail in Wyoming, I think it was, and he came up for parole and the Governor met with him and said, "I'll parole you if you'll promise to go straight." And Butch thought a moment and then said this: "I can't do that." In the stunned silence he went on: "But I'll make a deal with you—if you'll let me out, I promise never to work in Wyoming again."

And the Governor took the deal,

And Butch never robbed in Wyoming again.

Even today, that's probably the best character introduction I ever came across. When I was researching the material, reading whatever I could for all those years, I knew this was how we would meet Butch. And that kind of building block is essential when you're stumbling through material, trying to get a grip on the best way for you to tell this particular story. The entire Superposse chase, almost half an hour of screen time, was only writable for me because I knew the Sundance Kid couldn't swim, something I'd read was true of a lot of western figures of that period. I don't know how it is for others, but building up confidence is the single hardest battle I face every day of my life.

(As I sit writing this, I know that my next asssignment is John Grisham's novel about capital punishment, *The Chamber*. It is now July and the first draft is due October 15th and I will get it in on October 15th—I have only been late once in 30 years of this madness, and then by two weeks, and there was a good reason. And I got the next draft in two weeks early. Problem with *The Chamber*: I have zero idea how to write it. I know pretty much how it ends. I know most of the characters. But I cannot figure out where it begins. And until I have that, I have no idea what the spine will be, the structure. Since I don't know the first scene, I am just as in the dark as to the second. And the third and so it goes. In truth, I don't know much of anything. And since I am totally instinctive, I can't logic my way toward what the beginning should be. Confidence, as I said, is almost everything and I have less of it each July day.)

Anyway, I've got this wondrous Governor anecdote.

And it fell out of the movie. (It's included in the prequel *Butch and Sundance, The Early Years* that Allan Burns wrote and Richard Lester directed, a nice movie which I suggest you rent because I know you haven't seen it, because *nobody* saw it when it was in release.)

It works there because they were kids when that movie takes place. But I couldn't use it because it was off the spine. The movie I wrote was about these two legends who become legends all over again in a different country. I had no time to get Butch arrested, jailed, and then offered a pardon. And no Governor with a sniff at re-election is going to release the most famous outlaw of his time. Maybe you can figure out a way to fit it in. I sure wanted to and I sure couldn't. Faulkner said one of the great things: In writing, you must kill all your darlings. I'm not sure I totally subscribe to that but I do believe this: you damn well better be willing to.

*

A brief word about what follows.

The standard screenplay form is not only unreadable, it is something far worse, it is wrong. All those capital letters and numbers which stop our eye and destroy any chance at narrative flow, have nothing to do with writing. They are for the other technicians when the movie is actually in production so they will know what scenes they are doing that day. "Oh look, guys, we're shooting Scenes 104, 106, 109 this morning." I have never used them, hate them, always will.

I try to make my screenplays as readable an experience as I can, for a good and greedy reason—I want the executives, who read them and who have the power to greenlight a flick, to say, "Hey, I can make money out of this."

Obvious truism: we all want the movies we write to get made. And that's only going to happen if someone likes the script. Executives read a guh-zillion scripts a weekend. It would be idiotic for me not to have him try and enjoy the ride.

The screenplay is a limited form, as the sonnet is limited, as plays are limited, and as the epic poem and the novel are not. We cannot ramble. We are hemmed in by length. We do not handle aging well. If we attempt philosophical dialog, we empty theatres. In fact, any dialog is suspect that doesn't push us along.

If a character tries at length to tell us who he is, if he just stands there and talks, there is no law on earth that says we have to just sit there and listen. And we won't. We can get popcorn, have a pee, snooze, whisper, leave. We can do any number of things but the one thing we won't do is listen.

It gets harder and harder today to put new twists on old twists, which is a great part of the screenwriter's task. We do it as skillfully and hopefully as we can. But that damn audience is watching us. Teenagers today see more movies in a year—at theatres, on tape, on the tube—than anyone of my generation saw the first twenty years of life. We have an audience today that is more knowledgeable about their form of choice than any audience has ever been. One of the great early movie hits was simply of a cow eating grass. I don't think Mr. Paramount would greenlight that today. As screenwriters, it is our obligation to try and surprise.

This is a moment from the *Butch Cassidy* screenplay. At the end, they are trapped and out of ammunition. Butch has to run to get more while Sundance covers him. They are surrounded by a lot of Bolivian policemen who are firing at them.

CUT TO

BUTCH, *streaking, diving again, then up, and the bullets landing around him aren't even close as we*

CUT TO

SUNDANCE, *whirling and spinning, continuing to fire and*

CUT TO

SEVERAL POLICEMEN, *dropping for safety behind the wall and*

CUT TO

BUTCH, *really moving now, dodging, diving, up again and*

CUT TO

SUNDANCE, flinging away one gun, grabbing another from his holster, continuing to turn and fire and

CUT TO

TWO POLICEMEN, falling wounded to the ground and

CUT TO

BUTCH, letting out a notch, then launching into another dive forward and

CUT TO

SUNDANCE, whirling, but you never know which way he's going to spin and

CUT TO

THE HEAD POLICEMAN cursing, forced to drop for safety behind the wall and

CUT TO

BUTCH, racing to the mules, and then he is there, grabbing at the near mule for ammunition and

CUT TO

SUNDANCE, throwing the second gun away, reaching into his holster for another, continuing to spin and fire and

CUT TO

BUTCH, and he has the ammunition now and

CUT TO

ANOTHER POLICEMAN, screaming as he falls and

CUT TO

BUTCH, his arms loaded, tearing away from the mules and they're still not even coming close to him as they fire and the mules are behind him now as he runs and cuts and cuts again going full out and

CUT TO

THE HEAD POLICEMAN, cursing incoherently at what is happening and

CUT TO

SUNDANCE whirling faster than ever and

CUT TO

BUTCH, *dodging and cutting and as a pattern of bullets rips into his body he somersaults and lies there, blood pouring and*

CUT TO

SUNDANCE, *running toward him and*

CUT TO

ALL THE POLICEMEN, *rising up from behind the wall now, firing and*

CUT TO

SUNDANCE, *as he falls.*

You can say that is not Shakespearean and I would agree with you. You can say a lot of non-enthusiastic things about it and probably I would agree with you. But there is one thing I can say about it that you cannot disagree with and that is this: it's all one sentence.

Twenty cuts.

Three hundred words.

Why did I do that? (I don't know that I did it consciously. I do it a lot and I don't know that I ever do it consciously. It just feels right and I go with it. Do it in novels too. Probably do it too much. There it is.)

Look, that's a famous action scene. But it wasn't a famous scene when I wrote it. It was the first movie original of my life. I was in new and strange terrain. That's the peak of my story. All those years of research, of trying to figure just what the story should be, that's all climaxing here. I was killing my heroes, for chrissakes—and I didn't fucking want you looking away.

When I write a screenplay more than anything else I want this: I want to control your eye.

There is a tendency in collections of this kind to glorify the writer. I find that right and proper in a novel or a play or a poem, but it is pure bullshit in a movie. I have written this before and it is true, so tattoo it please behind your eyelids and remember it when you next read the director being serious in the *New York Times* or the star being cute on Letterman: movies are a group endeavor.

The bicycle scene in *Butch* will serve as an example.

I wrote the moment. In the early drafts, Butch takes Etta for a ride, as in the screenplay that follows and as in the finished film. And I had the notion of this visual: they ride through a ghost town and we see them not directly but rather intermittently, reflected in the windows of the empty stores.

George Hill read it, liked it, ran with it. He got the really remarkable notion that the bike ride not just be musicalized but should be a song. This had rarely been done before to my knowledge in a drama and certainly not in a Western. Hill had been a music major at Yale and was very strong in this area. He knew not only that it should be a song but the very song it should emulate: the

Gershwin's "Bidin My Time."

He told Burt Bacharach and Hal David what he required, and they came up with "Raindrops Keep Fallin' On My Head." Which has precisely the same loping feel and sense of the Gershwin.

That was a big moment in the movie—the song got famous, was the number one hit in the country. Good for Bacharach and David. Conrad Hall shot the scene sensationally. Good for him. The actors enjoyed the hell out of the sequence and it showed. Good for Newman and Ross. Good for the editors who cut it so well. Good for the art directors and, of course, good for Hill who came up with the musical notion. Not to mention me, good for me for beginning it all. Would my notion have worked? I think so. Would it have been as memorable as the final version? I don't think so.

Whenever you see a terrific moment in a movie, don't try and say anything but this: "Good for all of you. You gave me pleasure."

Which is all we are trying to do...all of us...all the time.

*

Two last Butch stories. I went to Russia a few years ago with a bunch of other screenwriters, and the high point of the trip for many of us was when we'd get invited into somebody's home, just sit around drinking vodka and talking with other screenwriters from across the world. And one night a few of us—I want to say the others were John Shanley and Larry Kasdan—were in a room talking with our peers and suddenly this one guy looked at me and you have to know this— they are nuts about movies in what used to be the Soviet Union. And of course, during the long terrible years they didn't get to see our movies, only the top Communists got to see those. But this strange thing began to happen: reels of film would be snuck out in the darkness and there were these impromptu black market screenings in the middle of the night and then the next morning the film would all be smuggled back.

This guy looked at me and he said these words. "Goldman," he said. "I see thees. I see thees weeth my eyes." And here he pointed to his eyes with his index finger. "I see man trade his bicycle for teeeket to Bootch Kessidy."

I made some standard self-deprecating horseshit reply but inside I was reeling. I remember I told myself it wasn't true, but the man's face said it was. Then I decided it was probably an old bicycle. But there was no such thing there then—any bicycle in that crumbling society was gold.

Finally I realized this: we have to be very careful what stories we tell. Because we have no idea what we might be holding in our hands.

Last Butch story: I was having dinner alone one night before a Knicks game at Quatorze Bis, my favorite French bistro, when one of the waiters came over. The staff there is mostly young, writers, actors. This guy said he had just seen the movie of *The Princess Bride* and how much he liked it and of course, I was pleased, and I thanked him and said it was one of my only two favorites of all the flicks I've been involved with, along with *Butch*. He kind of looked at me.

"*Butch*," I said. "*Butch Cassidy*."

Glass.

"*Butch Cassidy and the Sundance Kid*. It's a Western."

And then he said this: "I don't know that one."

After my initial shock, I realized there was no reason he should know it—it came out before he was born. We only sneak into people's memories for a very short time—no one gets to settle there. Every movie, no matter how it is received initially, is but a blip on the screen. As, alas, are we all...

CAST LIST

PAUL NEWMAN	BUTCH CASSIDY
ROBERT REDFORD	SUNDANCE KID
KATHARINE ROSS	ETTA PLACE
STROTHER MARTIN	PERCY GARRIS
HENRY JONES	BIKE SALESMAN
JEFF COREY	SHERIFF BLEDSOE
GEORGE FURTH	WOODCOCK
CLORIS LEACHMAN	AGNES
TED CASSIDY	HARVEY LOGAN
KENNETH MARS	MARSHAL
DONNELLY RHODES	MACON

Not that it matters,
but most of what follows is true.

FADE IN ON

THE ENTIRE SCREEN *is in deep shadow. Almost. The upper right-hand corner is white, a white that almost stings to look at. (The opening sequences of the film, until otherwise stated, are in a grainy black and white. Color comes later.)*

HOLD ON THE SHOT.

Eventually, it begins to come clear that the darkness is the side of a building, together with the shadow of that building on the ground, while the white is the afternoon sun. But if we don't know quite what it is that we're seeing at this point, that's all right. Now the shadow of a MAN *begins to fill the bright white corner. As the shadow lengthens—*

CUT TO

A MAN *idly walking around the building. He is* BUTCH CASSIDY *and hard to pin down. Thirty-five and bright, he has brown hair, but most people, if asked to describe him, would remember him as blond. He speaks well and quickly, and has been all his life a leader of men, but if you asked him, he would be damned if he could tell you why.*

CUT TO

BUTCH, *stopping by a window, giving it a glance.*

CUT TO

THE WINDOW. *It is heavily and magnificently barred.*

CUT TO

BUTCH *scowling briefly at the bars. He moves in toward the window to look through, and as he does, there begins a series of* QUICK CUTS. *(Butch, it might be noted here, is casing the bank, and what he is doing as his eyes flick from place to place inside is probing the place for weaknesses. But if we don't know quite what it is that's going on at this point, that's all right too.)*

CUT TO

A DOOR. *It is thick and solid metal and strong.*

CUT TO

PAPER MONEY *being counted by ten skilled fingers.*

CUT TO

A GUN IN A HOLSTER, *belonging to a* MAN *in a guard's uniform.*

CUT TO

A WINDOW HIGH UP ON ONE WALL. *It is, if anything, more heavily and magnificently barred than the first.*

CUT TO

THE DOOR OF A BANK SAFE. *It is behind shining bars and it is the kind of safe that has a time lock and*

CUT TO

BUTCH, *eyes expertly flicking from place to place. Then he starts to walk around the bank again, and he isn't happy.*

CUT TO

A BANK GUARD. *It is closing time now and he is slamming metal plates into place, the sound loud and sharp and final.*

PULL BACK TO REVEAL

BUTCH, *watching the Guard work.*

> **BUTCH**
> What was the matter with that old bank this town used to have? It was beautiful.

> **GUARD**
> *(continuing to slam things shut)*
> People kept robbing it.

CUT TO

BUTCH, *who starts to walk away across the street toward a barn of a building with a sign outside: "Macon's Saloon." In the middle of the street he turns and stares back at the bank. It is new, and ugly, and squat, and functional, and built like a tank.*

CUT TO

BUTCH: CLOSE UP.

BUTCH
(yelling back to the Guard)
That's a small price to pay for beauty.

And from this CLOSE UP of BUTCH:

DISSOLVE TO

A MUSTACHED MAN: CLOSE UP.

PULL BACK TO REVEAL

MACON'S SALOON.

It is a barn of a place, without much decoration, and it is all but empty now, giving an even greater impression of size. Almost the only action comes from a game of blackjack in which the MUSTACHED MAN is dealing. (There are other tables set up, ready for play, chips and cards neatly placed, but this is afternoon now, the sun slants in through windows, and the other tables are empty.)

CUT TO

THE BLACKJACK GAME. The mustached man is dealing to a PLAYER.

PLAYER
Hit me. *(The mustached man flicks a card.)* Over. *(He pushes back from the table. Hesitates. Then—)* Gimme credit, Mr. Macon?

CUT TO

JOHN MACON. He is a well-dressed, good-looking man in a big, rugged way. Not yet thirty, he gives the strong impression of power and maturity—he has come a long way through a tough world and he has come fast. He is a man who, at all times, knows whereof he speaks.

MACON
(shaking his head no)
You know my rules, Tom. *(He turns now, looks at the Mustached Man.)* You just about cleaned everybody, fella—I don't think you lost since you got the deal.

CUT TO

THE MUSTACHED MAN. He says nothing.

CUT TO

THE MACON.

                              MACON
What's the secret of your success?

CUT TO

THE MUSTACHED MAN.

                          MUSTACHED MAN
Prayer.

CUT TO

MACON. *And he isn't smiling.*

                              MACON
Let's just you and me play.

CUT TO

MACON AND THE MUSTACHED MAN. *The Mustached Man deals quickly, with no excess motion. The betting and the flicking out of the cards goes fast.*

                              MACON
Hit me. *(He gets another card.)* Again. *(Another card comes fast.)* Too much...

As the Mustached Man starts to take in the money—

CUT TO

MACON. *Smiling now.*

                              MACON
You're what's too much, fella. You're one helluva card player, and I know, because I'm one helluva card player, and I can't even spot how you're cheating.

CUT TO

The MUSTACHED MAN, *doing his best to ignore what has just been said. He continues to carefully stack his winnings into even piles.*

CUT TO

MACON, *on his feet. He wears guns, and his big hands are near them, relaxed and ready.*

                              MACON
                      (pointing to the money)
That stays—you go.

CUT TO

The MUSTACHED MAN. He sits almost sadly, slumped in his chair. His head is down. Now—

CUT TO

BUTCH tearing up to the card table, talking as he comes—

> **BUTCH**
> —we look a little short of brotherly love around here—

CUT TO

MACON standing there, his hands by his guns.

> **MACON**
> You with him, get yourselves out of here—

CUT TO

BUTCH AND THE MUSTACHED MAN. Butch pulling at the Mustached Man, who does not budge. As he pulls, he talks to Macon.

> **BUTCH**
> Yessir, thank you, sir, we were just on our way and—*(urgently now to the Mustached Man, who will not move)*—Will you come on?

CUT TO

BUTCH dropping down now beside the Mustached Man. This next is whispered and fast.

> **MUSTACHED MAN**
> I wasn't cheating...

> **BUTCH**
> *(trying to budge the other man)*
> ...move...

> **MUSTACHED MAN**
> I wasn't cheating...

CUT TO

MACON getting a little impatient now.

> **MACON**
> You can die—no one's immune—you can both die—

CUT TO

BUTCH AND THE MUSTACHED MAN. Lower and faster even than before:

                        BUTCH
—you hear that?—now you got him mad at me—

                    MUSTACHED MAN
—if he invites us to stay, then we'll go—

                        BUTCH
—we were gonna leave anyway—

                    MUSTACHED MAN
—he's gotta invite us to stick around—

CUT TO

The MUSTACHED MAN: CLOSE UP. *And here there will be a series of* QUICK CUTS *as his eyes take in everything around him. This will be not dissimilar in style to the moment with Butch casing the bank. While the cuts are going on, the following dialogue will continue overlapping and low between Butch and the Mustached Man. The cuts will include the following: (1) Macon's hands; (2) a window and sun streaming in and does it hit anybody's eyes; (3) the area behind the Mustached Man and is there anyone dangerous there; (4) Macon's eyes; (5) the area to the side of the Mustached Man and is there room to move. To repeat: While these quick cuts take place (and if we don't know what they're for, again, that's all right), camera returns constantly to the Mustached Man in* CLOSE UP, *with Butch beside him, moving in and out, both of them talking fast.*

                        BUTCH
—he'll draw on you—he's ready now and you don't know how fast he is—

                    MUSTACHED MAN
—that's just what I want to hear—

                        BUTCH
—face it—he don't look like he intends to lose—

                    MUSTACHED MAN
—you're really building up my confidence—

                        BUTCH
—well, I'm over the hill—it can happen to you—every day you get older—that's a law—

But the Mustached Man is clearly not leaving and Butch realizes this.

CUT TO

BUTCH RISING, *moving to* MACON.

> **BUTCH**

What would you think about maybe inviting us to stick around?

> **MACON**

What?

> **BUTCH**

—you don't have to mean it or anything—but if you'd just please invite us to stick around, I promise you we'll go and—

Macon gestures sharply for Butch to get the hell back out of the way and—

CUT TO

BUTCH. *He hesitates a moment, glancing down at the Mustached Man, who still sits slumped in his chair. Butch shakes his head, then moves back out of the way.*

> **BUTCH**
> *(softly)*

Can't help you, Sundance.

ZOOM TO

MACON *as the last word echoes. It registers, that word, and now Macon has a secret he tries desperately to keep behind his eyes: The man is terrified.*

CUT TO

THE SUNDANCE KID, *for that is the name of the Mustached Man. He sits slumped a moment more, his head down. Then he slowly raises his head. His eyes dazzle. He looks dead into Macon's eyes. Still staring, he stands. He, too, wears guns.*

CUT TO

MACON. *A brave man doing his best, he stands still and does not look away.*

CUT TO

SUNDANCE. *He says nothing.*

CUT TO

MACON, *and now the panic is slowly starting to seep out.*

> **MACON**

I didn't know who you were when I said you were cheating.

CUT TO

SUNDANCE. *He says nothing. His eyes are on* MACON'S HANDS *now.*

CUT TO

MACON'S HANDS. *Still close to his guns.*

CUT TO

SUNDANCE. *He says nothing. He just waits, stares.*

CUT TO

MACON.

> **MACON**
> *(The words burst out of him.)*
> If I draw on you, you'll kill me.

CUT TO

SUNDANCE.

> **SUNDANCE**
> There is that possibility.

CUT TO

BUTCH *moving in on Macon now.*

> **BUTCH**
> No sir, you'd just be killing yourself. *(urging now)* So invite us to stick around, why don't you?

CUT TO

MACON. *He starts to speak, stops, and*

CUT TO

BUTCH.

> **BUTCH**
> —you can do it—easy—come on, come on—

CUT TO

SUNDANCE. *The man does not make unnecessary motions. He stands now as before, silent and staring, eyes bright, ready.*

CUT TO

MACON.

>   **MACON**
>   *(He can barely get the words out.)*
> ...stick around, why don't you—

CUT TO

BUTCH *AND* SUNDANCE.

>   **BUTCH**
>   Thanks, but we got to be going.

And as they move along the path of gambling tables toward the door—

CUT TO

MACON *watching them go.*

>   **MACON**
>   Kid? *(a little louder now)* Hey, how good are you?

CUT TO

BUTCH, *between Sundance and Macon, but not for long, because the minute Macon asks his question, Butch gets the hell out of the way as fast as we*

CUT TO

SUNDANCE *diving left and dropping, and his guns are out and roaring, and as the sound explodes,*

CUT TO

MACON *as Sundance shoots his gun belt off, and as it drops*

CUT TO

SUNDANCE *firing on, and*

CUT TO

The GUNBELT *whipping like a snake across the floor as Sundance's bullets strike. Then, as the firing stops—*

CUT TO

JOHN MACON, *breathing the biggest sigh of relief anyone ever saw and*

CUT TO

SUNDANCE *standing now, his guns quiet.*

CUT TO

BUTCH AND SUNDANCE. Butch glances at Macon's gunbelt for a moment, then shakes his head.

BUTCH
(to Sundance as they move toward the door)
Like I been telling you—over the hill.

And they are gone.

CUT TO

BUTCH AND SUNDANCE riding. And as they ride, the film starts going into color. Faint at first, then, as the ride goes on, stronger. By the end, the effect should be considerable, not only because we will be in full color at that time, but also because by then we will be at Hole-in-the-Wall.

CUT TO

CLOUDS. They are white, just like clouds ought to be, and they are fluffy enough, and they hang there in the sky and then

PULL BACK TO REVEAL

BUTCH AND SUNDANCE riding along above the clouds, which spread out below them, filling a canyon. As Butch and Sundance begin riding down into the clouds—

CUT TO

A SMALL HERD OF DEER, startled and scared, veering wildly off as Butch and Sundance come riding along.

CUT TO

Butch and Sundance sitting by a dying fire, finishing coffee. Then—

CUT TO

Butch and Sundance riding along the crest, picking up their pace a little, because now they are getting there and

CUT TO

A ROCK FORMATION, strangely shaped, almost like a gated entrance to something, which it is: the entrance to Hole-in-the-Wall. And as WE DRAW NEAR,

CUT TO

HOLE-IN-THE-WALL. It is a sloping green valley, concave in shape, its upper rim coming in direct contact with a series of enormously high cliffs that rise almost vertically. At the bottom of the valley are a series of small lakes and streams.

CUT TO

Butch and Sundance, in the gated entrance made by the rock formation.

CUT TO

BUTCH: CLOSE UP. He stares out at all the glorious desolation.

> **BUTCH**
> Ahhhh; home.

And they start to ride down into the valley.

CUT TO

BUTCH AND SUNDANCE riding. As they move along, several of the cliffs behind them become momentarily visible, which is of interest for only one reason: The cliffs are filled with caves and every so often an armed lookout appears from a cave and signals and Butch, without ever breaking the rhythm of his speech, signals back.

> **BUTCH**
> Y'know, every time I see Hole-in-the-Wall again...

PAN TO

The VALLEY and the CLIFFS, glorious and desolate, breathtaking and lonely.

> **BUTCH'S VOICE** (off-screen)
> ...it's like seeing it fresh, for the very first time...

CUT TO

BUTCH riding along, SUNDANCE beside him.

> **BUTCH**
> ...and whenever that happens I ask myself the same question: How can I be so damn stupid as to keep coming back here?

> **SUNDANCE**
> *(He has heard this kind of speech before from Butch.)*
> What's your idea this time?

CUT TO

BUTCH: CLOSE UP.

BUTCH

Bolivia!

CUT TO

SUNDANCE.

SUNDANCE

What's Bolivia?

CUT TO

BUTCH AND SUNDANCE.

BUTCH

Bolivia's a country, stupid—in Central or South America.

SUNDANCE

Why don't we just go to Mexico?

BUTCH

'Cause all they got in Mexico is sweat and they sell plenty of that back here. Now listen: If we'd been in business during the California gold rush, where would we have gone to operate? California, right? Well, when I say Bolivia, you think California, because they're falling into it down there—silver mines, tin, gold; payrolls so big we'd strain our backs stealing 'em—

CUT TO

SUNDANCE. He looks at Butch, shakes his head.

SUNDANCE

You just keep thinking, Butch; that's what you're good at.

CUT TO

BUTCH.

BUTCH

I got vision and the rest of the world wears bifocals.

CUT TO

A shot of the base of the valley. Several plain cabins are visible. Outside the cabins there are a considerable number of men and horses.

CUT TO

BUTCH AND SUNDANCE *riding up.*

> **BUTCH**
> *(calling out, waving)*
>
> Hey, News—

CUT TO

NEWS CARVER, *a slender man of thirty. He is terribly busy taking care of his horse and makes no answer.*

CUT TO

BUTCH AND SUNDANCE *pulling up beside him.*

> **BUTCH**
>
> News, what're you doing?

> **NEWS**
> *(looking up, suddenly smiling)*
>
> Oh, hi, Butch. Nothing, nothing. Hello there, Sundance.

> **BUTCH**
>
> Sure y'are. You're getting ready to do something. What?

CUT TO

NEWS. *He is not happy and his words, when they come, come fast.*

> **NEWS**
>
> Just fixing to rob the Union Pacific Flyer, Butch, that's all we had in mind.

BUTCH *dismounts.* SUNDANCE *stays mounted, watching it all.*

> **BUTCH**
> *(as he gets down)*
>
> You got everything I told you wrong—when I left I said we might hit the Flyer, but even if we did, it wasn't this run but the one after, the return. Now, Sundance and me been out checking the bank situation and...

> **HARVEY LOGAN'S VOICE** (off-screen)
>
> No banks.

> **BUTCH**
> *(looking around, genuinely confused)*
>
> What?

CUT TO

HARVEY LOGAN in the doorway to one of the cabins. He was, in reality, a terrible man, vicious and frightening, and some of that should show.

LOGAN

The Flyer, Butch.

CUT TO

BUTCH looking around at his men as he talks.

BUTCH
(explaining as a patient teacher might)
Now, how many times have I told you people: Bad as they are, banks are better than trains. You can rely on a bank—they don't move. They stay put and you always know there's money inside and my orders were—

CUT TO

LOGAN moving away from the cabin toward Butch.

LOGAN

New orders been given.

BUTCH

Harvey, I run things here.

LOGAN

Use to, you did. Me now. *(pointing off suddenly)* This don't concern you.

CUT TO

SUNDANCE, silent, seated on his horse, looking down at them all.

CUT TO

BUTCH AND LOGAN.

LOGAN

Tell him to stay out.

BUTCH

He goes his own way, like always.

Then he suddenly whirls to face the gang of men who stand bunched, watching. Butch moves toward them, talking as he goes.

> **BUTCH**
>
> What's the matter with you people?—before I came here you were starving and you know it. You weren't even a gang—I formed you. News—News—read that damn clipping—

NEWS reaching into his pockets.

> **NEWS**
>
> Which one?

CUT TO

BUTCH hurrying to him.

> **BUTCH**
>
> Any of 'em.

News has taken out a batch of newspaper clippings. Unfolding the first...

> **NEWS**
>
> This here's from the Salt Lake Herald. *(He begins to read.)* "Butch Cassidy's Wild Bunch struck again today, looting the..."

> **BUTCH**
>
> That's enough right there. "Butch Cassidy's Wild Bunch"—hear that? That's you and that's me. Harvey gonna plan for you all? Harvey gonna do your thinking?

He turns back to News, who has kept right on reading throughout Butch's speech.

> **BUTCH**
>
> News, you can shut up now.

CUT TO

NEWS, looking up at Butch for a moment.

> **NEWS**
>
> Not till I come to the good part. *(reading away again)* "Also known to have participated in the hold-up are Flat Nose Curry and News Carver." *(folding up the clipping now)* I just love hearing my name in the papers.

CUT TO

BUTCH AND HIS MEN.

> **BUTCH**
>
> Now let's just forget about Harvey taking over. Okay, Flat Nose?

FLAT NOSE CURRY
(He has been nicknamed for obvious reasons.)
You always told us anyone could challenge you—

BUTCH
That's 'cause I figured nobody'd do it.

CUT TO

LOGAN smiling, starting toward Butch again.

LOGAN
Figured wrong, Butch.

CUT TO

BUTCH AND HIS MEN.

BUTCH
(a little desperate now)
You can't want Logan—

NEWS
...at least he's with us, Butch—you been spending a lot of time gone—

CUT TO

BUTCH: CLOSE UP.

BUTCH
That's 'cause everything's changing now—

CUT TO

LOGAN.

LOGAN
Guns or knives, Butch?

CUT TO

BUTCH hurrying rapidly on, doing his best to ignore Logan.

BUTCH
—everything's harder than it used to be—you got to plan more, you got
to prepare, you got to be damn sure what you're doing or you're dead—

CUT TO

LOGAN moving in front of Butch now.

                              LOGAN
Guns or knives?

                              BUTCH
Neither.

                              LOGAN
Pick!

                              BUTCH
I don't want to shoot with you, Harvey.

CUT TO

LOGAN SMILING.

                              LOGAN
Whatever you say, Butch.

And suddenly a KNIFE *is in his hand and—*

CUT TO

THE MEN, and with the appearance of the knife they start to get really excited, and from here on in, that excitement only builds as they surge toward Logan, who is calmly taking off his shirt. Butch moves to Sundance.

CUT TO

SUNDANCE on his horse, waiting quietly as Butch approaches.

                              BUTCH
Maybe there's a way to make a profit on this—bet on Logan.

                              SUNDANCE
I would, but who'd bet on you?

CUT TO

THE GANG clustered around Logan. He is stripped to the waist and his body is brutal. Suddenly he calls out—

                              LOGAN
Sundance—when we're done, if he's dead, you're welcome to stay.

CUT TO

BUTCH AND SUNDANCE looking out at Logan. Butch speaks quietly to Sundance.

BUTCH

Listen, I'm not a sore loser or anything, but when we're done, if I'm dead, kill him.

SUNDANCE

(This is said to Logan, but in answer to Butch.)

Love to.

CUT TO

BUTCH fidgeting a moment, then starting the long walk back toward Logan. LOGAN is younger and faster and stronger and Butch knows it. And knowing it doesn't make the walk any more pleasant. Still, Butch moves forward, unarmed as yet, toward the other man.

CUT TO

LOGAN WATCHING him come. In the sun his body glistens.

CUT TO

BUTCH moving through the gang toward Logan. He is unarmed and a knife is offered him by one of the gang.

BUTCH

Not yet. *(moving up to Logan now)* Not till Harvey and me get all the rules straight.

LOGAN

Rules? In a knife fight? No rules!

As he finishes speaking, Butch delivers the most aesthetically exquisite kick in the balls in the history of the modern American cinema.

CUT TO

LOGAN. For a moment he just stands there. Then he makes an absolutely indescribable sound, and as the look on his face moves from disbelief to displeasure, he sinks slowly to his knees.

CUT TO

BUTCH. He goes on as if nothing whatsoever had happened.

BUTCH

Well, if there aren't going to be any rules, I guess we might as well get this fight started. Somebody say "one-two-three-go."

CUT TO

SUNDANCE.

> **SUNDANCE**
> *(like a shot)*
> One-two-three-go.

CUT TO

LOGAN. He is green now, and still on his knees. BUTCH approaches, nods, locks his hands together, and as if swinging a baseball bat, delivers a stunning blow to Logan's jaw. LOGAN falls and lies there.

CUT TO

FLAT NOSE CURRY and several others, all hurrying to Butch.

> **FLAT NOSE**
> I was sure rooting for you, Butch.

> **BUTCH**
> I know, Flat Nose. That's what sustained me in my time of trouble. *(looking around)* News? Now what's all this about the Flyer?

CUT TO

NEWS, as he moves to Butch.

> **NEWS**
> Harvey said we'd hit 'em both, this run and the return. He said no one'd ever done that yet to the Flyer, so no matter what we got the first time, they'd be sure to figure the return was safe and load it up with money.

> **BUTCH**
> Harvey thought that up?

> **NEWS**
> Yessir, he did.

> **BUTCH**
> Well, I'll tell you something: That's just what we'll do.

CUT TO

LOGAN, who is still out, as Butch drops to his knees beside him.

> **BUTCH**
> *(slapping Logan's cheeks)*
> Good thinking, Harvey.

CUT TO

SUNDANCE, *and we don't know quite what he's doing. But he is dressed differently from the preceding, and the sun is at a different angle, so we do know this is a different time, perhaps a different place. There is a for-the-moment unidentified and continuing roar, and as it goes on, it becomes clear that Sundance isn't paying any attention to it. But whatever it is he is paying attention to, he is concentrating completely, almost like an Olympic high jumper before attempting a seven-foot leap. Sundance continues his intense concentration a moment more, because whatever he is about to do is damn dangerous, and then his quick body is in motion and*

CUT TO

A PASSING TRAIN,

curving below the rock from which SUNDANCE HURLS HIMSELF. *The train is not far below the level of the rock, so the drop isn't dangerous—what's dangerous is that the thing is moving like hell, and if he lands wrong, Sundance is going to roll off and*

CUT TO

SUNDANCE LANDING *wrong, but not completely, and he scrabbles his body back onto the center of the top of the train car and then*

CUT TO

SUNDANCE: CLOSE UP *and sweating and happy to be there. He stays where he is for a moment, getting collected, before standing and starting his precarious way up toward the engine.*

CUT TO

INSIDE THE ENGINE.

THE ENGINEER AND THE FIREMAN *are working. The Engineer is fifty and spare, almost a New England type. The Fireman is small, but with tremendous arms and shoulders and would speak a lot clearer if he had more teeth.*

CUT TO

THE EMPTY TRACKS AHEAD.

The landscape whizzing by on either side. All very PEACEFUL *and S.O.P. and*

CUT TO

THE ENGINEER. *Taut, and without a word, his hands start to rise as we*

CUT TO

SUNDANCE, quickly inside the engine, guns ready.

CUT TO

THE THREE OF THEM. *The Engineer has the responsibility for the train, and he acquits himself throughout as well as he can. The Fireman, frightened at first, stays close to the Engineer. Gradually, as the scene goes on, he gains confidence.*

> **ENGINEER**
> You want it stopped? *(Sundance nods once.)* Where?

> **SUNDANCE**
> Here would be fine.

CUT TO

THE ENGINEER *starting to slow the train.*

CUT TO

THE FIREMAN *looking at Sundance, maybe gathering courage to say something and*

CUT TO

A SHOT OF THE TRACKS *ahead from inside the engine. In the distance, a figure can be seen standing in the center of the rails.*

CUT TO

SUNDANCE, as the little Fireman goes to him and points to the distant Figure.

> **FIREMAN**
> I bet that's old Butch himself. *(Sundance gives him a look.)*

As the train continues to slow—

CUT TO

SUNDANCE. He drops to the ground, starts moving along the passenger cars. Behind him, the FIREMAN clambers to the ground. During this, other members of the gang are visible, some of them standing, guns drawn, in the doorways of the passenger cars. The Fireman hurries along, falling into step with Sundance.

> **FIREMAN**
> Thought I'd watch.

> **SUNDANCE**
> Bring the kids, why don't you?

CUT TO

THE EXPRESS CAR.

BUTCH, gun in hand, is banging at the door. While the following dialogue goes on, other members of the gang can be seen planting dynamite beneath the car.

> **BUTCH**
> *(He is clearly a little frayed.)*
> You're just gonna get yourself blown up, so open the door!

> **VOICE FROM INSIDE THE CAR** (off-screen)
> I can't do that on account of I work for Mr. E.H. Harriman of the Union Pacific Railroad and he entrusted me—

> **BUTCH**
> *(He has been hearing a lot of this these last few minutes.)*
> Will you shut up with that E.H. Harriman business and open the door.

CUT TO

SUNDANCE moving up to Butch. The FIREMAN IS HALF A PACE behind.

> **BUTCH**
> *(as Sundance approaches)*
> They got a patriot on their side.

> **FIREMAN**
> That's young Woodcock; he's awful dedicated.

> **NEWS**
> *(hurrying to Butch)*
> Dynamite's ready.

Butch nods. News goes.

> **BUTCH**
> Woodcock?

CUT TO

WOODCOCK INSIDE THE CAR.

He stands pressed against the door. Behind him is a good-sized safe. WOODCOCK is a young man with a soft western accent, an unexceptional but pleasant face. His sandy hair is slightly receding, and he is right now scared to death. But his voice—words well chosen, spoken calmly—belies that fact.

> **WOODCOCK**
> Yes sir?

> BUTCH'S VOICE (off-screen)
You know who we are?

> WOODCOCK
You're the Hole-in-the-Wall Gang, Mr. Cassidy. I understand that, but you gotta understand that Mr. E.H. Harriman himself of the Union Pacific Railroad gimme this job, and I never had such responsibility before, and since he entrusted me to get the money through, I got to do my best, don't you see?

CUT TO

BUTCH AND SUNDANCE OUTSIDE.

> BUTCH
Your best doesn't include getting killed.

CUT TO

WOODCOCK INSIDE. His eyes are closed now as he presses hard against the door.

> WOODCOCK
Mr. E.H. Harriman himself, he had the confidence in me—

> BUTCH'S VOICE (off-screen)
Open the door. Or that's it.

Woodcock makes no move.

CUT TO

BUTCH.

> BUTCH
Ya think he'd die for you, ya lousy amateur? *(There is no answer from inside the car.)* Now, Woodcock!

CUT TO

Woodcock huddled up, waiting for the blast.

> WOODCOCK
I work for Mr. E.H. Harriman of the Union Pacific Railroad...

CUT TO

THE RAILROAD CAR exploding, one wall just ripped away.

CUT TO

WOODCOCK'S BODY hurtling through the air, crashing down.

CUT TO

BUTCH AND SUNDANCE followed by the rest of the gang pouring into the car. While Sundance heads for THE SAFE,

CUT TO

BUTCH going to WOODCOCK, who is alive and crawling and not a little bloody.

> **BUTCH**
> You okay? *(Woodcock makes a nod.)* Whatever Harriman's paying you, it's not enough.

And as he helps Woodcock to get comfortable...

CUT TO

SUNDANCE kneeling beside the safe, deftly wedging several sticks of dynamite into place, lighting them, then backing off fast and

CUT TO

THE SAFE. There is a muffled explosion as the door bursts neatly open.

CUT TO

SUNDANCE as Butch approaches.

> **BUTCH**
> *(looking at the beautifully blown safe)*
> Dammitall, why is everything we're good at illegal?

CUT TO

NEWS taking money from the safe.

CUT TO

BUTCH AND SUNDANCE watching him.

> **NEWS**
> There ain't what I'd call a fortune in here, Butch.

> **BUTCH**
> Just so we come out ahead, News; that's the main thing.

CUT TO

A YOUNG, COMPETENT MARSHAL.

PULL BACK TO REVEAL

A CROWD OF CITIZENS standing in a street, looking up at the Marshal. It is dusk.

> MARSHAL
> *(Very businesslike, he speaks without much emotion.)*
> All right; they just robbed the Flyer outside our town, and that makes it our responsibility to get after them—

CUT TO

THE SECOND FLOOR PORCH OF A BUILDING DOWN THE STREET.

The building is FANNY PORTER'S, and it was as well known as any BROTHEL-SALOON of the period. Seated on the porch, listening to the Marshal talk, are BUTCH AND SUNDANCE. They are sprawled comfortably, hats pulled down. Between them on the table are two large steins and a bucket of beer. They are both a little buzzed.

> MARSHAL'S VOICE (off-screen)
> —now you'll have to bring your own horses—

CUT TO

THE MARSHAL AND THE CROWD.

> MARSHAL
> How many of you can bring your own guns?

CUT TO

THE CROWD. No one can. No hands are raised.

CUT TO

THE MARSHAL.

> MARSHAL
> Okay. Then how many of you will want me to supply them with guns?

CUT TO

THE CROWD. No hands are raised.

CUT TO

THE MARSHAL. It is beginning to dawn on him now that he is not getting through to his audience.

MARSHAL

Come on, now—it's up to us to do something.

CUT TO

THE MARSHAL AND THE CROWD.

FIRST CITIZEN

What's the point? They're probably half-way to Hole-in-the-Wall already.

MARSHAL

That's why we've got to hurry—we can head them off—

SECOND CITIZEN
(aghast)

Head 'em off? You crazy? We do that, and they'll kill us.

There is general vocal agreement on this point from the crowd.

CUT TO

BUTCH AND SUNDANCE.

BUTCH
(beaming)

I just eat this up with a spoon.

Sundance nods; as they fill their steins with more beer—

CUT TO

FANNY PORTER entering from a door behind them. It isn't easy running a successful brothel and she shows the strain.

FANNY
(moving up behind Butch and Sundance)

All right, you two; I want you at my party. *(She gestures to the open door through which she entered.)*

BUTCH

What party?

CUT TO

THE SCENE THROUGH THE DOOR.

A YOUNG MAN is by a piano with half a dozen GIRLS. A song of the period is being sung. A homemade sign —"Remember the Maine"—is amateurishly strung along one wall.

CUT TO

BUTCH AND SUNDANCE AND FANNY.

> **FANNY**
> I'm losing my piano player—he's going off to fight the war.

> **SUNDANCE**
> What war?

> **FANNY**
> The war against the Spanish.

> **BUTCH**
> Remember the Maine.

> **SUNDANCE**
> I could never forget it.

CUT TO

FANNY, as she exits.

> **FANNY**
> I'm giving him a send-off, so come on.

CUT TO

BUTCH AND SUNDANCE each taking a long drink of beer. Butch is really buzzed by this time; he gets up and glances back in at the party.

CUT TO

THE PIANO PLAYER. He is sitting on top of the piano now, the girls grouped around him, looking up at his face.

CUT TO

BUTCH AND SUNDANCE, Butch still staring inside.

> **BUTCH**
> Y'know, when I was a kid, I always figured on being a hero when I grew up.

> **SUNDANCE**
> Too late now.

> **BUTCH**
> You didn't have to say that—what'd you have to say that for? *(as he drains his glass)*

CUT TO

THE YOUNG MARSHAL, *still trying to gather his posse.*

MARSHAL

Listen—it's my job to go fight them—you want me to go off alone and fight the Hole-in-the-Wall Gang, fine with me—you want your kids to know you let me do that? Fine with me, but I don't think that's what you want, is it?

CUT TO

THE CROWD. *There is no negative outcry whatsoever.*

CUT TO

BUTCH, *excited—*

BUTCH

Hey—hey—let's enlist and go fight the Spanish—you and me in the war—*(Sundance just stares at him.)*—listen, we got a lot going for us: experience, maturity, leadership. Hell, I bet we'd end up officers—I'd be Major Parker—

CUT TO

SUNDANCE.

SUNDANCE

Parker?

BUTCH

That's my real name—Robert Leroy Parker.

SUNDANCE

No fooling? Mine's Longbaugh.

BUTCH

No fooling? ...long what?

SUNDANCE

Harry Longbaugh.

BUTCH

You'd be Major Longbaugh, then; what do you say?

SUNDANCE

You just keep thinking, Butch; that's what you're good at.

BUTCH
(into his beer)
I got vision and the rest of the world wears bifocals.

CUT TO

THE MARSHAL, and he is mad.

MARSHAL
You gonna go through life with your heads down? You gonna travel with your tail between your legs? You gonna shake at every sound you can't see what's makin' it? What do you say?

A NEW AND DIFFERENT VOICE (off-screen)
I say, boys and girls...

As the voice goes on,

CUT TO

THE SPEAKER. He is a Salesman and in a minute we will find out what he's selling.

SALESMAN
...friends and enemies...*(big)* Meet—the—future!

At the word "FUTURE"

CUT TO

A BRAND-NEW DAZZLING BICYCLE.

A VOICE FROM THE CROWD (off-screen)
The future what?

CUT TO

THE SALESMAN moving up alongside the Marshal.

SALESMAN
(The man has leather lungs.)
The future mode of transportation for the weary western world.

MARSHAL
Now just what in the hell do you think you're doing?

SALESMAN
You got the crowd together—that's half my work—I just figured I'd sell a little and—

MARSHAL

Well, I'm trying to raise a posse if you don't mind—

SALESMAN

I got a short presentation—*(to the crowd)*—the horse is dead!—*(to the Marshal)*—you'll see. This item sells itself—*(to the crowd)*—Soon the eye will see nothing but silk-ribboned bicycle paths stretching to infinity.

MARSHAL
(to crowd)
You gonna listen to him or you gonna come with me?

CUT TO

THE CROWD.

A CITIZEN

How much those things cost?

CUT TO

SALESMAN *mounting his machine.*

SALESMAN

An indecently paltry amount. *(starting to ride)* A bicycle is cheaper to buy than a horse, cheaper to maintain, as fast over short distances and I promise you this—*(And now he removes both hands from the bars.)*—the pleasure it provides can be equaled only by the love of your lady.

CUT TO

A GIRL *moving up behind Butch. She is reasonably pretty, a little used.*

GIRL

Fanny says for you to come right now to her party. *(Butch nods, stands. The girl comes into his arms.)*

CUT TO

SUNDANCE. *He stands.*

SUNDANCE

I think I'll get saddled up and go looking for a woman too.

CUT TO

BUTCH MOVING AWAY WITH THE GIRL.

BUTCH
Good hunting.

CUT TO

SUNDANCE.

SUNDANCE
Shouldn't be too hard; I'm not picky. Just so she's smart and pretty and sweet and gentle and soft and quiet and refined...*(as he continues his list of qualifications)*

DISSOLVE TO

ETTA PLACE. *As Sundance's list is spoken, her face, at first faint, becomes more and more clear. She is in her middle twenties, and has dark hair pulled back tight into a bun. She wears neat, starched clothing, and it is impossible to tell what her figure might be like.*

PULL BACK TO REVEAL

ETTA IN A SCHOOLHOUSE. NIGHT.

There isn't really enough light to work, but she works anyway, sitting at her desk, grading papers. From somewhere outside the schoolhouse comes a night sound, and it startles her.

CUT TO

The WINDOW AND THE NIGHT *beyond. Nothing moves.*

ETTA. *There is a* CLOCK ON HER DESK. *She glances at it, brings the papers into a neat pile, and gets up, goes to the door. As she opens it,*

CUT TO

A SMALL HOUSE. DARK.

She almost runs to it. The night is very dark and there is wind. The house is set off by itself behind the school. It is a one-story affair, obviously the kind of place built by the town to house the schoolmistress.

CUT TO

ETTA *entering her small house. Closing the front door, she moves across the tiny living room into the bedroom, undressing as she goes.*

CUT TO

ETTA *entering the bedroom, pulling off her blouse. There is a small light by the bed and as she gets it on, in this shadow-light, it is clear that she is really a terribly pretty thing.*

She wears a white slip, and it contrasts nicely with her sun-darkened skin. She has a fuller body than she showed before. She begins to take off her skirt and is almost done before she whirls and freezes and damn near screams and

CUT TO

SUNDANCE, GUN IN HIS LAP, seated happily in a corner of the room, watching.

SUNDANCE
(gesturing with his gun)

Keep going, teacher lady.

CUT TO

ETTA. She does not move.

SUNDANCE

It's all right, don't mind me—*(And now he gestures with his gun again.)*—keep right on going.

ETTA makes a nod, then nervously manages to undo her skirt and it slips to the floor.

CUT TO

SUNDANCE, enjoying himself.

CUT TO

SUNDANCE.

SUNDANCE

Don't stop on my account.

CUT TO

THE TWO OF THEM. She stares at him a moment, then begins to take off her slip. As she does so...

SUNDANCE

I'll tell you something, teacher lady—you're not so bad. Outside you're all stiff and starchy, but underneath, not so bad. *(Her slip is off now, and her body, while decently covered, is also revealed to him. It is a splendid body.)* Okay. Let down your hair.

CUT TO

ETTA. She hesitates a moment before reaching back behind her head with both hands. Her fingers work quickly, and in a moment her hair tumbles down over her shoulders.

CUT TO

SUNDANCE, watching appreciatively.

SUNDANCE
Shake your head.

CUT TO

ETTA. She shakes her head and her hair loosens up, covering her shoulders now, thick and gloriously black.

CUT TO

SUNDANCE. He tilts his head a moment, carefully examining the girl.

CUT TO

ETTA as she stands there. She looks wild.

CUT TO

SUNDANCE. Slowly he begins to rise from the chair and move across the silent room toward her.

CUT TO

ETTA, not looking away, watching him come.

CUT TO

SUNDANCE, very close to her now. Beside them is the bed.

CUT TO

ETTA. Unafraid, she stares at him.

ETTA
Do you know what I wish?

SUNDANCE
What?

ETTA
That you'd once get here on time.

And her arms go around him, her mouth finds his, and locked, they fall toward the bed. As their bodies fall...

CUT TO

BUTCH'S HEAD—just his head—gliding past a window at dawn. He might be a balloon floating by, for that is the impression his floating head gives. As his head goes past, Butch whispers a few words.

BUTCH
(in the style of the melodrama villains of the time)
You're mine, Etta Place; mine, do you hear me?

PULL BACK TO REVEAL

SUNDANCE AND ETTA asleep in bed. As her name is called out, Etta stirs.

CUT TO

BUTCH, as his head floats by another window, then disappears a moment before reappearing again, sailing gracefully past another window as, from inside, we watch his disembodied head circling the house.

CUT TO

ETTA, eyes open now, not entirely certain of the vision that confronts her and—

CUT TO

BUTCH, as he passes the window by the bed again.

BUTCH
Mine, I tell you; mine!

CUT TO

ETTA, as she gives a laugh, grabs a robe.

CUT TO

The FRONT DOOR OF THE HOUSE opening and Etta standing there. It is a beautiful early morning, barely dawn, and she turns, smiling as around a corner of the house comes Butch. He is riding a bicycle, which accounts for the gliding impression he has been giving.

BUTCH
(pulling up beside her)
Meet—the—future. *(And he gestures for her to get on the crossbar.)*

ETTA
Do you know what you're doing?

BUTCH
Theoretically.

CUT TO

BUTCH PUSHING OFF after Etta has hesitatingly gotten on the bike. It's downhill but it's still precarious at first and they almost tumble until he gets the hang of it, but once he's got it, he never loses it, and as they begin to pick up speed we are into:

MUSICAL INTERLUDE NUMBER ONE.

There are going to be three of them before the film is over. This, the first, is a song sung while Butch and Etta ride the bike. The song will be sung by male voices, and the feel of it is terribly contemporary, because in fact, the sounds of the songs of this period are shockingly close in feel to the popular music of today.

What we see during the song is a series of shots of Butch and Etta on the bicycle at dawn, and they are having just a marvelous time. Once Butch gains confidence, he tries stunting for Etta and more often than not, things don't work out quite as gracefully as he planned, but you can't win 'em all. She laughs and he clowns and they are aware of each other.

The song that we hear will not be along the lines of "A Bicycle Built for Two." None of the songs in the film will make a literal comment on scenes, but rather an emotional one. This song, for example, will not be loud. But it will be poignant. And pretty as hell.

As the song comes to an end:

CUT TO

BUTCH AND ETTA as he begins slowly now to ride back toward her house.

> ETTA
> You've come to get him for the Flyer?

> BUTCH
> *(nods)*
> And not a day too soon—I'm broke already.

> ETTA
> Why is there never any money, Butch?

> BUTCH
> I swear, Etta, I don't know; I've been working like a dog all my life, and I can't get a penny ahead.

> ETTA
> Sundance says it's because you're a soft touch, and you're always taking expensive vacations and buying drinks for everybody and you're a rotten gambler.

BUTCH

Well, I guess that has something to do with it.

CUT TO

BUTCH AND ETTA as they pedal along.

ETTA

And after the Flyer?

BUTCH

Sundance tell you about Bolivia? *(Etta nods.)* You think I'm crazy too?

ETTA
(She means this.)
Not with what they're finding in the ground down there; and if you happen to be a thief.

BUTCH

You're like me, Etta...

ETTA
(She has heard this before.)
...sure, sure, sure; I got vision and the rest of the world wears bifocals.

Butch laughs, leans forward, kisses her gently on the cheek. She looks at him for a moment. Then—

CUT TO

BUTCH.

ETTA

Butch? Do you ever wonder if I'd met you first if we'd been the ones to get involved?

BUTCH

We are involved, Etta; don't you know that?

CUT TO

ETTA. He has said this last straight and, for a moment now, she is absolutely uncertain of herself. Then—

BUTCH

I mean, you're riding on my bicycle—in certain Arabian countries that's the same as being married.

CUT TO

ETTA. She breaks out with a laugh, holds him very tight and—

                         SUNDANCE'S VOICE (off-screen)
Hey—

CUT TO

Sundance standing in the doorway to Etta's house.

                              SUNDANCE
What're you doing?

CUT TO

BUTCH AND SUNDANCE AND ETTA as Butch rides close to the house.

                               BUTCH
Just stealing your woman.

                              SUNDANCE
Take her, take her.

                               BUTCH
You're a romantic bastard; I'll give you that.

And on his words, there begins a series of QUICK CUTS, all adding up to the very clear impression that what is happening now is that the Flyer is being stopped a second time. Among the flash impressions are:

(1)   *Sundance moving along the train top*

(2)   *The Flyer's gigantic wheels starting to slow*

(3)   *Several outlaws jumping into position between the cars, guns drawn and ready*

(4)   *A train conductor, standing very still, his hands raised*

(5)   *A car full of passengers sitting deadly quiet and nervous as hell and now*

CUT TO

THE EXPRESS CAR,

as BUTCH approaches. Behind him comes Sundance.

                               BUTCH
Okay, okay, open up.

                 A VOICE FROM INSIDE THE CAR (off-screen)
I work for Mr. E.H. Harriman...

> BUTCH
> *(delighted)*

Hey, Woodcock.

CUT TO

WOODCOCK INSIDE THE CAR.

He is banged up and bandaged, but mobile.

> WOODCOCK
> *(He is not unhappy either.)*

Hi, Butch.

CUT TO

BUTCH OUTSIDE THE CAR.

> BUTCH

You okay?—that's wonderful—let's have a look at you—

CUT TO

WOODCOCK, and he isn't buying.

> WOODCOCK

Now, Butch, you got to have more respect for me than to think I'd fall for that—

CUT TO

BUTCH.

> BUTCH

You can't wait to get blown up again—

> WOODCOCK'S VOICE (off-screen)

Butch, if it was only my money, you know there's no one I'd rather have steal it, but I am still in the employ of Mr. E.H. Harr...

> A NEW AND VERY LOUD VOICE (off-screen)

Start this train!

CUT TO

AN ELEPHANT OF A WOMAN standing on the stairs of the nearest passenger car. She drops heavily to the ground and bulls her way toward Butch and Sundance.

>   VERY LARGE WOMAN
>   *(as she comes)*
> I'm a grandmother and a female and I've got my rights!

CUT TO

BUTCH *watching her come.*

>   BUTCH
> I got troubles of my own, lady, so...

>   VERY LARGE WOMAN
> You don't frighten me—no man frightens me—

CUT TO

SUNDANCE *as the* WOMAN PUSHES *by him to get at Butch. There is a strange expression on Sundance's face and it is hard to tell just what it is. But what it isn't is a smile.*

>   SUNDANCE
> We got no time for this.

CUT TO

WOODCOCK INSIDE THE CAR,

pressed against the door, listening.

>   VERY LARGE WOMAN (off-screen)
> You may cow the others, but I remain unafraid—I've fought against whiskey, I've fought against gambling, I can fight against you—

>   BUTCH (off-screen)
>   *(whispered)*
> Sundance, will you put your guns down—

>   SUNDANCE (off-screen)
> I'm telling you, we got no time—

>   BUTCH (off-screen)
> —but what's the point to violence?...

>   SUNDANCE (off-screen)
> It's the only thing that Woodcock understands. *(louder now)* Woodcock?

>   WOODCOCK
> I hear you.

VERY LARGE WOMAN (off-screen)
(almost incoherently)

...no...no...

WOODCOCK

What are you doing to do to her?

SUNDANCE (off-screen)

Whatever you force me to.

WOODCOCK

Well, leave her alone!—you're after the money—the money's in here—

VERY LARGE WOMAN (off-screen)

...help me—please...

CUT TO

BUTCH, SUNDANCE, AND THE VERY LARGE WOMAN.

Sundance holds her firmly, his hand over her mouth. Both his guns are in their holsters.

BUTCH
(going on with his imitation of the woman, just as he's been doing)
—oh, dear God, won't someone do something?

CUT TO

WOODCOCK, ANGUISHED.

WOODCOCK

Nobody kills innocent people.

SUNDANCE (off-screen)

You do, Woodcock—she's on your conscience, not mine—*(And now there is the sound of a gun being cocked.)*

CUT TO

BUTCH *going on* magnificently.

BUTCH

Our Father who art in heaven...

CUT TO

WOODCOCK: CLOSE UP.

WOODCOCK

Stop!!!

And as he throws the door open—

CUT TO

BUTCH AND SUNDANCE AND THE VERY LARGE WOMAN

standing there and—

CUT TO

WOODCOCK shaking his head as he realizes he has been had.

WOODCOCK

How'm I ever gonna explain this to poor Mr. Harriman?

CUT TO

BUTCH AND SUNDANCE getting into the car; Sundance carries a box of dynamite sticks, and as they are inside they both stop dead.

BUTCH

Woodcock—what did you have to go and get something like that for?

CUT TO

WOODCOCK standing beside the biggest railroad safe anyone ever saw.

WOODCOCK

I'm sorry, Butch, but you blew that last one so easy I just hadda do something.

CUT TO

BUTCH AND SUNDANCE, as Butch indicates the box of dynamite.

BUTCH

Gimme that and get some more. *(And as he reaches for the dynamite—)*

CUT TO

BUTCH working quickly, efficiently, inside the railroad car. He is beginning to perspire now, as he continues to wedge in the dynamite.

CUT TO

THE SAFE really loaded up with dynamite and—

CUT TO

THE CENTRAL DYNAMITE FUSE. *As Butch lights it, it begins to sizzle and burn toward the dynamite sticks and*

CUT TO

BUTCH *getting the hell out of the car. Then—*

CUT TO

THE SAFE—*just before a cataclysmic explosion rocks it. For a moment there is just the flash of blinding light, then deafening sound. The whole goddam railroad car has been blasted away to its foundation and as the sound diminishes, something fills the air: money.*

CUT TO

A view of the SKY, AS PIECES OF PAPER MONEY *flutter this way and that in the breeze.*

CUT TO

BUTCH AND SUNDANCE, *as Sundance starts to laugh.*

SUNDANCE

Think you used enough dynamite there, Butch?

CUT TO

The MONEY *fluttering this way and that on the breeze. It seems to fill the air. Then—*

CUT TO

THE GANG *starting off after the money, some of them crawling across the ground, others are jumping into the air, trying to clutch the fluttering bills.*

CUT TO

BUTCH, *starting to laugh at his own stupidity and*

CUT TO

SUNDANCE, *roaring and*

CUT TO

THE GANG *pursuing the money as the wind blows it along. They might almost be a convention of butterfly collectors, as they scramble around, jumping and crawling and turning and—*

CUT TO

BUTCH, as slowly his laughter dies. He is looking off at something.

CUT TO

In the distance, a TRAIN ENGINE *pulling one large, odd-looking car.*

CUT TO

BUTCH, still looking off at the engine and the strange single car. SUNDANCE *is beside him now, and they both watch. Around them, members of the gang still scramble around gathering up bits and pieces of money.*

CUT TO

THE ENGINE *pulling the single car, drawing closer and closer and*

CUT TO

BUTCH AND SUNDANCE watching it come.

BUTCH
Now what in the hell is that?

CUT TO

THE CAR, drawing closer, and now there is music under it all, nervous and fast, but not loud, not yet, as the train and the single car continue to come toward camera.

CUT TO

BUTCH AND SUNDANCE looking at each other in absolute bewilderment.

CUT TO

THE CAR. It is still some ways off, but the music is faster now and starting to get loud as the car continues to come toward camera, steadily and swiftly, and the music builds and builds and then, without warning, we are into:

THE LONGEST TRAVELING SHOT IN THE HISTORY OF THE WORLD.

The camera starts to move toward the car. As the camera starts, the car stops and just waits there, and the music is louder than ever now, as the camera picks up speed, moving toward the car, which stands dead still on the tracks as the camera comes and comes and now the camera is really moving, going like a shot toward the car and the car still waits, and now the music is starting to deafen, and Craig Breedlove must be driving the camera as it roars toward the car, close now, really close, right up almost on top of the goddam car and just as it seems as if it's going to smash right into the side of the car, the entire side of the car swings open and down, and the camera recoils, like a human face would recoil after receiving a terrible blow, and out of the car right into the eye of the camera comes riding—the SUPERPOSSE. *The superposse consists of perhaps a half-dozen men. Taken as a group, they look, act, and are, in any and all ways, formidable.*

CUT TO

BUTCH AND SUNDANCE.

BUTCH
Whatever they're selling. I don't want it—(*And he spins, shouting to the men gathering up the money.)*—leave it!

CUT TO

THE SUPERPOSSE *riding like hell. They are still a good distance away.*

CUT TO

SUNDANCE VAULTING *onto his horse, grabbing Butch's horse's reins and leading the animal over to* BUTCH, *who is in the midst of his men, urging them to leave the money and take off.*

CUT TO

THE SUPERPOSSE *at a distance, but closer now. One of them reaches for a rifle.*

CUT TO

BUTCH *dragging men away from the money, which still lies scattered thick across the ground. Gradually, most of* THE GANG *commence to run for their horses, but* NEWS AND FLAT NOSE *still chase the money.*

BUTCH
(*to News and Flat Nose*)
Ya crazy fools—(*gesturing wildly toward the Superposse*)—ya think they been sent here to help us?

As NEWS AND FLAT NOSE *mutter,* "Coming," "Right away," "Just one sec," *etc., Butch gets the hell on his horse and—*

CUT TO

THE SUPERPOSSE, *all of them with* RIFLES *out now and*

CUT TO

SUNDANCE, *riding.* SEVERAL MEMBERS OF THE GANG *form close beside him. Behind them now comes rifle fire.*

CUT TO

NEWS, and FLAT NOSE isn't moving anymore. NEWS, severely damaged, does his best to crawl. There is another shot. NEWS LIES STILL.

CUT TO

SUNDANCE, as BUTCH rides up to him. Sundance is staring back and Butch follows his stare.

CUT TO

NEWS and FLAT NOSE dead.

CUT TO

The SUPERPOSSE, bunched tight together.

CUT TO

BUTCH AND SUNDANCE, watching motionless for a moment. Then—

SUNDANCE

Butch?

BUTCH

What?

SUNDANCE

They're very good. *(And with that, they take off.)*

CUT TO

BUTCH AND SUNDANCE catching up with the rest of the Gang, then

CUT TO

A CAMERA SHOT FROM AN ENORMOUS HEIGHT. It is as if two great black centipedes were racing. In front, the Hole-in-the-Wall Gang, moving like crazy. Behind them, the Superposse, not losing ground. The terrain ahead of them is flat. On either side lie hills.

CUT TO

THE HOLE-IN-THE-WALL GANG, still from above but lower down. The sound of the horses is loud. Then BUTCH'S VOICE is heard—

BUTCH
(shouting it out)

Scatter!!!

And like a sunburst, the Gang fragments, every man taking a different direction, except Butch and Sundance, who ride together.

CUT TO

BUTCH AND SUNDANCE reaching the crest of a hill. Sundance is first and as he gets to the top, he pauses just for a moment, glancing back. Butch is just a step or two behind, almost to the top himself.

> BUTCH
>
> How many of 'em are following us?

> SUNDANCE
>
> All of 'em.

> BUTCH
> *(stunned)*
>
> All of 'em?

Butch is beside Sundance now at the top of the hill and he, too, pauses, looking back.

CUT TO

THE SUPERPOSSE, still bunched, coming after them. In the distance and safe, the rest of the Gang ride away.

CUT TO

BUTCH, FURIOUS, pointing out the rest of his men—

> BUTCH
> *(shouting at the Superposse, pointing at his men)*
>
> What's the matter with those guys?

CUT TO

SUNDANCE taking off, BUTCH a step behind.

CUT TO

The SUPERPOSSE. They just keep coming.

CUT TO

BUTCH AND SUNDANCE riding as fast as they can.

CUT TO

THE SUPERPOSSE. They are going at exactly the same pace as before. They are all in the same position in the pack. Nothing has changed. They are like a machine.

CUT TO

BUTCH AND SUNDANCE going, if anything, faster than before. But the strain is beginning to tell. The sun was high when this began. Now there are shadows. And on their faces, strain.

CUT TO

THE SUPERPOSSE coming on, more like a machine than ever.

CUT TO

BUTCH AND SUNDANCE. They are approaching a spot where several trails are indicated. At the last moment, they veer left, following the least likely path.

CUT TO

BUTCH AND SUNDANCE riding on. The shadows are deeper now. So is their strain.

CUT TO

BUTCH AND SUNDANCE. Abruptly they halt.

> **BUTCH**
> I think we lost 'em. Do you think we lost 'em?

> **SUNDANCE**
> No.

> **BUTCH**
> Neither do I.

And they are off again, riding flat out.

CUT TO

A WATERING PLACE.

SUNDANCE stands beside his horse. BUTCH sits slumped astride his. As the animals drink—

> **SUNDANCE**
> Horses aren't good for much more.

> **BUTCH**
> Me too. *(as Sundance remounts)* We just got to get to Fanny's, that's all. Once we get to Fanny's, we'll be fine.

CUT TO

FANNY PORTER IN HER BROTHEL,

looking concerned.

> FANNY

Trouble?

BUTCH AND SUNDANCE MOVING INTO THE SHOT. Butch nods.

> BUTCH

Bring me Sweetface.

CUT TO

A LONG SWIRLING SHOT that moves and moves across the main floor of the brothel to the stairs. No one is ever still—Butch and Sundance make their steady way to the stairs throughout the shot, and the rest of the activity spins around them.

> SUNDANCE
> *(this to a Bartender who has come running up)*

—get our horses—they're out back—

> BUTCH
> *(He is talking to Sweetface now. Sweetface has the visage of an aging cherub, soft and pink. Compared to him, Cuddles Sakall looks like Mike Mazurki.)*

—listen, you dirty old man—I know you're a lying thief and so do you, but who'd ever think it to look at you, so move yourself out front fast—

> SUNDANCE
> *(to the Bartender, almost at the stairs)*

—feed 'em good and get 'em out of sight—

> BUTCH
> *(on the stairs now, to Sweetface)*

—you seen us ride through town not ten minutes ago—you do this right, I'll get you an old dog to kick—

And as he and Sundance take the stairs two at a time, the swirling shot ends and we

CUT TO

An absolutely glorious tangle of LONG BLOND HAIR.

PULL BACK TO REVEAL

A ROOM UPSTAIRS.

There are WHISKEY BOTTLES and glasses on a table. SUNDANCE stands by the curtained window, looking out, BUTCH is in a chair, locked in a tight embrace with the owner of the blond hair. Her name is AGNES, and we met her already when she came to get Butch to come to the Piano Player's party. Agnes was not Phi Beta Kappa from Bryn Mawr.

CUT TO

BUTCH as the embrace ends. Eyes still closed, he gently rubs his cheek against Agnes'. Holding her close, he speaks in a soft tone.

> **BUTCH**
> Do you realize you're driving me crazy looking out that window? I swear to you, Sweetface can handle this easy. He wouldn't dare louse it up—he's that scared of me.

CUT TO

SUNDANCE still watching out the window.

CUT TO

THE VIEW OUTSIDE THE WINDOW.

SWEETFACE is visible across the street, whittling intently. It is dusk now, with the sun about to die.

> **BUTCH'S VOICE** (off-screen)
> How can I give Agnes the concentration she deserves with you with your nose all the time out the window?

CUT TO

INSIDE THE ROOM.

SUNDANCE has not moved from the window. BUTCH is still fondling AGNES.

> **AGNES**
> You're really something, Butch, you know that?

> **BUTCH**
> Could you be a little more specific there, Agnes?

CUT TO

THE VIEW OUTSIDE THE WINDOW.

SWEETFACE looks up quickly, then just as quickly he is back to his whittling. There is a pause. Then the SUPERPOSSE is visible. The second they appear—

CUT TO

INSIDE THE ROOM.

SUNDANCE
(sharp)

Butch!

BUTCH moves to the window and looks out. AGNES is still very much in his arms.

CUT TO

THE STREET OUTSIDE.

The SUPERPOSSE comes to a halt. SWEETFACE looks up.

BUTCH'S VOICE (off-screen)

Okay, Sweetface—give 'em the smile.

SWEETFACE SMILES. Then he stands and moves toward the Superposse with his hand cupped to an ear, indicating a hearing infirmity.

CUT TO

BUTCH, SUNDANCE, AND AGNES, watching.

BUTCH

I swear if he told me I rode out of town ten minutes ago, I'd believe him.

CUT TO

THE STREET OUTSIDE.

SWEETFACE is nodding now and pointing down the street. The SUPERPOSSE moves off. Sweetface sits back down and begins whittling again.

CUT TO

INSIDE THE ROOM.

BUTCH gives a genuine sigh of relief and even SUNDANCE relaxes. AGNES discreetly begins to undress. Sundance takes notice of this.

SUNDANCE

No, no, don't ask me to stay. *(And he leaves.)*

CUT TO

AGNES continuing to undress. As she does, she speaks of her feelings for Butch. Two things are a little odd about the moment: (1) they are across the room from each other, and not in bed, as the tone of her talk might logically indicate; and (2) there is a definite rote quality to Agnes's words.

> **AGNES**
> You're the only real man I ever met, Butch—it's not just because you got all that money to spend on people—it's you—

CUT TO

BUTCH, while this is going on. He is doing his best to get his boots off.

> **AGNES** (off-screen)
> The way you're always looking to see am I happy or not—a lot of the other girls—they might want you for when you got money to spend on people—me, I don't care for clothes and money and jewels and furs and— *(She stops, because from outside, there is the unmistakable sound of horses' hooves coming closer and closer.)*

CUT TO

SUNDANCE throwing the door of the room open, tearing across to the window, and as BUTCH joins him—

ZOOM TO

SWEETFACE, surrounded by the SUPERPOSSE. They draw their guns. Without a second's pause, Sweetface points dead at the window where Butch and Sundance are hiding, and as he does—

CUT TO

BUTCH AND SUNDANCE silhouetted against the glow left by the sun, as they race across a flat rooftop. They jump to a lower building, tear across that. Then—

CUT TO

BUTCH AND SUNDANCE with the camera at ground level, pointed up as their two bodies thud heavily to the ground.

CUT TO

SUNDANCE on his feet, helping BUTCH, then the two of them taking off around a corner and

CUT TO

BUTCH AND SUNDANCE racing toward the next corner of the building, reaching it, stopping dead.

CUT TO

A MEMBER OF THE SUPERPOSSE, his back to them, RIFLE IN HAND. He guards the

Superposse's horses, which are in the background.

CUT TO

BUTCH AND SUNDANCE, *as they dive for the* SUPERPOSSE GUARD. *Butch hits him around the middle, pinioning his arms, while Sundance clobbers the Guard's head with the butt end of his pistol. The Guard falls without a sound.*

CUT TO

SUNDANCE *moving off in one direction, beckoning for* BUTCH.

SUNDANCE
Our horses are over here—

CUT TO

BUTCH.

BUTCH
Get 'em, then get me. *(He breaks into a run toward the Superposse's horses.)*

CUT TO

The HORSES *as* BUTCH *reaches them. They are enormous animals, and they do not move as he comes up. Quickly he goes from one to the next, untying each in turn until they are all freed. Then—*

BUTCH
(his voice urgent, but not loud)
Okay, move. *(The horses stand there.)* Move, I told you. *(He leads one horse a few steps. Louder now—)* It's okay, go on now, go on. *(The horses do not budge. Louder than before—)* Get out of here! *(The horses stay where they are.)* Ya fathead beasts!! Get gone!!!

CUT TO

SUNDANCE *riding up, leading* BUTCH'S HORSE.

SUNDANCE
You're the fatheaded beast—quit shouting.

BUTCH *mounts, about to take off. He glances back one time.*

CUT TO

The SUPERPOSSE'S HORSES. *They stand very still, waiting.*

CUT TO

BUTCH AND SUNDANCE.

BUTCH
(shaking his head)

Somebody sure trained 'em.

CUT TO

BUTCH AND SUNDANCE riding off at top speed into the early darkness.

CUT TO

SOME WOODS. It is night now. Above, a little moon. Butch and Sundance ride by.

CUT TO

MORE WOODS. Thicker. It is dark here. Butch and Sundance appear, riding slowly. It is ugly riding, the branches of trees constantly whipping out at them.

CUT TO

DEEPER WOODS. The trees are attacking them now, as they ride slowly past, doing their best to protect themselves.

CUT TO

DARKNESS. The woods are still very deep. Abruptly, Butch reins up.

BUTCH

Why are we killing ourselves? It's night. What if they're not even after us?

SUNDANCE

What if they are? *(And he rides on without pausing.)*

BUTCH rides after him.

CUT TO

BUTCH AND SUNDANCE riding. Their FACES ARE CUT now, their clothes are torn.

CUT TO

A CLEARING.

SUNDANCE rides into it first, stops.

SUNDANCE

Which way?

BUTCH
(stopping beside him)

Hell, it doesn't matter—I don't know where we've been, and I've just been there. So they can't be following us. We're safe.

SUNDANCE

You really think so?

BUTCH

I will if you will. *(He rides off.)*

SUNDANCE *rides after him.*

CUT TO

Their TWO HORSES RIDERLESS.

PULL BACK TO REVEAL

THE CREST OF A HILL.

The horses are safely tied. It is still very much night. At the crest of the hill, BUTCH AND SUNDANCE *sit, staring out the way they came. For a moment nothing is said. Then—*

BUTCH

How long you figure we been watching?

SUNDANCE

A while.

BUTCH

How much longer before you think they're not after us?

SUNDANCE

A while longer.

CUT TO

BUTCH. *He stands, stretches.*

BUTCH

I haven't rode so much since I quit rustling. That's a miserable occupation; dusk to dawn, dusk to dawn, no sleep, rotten food—*(and suddenly his tone changes)*—Hey!!

SUNDANCE
(as Butch crouches down beside him)

I see it.

CUT TO

A LONG SHOT OF THE DEEP WOOD through which they have just come. And now, for the first time, the SUPERPOSSE *begins to take on an almost phantom quality. For what we see, very faintly in the distance, is a slowly moving glow. The glow never stops moving. It never moves fast, but it keeps coming toward them.*

> **BUTCH'S VOICE** (off-screen)
> *(whispering)*
> Torches, you think?

> **SUNDANCE'S VOICE** (off-screen)
> Maybe. Maybe lanterns.

> **BUTCH'S VOICE** (off-screen)
> That's our path they're following.

> **SUNDANCE'S VOICE** (off-screen)
> Dead on it.

> **BUTCH'S VOICE** (off-screen)
> I couldn't do that. Could you do that? How can they do that?

CUT TO

BUTCH: CLOSE UP. *Worried.*

> **BUTCH**
> *(the first mention of what will become a litany)*
> Who are those guys?

CUT TO

BUTCH AND SUNDANCE *riding.*

CUT TO

THE GLOW *behind them in the woods. It just keeps on coming.*

CUT TO

BUTCH AND SUNDANCE. *They are riding side by side along a trail, talking as they go.*

> **SUNDANCE**
> *(They have been going over and over this.)*
> —you sure this'll work?

> **BUTCH**
> Positive.

SUNDANCE

You were positive Sweetface was scared of you.

BUTCH

This'll work!

CUT TO

THE TRAIL WHERE IT DIVIDES.

BUTCH AND SUNDANCE come riding into view, side by side still, and Sundance takes a deep breath, times his move, then switches horses, clambering on behind Butch. When the trail divides, BUTCH AND SUNDANCE ON ONE HORSE go off one way, while Sundance's horse is supposed to take the other way, only the horse starts to follow them. Sundance takes a swipe at it with his hat and both shout for the animal to take off.

CUT TO

SUNDANCE'S HORSE stopping.

CUT TO

BUTCH AND SUNDANCE riding on.

CUT TO

SUNDANCE'S HORSE. It takes the other trail. It runs into the darkness and is gone.

CUT TO

BUTCH PACING.

PULL BACK TO REVEAL

THE CREST OF ANOTHER HILL.

This one is more rocklike than the one preceding, as the terrain is starting to change. SUNDANCE rests on his haunches, staring back down the way they've come. The ONE HORSE is in the background. It is still dark, but getting close to dawn now.

BUTCH
(continuing his nervous movement)

Once they divide up, we'll take 'em; no trouble at all, right?

SUNDANCE

Maybe. *(And with that, he snaps his fingers, points.)*

CUT TO

The GLOW OF THE SUPERPOSSE coming steadily ahead.

> **BUTCH'S VOICE** (off-screen)
> They should get to where we split any time now.

The GLOW OF THE SUPERPOSSE *stops.*

> **SUNDANCE'S VOICE** (off-screen)
> They're there.

> **BUTCH'S VOICE** (off-screen)
> I wonder how many'll come our way?—I wish we had rifles—they got rifles—but what the hell, we got surprise going for us, right?

The GLOW OF THE SUPERPOSSE *separates now. One glow moves toward camera. The other begins going in a different direction.*

CUT TO

Butch up and pacing again.

> **BUTCH**
> *(taking out his guns, starting to check them over as he moves)*
> —so far they're doing what we want, so do you think this is a good place to try and take 'em? Down closer to the trail maybe, or—

> **SUNDANCE'S VOICE** (off-screen)
> *(big)*
> Dammit!!

As Butch whirls—

CUT TO

THE SUPERPOSSE. *Slowly, the* TWO GLOWS *are moving back together. They join up, and now there is but a single glow again, and again, slowly, relentlessly, the glow begins moving toward the camera.*

CUT TO

CLOSE UP: SUNDANCE. *For the first time now, he is worried. And it shows.*

> **SUNDANCE**
> Who are those guys?

CUT TO

The GLOW OF THE SUPERPOSSE, *as it continues to move slowly toward them—*

CUT TO

SHERIFF RAY BLEDSOE ASLEEP IN HIS BED.

He is in a small room connected to a small jail. One window looks out at rocky terrain. RAY BLEDSOE is an aging hulk of a man, close to sixty.

CUT TO

BUTCH AND SUNDANCE entering. Bledsoe stirs, glances up, then suddenly erupts from his bed, clearly horrified at what he sees.

> **BLEDSOE**
>
> What are you doing here?

> **BUTCH**
>
> Easy, Ray—

> **BLEDSOE**
>
> *(riding roughshod through anything Butch starts to say to him)*
> —hell, easy—just because we been friends doesn't give you the right— what do you think would happen to me if we was seen together?—I'm too old to hunt up another job. *(glaring at them)* At least have the decency to draw your guns. *(As Butch and Sundance draw, Bledsoe grabs a rope, sits in a chair and tosses the rope to Sundance who hesitates a moment.)* Come on, come on—take it and start with my feet. Just don't make it so tight I can't wiggle loose when you're gone.

Through the remainder of the scene, Sundance binds and gags Bledsoe while Butch paces the room, keeping close track of the view out of the window, always aware of whatever it is that is following, somewhere behind them.

> **BLEDSOE**
>
> You promised you'd never come into my territory—

> **BUTCH**
>
> —and we kept our word, didn't we, Ray?

> **SUNDANCE**
>
> —we never pulled off anything near you—

> **BUTCH**
>
> —everybody in the business we told, "Leave old Ray Bledsoe alone."

> **SUNDANCE**
>
> —we been good to you, Ray—

> **BUTCH**
>
> —now you be good to us—help us enlist in the Army and fight the Spanish.

BLEDSOE

You are known outlaws.

SUNDANCE

We'd quit.

BLEDSOE
(exploding)
You woke me up to tell me you reformed?

SUNDANCE

It's the truth, Ray, I swear.

BUTCH

No, let's not lie to Ray. We haven't come close to reforming. We never will. *(He is desperately honest now.)* It's just—my country's at war and I'm not getting any younger, and I'm sick of my life, Ray.

BLEDSOE
(There is a pause. Then—)
Bull!!!

BUTCH

All right. There's a certain situation that's come up and—it could work, Ray—a lot of guys like us have enlisted; we could, too, if you'd help us— either fake us through or tell the government how we changed—they got to believe you; hell, you never done a dishonest thing yet and what are you, sixty?

BLEDSOE

You've done too much for amnesty and you're too well known to disguise; you should have got yourselves killed a long time ago when you had the chance.

SUNDANCE

We're asking for your help, Ray!

BLEDSOE

Something's got you panicked, and it's too late. You may be the biggest thing ever to hit this area, but in the long run, you're just two-bit outlaws. I never met a soul more affable than you, Butch, or faster than the Kid, but you're still nothing but a couple of two-bit outlaws on the dodge.

BUTCH

Don't you get it, Ray—something's out there. We can maybe outrun 'em awhile longer but then if you could—

BLEDSOE

—you just want to hide out till it's old times again, but it's over. It's over, don't you get that? It's over and you're both gonna die bloody, and all you can do is choose where. *(softer now)* I'm sorry. I'm getting mean in my old age. Shut me up, Sundance.

CUT TO

SUNDANCE—THE GAG *in his hands.*

CUT TO

The GLOW OF THE SUPERPOSSE, *seen in the distance now.*

CUT TO

BUTCH *reaching the rear door, opening it, going out. A moment later,* SUNDANCE *follows him.*

CUT TO

BLEDSOE, *gagged, staring after them; he is terribly moved. Camera holds on the old man a second. Then—*

CUT TO

THE SUN AND IT IS BLINDING.

CUT TO

BUTCH AND SUNDANCE *riding the one horse and riding as fast as they can, considering the terrain, which is a narrow path bordered on both sides by enormous boulders. This is mountainous terrritory starting now and the horse slips, rights itself, and they continue to move with no slowing of pace until we—*

CUT TO

A MOUNTAIN STREAM.

BUTCH AND SUNDANCE *ride across it, then double back almost immediately into the stream and ride in the water for a while. Then they move out of the stream, and almost immediately double back again, re-crossing it surprisingly, picking up the pace now, and then*

CUT TO

BUTCH AND SUNDANCE, *seated on the horse. They are motionless and so is the animal, as they all three wait in a narrow part of the all but invisible path they have been following.*

CUT TO

BUTCH AND SUNDANCE: CLOSE UP. *This shot takes a long time, as they wait, hardly breathing, listening for the least conceivable sound. First there is nothing. Then, as their ears get accustomed, there is wind. The wind picks up. It dies. It starts up again, and Butch and Sundance still wait, motionless, wanting to be damn sure they are safe, and on the wind another sound begins to drum in now: faint but always growing. It is* THE HOOVES OF THE SUPERPOSSE.

CUT TO

BUTCH AND SUNDANCE'S HORSE *starting off in overdrive and—*

CUT TO

BUTCH AND SUNDANCE *going as fast as they can along a difficult trail. They are more worried than before and neither of them bothers to hide it, as they work their horse along as best they can and*

CUT TO

BUTCH AND SUNDANCE *making a difficult cut on their horse, moving into an area that is bounded by boulders, and it's miserable terrain to ride through, but they keep on going, sweaty and beat and*

CUT TO

BUTCH AND SUNDANCE *riding along faster than before, trying another change of direction, then another, never slowing for a second and*

CUT TO

BUTCH AND SUNDANCE, *seated motionless on their horse again. This is another long, long listening shot only they are breathing a little harder now from their efforts, and it's hard to get perfectly quiet, but they make it and then, as before, there is no sound, nothing. Then again, as before, there is wind. Then the wind dies. Then as it starts to build again, there comes the sound right behind them of a rock slipping down and the sound means the Superposse has them dead, but Butch jerks around desperately, getting his guns out, and Sundance's are already free and he fires and fires and as the sound explodes off the boulders—*

CUT TO

A LITTLE DEAD LIZARD. *It has caused the sound they'd heard, the little rock rolling a little way and*

CUT TO

BUTCH AND SUNDANCE looking at each other, both of them with their guns out, and there isn't anything to say, because they are both of them scared and they know it and it shows. Sundance puts his gun back. Butch does the same. They look away from each other and start to ride.

CUT TO

THE HORSE, RIDERLESS. It stands still.

CUT TO

BUTCH AND SUNDANCE scrambling and scratching their way up a boulder. It is terribly bright, the light bouncing viciously off and, as they sweat their way to the top—

CUT TO

THE SUN, more blinding now than ever, and

CUT TO

A LONG LONG SHOT, with the blinding sun bouncing off rocks, making everything hard to see. But there, in the great distance, is the SUPERPOSSE. Looking at them is like looking at a mirage.

CUT TO

BUTCH AND SUNDANCE squinting, shielding their eyes, trying desperately to see.

CUT TO

MIRAGE SHOT. It is very hard to make out what is going on, but perhaps all the Superposse, save ONE MAN, are on horseback, and perhaps that ONE MAN is on his haunches, staring at the ground.

CUT TO

BUTCH AND SUNDANCE squinting out.

> **BUTCH**
> Don't they know it's stupid trying to follow people over rocks?

> **SUNDANCE**
> Yeah, they've sure been acting awful dumb.

> **BUTCH**
> *(genially)*
> They're beginning to get on my nerves.

> **SUNDANCE**
> *(not so genially)*
>
> Who are those guys?!

> **SUNDANCE**
>
> You remember when you and Etta and me went to Denver last summer for a vacation?

CUT TO

BUTCH: CLOSE UP. He is absolutely stupefied by the question.

> **BUTCH**
>
> Now, there's a really important topic, considering our situation—I'm sure glad you brought that up.

CUT TO

SUNDANCE: CLOSE UP. He is as pensive right here as Butch is agitated.

> **SUNDANCE**
>
> That night we went gambling, remember?

CUT TO

BUTCH AND SUNDANCE.

> **BUTCH**
>
> Sure, Kid, I remember. We ate supper at the hotel first. I had the roast beef and Etta ordered chicken, and if I could only remember what you had, I'd die a happy man.

> **SUNDANCE**
> *(ignoring Butch; going right on)*
>
> Look out there—*(and as he points—)*

CUT TO

MIRAGE SHOT. It is still very hard to make anything out with clarity, but it appears that all the Superposse are still on horseback, save ONE, who is still on his haunches, staring at the ground.

> **SUNDANCE'S VOICE** (off-screen)
>
> We got to talking with some gambler that night. And he told us about the Indian. A full-blooded Indian except he called himself with an English name. Sir somebody...

> **BUTCH'S VOICE** (off-screen)
>
> Lord Baltimore.

SUNDANCE'S VOICE (off-screen)

That's right. He called himself Lord Baltimore, and he could track any-body. Over anything. Day or night.

CUT TO

BUTCH *AND* SUNDANCE *LYING on the boulder, staring out.*

BUTCH

So?

SUNDANCE

That guy on the ground—I think it's him...

CUT TO

MIRAGE SHOT—THE MAN ON THE GROUND. *It is as if Butch and Sundance are strain-ing their eyes to the point of pain, trying to see clearly. The Man on the Ground might indeed be an Indian, but the sun bouncing off the rocks is just too strong, the distance just too great. During this—*

BUTCH'S VOICE (off-screen)

I can't quite see him clear.

SUNDANCE'S VOICE (off-screen)

Me either. But it might be.

CUT TO

BUTCH *AND* SUNDANCE. *Sundance still stares out. Butch turns to him.*

BUTCH

Except he works out of Oklahoma—Lord Baltimore's strictly an Oklahoma man and I don't know where we are, but it isn't Oklahoma, so it couldn't be him, it couldn't be him.

SUNDANCE
(nodding)

I guess.

CUT TO

MIRAGE SHOT. *The Man on the Ground stands slowly, then gestures dead in the direc-tion of Butch and Sundance. As he does—*

SUNDANCE'S VOICE (off-screen)

But whoever he is, he sure the hell is somebody.

THE MAN ON THE GROUND *mounts. The Superposse begins to move forward again, steadily, inevitably, and*

CUT TO

BUTCH AND SUNDANCE, *both of them on the one horse, riding as fast as they can.*

CUT TO

A VERY HIGH SHOT *of a trail leading through a canyon. The terrain now is wilder, rockier, increasingly isolated, increasingly beautiful. Below now, Butch and Sundance can be made out.*

PULL BACK TO REVEAL

THE SUPERPOSSE *behind them, closer now, moving as steadily and smoothly as a machine.*

CUT TO

BUTCH AND SUNDANCE *on the horse. Butch is going on nervous energy now, and it shows. They come to a break in the rocks, and he stares back—we know at what.*

> **BUTCH**
> Damn them anyway. Aren't they hungry?—aren't they tired?

> **SUNDANCE**
> Got to be.

> **BUTCH**
> *(anger building)*
> Then why don't they slow down? Hell, they could speed up and that'd be fine too—it'd be a change. They don't even break formation—*(shouting)*—Do something!

CUT TO

MIRAGE SHOT. *The Superposse moves on as before.*

> **SUNDANCE'S VOICE** (off-screen)
> They're like their horses—somebody sure trained 'em.

CUT TO

An extremely rocky area.

CUT TO

BUTCH AND SUNDANCE. Sundance leads the horse now, as they scramble along as fast as they can. When the terrain allows for it, they run.

CUT TO

BUTCH AND SUNDANCE running until, without warning, Butch trips and falls heavily down.

> **BUTCH**
> *(grabbing the rock that tripped him)*
> Ya stupid rock!! *(and he smashes it down against a boulder)*

BUTCH AND SUNDANCE walking, terribly out of breath. Their faces drip sweat.

> **BUTCH**
>
> Hey!

> **SUNDANCE**
>
> What?

> **BUTCH**
>
> Who's the best lawman?

> **SUNDANCE**
>
> Best how? You mean toughest or easiest to bribe?

> **BUTCH**
>
> Toughest.

> **SUNDANCE**
>
> Joe Lefors.

> **BUTCH**
> *(nodding)*
>
> Got to be.

> **SUNDANCE**
>
> Why...?—*(answering the question himself)* You crazy? Joe Lefors never leaves Wyoming—never, and you know it.

> **BUTCH**
>
> But he wears a white straw skimmer, doesn't he? That's how you know it's Joe Lefors, by that white straw skimmer.

CUT TO

MIRAGE SHOT.

                                 BUTCH'S VOICE (off-screen)
      Well? That guy in the middle...?

THE SUPERPOSSE is too far away to tell anything exactly. But the Man in the Middle does appear to be wearing a hat that might indeed be white, that might be made of straw.

CUT TO

BUTCH AND SUNDANCE, wedged between some rocks, staring out at the Superposse—

                                 SUNDANCE
                             (almost a whisper now)
      Who are those guys?

CUT TO

A SHOT OF THE TERRAIN. It is even rougher now, verging on the mountainous. And really very beautiful.

CUT TO

BUTCH AND SUNDANCE stumbling along, leading the horse. The way they are taking is the flattest way possible, but now, more and more, there are paths that lead up into the mountains.

CUT TO

BUTCH AND SUNDANCE making their way. They are completely exhausted, beat down to the ground. Their clothes are ragged and torn and so are they. They pause for a moment, gulping down air, pulling it into their lungs and

CUT TO

MIRAGE SHOT. THE SUPERPOSSE is moving on foot now, their horses following along behind them. But they move fast and seemingly without effort, as if in a dream.

CUT TO

BUTCH AND SUNDANCE glancing back, pushing on.

CUT TO

A SHOT OF THE MOUNTAINS. It's later in the afternoon now.

CUT TO

BUTCH AND SUNDANCE sending their horse the way they have been going while they cut off and up, into the mountains.

CUT TO

The HORSE *going.*

CUT TO

BUTCH AND SUNDANCE *moving up higher into the mountains.*

CUT TO

THE TWO OF THEM *making their way. They are following a fairly wide path and making good time. Below them, a mountain stream is occasionally visible.*

CUT TO

BUTCH AND SUNDANCE *catching their breath a moment, glancing back the way they came.*

                              BUTCH
         I figure they followed the horse, don't you?

                             SUNDANCE
             No.

CUT TO

THE PATH *far below them. The* SUPERPOSSE *moves into view, on foot.*

CUT TO

BUTCH AND SUNDANCE *watching as the Superposse becomes visible.*

CUT TO

THE SUPERPOSSE. *They move on foot as they moved on horseback: bunched together, silently, without strain.*

CUT TO

BUTCH AND SUNDANCE *going like sixty.*

CUT TO

The PATH THEY ARE FOLLOWING, *as it curves along. Below, the stream is widening and going faster, something it continues to do.* SHADOWS *are starting to lengthen. Soon, dusk.*

CUT TO

BUTCH AND SUNDANCE *doing their best. The path is narrower now, but still wide enough for them both to move side by side and they force themselves along it.*

CUT TO

The path curving up. They race along it, then begin to slow as the path starts to narrow.

CUT TO

The path. They are moving Indian file now, Sundance leading.

CUT TO

A shot of the two of them from the stream below. At this distance, perhaps fifty feet, as they move through sunlight and shadow, they seem very, very small.

CUT TO

The path widening, and they pick up the pace.

CUT TO

The path widening more, and they are both of them running flat out, heedless of where they are, and

CUT TO

THE SUN, just starting to edge down over the mountains and

CUT TO

THE STREAM, quite wide and fast now, and still in sunlight, while all around it there is shadow; the effect is stunning as it swirls around and around—

CUT TO

THE PATH, ENDING.

CUT TO

BUTCH AND SUNDANCE standing there, just standing there, gaping at the dead end the path has led them into.

BUTCH AND SUNDANCE
(together)

DAMMIT!

CUT TO

A LONG SHOT of the two of them standing there stunned, the sound echoing over and over and

CUT TO

BUTCH AND SUNDANCE whirling, starting back the way they came and

CUT TO

The S<small>UPERPOSSE</small> *moving up toward them.*

CUT TO

B<small>UTCH AND</small> S<small>UNDANCE</small> *watching them come.*

> **BUTCH**
> What I figure is we can fight or we can give. *(Sundance nods.)* If we give, we go to jail.

CUT TO

C<small>LOSE</small> U<small>P</small>: S<small>UNDANCE</small>, *shaking his head.*

> **SUNDANCE**
> *(with all the meaning in the world)*
> I been there already.

CUT TO

B<small>UTCH</small> *nodding in agreement.*

> **BUTCH**
> Me too. If we fight, they can stay right where they are and starve us out—
> *(He glances up now and—)*

CUT TO

T<small>HE</small> M<small>OUNTAIN</small> *above them. High up, there are open flat places where a man could fire down on them.*

> **BUTCH'S VOICE** (off-screen)
> —or they could go for position and shoot us—

CUT TO

B<small>UTCH AND</small> S<small>UNDANCE</small>.

> **BUTCH**
> —or they could start a little rockslide and get us that way. What else could they do?

> **SUNDANCE**
> They could surrender to us, but I don't think we oughtta count on that.

CUT TO

B<small>UTCH</small>. *He laughs, but the moment won't hold.*

> **BUTCH**
> *(flat and down)*
>
> What're we gonna do?

CUT TO

BUTCH AND SUNDANCE.

> **SUNDANCE**
>
> You always been the brains, Butch; you'll think of something.

> **BUTCH**
>
> Well, that takes a load off; for a while there, I was worried. *(He looks back down the way they came and—)*

CUT TO

The SUPERPOSSE. THE MAN IN THE WHITE HAT *is gesturing and now the Superposse begins to split, some of them moving into a higher path that leads above where Butch and Sundance are.*

CUT TO

BUTCH AND SUNDANCE *watching them climb.*

> **SUNDANCE**
>
> They're going for position all right. *(He takes out his guns, starts to examine them with great care.)* We better get ready.

> **BUTCH**
> *(getting his guns ready)*
>
> The next time I say let's go somewhere like Bolivia, let's go somewhere like Bolivia.

> **SUNDANCE**
>
> Next time.

CUT TO

THE SUPERPOSSE. *They continue to make their way up, moving quickly and silently across the mountain.*

CUT TO

SUNDANCE.

> **SUNDANCE**
> *(watching them get into position)*
>
> You ready, Butch?

BUTCH'S VOICE (off-screen)

No!!

And as Sundance turns—

ZOOM TO

CLOSE UP: BUTCH. *He is smiling.*

BUTCH

We'll jump!

CUT TO

THE STREAM BELOW. *It is fifty feet down and going very fast.*

CUT TO

BUTCH AND SUNDANCE.

SUNDANCE

Like hell we will.

BUTCH
(really excited now—all this next is overlapping and goes like a shot)

No, no, it's gonna be okay—just so it's deep enough we don't get squished to death—they'll never follow us—

SUNDANCE

—how do you know?

BUTCH

—would you make that jump if you didn't have to?

SUNDANCE

I have to and I'm not gonna—

BUTCH

—it's the only way. Otherwise, we're dead. They'll have to go all the way back down the way we came. Come on—

SUNDANCE
(looking up at the mountains)

—just a couple decent shots, that's all I want—

BUTCH

—come on!

                              SUNDANCE
—no—

                              BUTCH
—we got to—

                              SUNDANCE
—no—

                              BUTCH
—yes—

                              SUNDANCE
—get away from me—

                              BUTCH
—why?

                              SUNDANCE
—I wanna fight 'em—

                              BUTCH
—they'll kill us—

                              SUNDANCE
—maybe—

                              BUTCH
—wanna die?

                              SUNDANCE
—don't you?

                              BUTCH
—I'll jump first—

                              SUNDANCE
—no—

                              BUTCH
—okay, you jump first—

                              SUNDANCE
—no, I said—

                              BUTCH
                              (big)
What'sa matter with you?!

> **SUNDANCE**
> *(bigger)*
> I can't swim! *(Blind mad, wildly embarrassed, he just stands there.)*

CUT TO

BUTCH, *starting to roar.*

CUT TO

SUNDANCE, *anger building.*

CUT TO

BUTCH.

> **BUTCH**
> You stupid fool, the fall'll probably kill you.

CUT TO

SUNDANCE, *starting to laugh now and*

CUT TO

THE TWO OF THEM. *Butch whips off his gun belt, takes hold of one end, holds the other out. Sundance takes it, wraps it once tight around his hand. They move to the edge of the path and step off.*

CUT TO

BUTCH AND SUNDANCE *falling through the twilight.*

CUT TO

THE BIGGEST SPLASH EVER RECORDED.

CUT TO

THE STREAM *going like hell. Then—*

CUT TO

BUTCH AND SUNDANCE ALIVE *in the water. Music begins, the same music that went on during Butch and Etta's bicycle ride, and as the music picks up, so does the speed of the current as it carries them along, spinning and turning and*

CUT TO

THE SUPERPOSSE, FROZEN *in the twilight on the mountainside. As they stand there—*

CUT TO

BUTCH AND SUNDANCE *from high above, swirling happily along.*

HOLD ON

BUTCH AND SUNDANCE *in the twilight. They move in and out of shadow, sputtering, coughing, holding tight to the gun belt as the music hits a climax and they are swept safely from view....*

FADE OUT.

FADE IN ON

ETTA PLACE ON HER DOORSTEP. LATE NIGHT.

ETTA'S ARMS *are locked around her legs; her chin rests on her knees. She looks half dead.*

CUT TO

CLOSE UP: ETTA. *She just sits there, waiting, hunched over, motionless. One gets the feeling she was born in that position, and when she dies, she will never have moved.*

CUT TO

THE NIGHT. *It is too dark to make anything out clearly until we—*

CUT TO

BUTCH AND SUNDANCE *moving out of the darkness toward Etta. They have come a long way now, and there is nothing left. They manage to keep walking.*

CUT TO

ETTA RISING *as they close the gap. Without a word, she moves to meet them and her arms go around them both. They stand that way a moment,* ETTA AND HER MEN. *Then—*

> ETTA
>
> The papers said they had you.

> SUNDANCE
>
> Was it Lefors, did they say?

> ETTA
> *(a little hesitant nod)*
> Joe Lefors...? I think that was the name.

> SUNDANCE
>
> And their tracker?

ETTA

Tracker?

BUTCH

Was it Lord Baltimore?

ETTA

I think so—the paper's inside.

BUTCH hurries into the house. For a moment, ETTA holds just SUNDANCE, but their game has never been to show anything, no matter what, so she drops her arms.

SUNDANCE

Got enough to feed us?

ETTA

Don't you know I do?

CUT TO

ETTA turning. She starts toward the front door. With her back to SUNDANCE—

ETTA

They rumored you were dead and—

CUT TO

SUNDANCE.

SUNDANCE

—don't make a big thing out of it.

CUT TO

ETTA. She nods once, continues silently toward the house. Then—

CUT TO

SUNDANCE watching as Etta moves away.

SUNDANCE

No—it's okay; make a big thing out of it.

ETTA starts to whirl toward him but, before the move is half done, he has her and she completes the spin with his arms already around her, and it's dark, and they don't embrace for long, but still, we can see it: They care for each other. They care.

CUT TO

BUTCH INSIDE THE HOUSE,

sitting at the dining table, looking at a paper.

> BUTCH
> *(calling out)*
> Hey—it was Lefors and Baltimore and you know who else?

CUT TO

SUNDANCE AND ETTA ENTERING. Etta goes to the stove, where a large pot is simmering and probably has been for days. She reaches for plates and during this—

CUT TO

BUTCH AND SUNDANCE.

> BUTCH
> *(reading: the names are enormously impressive to him)*
> Jeff Carr, George Hiatt, T.T. Kelliher...

> SUNDANCE
> *(The names register on him too; as he sits across from Butch)*
> We lucked out, getting away, you know that? *(Butch nods.)* Now, why would those guys join up and take after us?

> BUTCH
> *(folding the paper away)*
> Forget it—a bunch like that won't stay together long.

CUT TO

ETTA CONCENTRATING very hard on fixing their food.

> ETTA
> You didn't finish the article, Butch—they're hired till you're dead.

CUT TO

BUTCH AND SUNDANCE, stunned.

CUT TO

ETTA. She looks at them briefly, nods.

CUT TO

BUTCH AND SUNDANCE

> SUNDANCE

Who by?

CUT TO

ETTA, piling food onto two plates, being very careful not to spill.

> ETTA

Mr. E.H. Harriman of the Union Pacific Railroad. He resents the way you've been picking on him, so he outfitted a special train and hired some special employees—you've spent the last few days avoiding them—it's really sort of flattering, if you want to think about it that way.

CUT TO

BUTCH AND SUNDANCE AND ETTA.

> BUTCH

Hell, a setup like that's costing him more'n we ever took—

> ETTA

Apparently he can afford it.

CUT TO

BUTCH. CLOSE UP. Wild and upset and angry.

> BUTCH

That crazy Harriman—it's bad business—how long do you think I'd stay in operation if every time I pulled a job it cost me money?—if he'd just give me what he's spending to make me stop robbing him, I'd stop robbing him. He probably inherited every penny he's got; those inherited guys, what do they know?

CUT TO

SUNDANCE AND ETTA.

> SUNDANCE

You say they're hired permanent?

> ETTA

No, no, no—just till they kill you. (*She brings the food to the table and—*)

CUT TO

SUNDANCE, up fast, moving to the door—he is upset now too.

> **SUNDANCE**
> That means they're still after us, Butch—it's gonna be like yesterday all over again—they'll show here sooner or later—

CUT TO

BUTCH.

> **BUTCH**
> I vote for later. *(And as he begins ravenously to eat—)*

CUT TO

Two plates rapidly emptying of food.

CUT TO

ETTA, *sitting on the front steps, while behind her at the table* BUTCH AND SUNDANCE *eat.*

> **SUNDANCE**
> Hey, Etta—

> **ETTA**
> *(Very pensive, she stares out, in the same waiting position as when they came back.)*
> I'll get you some more.

CUT TO

Butch and Sundance, as they move out into the darkness with her.

> **SUNDANCE**
> Butch and me been talking and wherever the hell Bolivia is, that's where we're off to.

> **BUTCH**
> We're just gonna hide out till it's safe and maybe keep our hand in a little.

> **SUNDANCE**
> Butch speaks some Spanish—

> **BUTCH**
> You know, I can wrestle with a menu okay.

CUT TO

SUNDANCE

> **SUNDANCE**
> *(to Etta)*

You speak it good. And it'd be good cover for us going with a woman—
no one expects it—we can travel safer. So what I'm saying is, if you want
to come with us, I won't stop you, but the minute you start to whine and
make a nuisance, I don't care where we are, I'm dumping you flat.

CUT TO

BUTCH.

> **BUTCH**

Don't sugarcoat it like that, Sundance—tell her straight—

CUT TO

ETTA: CLOSE UP.

> **ETTA**
> *(For a moment, she says nothing. Then, starting soft, building as she goes—)*

I'm twenty-six, and I'm single, and I teach school, and that's the bottom
of the pit. And the only excitement I've ever known is here with me now.
So I'll go with you, and I won't whine, and I'll sew your socks and stitch
you when you're wounded, and anything you ask of me, I'll do, except
one thing: I won't watch you die. I'll miss that scene if you don't mind...

HOLD ON ETTA'S LOVELY FACE a moment—

DISSOLVE TO

A SMALL SUITCASE.

PULL BACK TO REVEAL

*ETTA dressed for travel. The house is dark as she picks up the suitcase, goes to the door,
looks around her little home one final time, then—*

CUT TO

BUTCH AND SUNDANCE WAITING OUTSIDE.

*ETTA goes to SUNDANCE who reaches for her bag. BUTCH takes a final glance around and,
as he turns his head—*

PAN TO

*THE NIGHT. It is a GIGANTIC LONG SHOT and very beautiful, and as THE CAMERA MOVES
along, it comes to Butch's bicycle, leaning against the side of Etta's house.*

CUT TO

BUTCH *going to the bicycle, picking it up, giving it a shove with all he has and*

CUT TO

THE BICYCLE ROLLING ALONG, *then beginning to totter, then crashing down onto its side. As the wheels continue to spin—*

CUT TO

BUTCH: CLOSE UP. *Bawling it out big:*

BUTCH
The future's all yours, ya lousy bicycles!!!

CUT TO

THE BICYCLE WHEELS, *spinning slower and slower in the darkness until there comes an almost blinding flash of hard white light, and we are into*

MUSICAL INTERLUDE NUMBER TWO.

This is the New York sequence, and the flash of hard white light mentioned above is the flash from the equipment of a Portrait Photographer, as he takes a picture of Butch, Sundance, and Etta. (In fact, it was perhaps the leading society photographer of the day who photographed them when they visited—much of what they did in New York is documented in some way or other.) This sequence is in black and white, and over the song is a series of actual still photographs of New York at this time—lower Fifth Avenue, Central Park, etc.—with Butch and Sundance and Etta processed into the photos. The camera moves over the stills, picking out the various emotional moments. And it was an emotional time for them—kind of sad, since they were leaving their country; kind of exciting, since they were able to lead the sort of civilized life impossible in the West at this time. None of them had ever enjoyed such elegance before, and this feeling of elegance grows and grows and, as the song ends, we have moved in time and space and are in Bolivia.

CUT TO

A SMALL PATCH OF SAND.

(We are back in color now.) A pair of boots walk onto the patch, stand there. Then another pair of boots move up to the first; finally, a pair of shoes encasing a lady's feet move up and stop. There is a moment's pause before we

PULL BACK TO REVEAL

BUTCH AND SUNDANCE AND ETTA, standing on what might be called a street in a pit of a town that in no way resembles the French Riviera—horrid little low adobe huts stretch out and an occasional pig grunts by. Butch glances at Sundance, who is close to a Homeric anger. In the distance, a stagecoach pulls away.

> BUTCH
> *(to Etta)*
> Just think, fifty years ago there was nothing here. *(Sundance just stares at Butch.)* It's not as bad as it might be—you get more for your money in Bolivia than anywhere—I checked—

> SUNDANCE
> —what could they sell here you could possibly want to buy?

CUT TO

THE STREET.

It really is terrible. You wouldn't wish the place on your mother-in-law.

CUT TO

BUTCH AND SUNDANCE.

> BUTCH
> All Bolivia can't look this way—

> SUNDANCE
> How do you know?—this might be the garden spot of the whole country—people might travel hundreds of miles just to get where we're standing now—this might be the Atlantic City, New Jersey, of all Bolivia, for all you know—

> BUTCH
> I know as much about Bolivia as you do about Atlantic City, New Jersey, I'll tell you that much—

> SUNDANCE
> You do? I was born in New Jersey; I was brought up there, so—

CUT TO

BUTCH, genuinely surprised.

> BUTCH
> You're from the East? I didn't know that.

CUT TO

SUNDANCE.

> **SUNDANCE**
> The total tonnage of what you don't know is enough to—

CUT TO

ETTA, *moving to them, doing her best to pacify them.*

> **ETTA**
> I'm not sure we're accomplishing as much as we might. Now—

> **SUNDANCE**
> Listen: Your job is to back me up because you'd starve without me.

> **ETTA**
> *(biting the words out)*
> I—shall—commit—that—to—memory.

> **SUNDANCE**
> *(to Butch now)*
> And you—your job is to shut up.

CUT TO

BUTCH *moving to* ETTA.

> **BUTCH**
> *(softly, consoling)*
> He'll feel a lot better once we robbed a couple banks.

CUT TO

SUNDANCE *staring around him.*

> **SUNDANCE**
> Bolivia!

CUT TO

A SMALL BANK

We're in a different, bigger town. The bank is on the town's busiest street. A few people straggle by.

PULL BACK TO REVEAL

BUTCH AND SUNDANCE *casually watching the bank from across the street.*

BUTCH
(as they start toward the bank)
Now, when we get inside, remember, the first thing we do is to check to
make sure that—

SUNDANCE
—I know how to rob a bank—don't tell me how to rob a bank—

BUTCH
Boy, a few dark clouds appear on your horizon, you just go all to pieces.

CUT TO

INSIDE THE BANK

BUTCH AND SUNDANCE appear in the doorway.

CUT TO

BUTCH AND SUNDANCE peering around, trying to get their bearings.

CUT TO

A LARGE ARMED GUARD watching them. He is seated but now stands, begins moving forward.

CUT TO

BUTCH AND SUNDANCE, watching the Guard approach, both of them ready.

CUT TO

THE ARMED GUARD. He stops. There is a pause. Then—

ARMED GUARD
Buenos días; le puedo servir?

CUT TO

BUTCH AND SUNDANCE. Sundance looks at Butch, waiting for him to say something.
Butch just stands there stunned. Then—

CUT TO

A CHEAP HOTEL ROOM.

BUTCH AND SUNDANCE AND ETTA SIT, huddled together. Etta is teaching them Spanish.

ETTA
All right, pay attention now. This is a robbery: Esto es un robo.

BUTCH

Esto es un robo.

ETTA
(to Sundance)

We're supposed to be doing unison recitation.

SUNDANCE

I don't know why I have to do any of this—he's the one claimed he knew the damn language—

ETTA

We've gone over this before—your line of work requires a specialized vocabulary—

BUTCH

That's right—I got nervous—I didn't know the words—shoot me—

SUNDANCE

You've had worse ideas lately.

CUT TO

ETTA. She means what she's saying—

ETTA

I simply cannot tolerate this kind of outburst—both together, now—this is a robbery: Esto es un robo.

CUT TO

BUTCH AND SUNDANCE.

BUTCH AND SUNDANCE
(together—Sundance a trifle sullen)

Esto es un robo.

CUT TO

ETTA. Throughout, her vocal intonations are of the same machine-like quality achieved by Berlitz instructors.

ETTA

Raise your hands: Manos arriba.

CUT TO

BUTCH AND SUNDANCE AND ETTA. DAY.

They are walking along a HOT, QUIET STREET *now. The lesson goes right on.*

BUTCH AND SUNDANCE
(together)

Manos arriba.

ETTA

Raise them!—Arriba!

BUTCH AND SUNDANCE
(together)

Arriba!

CUT TO

CLOSE UP: ETTA.

ETTA
(to Butch)

All of you—back against the wall.

PULL BACK TO REVEAL

BUTCH AND SUNDANCE AND ETTA.

They are eating in a CRUMMY RESTAURANT.

BUTCH
(doing his best)

Todos ustedes—arrimense a la pared.

ETTA
(to Sundance now)

Give me the money.

CUT TO

SUNDANCE: CLOSE UP. *The answer's on the tip of his tongue.*

PULL BACK TO REVEAL

SUNDANCE AND ETTA IN BED.

SUNDANCE

What was that again?

> ETTA
> *(impatient)*

Give me the money.

SUNDANCE embraces ETTA suddenly. He's all over her, nuzzling her, holding her to him.

> ETTA

That's not going to work, and we're going to stay up all night till you get this: Give me the money. *(She knocks on the wall by the bed.)* You still thinking in there?

> BUTCH'S VOICE (off-screen)

What the hell else is there to do?

> ETTA
> *(to the wall)*

Try this one: Where's the safe? Open it.

CUT TO

THE NEXT ROOM.

BUTCH is rapidly running his finger down a crib sheet.

> BUTCH

That's a hard one—just lemme think, now—*(And he's found it on his sheet.)*—Dónde está la caja? Abrala.

> ETTA'S VOICE (off-screen)

That's very good, Butch.

CUT TO

ETTA AND SUNDANCE IN BED.

> BUTCH'S VOICE (off-screen)

You're just a good teacher, Etta.

> ETTA
> *(to Sundance)*

For the last time: Give me the money.

CUT TO

SUNDANCE. The answer is so close now it's killing him.

CUT TO

ETTA.

ETTA

You'd starve without me.

DISSOLVE TO

A BOLIVIAN STREET. DAY.

PULL BACK TO REVEAL

BUTCH *AND* SUNDANCE *AND* ETTA. *She is dressed, purse in hand, looking out the window.*

ETTA

Someplace out there must sell horses. I'll get the best I can with what we have left. *(going to the door)* And don't expect much. *(as she exits)*—And don't stop—begin at the beginning and go right through: This is a robbery. *(And on these words—)*

CUT TO

THE SAME ARMED GUARD AS BEFORE.

As before, he speaks:

GUARD

Buenos días, le puedo—

SUNDANCE'S GUN *hits him once on the head and as he falls senseless,*

PULL BACK TO REVEAL

BUTCH *AND* SUNDANCE *in the bank, guns drawn.*

BUTCH

Esto es...es...*(He yanks out his crib sheet.)* Robo!

CUT TO

EVERYONE IN THE BANK. *Before Butch can even finish, they all quietly raise their hands and back quickly against the wall.*

CUT TO

BUTCH.

BUTCH
(jumpy as hell—reading, first more or less to himself,
making sure he's got it right, then out loud. To himself—)

Raise your hands. *(out loud)* Manos arriba.

CUT TO

SUNDANCE MOVING NERVOUSLY among the People in the bank, frisking them for weapons as he goes.

> **SUNDANCE**
> They got 'em up—skip on down—

CUT TO

BUTCH READING.

> **BUTCH**
> *(to himself)* Raise them! *(out loud)* Arriba!

CUT TO

SUNDANCE.

> **SUNDANCE**
> Skip—on—down!

CUT TO

BUTCH.

> **BUTCH**
> *(to himself)* Back against the wall. *(out loud)* Arrimense a la pared.

CUT TO

SUNDANCE.

> **SUNDANCE**
> They're—against—the—wall—already!!

CUT TO

BUTCH, furious.

> **BUTCH**
> Don't you know enough not to criticize someone who's doing his best? *(going to Sundance, shoving the paper at him)* Here—you're so damn smart, you read!!

CUT TO

THE BANK PEOPLE standing quietly confused, hands raised, looking at each other.

CUT TO

BUTCH AND SUNDANCE, each of them carrying small bags of money, tearing out of the bank and—

CUT TO

ETTA, IN THE SHADOWS OF A BUILDING.

She is dressed in men's clothing and she waits expectantly, staring out of the shadows. She holds the reins of three horses, none of them much worth looking at. As BUTCH AND SUNDANCE come running into view, she quickly mounts her horse, leads the other two toward them and

CUT TO

PEOPLE FROM THE BANK.

Pouring out onto the street, they look around, then start to call out:

> **BANK PEOPLE**
> Bandidos—bandidos Yanquis!!—

CUT TO

BUTCH AND SUNDANCE AND ETTA, riding just as fast as their horses will go out of town and

CUT TO

HALF A DOZEN BANK PEOPLE running into the office of the local constabulary—"corregidores," as they were called.

> **BANK PEOPLE**
> *(jabbering to the Chief Corregidor, a lean, uniformed officer)*
> —bandidos Yanquis—bandidos Yanquis...!!!!!

CUT TO

BUTCH AND SUNDANCE AND ETTA, riding on, except all the horses are rotten and already starting to show strain.

CUT TO

THE CHIEF CORREGIDOR racing into a room where three assistants sit playing cards.

> **CHIEF CORREGIDOR**
> Bandidos Yanquis! *(And as the men quickly stand—)*

CUT TO

THE FOUR CORREGIDORS riding out of town. Their horses are fresh and powerful-looking, and there is no question that they look competent as hell and

CUT TO

THE FOUR CORREGIDORS, in open country now, riding quickly and well and...

CUT TO

THE TERRAIN. There are rocks and groves of trees now as the four corregidors continue their efficient way and

CUT TO

THE FOUR CORREGIDORS riding like hell in one direction, a no-nonsense quartet, and as a terrible barrage tears into them, a hat flies off, their horses rear in sudden panic, and the three assistants take off without a moment's hesitation back in the opposite direction, back the way they came. The CHIEF CORREGIDOR hesitates for only a moment, but when another barrage of bullets sounds, he takes off in the same direction as his men: away.

CUT TO

BUTCH AND SUNDANCE AND ETTA, staring after the disappearing corregidors.

> **BUTCH**
> *(gesturing after them)*
> Isn't that a beautiful sight? *(on a note of triumph)* We're back in business,
> boys and girls—it's just like the old days! *(And with these words, begins—)*

MUSICAL INTERLUDE NUMBER THREE.

This accompanies a SERIES OF SOUTH AMERICAN ROBBERIES. There is dialogue in and out, and it is entirely possible that the song, for example, would be entitled "Bandidos Yanquis" and would be loud and rhythmic, like one would expect a Spanish-titled song to be. But not necessarily—again, here as before, the connection is not literal between scene and song: The song might be a simple Quaker-type tune extolling the virtues of labor. Whatever the case, the robberies go like this:

CUT TO

INTERIOR OF BANK #2.

TWO BOLIVIAN BANK CLERKS. Their hands are raised, their backs against the wall, and they are watching as, in the background, BUTCH AND SUNDANCE busily rob the bank.

> **FIRST BANK CLERK**
> *(whispering to the Second Clerk)* Bandidos Yanquis. *(The Second Clerk looks blank. The First Clerk repeats, a little louder.)* Bandidos Yanquis. *(The Second Clerk just shrugs—he's never heard of them.)*

CUT TO

INTERIOR OF BANK #3.

An ELEGANTLY DRESSED BANK EXECUTIVE, moving toward an enormous bank vault. As he goes, he gestures about proudly, showing off his bank.

CUT TO

BUTCH AND SUNDANCE, dressed extremely well. Sundance carries a satchel and both he and Butch are clearly very impressed with the quality of the bank they are depositing their money in.

As they approach the vault door, Butch gestures and Sundance hands the Bank Executive their satchel. The Bank Executive smiles and—

CUT TO

The VAULT DOOR swinging open.

CUT TO

BUTCH AND SUNDANCE AND THE BANK EXECUTIVE.

> **BANK EXECUTIVE**
> *(still smiling)*
> So you see how foolish your fears were?

> **SUNDANCE**
> *(as they enter the vault)*
> No one could get in here, that's for sure.

And suddenly there is A GUN IN HIS HAND and—

CUT TO

THE BANK EXECUTIVE.

> **BANK EXECUTIVE**
> Who are you?

CUT TO

BUTCH happily scooping up money, stuffing it into their satchel.

> **BUTCH**
> We're from the Red Cross.

CUT TO

INTERIOR OF BANK #4.

TWO BOLIVIAN BANK CLERKS *(not the same two as before). Their hands are raised, their backs against a wall, and they are watching as, in the background,* BUTCH AND SUNDANCE *busily rob the bank.*

> FIRST BANK CLERK
> *(whispering to the Second Clerk as he nods toward Butch and Sundance)*
> Bandidos Yanquis.

> SECOND BANK CLERK
> *(Interested, he's heard of them.)*
> Sí?

> FIRST BANK CLERK
> Sí.

CUT TO

THE BOLIVIAN COUNTRYSIDE.

A BAND OF CORREGIDORS *riding like crazy in one direction before getting blasted. They immediately wheel around and take off like hell back the way they came as the third Musical Interlude ends.*

CUT TO

BUTCH AND SUNDANCE AND ETTA *dining in as nice a restaurant as Bolivia has to offer. It is early evening, a lovely night, and the restaurant offers a fine view of the street. Butch and Sundance are looking just a little older now; not much, just a little.*

> BUTCH
> *(raising a glass)*
> I'd like to propose a toast to Bolivian law enforcement.

They drink; a WAITER *appears with a large tray of food, puts it down nearby.*

CUT TO

BUTCH AND ETTA *watching as the* WAITER *sets about serving them. The food looks really good. Etta glances toward Sundance and*

CUT TO

SUNDANCE, *only he isn't there now, just an empty chair, and then quick—*

CUT TO

BUTCH AND ETTA *looking around confused and—*

CUT TO

SUNDANCE and he is doing something very strange: His body pressed flat, he is standing against the closest wall of the restaurant, hiding, and he cannot take his eyes from the street.

CUT TO

THE STREET. It is dark, but not too dark to make out the figures of THREE MEN *moving down the street by the restaurant. The* MAN *in the middle wears a white straw skimmer.*

ZOOM TO

BUTCH frantically saddling up a horse.

PULL BACK TO REVEAL

SUNDANCE AND ETTA watching him. We are in a dimly lit stable and Sundance guards the door. Etta moves between the men.

> **SUNDANCE**
> —I say let's go find him—let's get it done—

> **BUTCH**
> —We might lose—we just saw two men with him—he might have twenty, we don't know—

> **ETTA**
> You don't even know for sure it was Lefors—

> **BUTCH**
> I'm one helluva guesser.

> **ETTA**
> He can't arrest you here—there are laws against that. And he can't take you back either.

> **SUNDANCE**
> He's not about to take anybody back—he's going to finish us right here. He's just gonna wait until we pull another job and then hunt us down like before, and if he misses us, he'll wait for the next job and get us then. So let's finish it now, Butch; one way or the other.

CUT TO

BUTCH, and he is smiling.

BUTCH

He's waiting for us, right? Well, let him—we'll drive him crazy—we'll outlast the bastard—we'll go straight!

And on the word "straight"—

CUT TO

PERCY GARRIS: CLOSE UP.

GARRIS

So ya want jobs—

PULL BACK TO REVEAL

GARRIS, *standing on the steps in front of his office at the Concordia Tin Mines high in the Bolivian mountains. He is a flinty bantam rooster of a man, with an incongruously mellifluous voice.*

GARRIS

—you're from the U.S. of A. and you're seeking after employment. Well, you couldn't have picked a more out-of-the-way place in all Bolivia, I'll tell you that.

CUT TO

BUTCH AND SUNDANCE, *standing at the foot of the steps below him.*

BUTCH

We're awful interested in learning about mining without any of those big-city distractions.

CUT TO

GARRIS.

GARRIS

Ordinarily you got to wait to work for Percy Garris, but this ain't ordinarily—bingo!

It might be mentioned here that GARRIS IS A WORLD-CLASS TOBACCO SPITTER, *and his speech is punctuated with the words "dammy" or "bingo," depending on his accuracy.*

CUT TO

BUTCH AND SUNDANCE.

BUTCH

Then there are jobs?

CUT TO

GARRIS, *advancing on them.*

> **GARRIS**
> Yes, there are jobs, there are lotsa jobs, don't you wanna know why?

> **SUNDANCE**
> Okay. Why?

> **GARRIS**
> Dammy—'cause I can't promise to pay you, don't you wanna know why?

> **BUTCH**
> Okay. Why?

> **GARRIS**
> On account of the payroll thieves, fellow citizens, that's why—bingo! Every mine around gets its payroll from La Paz and every mine around gets its payroll held up.

CUT TO

BUTCH AND SUNDANCE *as* GARRIS *moves toward them again.*

> **GARRIS**
> Some say it's Bolivian bandits, some say the bandidos Yanquis; can you hit anything? *(And he points to their guns.)*

> **SUNDANCE**
> Sometimes.

> **GARRIS**
> Hit that—

And he pitches a plug of tobacco a good distance away.

CUT TO

SUNDANCE *stepping back, getting ready to draw. Then—*

> **GARRIS' VOICE** (off-screen)
> No, no. *(And he moves into view.)* I just want to know if you can shoot.

He grabs one of SUNDANCE'S *PISTOLS from its holster, shoves it to Sundance.*

> **GARRIS**
> Shoot.

SUNDANCE grabs the gun, fires, and

CUT TO

THE TOBACCO PLUG, undisturbed as the shot misses.

CUT TO

BUTCH, stunned, looking at SUNDANCE.

> **SUNDANCE**
> Can I move?

CUT TO

SUNDANCE AND GARRIS.

> **GARRIS**
> *(confused)*
> Move? What the hell you mean, move?

But before the words are half-finished—

CUT TO

SUNDANCE dropping, drawing, firing, all in one motion and as his gun erupts—

CUT TO

THE TOBACCO PLUG, obliterated.

CUT TO

SUNDANCE, rising.

> **SUNDANCE**
> *(explaining, simply)*
> I'm better when I move.

CUT TO

BUTCH AND SUNDANCE AND GARRIS.

> **GARRIS**
> *(He is not unimpressed.)*
> Considering that I'm desperate and you're just what I'm looking for, on top of which you stem from the U.S. of A., we'll start in the morning.

> **BUTCH**
> You mean you're hiring us?

>   SUNDANCE
>   *(as excited as Butch)*
>
> We got jobs?

>   GARRIS
>   *(nodding)*
>
> Payroll guards.

And as the occupation is named,

CUT TO

THREE MEN ON MULEBACK *riding back down the mountain.* GARRIS *rides ahead, singing "Sweet Betsy from Pike" in a loud and lovely voice.* BUTCH AND SUNDANCE *lag behind.*

CUT TO

BUTCH AND SUNDANCE. *They have never done this kind of thing before and are both in a sweat, anticipating attack.*

>   BUTCH
>   *(low and tense)*
>   I think they're in those rocks up ahead—

>   SUNDANCE
>   *(pointing to the other side of the trail)*
>   No—the shrubs—*(a whisper)*—Butch, I see them moving—

CUT TO

GARRIS, *glancing balefully around at the two of them.*

CUT TO

BUTCH AND SUNDANCE, *riding nervously on.*

>   BUTCH
>   I'm telling you they're in the rocks—

>   SUNDANCE
>   You take the rocks, I'll take the shrubs—

CUT TO

THE ROCK-SHRUBS *area as* BUTCH AND SUNDANCE *ride slowly through*—GARRIS *has ridden through it already and has stopped up ahead of them, still glaring back.*

>   GARRIS
>
> Will you two beginners cut it out!

CUT TO

Butch and Sundance riding up to him.

> **BUTCH**
> We're just trying to watch out for ambush, Mr. Garris.

> **SUNDANCE**
> We've never done this kind of work before—we want to get it right—

> **GARRIS**
> *(exploding)*
> Morons! I got morons on my team!! Nobody's gonna rob us going *down* the mountain—we got no money going *down* the mountain—when we get the money, on the way back, then you can sweat!

CUT TO

Four payroll bags being pushed across a counter.

PULL BACK TO REVEAL

THE COUNTER IN A BANK.

Garris is signing for the payroll money as Butch and Sundance stand aside, watching him.

> **GARRIS**
> *(taking the bags)*
> Jones—gimme a hand with these—

> **SUNDANCE**
> *(whispered)*
> Which are you, Smith or Jones?

> **BUTCH**
> *(shrugging)*
> Live.

And as he starts toward Garris—

CUT TO

The three of them riding out of La Paz, starting back up toward the mountains.

CUT TO

Butch and Sundance and Garris in the mountains now.

GARRIS rides with the payroll bags. BUTCH AND SUNDANCE are more nervous than ever, whirling and turning as they ride.

> GARRIS
>
> 'Bout a half hour more we can start to worry. *(He points to an enormous rock a considerable distance up ahead of them.)* Once we pass that rock.

> SUNDANCE
>
> They might try something here.

> GARRIS
> *(shaking his head)*
>
> Better cover up there.

They are riding through an area with smaller rocks and boulders around them, and BUTCH AND SUNDANCE finger their guns, constantly on the alert. GARRIS rides calmly ahead. Then—

> GARRIS
>
> Got to relax, you fellas; got to get used to Bolivian ways; got to go easy, dammy, like I do...

CUT TO

BUTCH AND SUNDANCE, continuing their constant straining around.

> GARRIS
> *(chattering on)*
>
> —'course you probably think I'm crazy but I'm not—bingo! I'm colorful; that's what happens to you when you live ten years alone in Bolivia—you get colorful—

And as a sudden unexpected blast of gunfire starts—

CUT TO

BUTCH AND SUNDANCE AND GARRIS, rolling off their mules.

CUT TO

The area around them, as MORE SHOTS ring out. No one is visible.

CUT TO

BUTCH AND SUNDANCE, wedged together behind one rock as the firing at them continues.

> BUTCH
>
> It's not us so it must be the Bolivians.

CUT TO

The area around them. Still MORE SHOTS *pour down, narrowly missing them, but still no one is seen.*

CUT TO

BUTCH AND SUNDANCE, *wedged behind the rock. Butch's face is visible. Sundance's, behind him, is not.*

> SUNDANCE

Butch—

> BUTCH
> *(He is trying desperately to locate where the firing is coming from.)*

What?

> SUNDANCE

Butch!!

> BUTCH

I'm right beside you—*(Suddenly Sundance hits him on the back.)*—Hey—*(As Sundance hits him again)* Cut it out!

SUNDANCE, *turning—we see his face now—he is terribly moved.*

> SUNDANCE

What are we doing here? *(Butch says nothing.)* You got to tell me—I got to know—what are we doing? I'm not sure anymore—are we outlaws? You're smart, Butch, so you tell me—

> BUTCH
> *(And now he too is moved.)*

We're outlaws. Outlaws. I don't know why. 'Cause we're good at it. I been one since I was fifteen, and my wife left me on account of it, and she took our kids on account of it, and I'm not sure anymore either.

CUT TO

SUNDANCE: CLOSE UP.

> SUNDANCE

You had a family? I didn't know that.

CUT TO

BUTCH: CLOSE UP. *He says nothing.*

CUT TO

SUNDANCE.

SUNDANCE
Let's find Garris and get the hell out of here.

He gestures toward a neighboring rock and as the firing continues—

CUT TO

BUTCH AND SUNDANCE, diving from their rock to Garris's, rolling over and up and

CUT TO

GARRIS, dead. The payroll bags are beside him.

CUT TO

BUTCH AND SUNDANCE. They hover over Garris for just a moment until the firing increases in intensity. Then Sundance grabs for a payroll bag, brings out a knife, and as he begins to slit the bag—

CUT TO

The rock behind which they are hiding. The firing continues. Suddenly a payroll bag comes flying out from behind the rock and soaring high into the air.

CUT TO

THE PAYROLL BAG. It arcs down and as it hits, coins come spilling out through a cut in the side.

CUT TO

The SECOND OF THE FOUR BAGS flying through the air, landing and

CUT TO

The THIRD AND FOURTH BAGS, and while they are still in the air,

CUT TO

BUTCH AND SUNDANCE, breaking from cover and running away like crazy down the mountain. A few scattered shots land near them as they continue to run away—

DISSOLVE TO

A LARGE PILE OF COINS and, beside it, several smaller piles.

PULL BACK TO REVEAL

HALF A DOZEN ARMED BOLIVIAN BANDITS. They sit silently on their haunches, watching as one of them, the Leader, carefully divides up the money. The only sound is that of the coins falling.

CUT TO

BUTCH AND SUNDANCE, moving onto a flat piece of ground, a bit above the bandits. They stand still, their guns in their holsters.

CUT TO

THE LEADER. He glances up, sees them. He makes no move to draw, but points instead.

CUT TO

BUTCH AND SUNDANCE, motionless and still, as the other Bandits look up at them.

CUT TO

THE BANDITS WAITING, still on their haunches. There is no sound.

> **SUNDANCE**
> Tell him we were hired to take it back—it's our job—tell him the money isn't ours.

> **BUTCH**
> El dinero...no es nuestro—

> **SUNDANCE**
> Tell him we need it.

> **BUTCH**
> El dinero...lo necesitamos...

CUT TO

THE LEADER. He cannot believe what he is hearing.

CUT TO

BUTCH AND SUNDANCE and the Bandits. No one makes a move.

> **SUNDANCE**
> Leave the money and go.

> **BUTCH**
> Dejan el dinero y vayanse.

> **LEADER**
> Dejan el dinero y vayanse?

                              BUTCH

Sí.

CUT TO

THE BANDIT LEADER. *Slowly he stands.*

                              BUTCH

What do you think?

                            SUNDANCE

Not so good. Try telling him again it's not our money.

                              BUTCH

El dinero...no es nuestro.

                            SUNDANCE

No es nuestro...!

CUT TO

THE BANDITS. *A SECOND MAN stands now. Then a THIRD. Still no sound.*

CUT TO

BUTCH AND SUNDANCE.

                            SUNDANCE

Can you take the two on the right?

                              BUTCH

Listen, there's something I think you ought to know—I've never shot anybody.

                            SUNDANCE

This is one helluva time to tell me—

CUT TO

THE BANDITS. *They are all standing now. Silent.*

CUT TO

BUTCH AND SUNDANCE.

                            SUNDANCE

—try the two on the right—I'll work my way over if I can—go for the gut, dead center—that way if you miss a little you'll still hit something—

CUT TO

SUNDANCE: CLOSE UP.

> **SUNDANCE**
> —you got a wife and kids and you never shot a soul—*(bewildered; almost sad)* I just don't understand anything anymore.

CUT TO

THE BANDITS. The Leader is saying something to his men but the words aren't clear.

CUT TO

BUTCH AND SUNDANCE.

> **SUNDANCE**
> Please go. Please. Por favor.

CUT TO

THE BANDITS.

> **THE LEADER**
> Por favor? *(It strikes him as funny.)* Por favor?

And as he goes for his guns—

CUT TO

BUTCH AND SUNDANCE, drawing and firing. Sundance first, Butch after him and

CUT TO

THE BLOODBATH. Camera stays on the BANDITS, and in the next sixty seconds, the action freezes sixty times, and the first sound that we hear is the deafening blast of gunfire as Butch and Sundance's bullets thud home and from left to right, the Bandits start to die.

And the left-to-right move is the first move the camera makes, panning across the dying men, some of them with their guns still in their holsters, and then, as the gunfire ends, another sound begins, just as loud and just as terrifying and this sound is a scream. It doesn't come from any one Bandit, it isn't even connected in any actual way with any one man, but it is the loudest scream anyone ever heard, and it peaks almost immediately and then it really starts to build as the blood starts pouring from the Bandits, from their chests, mouths, eyes.

And once the left-to-right move is over, the camera begins its second move, and the direction of the second move is down, as gradually, the Bandits, no longer able to stand, start slipping gracelessly to earth. And every second, the action freezes them in their final trip, and the scream keeps them company, and even though the trip is short, it still takes time for all six to slip and stagger and crumble awkwardly to their knees and beyond, toppling sideways and backwards and forwards, but always down, colliding finally with the hard earth, which is red now with their blood as it leaves the dying bodies and as the scream ends, the blood continues to drain ceaselessly into the ground—

CUT TO

BUTCH AND SUNDANCE, *staring at the holocaust. Butch is shattered; Sundance is numb.*

> SUNDANCE
> *(very quiet)*
> Well, we've gone straight; what'll we try now?

CUT TO

THE CONCORDIA MINES. NIGHT.

GARRIS'S MULE *moves into view. Garris is strapped to it. As the mule comes close to camera, the payroll bags are visible, strapped tight to Garris's body. As the mule moves on...*

CUT TO

ETTA BY THE FIRE. *She is pouring coffee.*

PULL BACK TO REVEAL

A CAMPSITE.

It is night and it is cold. SUNDANCE *sits near the fire, finishing a plate of food. He nods when* ETTA *puts his coffee down beside him.*

CUT TO

ETTA *moving to* BUTCH *with another cup of coffee. He sits off by himself.*

CUT TO

BUTCH, *as* ETTA *comes up. He and Sundance both look a little older now. Not much. Just a little.*

> ETTA
> *(as she gives him his coffee)*
> Done?

BUTCH *nods.*

> ETTA
> I'll take your plate then. *(She picks it up—the food is untouched.)* Full?

Butch nods again.

                              ETTA
Good. *(She starts away. As she goes—)* There's other ways of going straight,
you know.

CUT TO

BUTCH. *He makes no reply.*

CUT TO

ETTA *pouring coffee for herself, sitting beside* SUNDANCE.

                              ETTA
There's other ways of going straight, you know. *(She sips her coffee.)*
There's farming—we've got the money; we could buy a little place.

                            SUNDANCE
I don't know how to farm.

                              ETTA
What about a ranch then?

                    BUTCH'S VOICE (off-screen)
Closest we ever came to ranch work was back in our rustling days—

CUT TO

BUTCH.

                              BUTCH
We weren't much at it even then, and it's hard. The hours are brutal. No,
you got to be a kid to start a ranch.

CUT TO

ETTA.

                              ETTA
It was a silly idea. Sorry.

CUT TO

SUNDANCE *watching the fire.*

CUT TO

BUTCH *watching the night.*

CUT TO

ETTA sipping her coffee. After a moment, she closes her eyes...

DISSOLVE TO

THE CAMPSITE. The fire is out now; it is very late and very cold—when they speak, the three of them, you can see their breath white in the darkness. SUNDANCE AND ETTA lie under one blanket, their backs to each other. BUTCH, wrapped in a blanket, is off by himself. This scene is written for the camera to be in constant motion above the three people lying below; sometimes it comes down close to them, sometimes it rises away. But it never stops moving.

ETTA
(wide awake)

Hey?

SUNDANCE
(wide awake too)

Hmmm?

ETTA

Maybe I might go back ahead of you.

SUNDANCE

You mean home?

ETTA

I was thinking of it.

SUNDANCE
(He doesn't want her to go.)

Whatever you want, Etta.

ETTA

Then maybe I'll go.

SUNDANCE
(to Butch)

Hey?

BUTCH
(He is also wide awake.)

Hmm?

SUNDANCE

Etta's thinking of maybe going home ahead of us.

> BUTCH
> *(He doesn't want her to go either.)*

Whatever she wants.

> ETTA

I'll go then.

> BUTCH

Hey?

> ETTA

Hmm?

> BUTCH

Remember what you said once about leaving us?

> ETTA
> *(She remembers.)*

No; what did I say?

> BUTCH

That you wouldn't stick around to watch us die.

> ETTA

Now, Butch, you know I never said anything like that.

> BUTCH

Then that's not why you're going?

> ETTA
> *(Of course it is.)*

Of course it isn't.

> BUTCH

I didn't think it was—

And now, as the CAMERA MOVES TO THE NIGHT, it holds for just a moment on the silent darkness. Then, as a very distinct hissing sound becomes increasingly audible—

CUT TO

The FAINT FLICKERING IMAGE of an evil-looking man.

CAMERA PULLS BACK TO REVEAL a makeshift movie theatre—it really is nothing more than a large-sized tent—on the edge of a decent-sized Bolivian town. The theatre is crammed with Bolivian peasants, all of them hissing the evil-looking man on the screen. Seated among the Bolivians are BUTCH AND SUNDANCE AND ETTA. The hissing stops suddenly, turns to a gasp, and

CUT TO

THE SCREEN. An innocent, beautiful, helpless young girl is totally unaware that the evil-looking man is creeping up behind her.

CUT TO

BUTCH AND SUNDANCE AND ETTA. Butch and Sundance are drinking more than a little. Etta is dressed for travel. She looks weary.

> ETTA
> *(opening her purse, consulting a timepiece)*
> I ought to get over to the station...

> SUNDANCE
> We'll walk you.

> ETTA
> It's just down the street.

The hissing grows louder and—

CUT TO

THE SCREEN. The evil-looking man is carrying the girl across a moor.

CUT TO

BUTCH AND SUNDANCE AND ETTA.

> BUTCH
> Listen, if there's one thing about us, we got manners—

> ETTA
> *(firmly)*
> It's just down the street. *(softer)* Really.

There are cheers from the audience now, so

CUT TO

THE SCREEN. A blond handsome man appears, begins chasing the evil-looking man and girl. A title comes on reading: "The Cliff," and then the evil-looking man is visible, holding the girl over a precipice. Then another title comes on reading: "In the Nick of Time."

> SUNDANCE'S VOICE (off-screen)
> *(while the title is on)*
> These guys can't read English.

> **BUTCH'S VOICE** (off-screen)
> These guys can't read Spanish.

CUT TO

The AUDIENCE *cheering wildly now.*

CUT TO

BUTCH AND SUNDANCE AND ETTA watching the screen as the hero and villain struggle on the precipice. The hero falls, clutches the edge with his fingertips. The villain stomps on them, but the hero fights his way back, and now it is the villain's turn to fall and clutch the edge. The hero does his best to save him, but too late. The villain falls to eternity. The cheering is tumultuous. During all this—

> **ETTA**
> They just ship them straight down from America—they're supposed to be very popular up there now.

ON THE SCREEN: *The hero holds the girl. Then the title: "The End." Then a plain white light beams onto the screen as the next picture is gotten ready.*

CUT TO

ETTA, slowly starting to stand.

> **ETTA**
> There's something I'd like to say to you both...

CUT TO

BUTCH AND SUNDANCE looking at her.

CUT TO

BUTCH AND SUNDANCE AND ETTA, with Etta on her feet now.

> **ETTA**
> *(catching their look)*
> Oh, you thought I was going to be sentimental and embarrass you, admit it. *(shaking her head)* All these years and we don't know each other at all.

She starts to go, stops suddenly, as the next one-reeler begins and the title "The Hole-in-the-Wall Gang" flickers on the screen.

CUT TO

Butch and Sundance, riveted.

CUT TO

A TITLE *reading: "The Hole-in-the-Wall Gang Are All Dead Now but Once They Ruled the West." This is followed by a picture of a gang of men in shadow, watching the approach of an oncoming train.*

CUT TO

THE AUDIENCE *starting to hiss.*

CUT TO

THE SCREEN AND A TIGHT SHOT OF THE GANG. *(In this "movie," all the actors should be dressed as the real people were dressed, and they should look like the real people as much as possible.)*

CUT TO

The AUDIENCE HISSING *louder now.*

CUT TO

BUTCH AND SUNDANCE.

> **BUTCH**
> *(to Sundance)*
> Did it say we're dead? We're not dead.

CUT TO

THE SCREEN AND A TITLE *reading, "Their Leaders Were Butch Cassidy and the Sundance Kid." This is followed by a shot of "Butch and Sundance" grappling with a small child.*

CUT TO

The AUDIENCE, *as suddenly the hissing doubles in volume and*

CUT TO

THE SCREEN, *as "Butch and Sundance" are tying the child to the railroad tracks in order to stop the oncoming train—*

CUT TO

BUTCH AND SUNDANCE.

> **SUNDANCE**
> —we didn't do that—never—

> **BUTCH**
> —damn right we didn't—Etta, you tell 'em—

CUT TO

ETTA: CLOSE UP. *She is just leaving the theatre now and this is the first of a series of shots of her—all of them walking shots as she moves away and into the night—all of them close and getting closer.*

CUT TO

BUTCH AND SUNDANCE, *and Butch whirls back to the screen, as suddenly the* AUDIENCE *is cheering like crazy and—*

CUT TO

THE SCREEN, *as "the Superposse" appears. The cheering grows louder as "the Superposse" takes out guns and begins firing.*

CUT TO

THE SCREEN, *and* BUTCH AND SUNDANCE *watching it.*

BUTCH
(as "Harvey Logan" is gunned down)
Hey, that's Harvey—*(grabbing Sundance now)*—They didn't get Harvey, then—you think they got him later?

SUNDANCE
—I don't know, I don't know—

As "News Carver" is shot:

SUNDANCE
—they just got News—

He turns quickly, glancing back to where Etta exited.

CUT TO

ETTA: CLOSE UP. *Walking. The sound of the crowd inside the theatre is terribly loud in the night. She continues to move away.*

CUT TO

BUTCH AND SUNDANCE WATCHING *the screen. As "Flat Nose Curry" dies:*

BUTCH
—There goes Flat Nose—My God, they're getting everybody—

The audience is screaming now and Butch turns on them.

BUTCH

—shut up, you people—

CUT TO

SUNDANCE: CLOSE UP.

SUNDANCE
(riveted on the screen)

Butch—

CUT TO

BUTCH AND SUNDANCE.

SUNDANCE
(grabbing Butch now)

Look—they're coming after us!

CUT TO

THE SCREEN, as "the Superposse" takes off after "Butch and Sundance."

CUT TO

Butch turning again to the screaming audience—

BUTCH

This isn't how it was—it wasn't like that—shut up—

CUT TO

THE SCREEN. "The Superposse" is closing the gap on "Butch and Sundance."

CUT TO

BUTCH AND SUNDANCE, staring at the screen and—

CUT TO

THE SCREEN, as "the Superposse" draws nearer, nearer and

CUT TO

BUTCH AND SUNDANCE on their feet now, caught up in the action on screen, talking softly, almost in spite of themselves.

BUTCH

—They'll never get you—

SUNDANCE

—move—you can do it—move—

BUTCH

—come on, you guys—

SUNDANCE

—all the way—

BUTCH AND SUNDANCE
(together)

—come—on—you—guys—

But ON THE SCREEN, *"the Superposse" continues to close in.*

CUT TO

A SERIES OF SHOTS. *And this next sequence consists of* QUICK CUTS *to:*

(1) Butch and Sundance watching the screen

(2) The action on the screen

(3) The audience cheering wildly, the sound always building

(4) Etta walking away, her face always growing as the camera comes closer and closer to her.

On the screen, "the Superposse" forces "Butch and Sundance" into a corner where they can't ride anymore and "Butch and Sundance" get off their horses and try to climb to safety up the rocks that have cornered them, but "the Superposse" is too quick for them, too smart, and before "Butch and Sundance" are halfway up the rocks, "the Superposse" is already firing and the audience is screaming itself crazy as "Butch" gets winged and the explosive nature of the sound carries through the night to Etta, who continues her walk away from it all, and on screen now, "Butch" is hit again—"Sundance" too—and they slip and slide down the rocks as "the Superposse" continues to fire on them. "Butch" is dead as he slides to earth. As "Sundance" dies, Etta's stunning face fills the screen. HOLD *on Etta.* HOLD...

FADE OUT.

FADE IN ON

A shot from above of a mule train moving slowly along a Bolivian jungle trail. It is a payroll train and the four men who accompany it are armed. The trail is narrow, the going slow. The sun is blistering.

CUT TO

A SECTION OF JUNGLE.

Foliage is terribly thick and nothing is visible beyond it. Then something moves and

CUT TO

BUTCH AND SUNDANCE, crouched in the jungle beside the trail. They both look older now. Not a little. A lot. Butch is nervous, continually swatting away flies.

BUTCH
(Whispering—the payroll train is close.)

No more of this jungle work for me.

SUNDANCE
(whispering back)

You're getting to be an old maid.

CUT TO

THE FOUR PAYROLL GUARDS. They stand tightly together, arms raised. Sundance covers them, while in the background, Butch gathers up the payroll money. The Guards look at each other, silently mouth the words "Bandidos Yanquis," and stand very still.

CUT TO

BUTCH, as he works away.

BUTCH

You can keep your old-maid remarks to yourself, if you don't mind, because I got a right to my opinion and my opinion is there's snakes around here, so I'll work in the mountains and I'll work in the cities, but from now on, jungle work is out. Hey, c'mere.

CUT TO

SUNDANCE moving to BUTCH, always watching the Guards.

SUNDANCE

What?

BUTCH

Whoever owns this Alpoca Mine must be a millionaire—*(He points to the payroll—it is big.)* We'll never be able to carry it all. *(He reaches for the nearest mule. It is a large, silver-gray animal. They start to work, transferring payroll bags to the mule.)* If it isn't one thing, it's another.

CUT TO

The MULE, LOADED with the payroll. Butch starts to lead it off.

CUT TO

BUTCH AND SUNDANCE.

> **BUTCH**
> *(as he goes)*
> Tell them not to move.

> **SUNDANCE**
> What's the word?

> **BUTCH**
> Quietos.

And he disappears into the jungle.

> **SUNDANCE**
> *(to the Guards)*
> Quietos!

CUT TO

THE FOUR GUARDS. *They are alone with their mules now. Sweat pours down their faces. They do not move.*

DISSOLVE TO

A STREET IN A SMALL TOWN.

BUTCH AND SUNDANCE LEAD TWO MULES, *the large silver-gray one and one other. The silver-gray mule carries the payroll money, which has been adequately concealed beneath a blanket.*

> **BUTCH**
> This must be San Vicente, you think?

> **SUNDANCE**
> *(nods)*
> Isn't there supposed to be a good place to eat here?

CUT TO

A SMALL, WHITE-HAIRED MAN. *He owns the restaurant.*

PULL BACK TO REVEAL

BUTCH AND SUNDANCE, *talking to him.*

> BUTCH
> *(miming eating)*

Comer? Sí?

> WHITE-HAIRED MAN
> *(He gestures toward a patio.)*

Sí.

BUTCH AND SUNDANCE start off in the direction the man indicated, leading their mules. The MAN smiles as they go. Then his smile abruptly dies and—

CUT TO

THE SILVER-GRAY MULE. It is branded.

CUT TO

BUTCH AND SUNDANCE, seated alone in a tiny restaurant, starting to eat.

CUT TO

THE SILVER-GRAY MULE.

PULL BACK TO REVEAL

The RESTAURANT OWNER AND TWO POLICEMEN, peering from behind cover at the mule.

> RESTAURANT OWNER
> *(whispering as he points to the mule)*

El mulo es de Alpoca Mines.

> FIRST POLICEMAN

Cierto?

> RESTAURANT OWNER
> *(raising his right hand)*

Sí.

THE FIRST POLICEMAN whispers something to the SECOND, who moves off quickly.

CUT TO

BUTCH AND SUNDANCE. Sundance manages to eat. Butch stares at his food, then shoves his plate away, standing.

> BUTCH

The speciality of the house and it's still moving.

SUNDANCE

—bitch, bitch, bitch—

CUT TO

THE DOORWAY OF THE TINY RESTAURANT.

BUTCH moves into it and stands there in the sunlight until a shot almost takes his head off, and

CUT TO

BUTCH diving down back inside the room. SUNDANCE is crouched, guns ready.

BUTCH

That settles it—this place gets no more of my business.

CUT TO

SUNDANCE moving around the room, from window to window.

CUT TO

THE VIEW OUTSIDE THE WINDOW.

There is a WALL THAT SURROUNDS THE RESTAURANT with just the open patio in between. Beyond the wall no one is visible.

CUT TO

BUTCH moving close alongside SUNDANCE as he completes his circle around the tiny room.

BUTCH

What do you think?

SUNDANCE

Can't tell.

BUTCH

I bet it's just one guy.

SUNDANCE takes off his hat, raises it to a window. As he does this—

CUT TO

HALF A DOZEN POLICEMEN rising up behind the wall, blasting away.

CUT TO

BUTCH AND SUNDANCE.

> SUNDANCE
> *(pulling his hat back)*
> Don't you get tired of being right all the time?

CUT TO

THE WINDOW *as seen from beyond the wall.*

Again the hat appears and again, half a dozen policemen rise and fire and

CUT TO

A NEIGHBORING WINDOW, *and* SUNDANCE *framed there, firing back, and*

CUT TO

A TALL POLICEMAN *spinning and falling, lying quiet on the ground.*

CUT TO

THE MULES *in the far corner of the patio. The sound of gunfire increases steadily. The mules stand motionless.*

CUT TO

The TALL POLICEMAN *lying on the ground. Then—*

PULL BACK TO REVEAL

SEVERAL OTHER POLICEMEN *lying sprawled out too. It's later.*

CUT TO

INSIDE THE RESTAURANT.

It has been all shot up. The tables are turned over for protection. BUTCH *is crouched behind one window,* SUNDANCE *behind another.*

> SUNDANCE
> *(loading his pistols)*
> This is all I got left.

> BUTCH
> Me too. *(He starts to crawl along the floor to a different window.)* Now, we can either stay here until we run out and get killed, or we can go get some more. *(He points.)*

CUT TO

THE MULES, *all the way across the patio from the tiny restaurant.*

CUT TO

BUTCH AND SUNDANCE, crouched by a window, staring at the animals. The silver-gray mule is behind the smaller pack mule.

>   **SUNDANCE**
> Which one's got the bullets?

>   **BUTCH**
> The little one.

>   **SUNDANCE**
>   *(starting to crawl toward the door)*
> I'll go.

CUT TO

BUTCH.

>   **BUTCH**
> This is no time for bravery: I'll let you.

CUT TO

THE PATIO.

From where they are, the mules are a long, long way.

CUT TO

INSIDE THE ROOM.

SUNDANCE is by the door now. BUTCH, across the floor, watches him.

>   **BUTCH**
> Hey? *(Sundance glances at him.)* I gotta be the one to go.

>   **SUNDANCE**
> Why you?

>   **BUTCH**
> I could never give you cover. You can cover me. *(Sundance says nothing.)*
> I'm right. You see that, don't you?

CUT TO

SUNDANCE: CLOSE UP.

>   **SUNDANCE**
> You go.

CUT TO

BUTCH: *CLOSE UP.*

> **BUTCH**
> Why am I so damn smart all the time?

And as he shakes his head—

CUT TO

THE PATIO.

—and far across, the mules.

CUT TO

THE HEAD POLICEMAN, rifle in hand, staring in at the room where Butch and Sundance are.

CUT TO

INSIDE THE ROOM.

BUTCH AND SUNDANCE stand by the door. Silently, Butch hands Sundance his pistols.

CUT TO

THE HEAD POLICEMAN staring in across the patio toward where Butch and Sundance are. Then, as he watches, the door to the room silently opens. The Head Policeman raises his rifle, aims it dead at the door.

CUT TO

THE DOOR: Completely open now.

CUT TO

THE HEAD POLICEMAN waiting. Then—

CUT TO

SUNDANCE, vaulting through a shattered window, moving out into the sunlight of the patio, two guns in his hands, two more in his holsters, and as he comes he fires and starts to turn and as the first turn happens—

CUT TO

BUTCH barrel-assing out the door.

CUT TO

SUNDANCE now, firing with both guns, turning around and around, firing as he spins and maybe he wasn't the greatest gunman that ever lived, but then again, maybe he was and

CUT TO

BUTCH running like hell, then diving to the ground, rolling up and running again and

CUT TO

THE HEAD POLICEMAN with SUNDANCE in the background. He is about to fire when suddenly Sundance changes the direction of his turn, and the Head Policeman has to drop for safety behind the wall.

CUT TO

BUTCH, streaking, diving again, then up, and the bullets landing around him aren't even close as we

CUT TO

SUNDANCE, whirling and spinning, continuing to fire and

CUT TO

SEVERAL POLICEMEN dropping for safety behind the wall and

CUT TO

BUTCH really moving now, dodging, diving, up again and

CUT TO

SUNDANCE flinging away one gun, grabbing another from his holster, continuing to turn and fire and

CUT TO

TWO POLICEMEN falling wounded to the ground and

CUT TO

BUTCH letting out a notch, then launching into another dive forward and

CUT TO

SUNDANCE whirling, but you never know which way he's going to spin and

CUT TO

THE HEAD POLICEMAN cursing, forced to drop for safety behind the wall and

CUT TO

BUTCH *racing to the mules, and then he is there, grabbing at the near mule for ammunition and*

CUT TO

SUNDANCE *throwing the second gun away, reaching into his holster for another, continuing to spin and fire and*

CUT TO

BUTCH, *and he has the ammunition now and*

CUT TO

ANOTHER POLICEMAN *screaming as he falls and*

CUT TO

BUTCH, *his arms loaded, tearing away from the mules and they're still not even coming close to him as they fire and the mules are behind him now as he runs and cuts and cuts again, going full out and—*

CUT TO

THE HEAD POLICEMAN *cursing incoherently at what is happening and*

CUT TO

SUNDANCE *whirling faster than ever and*

CUT TO

BUTCH *dodging and cutting and as a pattern of bullets rips into his body, he somersaults and lies there, pouring blood and*

CUT TO

SUNDANCE *running toward him and*

CUT TO

ALL THE POLICEMEN *rising up behind the wall now, firing and*

CUT TO

SUNDANCE *as he falls.*

CUT TO

BUTCH crawling.

CUT TO

SUNDANCE, half up now, going the best he can, and

CUT TO

THE POLICEMEN pumping bullets and

CUT TO

SUNDANCE, his left arm hanging, going for BUTCH, starting to pull him toward the safety of the room, and it's not far away, but bullets are landing all over now, and first one of them is hit again, then the other and

CUT TO

INSIDE THE ROOM.

BUTCH AND SUNDANCE come falling through the door and lie there. The firing continues. Sundance manages to get the door shut and then there is no sound except for their agonized breathing. They are both wounded terribly, but that fact never for a moment enters into their conversation, either here or later.

> **BUTCH**
> *(as he forces himself up into a sitting position)*
> —I thought you were gonna cover me—

> **SUNDANCE**
> *(sitting now too)*
> —I thought you were gonna run—if I'd known you were just gonna stroll along—

> **BUTCH**
> Stroll!—You never could shoot; not from the beginning—

> **SUNDANCE**
> —you are all mouth...

They are doing what they can with their wounds now, muttering to themselves as we

CUT TO

THE HEAD POLICEMAN. He is standing nervously at attention, saluting.

PULL BACK TO REVEAL

OVER A HUNDRED MEMBERS OF THE BOLIVIAN CAVALRY. A young Captain rides at their head; beside him is the Policeman who had been dispatched earlier.

HEAD POLICEMAN

Mi Capitán.

THE CAPTAIN is a young, energetic man, handsome and volatile. He dismounts rapidly while behind him, his troops remain on horseback. As he looks around—

CAPTAIN

El enemigo?

THE HEAD POLICEMAN points to the small room where Butch and Sundance are. The Captain glances at it briefly, then back to the Head Policeman.

CAPTAIN

Quantos hombres?

HEAD POLICEMAN
(holding up two fingers)

Dos.

CAPTAIN
(furious)

Dos hombres?

HEAD POLICEMAN
(trying to get a word in)

Capitán, por favor—

CAPTAIN

Dos hombres?

HEAD POLICEMAN

Bandidos Yanquis!

He points to the room where Butch and Sundance are.

CAPTAIN

Bandidos —bandidos Yanquis?

HEAD POLICEMAN

Sí, mi Capitan.

CUT TO

THE CAPTAIN: CLOSE UP.

CAPTAIN

Ahhhhhhhhhhhh............

CUT TO

THE CAVALRY dismounting, beginning to move into position around the outside of the patio and

CUT TO

BUTCH AND SUNDANCE watching; quick glimpses of the running Cavalrymen are visible. Butch and Sundance are still bleeding as badly as before.

CUT TO

THE SUN, crimson and falling. There is a sharp metallic sound and

CUT TO

ONE OF THE FOUR SIDES OF THE PATIO.

THE TROOPS are sharply slipping their bayonets onto their rifles. The Captain moves quickly along his men, making sure that everyone and everything is ready and as he turns a corner—

CUT TO

ANOTHER WALL LINED WITH TROOPS.

As THE CAPTAIN approaches, THIS GROUP snap on bayonets, and again there is the sharp metallic sound. As the Captain continues his efficient military way—

CUT TO

BUTCH AND SUNDANCE, crouched close together by a window, peering out toward the setting sun.

> **BUTCH**
> I got a great idea where we should go next.

> **SUNDANCE**
> Well, I don't wanna hear it.

> **BUTCH**
> You'll change your mind once I tell you—

> **SUNDANCE**
> Shut up.

> **BUTCH**
> Okay, okay.

> **SUNDANCE**
> It was your great ideas got us here.

                          BUTCH
Forget about it.

                        SUNDANCE
I never want to hear another of your great ideas, all right?

                          BUTCH
All right.

                        SUNDANCE
Good.

                          BUTCH
Australia.

CUT TO

SUNDANCE. He just looks at Butch.

CUT TO

BUTCH.

                          BUTCH
I figured secretly you wanted to know, so I told you—Australia.

CUT TO

BUTCH AND SUNDANCE.

                        SUNDANCE
That's your great idea?

                          BUTCH
The latest in a long line.

                        SUNDANCE
             (exploding with everything he has left)
Australia's no better than here!

                          BUTCH
That's all you know.

                        SUNDANCE
Name me one thing.

                          BUTCH
They speak English in Australia.

                              SUNDANCE
They do?

                               BUTCH
That's right, smart guy, so we wouldn't be foreigners. And they ride horses. And they got thousands of miles to hide out in—and a good climate,
nice beaches, you could learn to swim—

                              SUNDANCE
Swimming's not important, what about the banks?

                               BUTCH
Easy, ripe, and luscious.

                              SUNDANCE
The banks or the women?

                               BUTCH
Once we get the one we'll get the other.

                              SUNDANCE
It's a long way, though, isn't it?

                               BUTCH
                           (shouting it out)
Everything always gotta be perfect with you!

                              SUNDANCE
I just don't wanna get there and find out it stinks, that's all.

CUT TO

BUTCH.

                               BUTCH
Will you at least think about it?

CUT TO

SUNDANCE. He considers this a moment.

                              SUNDANCE
All right, I'll think about it.

CUT TO

BUTCH AND SUNDANCE: CLOSE UP.

BUTCH

Now after we—*(And suddenly he stops.)*—Wait a minute—

SUNDANCE

What?

BUTCH

You didn't see Lefors out there?

SUNDANCE

Lefors? No.

BUTCH

Good. For a minute I thought we were in trouble.

CUT TO

THE SUN dying.

PULL BACK TO REVEAL

THE SOLDIERS, tense and ready and

CUT TO

THE CAPTAIN moving swiftly around the perimeter, gesturing his men forward, and as he does

CUT TO

ONE GROUP OF MEN vaulting over the wall, then

CUT TO

ANOTHER GROUP OF MEN vaulting over the wall, rifles at the ready.

CUT TO

BUTCH AND SUNDANCE on their feet. Slowly, they move toward the door as we

CUT TO

More and more soldiers vaulting the wall.

CUT TO

BUTCH AND SUNDANCE into the last of the sunlight and then comes the first of a painfully loud burst of rifle fire and as the sound explodes—

The CAMERA FREEZES BUTCH AND SUNDANCE.

Another terrible barrage. Louder. Butch and Sundance remain frozen. Somehow the sound of the rifles manages to build even more. Butch and Sundance stay frozen. Then the sound begins to diminish.

And as the sound diminishes, so does the color, and slowly, the faces of Butch and Sundance begin to change. The song from the New York sequence begins. The faces of Butch and Sundance continue to change, from color to the grainy black and white that began their story. The rifle fire is popgun soft now, as it blows them back into history.

FINAL FADE OUT.

THE END

MARATHON MAN

DIRECTOR	JOHN SCHLESINGER
PRODUCERS	ROBERT EVANS
	SIDNEY BECKERMAN
CINEMATOGRAPHER	CONRAD HALL
EDITOR	JIM CLARK
PRODUCTION DESIGNER	RICHARD MacDONALD
MUSIC	MICHAEL SMALL
SCREENPLAY	WILLIAM GOLDMAN
	(FROM HIS NOVEL)

Since this entire book is clearly not without ego, I'm sure you won't be surprised if I start quoting myself. I once ended a novel with the notion that life was material—everything was material, you just had to live long enough to see how to use it. I believed that then, still do, and it is certainly true of the dental scene which was written in Manhattan in 1973 but began life thirty-five years earlier in the town of Evanston, in the state of Illinois.

That being when I first encountered Meyer P. Cohn (not his real name).

A handsome man, a good and loving father, pillar of the community, hale fellow well met, all that shit. I didn't care, I hated him. Because I was eight years old and, though it may seem petty for one human to dislike another over something as trivial as this, so be it. The son of a bitch scared me. Hurt me. Made me scream. Made me cry.

Cohn, need I add, was a dentist.

Who did not believe in novocaine.

Half a century after I escaped him, I can still see him in his white jacket, his knee on my chest (believe it), doing these awful things. (He explained the knee to my mother by saying that I had a very strong tongue and needed to be firmly held down.) We lived in a neighboring small town and I used to beg not to go back, fake the most amazing ailments. Didn 't work. (Anybody under forty won't know this, but the only thing in the universe that has improved on our watch is dentistry.) Eventually, my family found a fellow close to home, and Cohn took his place in memory.

I thought that Hiram Haydn was the outstanding editor in New York in the Fifties and Sixties. He was certainly the one I most wanted to work with and, starting with my third book, *Soldier in the Rain*, I got lucky. I have a thing for father figures and I worshipped Hiram, stayed with him until he died, just after he edited *The Princess Bride*. He had been a college professor, came late to publishing, edited *The American Scholar*, cared remarkably little for standard popular fiction. (Book publishing is sort of the reverse of dentistry.) The only novel of mine during our fifteen-year period that seemed like it might be, ugh, popular, was *No Way to Treat A Lady*. Hiram read it, liked it well enough, said this: "Bill, I have no idea how to edit this. Why don't you take it somewhere else and do it under a pseudonym?"

Which is what I did. And that book's author became Harry Longbaugh, which happens to be the real name of The Sundance Kid. (Since this was 1963, it's clear I was aware of the Butch Cassidy material well before I wrote the screenplay.) I stayed with Hiram ten more years, would have stayed forever. When he died, I was shocked and saddened, didn't know quite what I wanted to write, but I did know there was a world of material I was fascinated with that I was never allowed to try when he was mentoring me. (Much of what I've written since 1974, beginning with *Marathon Man*, is of a more openly commercial nature than anything Hiram would have accepted.)

With his death, I began to try a thriller. If you love a genre, as I love thrillers (and spy novels and hard-boiled detective novels), you're stuck with your passion and what you hope for is someday to be classed with those writers who moved you. (I remember during the two month run-up to *Butch*, George Roy Hill and I hoped the movie would be thought of in twenty years as being as good as *Shane* and *The Gunfighter*.) My guy was Graham Greene. Of course you know you can't reach that level, but hope is a thing with feathers and away you go.

In a thriller you start with the villain. (Obviously, that's not a rule, there are no rules, but it's what I did and I bet if I ever write another one, I'll do it again.) I started with Mengele, the most intellectually startling of the Nazis (an M.D. plus a Ph.D.) And I knew this: I needed to get him to America. But why in the world would he come? (Mengele, when I began fiddling with this story, was either alive in South America or had been alive in South America, choose one. Living secretly or palatially—I chose palatially.)

But this was one of the brilliant minds of his generation. Why would he be so dumb as to risk his world to visit America? I was reading the papers one day when the answer came. An American doctor in, I think, Cleveland had begun doing a then-revolutionary operation, heart sleeve surgery, and people were streaming in from all over the world. Mengele would be among the needy.

From the start I have had an unerring brilliance when it comes to narrative and here was just another shining example. Mengele would come to Cleveland for surgery. Mengele had to come to America, the reasoning was rock solid perfect. I had scored another coup.

One day I was just walking around—I get a lot of ideas just walking around as well as at the ballet, just sitting there drifting—when, thank God, reality thudded home. Schmuck, what kind of a villain is he if he's so fucking frail he needs heart surgery? Asshole, what kind of a thriller do you have if the villain is already dying? Ahhhhhhh.

I don't know if it's true for other writers, but for me, when a piece of material becomes urgent, there is only a certain window of time in which it can be put down. If that passes, the window shuts, the material is dead, often forever. I had never tried a spy thriller, owned the standard lack of confidence, felt a certain sense of panic setting in.

Then I read an article about how some Nazi leaders had accumulated great fortunes by knocking the teeth out of their prisoners and melting the gold down, or taking jewels from their colons where desperate men and women had been hiding their valuables for centuries. It all fell in. The name, Szell, I chose from the great conductor—just saying it made me feel sadistic. The reason for visiting: to get his diamonds. (The only man he trusted, his father, the man who had been in charge of the fortune in America, is killed in a car crash in the opening.)

So Szell has to come. A doctor, a monster, a Nazi, but I wanted worse, I wanted more. So bless you, Meyer P. Cohn, because Szell became, one afternoon, suddenly and forever a dentist. I had my villain. And I knew he had to torture someone because I remembered the pressure from my childhood, of being helpless in the chair with that knee forcing me down, unmindful of my pain.

Babe, the hero, (Dustin Hoffman in the flick, Olivier played the dentist) appeared because I had become fascinated with this notion: what if someone close to you was something totally different from what you thought? In the story, Hoffman thinks his brother (Roy Scheider) is a money-driven businessman, whereas in reality the man is a spy. Who has been involved with the Nazi, Szell.

Once I had that, the rest was essentially mixing and matching, figuring out the surprises, hoping they would work. (You never know. I don't, anyway. Same is true of screenplay writing. Each time out is just as scary. I wish it weren't so, but there it is.) So now I had my torturer, my method, and my victim and early on in the novel I gave Babe a toothache. At the time I was building this into the book, I went to see my gum guy, a wonderful periodontist, a joy. He never hurts people, plays Bach on the radio, is fascinated with restaurants as am I. We are talking about a genuinely kind and decent human being.

He asks what I am writing and when I am about to leave I tell him and mention that Babe has a cavity and what I am about to do to him—

—and I will never forget the look that dropped onto his face. "Oh, no," he said, quietly, his eyes all dreamy. "No, Bill. Forget the cavity. You want pain. You want genuine unforgettable pain. You want pain that would make you want to die. Bill, listen to me—have him drill into a healthy tooth."

On and on this sweet man went, talking to me of the glory of anguish, of how it would be impossible to keep any secrets if someone were drilling into a fine, strapping tooth. I have rarely been more frightened. Here this sweet fellow I'd known for twenty years was Jekyll-Hyding as I watched. He wouldn't stop. The level of agony would be unsurpassable. Death would be preferable. The memory of being destroyed in the chair would never leave you...bliss...

He's still my gum guy. But now I get nervous when we're alone.

Since my villain was, hopefully, the worst guy in the world, figuring out the hero was easier. If the worst guy in the world gets in the ring with the toughest guy in the world, that's Stallone territory, and I can't write that. I don't mean that I am pristine and above it all—obviously I could write it—anyone can write it—

—because anyone can write anything badly.

I mean that and I think it's true. I could write an Elizabethan tragedy— couplets and all. This week. And it would be so painful, audiences would beg to leave. The only hope we have is to write what we care about, to stay emotionally close to our wheel house. And pray.

Anyway, I've got this Nazi dentist coming to America. (If I were English, he would have come to London, but I live in New York so here came Szell.) And there had to be an adversary for him who is interesting. Interesting for me to write, hopefully for you to read.

The hero needed to be this: a total innocent. So I made Babe—the Hoffman part in the flick—as virginal as I could. A grad student at Columbia, a scholar, crazed and brilliant and driven. But what chance would a guy like that have against a master?

Zip. So I gave him blood lines: a beloved brother who killed for a living.

*

I wrote the novel over Summer, '73. In my pit in the fashionable Upper East Side of the city. Few ever saw my office. Somehow George Hill got in one day, looked around and termed the place "scrofulous" and, although I wasn't quite sure of all the meanings, the sound matched the chaos.

I worked in a place that was scrofulous.

Late one afternoon—(I always worked regular hours. It was important to me to pretend to have a real job.)—as I was waiting for the elevator, a neighbor left her place, moved alongside. She had the contiguous apartment, was reputed to be a shrink, and we had disliked each other for a very long time, owing to a swimming accident (There was a pool in the basement of the building.) when she felt I had been unruly and cut off her lane.

So we are standing there.

And she turns to me.

Glares.

Speaks thusly: I CHUST VANT YOU TO KNOW (She was from Europe.) ZAT I KNOW EFFERY-SING ZAT IS GOING ON IN ZERE.

I don't know that I was ever more surprised.

Because NUSSING was going on IN ZERE. NUSSING ever went on IN ZERE. Just me and my pit trying to make it through another day. The elevator came and we rode down in silence. And I still remember her total contempt for me.

I get home, tell my then wife and we instantly agree the woman is mad.

Later that summer we rented a house in Massachusetts, a nightmare of a place with a murky pond owned by an architect /builder who must have hated children. He built his dream palazzo without bannisters. Coming down for breakfast was an adventure. But we survived, and one day I am tippy-toeing to lunch with my kiddoes, Jenny and Susanna, then ten and seven.

And they cannot stop giggling.

I ask why and finally they manage to ask me this question: did I know that I talked when I wrote? I was reworking *The Great Waldo Pepper*, and I said that I absolutely did not talk when I wrote. They said I did. I, being mature, replied 'did not.' Did. Not. Did. And then, in triumph, they started quoting back some of the morning's dialog. (Until that moment I had no idea that I did that.)

But all I thought of at that moment was the woman who knew EFFERY-SING ZAT WAS GOING ON IN ZERE. Because, you see, she was just on the other side of a very thin wall.

And I had been writing the dental scene that day.

Is it safe?

Huh?

Is it safe?

What?

Is it safe?

Is what safe?

Is it safe?

Is it safe?

Is it safe.?

And later, Szell going, "You seem a bright young man, able to distinguish light from darkness, heat from freezing cold. Surely, you must prefer anything to my brand of torment, so I ask you, and please take your time before answering: Is it safe?"

And then Babe screaming and the top of his head coming off and...

...and at last I realized why she looked at me that terrible way...

*

We were more than anxious that Olivier play Szell but when the director John Schlesinger went to see him, he was dying again, and could barely move one side of his face. The part was his if he could play it, but who knew? I was working in London with Schlesinger one day when the phone rang. It was Richard Widmark asking could he read for the part, yes he knew about Olivier. (Widmark had made one of the memorable film debuts in *Kiss of Death* playing the madman Tommy Udo who pushed a crippled woman down a flight of stairs. In today's bloodbath era of violence, that would probably be a comedy scene. But back then, no one who saw it forgot it.)

Widmark came to Schlesinger's home. Tall, educated, a perfect gent, he had pretty much memorized the role and when he read the dental scene with a slight German accent, he was sensational. We took a cab back to his hotel together afterwards and talked of Sandy Koufax, whom his daughter had married.

I never saw him before that afternoon and have never seen him since. But no one who was almost in a movie I've been involved with has been as fine.

*

The only two moments from the novel that wrote easily for the movie were the one near the end with Szell in the diamond district finally being spotted by the Jews and the dental scene. I've written about the rehearsals with Hoffman and Olivier in *Adventures in the Screen Trade*. But this happened too. We had hired a dentist to be there to assist Olivier and we all sat around this large table, for the first script reading. A big moment for me. An Oscar winning director, Schlesinger. Wonderful actors like Hoffman and Scheider and Bill Devane and of course Olivier, one of my heroes, along with Willie Mays and Sandy Koufax and Irwin Shaw.

And I am, as I always am at such moments, tired and scared.

I'd written several drafts of the novel and a lot of versions of the movie and I was whipped and I hoped, at last, I'd gotten it down ok. Because I didn't have much more to give the project. That happens to a screenwriter, at least to this one. You've thought about it so long, done it so often, in your head or on paper, that you start to get punchy, silly, dry. I wanted the reading to work so I could leave it behind, begin to rebuild my head.

The reading more than worked, it went wonderfully. There was a pause after the ending. A treasured pause. A sense of contentment in the air—

—and then, from some dimwitted blue, this dentist starts talking. "I don't know about the rest of you, but frankly, I have a lot of problems with the screenplay—"

—*nightmare.*

If you write movies, you never know who the enemy is. Someone is going to fuck you , that's a given. I knew Hoffman was the enemy—he felt he was too young for the role and he was right, of course. I knew Schlesinger could be an enemy; he only took such a commercial piece of work for the same reason that all the good ones do—fear their careers are in trouble. But those two were momentarily happy. I was free, I was home and dry. Until this dentist turns into Brooks Atkinson.

I screamed at him. "You're here for teeth. Leave the goddam script alone." He did not know how crazy writers can be. The fact is truly this: if I'd had a gun and thought I could get away with it, the guy was dead.

I was out of the loop during shooting and post production; I was out of the country when the film opened, working in Holland on *A Bridge Too Far*. But the first Saturday night after I landed, I went to a big Times Square theatre and sat in the back on the right, my preferred spot when I am involved with a flick, easy for fleeing.

Lights down, picture starts. Certain things are immediately clear: you don't get people of that talent to work on a genre film very often. Hoffman was wonderful, so were the others, I wanted to marry Sir Laurence. I kind of relaxed, sitting there in the dark with my popcorn. It was an absolutely decent film. I kind of liked it.

But a little over halfway, I realized something awful: the audience hated it. The aisles were crammed with people leaving. I was stunned. "Wait," I wanted to shout out to them. "It's not so terrible. There's good stuff coming up. Please. Don't go." (This is a screenwriter's worst fear—that you have misconstructed so badly and they hate you so much, they cannot even survive another hour before resuming their normal lives.)

"Please," I almost cried to them, "I've got surprises for you."

Nothing would stop them.

I slumped in my seat. I had never missed my target by so much before. The aisles were emptying now with the dental scene hard on the horizon.

Hmmm.

I was caught up in it. Delighted by the way Schlesinger had done it, all of it indirection, no bloodbath moments. Just shots of eyes and faces filled with fear.

Very classy. The audience would have liked it if they had stayed around.

In point of fact, they had stayed around. They didn't hate the movie, it was just that they had heard about the dental scene and decided not to risk it, had gone for popcorn. Back they trooped when it was done, sitting happily, as did I, until the movie ended.

*

Final dental scene memory.

I was Out There in '92 when I got a twinge of pain that I knew meant this: root canal. I chose to ignore it, hoped it would stay bearable until the end of the week when I could get back to New York.

It didn't. I asked around, got a specialist, went to see him. This fellow worked in an office of specialists—a long railroad car of root canal guys. I sit in the chair, he starts to work.

And to chat. "What brings you to Los Angeles?" he starts, and I already know the, you should pardon the expression, drill. I either lie and say I sell corn futures or tell the truth. Which is no fun because I am waaay too old to be giving my credits, which is how this scenario usually ends. I decide to buy time.

"Business."

"And what kind of business might that be?"

The crossroads question. I go for it. "I'm a writer."

"What kind of writing is it that you do?"

Pause. "Books and movies."

"Hmmm. Interesting." And now the most hated question of all. "What movies have you written that I might have seen?" (Often they haven't seen any.)

I am totally in his power, understand. Tilted way back. He is a big man and seems bigger looming over me. To hell with it, I decide. Go for the gold.

"*Marathon Man*. Both the book and the movie..."

Pause.

The information registers. Every dentist on both sides of the Iron Curtain knows *Marathon Man*. Excuse me, he says. He is gone, but after a while he comes back, gently works at my mouth until he is done. I thank him. Get up to go.

And as I walk into the hallway I see this whole corridor of dentists, all of them staring at me from their cubicles. He had told them all who he was punishing. I was not used to the attention. All these men, staring at me. I was, within the confines of that suite, famous.

Everyone in the movie business is a star fucker. Never happened like that to me before, never since. But right then, at last, I was twinkling...

CAST LIST

DUSTIN HOFFMAN	BABE
LAURENCE OLIVIER	SZELL
ROY SCHEIDER	DOC/SCYLLA
WILLIAM DEVANE	JANEWAY
MARTHE KELLER	ELSA
FRITZ WEAVER	BIESENTHAL
RICHARD BRIGHT	KARL
MARC LAWRENCE	ERHARD

FADE IN ON

TIGHTSHOT: BABE

We are looking at an exhausted boy, drained; maybe twenty-five. We don't know where we are or what's going on exactly, but he's sitting in a chair in a corner of a room, staring straight ahead. And he's not alone—from other parts of the room there are mutterings which we can't make out. And he is talking to someone whom we don't see. BABE sits there, not moving. His eyes blink, again, again. (We'll be returning to this TIGHTSHOT occasionally, and what's going on will come clearer as we do. The feeling should be that we're being told something, but it all doesn't fit together. In other words, what he says will not be connected necessarily with what follows; he's not a plot device—we're dealing here, as much as possible, with emotion.)

BABE
(looks at camera, says something)

VOICE *(off-screen)*
(Irish-American accent; gentle)

I didn't quite hear you.

BABE
(Same as before, only now we understand it.)

Water? *(His eyes blink.)* I'd like some water please...

The MUTTERINGS OFF CAMERA *go on. BABE sits as before. He is wearing pants and a white shirt, and now we* PULL BACK *just enough to make out one thing that wasn't clear before: the boy is absolutely sopping with blood. Now—*

CUT TO

A BANK VAULT.

A GUARD *is replacing a large safe deposit box, locking it back up.*

Watching him carefully is a VERY OLD MAN *whose most noticeable feature are his deep, deep blue eyes. The* OLD MAN *is not dressed expensively enough to look like he has much need for a safe deposit box as big as the one the BANK GUARD is locking away. The GUARD finishes, hands the VERY OLD MAN the key. The VERY OLD MAN nods, studies the key a moment, then, before he turns to leave, puts the key carefully into his right hand pocket.*

CUT TO

A GARAGE.

A car is being examined, the hood up, the MECHANIC, *only half visible, tinkering away. Watching is* ANOTHER OLD MAN, *this one named* ROSENBAUM, *and his most distinguishing feature is his nose.*

> MECHANIC

What can I tell you, Rosenbaum.

> ROSENBAUM
> *(clearly a choleric type)*

You can tell me why you sold me an air-conditioner that only works in the winter—

> MECHANIC

—it was factory tested—don't lose your temper at me. *(He closes the hood.)*

> ROSENBAUM
> *(He always loses his temper.)*

—it's ninety degrees in late September, I got to drive to Jersey with a factory tested piece of dreck that don't like hot weather, you want me to tap dance? *(mutters)* Goddam Thursday. *(The* MECHANIC *looks at him, as* ROSENBAUM *gets in.)* Everything horrible in my life has took place on a Thursday—I got married on a Thursday, my teeth got pulled on a Thursday—*(starting the car)*—you know the song that says Saturday night is the crummiest night of the week? Well, that's bullshit; Thursday's the one you got to watch out for. *(and as he drives violently off—)*

CUT TO

ROSENBAUM, *weaving his way up First Avenue. It's heavily trafficked but that doesn't bother him—he drives with the same anger that is evident when he speaks, constantly honking, shaking fists at cars he passes. As he moves along—*

CUT TO

THE SHOPS *on First Avenue and here is the initial indication of one of the images we're going to be seeing throughout, and it's this: cities in crisis. Stores are empty. A lot of them. And a lot of others have "sale" signs across the fronts. And others have their steel gates pulled across the doorways even though it's the middle of the day. You can see the salespeople looking out from behind the gates, but no one appears very happy.*

HOLD ON THE SHOPS *as we pass them by. Inflation, depression, recession, call it what you will; clearly this is crisis time. From the nature of the signs above the storefronts, we can tell that we are in an area that, at least once, was heavily German. Now—*

CUT TO

A VOLKSWAGEN *stalled in the middle of 87th Street. There are cars parked on both sides and the street is narrow, so no one can drive past. There comes, from behind the VOLKSWAGEN, the sound of someone honking. The VOLKSWAGEN DRIVER, whom we met before—he's the VERY OLD MAN from the bank—is trying to make his car go, but the motor won't quite catch.*

*There are a number of people walking by, the usual New York mix, Spanish and Blacks and Whites and, interestingly, Jews, many of them in skullcaps. It's Jewish holidays— probably a synagogue is nearby. The honking sound becomes more insistent, the horn held longer—*HOOOONNK, *then again,* HOOOOOONNK! *Then a man's* VOICE *is* HEARD *and as it is—*

PULL BACK TO REVEAL

ROSENBAUM, *sweating in his* CHEVY, *trapped behind the* VOLKSWAGEN *guy.*

ROSENBAUM

—move that heap—*(louder)*—I'm talkin' to you, Mister, mooooooove!

The Volkswagen almost catches, but then subsides. ROSENBAUM *leans out of his Chevy window, shouts at the old man ahead of him.*

ROSENBAUM

You're a goddam menace, you know that, you senile *cocker?*

VOLKSWAGEN DRIVER
(sticks his head out too, says one word)

Langsamer!

ROSENBAUM

Don't you tell me "take it easy," you kraut meathead. *(yelling louder)* Don't you tell me "langsamer," you kraut meathead!

VOLKSWAGEN DRIVER
(louder)

Langsamer!

In reply, ROSENBAUM *backs up his car a few feet, then drives sharply forward and knocks the Volkswagen forward maybe half a foot. The sound is very satisfying to* ROSENBAUM *who leans out the window now as the* VOLKSWAGEN DRIVER *stares back at him, shaking an ancient withered fist.* ROSENBAUM *goes into reverse again, but just before he starts forward, he leans out the window and shouts something clearly insulting, this time in German. The* OLD GUY IN THE VOLKSWAGEN *shouts something back in German and in a second, they're insulting the hell out of each other in this other tongue. Then* ROSENBAUM *drives forward again and really clobbers the other car, knocking it at least a yard this time.* ROSENBAUM *almost beams, he's really in heaven.*

THE OLD GUY IN THE VOLKSWAGEN *tries again and again to make his car start.*

CUT TO

ROSENBAUM, *still smiling. He backs his car up a third time, but suddenly the smile is gone, replaced with surprise as we*

CUT TO

The VOLKSWAGEN, *as finally the motor catches and it takes off, leaving the* CHEVY *far behind.* ROSENBAUM *is stunned at this turn of events, but he jams his car into forward and guns it and as he does, THE TWO OLD CARS AND THE TWO ANCIENT DRIVERS begin their lunatic race.*

CUT TO

THE PEOPLE ON THE SIDEWALKS, *and it's dangerous because the two cars are roaring, and people can get hurt that way and as they turn to watch—*

CUT TO

The CHEVY *catching up, and the* VOLKWAGEN *is shaking almost as if it will come apart, but it cannot keep pace with the Chevy and now* ROSENBAUM *tries to inch by on the right but he can't because—*

CUT TO

The VOLKSWAGEN DRIVER, *and he spots through the rear view mirror what the* CHEVY *is up to and swerves right, blocking the other car and*

CUT TO

ROSENBAUM, *trying to get a run at going by on the left and*

CUT TO

PARK AVENUE UP AHEAD, *the lights switching from red to green and*

CUT TO

THE TWO OLD MADMEN IN THEIR CARS, *flashing across the intersection, honking, motors roaring and from the noise —*

CUT TO

WHAT MIGHT BE A STILL PHOTO OF A TRUCK. *It happens to be an oil truck. It is parked in front of a building, we don't know where. There is absolutely no connection between this shot and anything that's gone before. All is silent.*

CUT TO

THE TWO CARS, *gunning past Park now, heading along 87th and*

CUT TO

ROSENBAUM, *trying to get by and*

CUT TO

THE VOLKSWAGEN DRIVER, *blocking him and*

CUT TO

THE CHEVY, *shaking from the chase and*

CUT TO

THE VOLKSWAGEN, *weaving dangerously, and now*

CUT TO

THE SHOT OF THE MOTIONLESS OIL TRUCK AGAIN. *Only this time it's not so silent: we can't see anything yet, but we can start to hear the roaring of the engines of the two cars, and now we know it's inevitable, nothing can stop it, there is going to be some terrible connection between the* TWO OLD MEN *in their cars and this gigantic truck and*

CUT TO

ROSENBAUM, *and for the first time he realizes he's going beyond control but he won't stop, and as they roar past Madison toward Fifth,*

CUT TO

THE VOLKSWAGEN DRIVER, *frightened because the car is making terrible sounds from the punishment it's taking, but he won't stop either and*

CUT TO

THE OIL TRUCK, AND THE REST OF WHAT WE SEE, WE SEE FROM THIS POINT OF VIEW. *The cars are visible now, coming closer, jockeying, trying to pass or block, feint or dodge, and the truck just stands there and as the* VOLKSWAGEN *starts to slow to miss the truck, it locks with the* CHEVY *behind it and here they come, seconds from the wipe out, six, five, four— the cars are spinning, all control gone —three, two, one—and as they cream into the oil truck, it flames, and the explosion is dreadful and deafening and*

CUT TO

A NANNY AND A RICH LITTLE KID, *and the nanny shields the child, as they both start screaming and*

CUT TO

THE DISASTER, *the flames shooting God knows how many stories into the air and*

CUT TO

A KNOT OF PEOPLE, *most of them Jewish in skullcaps, standing in front of a synagogue.*

They move toward the crash. They can't get too close, the heat precludes that, but they stand there all the same, gaping, more and more of them pouring out of the building toward the holocaust.

CUT TO

ROSENBAUM, *crumpled and dead and*

CUT TO

THE VOLKSWAGEN DRIVER, *and he should be dead too, maybe he is, but he's moving, he's trying with all the desperation left in his aged shattered body to get something out of his pocket and finally he does and*

CUT TO

WHAT'S IN HIS HAND, *and it's the safe deposit key. He tries to protect it but it's too much, and as he sprawls across the seat dead, his hand opens, the key falls, the flames begin to destroy it.*

CUT TO

A BLACK GUY IN HIS EARLY TWENTIES; *he's got a camera and he's excited as hell as he moves around snapping pictures like crazy.*

CUT TO

THE OIL TRUCK. *It's right near Fifth, and it's the same peaceful shot as when we first saw it. Not so peaceful anymore...*

CUT TO

THE RESERVOIR IN CENTRAL PARK.

It's several hours later, getting on toward evening.

A COUPLE OF PUDGY GUYS IN SWEAT SUITS COME PUFFING ALONG. *As they reach a spot nearest Fifth Avenue, they stop, stare off and we follow their gaze.*

They're watching the remains of the accident. The flames are gone now, the crowd too. All that's left is a large vehicle that is disengaging the two cars from each other and from the cinder-like remains of the oil truck. The vehicle goes about its work noisily.

THE FAT MEN *continue to watch, fascinated. Now, behind them,* BABE *comes running. He's in track shorts and Adidas shoes and a track shirt and on his head is a long-billed golf cap. Babe clearly runs well. He may not be the most graceful thing we've ever seen, but he gets there. He looks kind of colorful in his outfit, golf cap and all. He pauses behind the fat men, looks out in the same direction.*

The VOLKSWAGEN *and the* CHEVY *are locked in some kind of final confrontation and it's impossible to separate them.*

BABE *presses a finger against one of his upper front teeth, briefly grimaces. He watches a moment more, then starts to run again.*

Up ahead now is an experienced runner, going fast. BABE *picks up his pace, begins to close. The other runner is good, but Babe keeps after him, won't let up.*

In the semi-darkness of the running track now, A DRUNK *suddenly appears from the bushes on the right, standing weaving in the center of the track, a bottle in one hand.* ANOTHER DRUNK *is sprawled against a tree; their appearance here in the dimness is scary.*

BABE *sees the guy in the path—the guy doesn't move, it's almost as if he'd welcome trouble, but* BABE *fakes left, goes right, and the* DRUNK *spins around after him but* BABE *is past. Ahead, the experienced runner has gotten his old lead back.* BABE *increases his pace but it's starting to get punishing. He takes in air more audibly now but he doesn't slow, he's just having trouble gaining, his running rhythm upset by the drunk, and now the experienced runner is going even faster and it looks like Babe will never catch the guy and as that moment happens—*

CUT TO

ANOTHER TIME, ANOTHER PLACE.

A LITTLE BOY *is running in a field. At the top of a hill at one end,* A MAN *stands—we haven't seen the man before, but he wears rimless glasses and his arms are stretched out in the direction of the little boy. Now, his words, on this sunlit remembered day, come softly on the wind—*

> **MAN WITH RIMLESS GLASSES**
> ...all the way, Babe...

As he hears the words, the LITTLE BOY *starts running faster and as he does—*

CUT TO

BABE IN THE PRESENT AT THE RESERVOIR, AND HE STARTS RUNNING FASTER TOO. *He's really moving now, his rhythm back and the guy ahead begins to falter and when that happens, Babe flashes past, leaving the guy way behind.*

The sun is lowering now. BABE *keeps at it, as a* KID ON A BICYCLE *comes tearing by, damn near knocking Babe off balance and Babe sets out after him, and naturally, you wouldn't expect him to be able to catch the kid, but he tries. And as we hold, Babe slowly begins to cut the bike rider's lead.* THE KID ON THE BIKE *half turns in his seat, sees Babe coming and is startled enough to turn back and start pedaling like crazy. He churns away at his pedales.*

But he can't shake BABE. *And maybe you can't tell a lot about people from just seeing them run, but you sure can tell this much about Babe: he doesn't give up easily.*

HOLD ON *the bike,* BABE *in pursuit, as the sun sets across the quiet water of the reservoir.*

CUT TO

HALF A DOZEN PUERTO RICANS.

They are in their middle to late teens, sit bare-chested on the steps of a brownstone, swilling beer, smoking. They are not, in any way, cherubic. One of them sits on a higher step than the others and is slightly larger and brighter seeming. His name is MELENDEZ.

> **FIRST STOOP KID**
> *(to Melendez)*
> Hey, Melendez —*(gesturing down the street)*—it's the Creep.

BABE *is visible now, jogging toward them, past them to a brownstone two houses farther from the Park.*

> **MELENDEZ**
> Whad'ya say, Creepy? *(Babe says nothing.)* Fun running in the heat, was it? *(Babe is at his steps now, starts up. He continues to ignore their baiting. Melendez suddenly mimes having a hat on and speaks very hoity-toity.)* I just adore his chateau.

Involuntarily, BABE *adjusts his cap, and as soon as he does, they start laughing.* BABE *heads up the stairs, away from their laughter.*

CUT TO

BABE'S ONE-ROOM APARTMENT.

We're a long way from House Beautiful. *Not that the place is dirty, it's just strewn with books, shelves full of them, stacks of them on the floor. There's a hi-fi, a TV, desk, bed, couch, etc.*

BABE *emerges from the bathroom where he's just turned on the tub spigots. He's wearing a towel around his waist now and still has his golf cap on. He heads for his desk, picks up a heavy volume, flips it open. We catch a glimpse of a framed photo on the desk—it's the man we saw briefly during Babe's run, the man from another time and place who had his arms out to the little boy.*

Book in hand, BABE *turns, starts reading as he walks toward the small icebox. Clearly, he walks and reads a lot, because he manages to skirt any obstacles in his way. Before he reaches the icebox, he passes the TV and he flips it on without breaking stride. The* BLACK KID *we saw taking pictures of the crash is being interviewed—it's six o'clock news time—*

TV ANNOUNCER

And what happened next?

BLACK KID

BOOM!—that's what happened next.

BABE is at the icebox now. He opens it, revealing some bottles of Gatorade, some cans of tuna and peanut butter and Ritz crackers and instant coffee and candy bars. He grabs up a couple of candy bars. The TV interview is still going on.

ANNOUNCER (off-screen)

What else can you tell us?

BLACK KID (off-screen)

I took the first pictures—*Daily News* may use 'em—

ANNOUNCER (off-screen)

I meant your feelings—was it a terrible thing to have to see?

BLACK KID (off-screen)

Oh yeah, it was even worse than Towering Inferno.

There is a hook on a wall. On either side are formal framed pictures of runners, with legends below. One of the men is black, one white.

PAAVO NURMI   ABEBE BIKILA
"The Flying Finn"   "The Barefoot Wonder"
Winner 7 Olympic Golds   Winner 2 Marathon Golds
1920-1928   1960-1964

BABE glances up from the book at the two other runners. He studies them briefly, then puts his golf cap on the hook between the two. Then he heads toward the bathtub, reading away. As he goes, the TV set is still on. Now, the interview is over. The crash is being shown. The flames still rise over the oil truck, firemen work on the thing, trying to make it stop burning.

HOLD ON THE FLAMES, *then*

CUT TO

TIGHTSHOT: BABE

Same set up as before. He sits in the chair, covered with blood. Now he is draining a glass of water with great gulps. Finished, he fidgets with it.

BABE

Babe.

IRISH VOICE (off-screen)

Hmm?

BABE

Didn't you ask what my name was? Babe's what people call me. *(puts the glass down)* Listen—I'm just a grad student, I don't know what's going on, I'm an historian. I come from a family of historians—*(getting out his wallet)* You call Columbia, they'll tell you—*(He pulls out a card like a credit card.)* See? That's my picture and my signature and it says where I go and everything. That's all there is about me...

He holds the card in front of him toward the camera. It has a passport type picture, unflattering and flat, and his name and signature and the name of the University stamped across the front.

CUT TO

A PAN AM DEPARTURE BOARD AT LOS ANGELES INTERNATIONAL.

A lot of muttering goes on off camera, only it doesn't stay off camera for long because we quickly pull back to reveal A CROWD staring at the board, and are they ever unhappy— every plane has been delayed. The airport looks like it's in a state of siege and the passengers are hostages to fortune. Now a voice comes over the loudspeaker, and the voice is a little frayed. You get the feeling he's made this kind of announcement a lot lately.

LOUDSPEAKER

Pan American regrets to announce the further delay of 747 Service flight 909 to Hawaii. Plane 909 should be ready to depart in three hours. *(There is a horrendous groan from the crowd.)* Folks, thanks for understanding—the traffic controllers' slow-down has made all our lives a little difficult, but you've been terrific and we at Pan Am really appreciate it.

He clicks off now. While he's been talking, we've taken looks at the crowd—sitting, standing around, couples arguing angrily with one another, finger-pointing; there is the steady accompaniment of children crying "I'm huuuuungry." It's like the land of plenty has suddenly been overrun with refugees.

Now a RUGGED LOOKING GUY comes into view, quickly studies the Departure Board. What can you say about him? He's not particularly large, but he can't help giving the impression of power. He's not that handsome, but it would be hard to imagine him having trouble with women. He's well dressed but not conservatively so; Tasteful Californian you might call it. Between thirty-five and forty, he's obviously successful at whatever he does. Now he turns, heads for the sign saying "Bar."

CUT TO

THE BAR.

Tacky and plastic, and doing business—a lot of angry people sitting around drinking, some playing cards, more playing backgammon on small portable sets. At the far end of the bar itself, a SMALL MAN is drinking alone. His wig, from even this distance, is clearly a sad, ill-fitting thing.

THE RUGGED LOOKING GUY stands in the doorway of the bar, and for a moment, he hesitates. Then, with no warning he starts to move at a faster pace than expected.

THE MAN WITH THE WIG sits drinking until suddenly the RUGGED LOOKING GUY wraps his arms around him, and from a distance it might look like a couple of Rotarians locked in secret greeting. But close up we can see that the MAN WITH THE WIG is totally pinioned and helpless.

RUGGED LOOKING GUY

Peace, Ape.

APE
(quickly)

I'm unarmed.

RUGGED LOOKING GUY
(releasing him, sitting alongside)

How's life with the Arabs, rich and gaudy?

APE
(He doesn't answer the question.)

I'm glad you sat down, Scylla.

SCYLLA
(For that is the Rugged Looking Guy's name,
just as Ape is the man with the wig.)

Good. I wasn't sure you'd want me to.

APE

Why wouldn't I ?

SCYLLA

Maybe because the last time out we tried to kill each other.

APE

Brussels, you mean? *(Scylla nods.)* Oh that was work, work isn't personal, you know that. I've always wanted to meet you, Scylla, truly. *(to the Bartender)* The same for me, and—*(looks at Scylla)*—scotch, rocks, lemon twist. That's all you ever drink, yes? *(Scylla nods, the Bartender goes.)* Our file on you is really very thick. "Glorious career you're having," he said, enviously. You and Chen are the best now.

SCYLLA

When I came in the business, there was you and there was Fidelio. I read every file we had about the both of you—I was like a Willie Mays fan thumbing through old baseball magazines.

CUT TO

THE BARTENDER *returning. APE immediately takes his new drink, drinks too much of it. SCYLLA sips his, watching.*

SCYLLA

Why did you miss me in Brussels? Not that I'm sorry, understand, but it wasn't that hard a shot for someone like you.

APE

Shadows, I expect. I went for your brains and got the wall.

SCYLLA
(toasts)

To more shadows.

APE
(drinks again)

You should have known me at the beginning, Scylla. When I retired Fidelio, I was something.

SCYLLA

You retired Fidelio?

APE

Best shot I ever made—*(drinks again)*—it was an incredible story, truly.

SCYLLA

Tell me.

APE

It would take too long.

SCYLLA

Where are you going from here?

APE

London.

SCYLLA

So am I, we'll sit together, you can tell me on the plane.

CUT TO

APE: CLOSE UP. *He finishes his drink.*

> **APE**
>
> They're sending me coach.

CUT TO

SCYLLA. *For a moment he says nothing.*

> **SCYLLA**
>
> For cover? *(Ape shakes his head.)* Mistake, probably. *(Another head shake; Ape signals for another drink.)*

> **APE**
>
> I've had a better run than most, I expect.

> **SCYLLA**
>
> It's shitty—why give you hints that your work ratings are going down, why not just send you on a job you can't survive, retire you that way?

> **APE**
> *(as his new drink arrives)*
>
> Do you know what I was thinking before you sat down? There's never been a woman I didn't pay for, or a child who knew my name—*(He touches his dreadful wig.)*—or a wig that enhanced me.

> **SCYLLA**
> *(without a pause)*
>
> Sentimental crap.

> **APE**
> *(stung)*
>
> You can't imagine being retired—people like you and that goddam glass-eyed Chen, you think it won't happen to you but I promise you—*(stares at Scylla)*—they'll be sending you coach someday.

CUT TO

SCYLLA: CLOSE UP. *There is a pause. Then he looks at Ape.*

> **SCYLLA**
>
> Give me your ticket —

> **APE**
>
> —why?

> SCYLLA

Just give it to me—I'll change you to First Class. Don't worry, I'll pay the difference.

> APE

Sentimental crap. *(But he's starting to get excited as he shoves his ticket over.)* Here, here, take it. *(Scylla does.)* God damn, Scylla, but I'm glad you sat down—and I will tell you the Fidelio story—*(faster now)*—and I retired Trench too, same year. I've never even admitted I did that before—I'll tell you what the world was like before there were shadows...*(hops off his stool, almost happy)*. Obviously you know where I'm going—my intestinal difficulties must be noted in your files...

> SCYLLA
> *(nods)*

Rest assured. *(as Ape scurries away)*

CUT TO

SCYLLA AT THE PAN AM TICKET WINDOW.

As he slides Ape's ticket across the counter, the Ticket Man nods, takes it and

CUT TO

THE AIRPORT.

More like a refugee camp than ever. Now as the loudspeaker voice comes again, the groan of anger begins even before the message is totally audible.

> LOUDSPEAKER

Pan American regrets to announce that Flight 88 to New York—*(He knows he's drowned out—even over the loudspeaker, he sounds tired.)* Folks, we're not doing this on purpose, believe me.

CUT TO

SCYLLA, at the counter, receiving the new ticket from the agent, starting back toward the bar and

CUT TO

THE BAR.

SCYLLA approaches. Ape's seat is still empty. Scylla hesitates, then turns and

CUT TO

THE MEN'S ROOM.

A MAN APPROACHING THE DOOR, pushing it.

It's locked. There is a sign. The man glances at it as SCYLLA comes up. The man leaves. SCYLLA looks at the sign which is typed on official airline paper and taped to the door.

INSERT: THE SIGN

> Sorry for the inconvenience. Pipe trouble. Please use
> the facilities located at the bottom of the escalator.
> Thank you.

CUT TO

SCYLLA, studying the sign a moment. He half starts away, then is drawn back, looks at it again, especially the word "facilities."

Suddenly there's a tiny knife in his hand, a pocket knife and the smallest blade has been filed into a slight hook. SCYLLA slips it into the lock, rakes it up and down and

CUT TO

INSIDE THE MEN'S ROOM.

SCYLLA, obviously blind drunk, comes staggering in, makes it to the sink. TWO MEN look at him, surprised. ONE, AN ENGINEER WITH A WRENCH, plus other tools, is white. THE SECOND, A JANITOR who is pushing an enormous canvas garbage bag, is black. The bag is stuffed with linens, those long towels used to dry hands, etc.

> SCYLLA
> *(slurred)*
> Martinis're killers. *(He manages to get the "cold" spigot turned on, the water runs smoothly.)* Martinis're killers.

> ENGINEER
> *(very politely)*
> You'll have to turn that off, sir. *(He gestures with his wrench, explaining.)* These facilities aren't functioning properly.

> JANITOR
> There was a sign on the door, didn't you see it?

> SCYLLA
> *(perplexed)*
> Said "Men's Room"—course I saw it, ya think I wanna have a buncha women screamin' at me?! *(blinks drunkenly)* Martinis are killers.

CUT TO

THE ENGINEER *turns off the spigot. He couldn't be more polite.* SCYLLA *is looking at the mirror over the sink. The* JANITOR *moves to the door.*

> **ENGINEER**
> I really can't let you use the water, sir, I'm sorry.

CUT TO

THE LARGE CANVAS BAG WITH THE LINEN CRAMMED AT THE TOP. *Beneath the linen, out of sight, it's not hard to guess that Ape is lying dead; there is an outline visible of what undoubtedly is his body.*

> **SCYLLA**
> *(looking at the bag through the mirror)*
> I'm sorry too.

> **JANITOR**
> *(coming back from the front door)*
> Sign's still there—

> **ENGINEER**
> You shouldn't have come in—

> **SCYLLA**
> —I'm goin', I'm goin'—*(and as he takes a last glance in the mirror—)*

CUT TO

A TOILET STALL. *In one corner, Ape's ill-fitting wig is on the floor and*

CUT TO

SCYLLA, *suddenly exploding wildly—*

> **SCYLLA**
> You should have waited, Jesus Christ!

CUT TO

THE ENGINEER AND THE JANITOR, *surprised, and before the* ENGINEER *can even get his wrench half raised—*

CUT TO

SCYLLA, *moving like fire—his right hand comes up with the fingers stiff under the chin of the* ENGINEER, *lifting the other man off his feet, sending him gasping to the floor, and as the* JANITOR *tries to defend himself, he's just too slow as* SCYLLA *clubs him with the hard edge of his left hand near the neck and there is the sound of bones snapping as the* JANITOR *crumbles, falling near the* ENGINEER.

> **SCYLLA**
> You killed him with his pants down, you humiliated a legend—*(huge)*—why didn't you wait?!

CUT TO

THE ENGINEER AND THE JANITOR, *both of them in agony; the* ENGINEER *can only gasp and hold his ruined throat, the* JANITOR *just lies there, eyes glazed, as* SCYLLA *comes to them.*

> **SCYLLA**
> I think I'll take your pants down, would you like that?—and then put you on the squat, would you like that?—and kill you, would you like that?

The ENGINEER *continues his terrible gasping. The* JANITOR *manages a word.*

> **JANITOR**
> ...orders...

> **SCYLLA**
> I don't know whose side you're on and I don't care, you remember what I tell you: always—leave—a—person—something. *(to the janitor)* Understand? *(The janitor nods. Scylla looks at the engineer.)* Say it!!

> **ENGINEER**
> *(The rasp is barely audible.)*
> ...al...ways...le-leave...a per...son...suh...some...*(a breath)*...something...
> *(Scylla continues to stare, his eyes will not stop blazing.)*

HOLD ON SCYLLA. *Then*—

CUT TO

ANOTHER MAN WITH BRIGHT EYES. *He is sitting in a book-lined office, reading. Fifty-five, maybe sixty, he is whip thin, perfectly dressed. It is, as we'll soon know,* BIESENTHAL, *and there is no doubt about his brilliance. Outside it's day,* COLLEGE STUDENTS *can be seen walking. Then a knock at the door and* BABE'S VOICE *is heard. The door is opened a crack.*

> **BABE** (off-screen)
> Professor Biesenthal? *(sticking his head into view)* You sent for me?

BIESENTHAL *nods,* BABE *comes in, sits by the desk. He's wearing khakis, a levi shirt, badly knotted tie, old jacket. He looks, as he often does, attractively schlocky.*

> **BIESENTHAL**
> I finished your latest chapter. I'm a bit worried.

> BABE
> *(surprised)*

I thought it was the best so far.

> BIESENTHAL

I didn't say it lacked quality. *(opens a desk drawer)* Let's backtrack a moment. *(pulls out a single sheet of paper)* Title page: Modern American Fascism. Certainly a dull enough subject for a doctoral dissertation. *(pulls out papers, not many)* Introduction: 12 pages, cleanly written, objectives stated. *(more pulled out, not many)* Chapter One: Coolidge and the Boston Police Strike. 27 pages. A reasonable summary. *(puts them down)* Chapter Two: F.D.R. and the California Concentration Camps. 23 pages, again reasonable, since the subject is so well known. *(pauses)* Chapter Three: Joseph McCarthy and the Purges of the Fifties. *(And now he pulls out a whopping bundle of sheets tied together.)* 385 pages. *(looks at Babe)* I ask you, Levy, does anything about the balance strike you as being a trifle strange?

BABE sits tense, says nothing.

> BIESENTHAL

I get the feeling that you're trying to either recreate the past or alter it to your liking. Which?

> BABE

Neither.

> BIESENTHAL

Oh, come now, sir. Your father went to Denison, you went to Denison; he won a Rhodes Scholarship, you won a Rhodes Scholarship; he came here for his doctorate, look who's sitting across from me now. *(thumping the enormous chapter)* He was destroyed by McCarthy, and now you hand in this. *(watches Babe)* There's nothing you can do to clear him.

> BABE

I know that—he wasn't guilty. *(as he stares back at Biesenthal)*

CUT TO

THE TWO OF THEM walking across the Columbia campus. They pass buildings, the typical university stone-type things, the buildings have been covered with graffiti. Nothing vulgar, but not clever either, just scarring.

> BIESENTHAL

Ordinarily I don't involve myself in my students' neuroses—I've plenty of my own to go around. But since your father was my mentor—

> BABE
> *(cutting in)*

—listen, really, I'm fine.

> BIESENTHAL

Is your brother also involved in your crusade?

> BABE
> *(half smiles)*

Doc?—he's a money grubber, he works in the oil business, dreams about tax shelters and talks about French wines. That's all he ever drinks, and he only wears these hand-tailored Brooks Brothers suits. He's kind of a world class dilettante. *(shakes his head)* Why I should think he's so terrific baffles me, but it must have something to do with—*(starting to get into a difficult thing now)*—with, well, you know, he brought me up after—*(And now he kind of falters a bit.)*—you know, the incident with my father. *(shrugs, lapses into silence)*

> BIESENTHAL
> *(The silence goes on briefly, then—)*

I want you to know something, I wept when he died.

> BABE

It wasn't a good day for any of us.

And from that, very quickly—

CUT TO

TIGHTSHOT: *BABE.*

> BABE
> *(confused)*

Weapons? Why do you want to know if I have any weapons?

> IRISH VOICE (off-screen)

Well, do you? *(Babe nods.)* What?

> BABE

Gun. *(points)* There—in my bottom desk drawer, but it's licensed, it's all legal—

> IRISH VOICE (off-screen)

Why does a grad student have a gun?

> BABE

No reason—

CUT TO

ANOTHER TIME, ANOTHER PLACE.

The BOY *we saw running through the field is in a room now—playing with whatever ten-year-old smart kids play with—great masses of toy soldiers maybe, laid out according to some battle plan, and on the wall is a map of the battle and as the boy concentrates, there comes the altogether terrifying sound of a shot and the boy bolts out of the room and down the hall of a house and stops at another doorway and stands there and as he looks into the room, so do we and there's just a bed visible, nothing else, no one.*

Then, slowly, inexorably, a blood puddle becomes visible behind the bed, dark red and growing and the BOY *cries out, runs forward, stops and now we see sprawled behind the bed the* MAN *who stood on the top of the hill and the blood puddle comes from the man's head and near the man's right hand there is a gun, a pistol. The* BOY *begins to shriek.*

CUT TO

BABE: BACK IN THE TIGHTSHOT.

BABE
(eyes dead at the camera)

It was my father's.

HOLD ON BABE, then—

CUT TO

BIG BEN announcing the hour on a glorious sunny day, and as the sound echoes, we quickly go to Buckingham Palace and the changing of the guard and then we see the pigeons flying across Trafalgar Square and it's England, obviously, Merrie and Olde and just like it's always been—

—only maybe it isn't because now, as we see the front of Harrods, there is visible great mounds and piles of garbage. A strike is clearly going on, and as we look around at all the refuse it's clear that America isn't the only place that's stopped working with Swiss-type efficiency.

CUT TO

SCYLLA walking along by Harrods—there is a line of people waiting to get in, not so much because business is booming as because everyone has to be carefully searched before they are allowed into the store. Scylla pauses, watching as a wealthy elderly woman has her purse examined.

> WEALTHY WOMAN
> *(to the examiner)*

I resent this. *(really put out)* Don't think I don't resent this. *(She passes— her purse is handed back. She sweeps into the store.)* There will be repercussions.

Scylla half smiles, crosses the street, goes along, stops at a gift shop, a lovely small Knightsbridge type establishment. He is studying the merchandise in the window when, with no warning whatsoever, a bomb goes off inside.

There is a great and sudden CLOUD OF DEBRIS *billowing out and along with the cries and the wild echo of the explosion, there is a moment of considerable confusion. What Scylla thinks or does we can't tell—he's disappeared, covered by the* CLOUD, *gone—*

CUT TO

A WILDLY BUSY LONDON PUB AT LUNCH.

Jammed. At a table set for three, TWO MEN *sit drinking pints of beer.*

One of them, KAVANAUGH, *is unimportant, average, nondescript.*

The other guy, THE COMMANDER, *is blonde, mid-thirties, handsome and has about him—he can't help it, it's just there—the air of the hero. Now he glances up.*

CUT TO

THE DOORWAY. SCYLLA *enters. He is dressed as before, but not as clean, and his jacket is torn at the shoulder. He looks around.*

THE COMMANDER gestures, SCYLLA *approaches.*

> SCYLLA
> *(sitting, nods a greeting)*

Commander.

> COMMANDER

What happened?

> SCYLLA

Bomb went off across from Harrods.

> KAVANAUGH

Goddam Irish.

> COMMANDER

Kavanaugh—get the man a double scotch, why don't you. And take your time about it.

KAVANAUGH

Yessir. *(He rises.)*

COMMANDER
(when he is alone with Scylla)

All right—what happened?

SCYLLA

I don't think it was the Irish—*(before the other man can speak)*—I think the bomb was for me.

COMMANDER

You've really got to get hold of your paranoia, Scylla.

SCYLLA

I used that shop—a lot—I bought gifts there—

COMMANDER

—for Janey I imagine—*(Scylla nods.)*—oh Christ, Scylla—you eat at Rules, is that going next? Are they blowing up the Dorchester too? Why the hell would anybody want you so badly?

SCYLLA

I don't know, but I am not trusted. I'm telling you, something's happened I don't know about.

CUT TO

KAVANAUGH, scotch in hand, waiting by the bar to be beckoned. He watches the two men closely as they continue talking fast.

CUT TO

THE TABLE.

COMMANDER

I'll check around but I promise you, it's nothing—you are the best! That's agreed on.

SCYLLA

The last man who said that died in a sack in a men's room, take care. *(leaning forward)* You're going back tomorrow. *(The Commander nods.)* Call me if there's anything.

COMMANDER

I'll call the States this afternoon if you'll feel better.

SCYLLA

I'd feel better. *(rubs his eyes)* I just hate all this. It's such shit.

COMMANDER

We knew that when we got involved.

SCYLLA

(nods)

When I was twenty, I didn't mean to be here when I was forty. *(stares at The Commander)* Deliver a message?

COMMANDER

For Janey? *(Scylla nods again.)* If it isn't too mushy. *(Scylla suddenly is emotionally full and silent.)* Well, let's have it, what's the message?

SCYLLA

Not important.

COMMANDER

When you get hooked, you stay hooked.

SCYLLA

No one ever said I had taste.

They both laugh and THE COMMANDER *gestures for* KAVANAUGH *who brings the scotch.*

KAVANAUGH

What was so important that I couldn't hear?

COMMANDER

We were talking about charades—*(looks at Scylla)*—wouldn't you agree?

KAVANAUGH

Good game.

HOLD FOR A MOMENT *on* KAVANAUGH, *looking first from the blonde heroic* COMMANDER *to the powerful* SCYLLA. *Scylla glances at the commander, downs the double without the least difficulty.*

CUT TO

ISLINGTON.

A trendy section, a good cab ride's distance from the center of London. Dusk. Lots of antique shops, one of which is Robertson's. SCYLLA *comes walking along, approaches Robertson's shop, enters.*

CUT TO

INSIDE THE STORE.

Lots of bric-a-brac. The store is dimly lit and ROBERTSON *is visible at the rear of the store, rocking back and forth in his rocking chair. He is a fat man, his hands in his lap, his legs covered by a robe.*

CUT TO

SCYLLA *waving in greeting to* ROBERTSON.

CUT TO

ROBERTSON, *rocking. He does not gesture back and now—*

ZOOM TO

SCYLLA *as he breaks into a sudden run toward the fat man, and even before he reaches him, it's clear* ROBERTSON *is dead, and recently so, because the rocker is still in motion and as* SCYLLA *touches his shoulder, his neck lolls like a dead chicken and he's been garroted and* SCYLLA *looks around, tears like a madman out the nearby back door and*

CUT TO

AN ALLEY AT DUSK.

SCYLLA *listens. Silence. He starts down the alley, ready. Silence. He comes to an abandoned building. Broken glass. Dark. He stops, stares inside and as he does —*

Slooooooowly move into the building. Silence. Nothing. We go deeper and deeper into the darkness. Finally something becomes visible. A glass eye set in an Oriental face. It is CHEN. *He stands in darkness, staring out through the broken glass at* SCYLLA. *It's all chilling now.*

CUT TO

SCYLLA, *staring in.*

CUT TO

CHEN, *staring out.*

CUT TO

THE TWO MEN *staring and either they see each other or it's too dark, and they can't. But they both sense the presence of something, because, for the longest time, they do not move...*

HOLD. *Then —*

CUT TO

AN ENGLISH PARK IN THE MIDDLE OF THE NIGHT.

A YOUNG GIRL *walks quickly along. She could have gone to Bryn Mawr. It's cold. She pulls her coat more tightly around her, moves faster through the darkness until we*

CUT TO

A PARK BENCH. *Empty. She sits and we pull back to reveal* SCYLLA *seated on the bench opposite. Behind Scylla is a dark, heavily bushed area. Not even the wind stirs.*

> GIRL
>
> I seem to be out of cigarettes—I only smoke American.

> SCYLLA
>
> Oh, don't make us go through all that password gibberish, please. Who the hell else do you think would be sitting here freezing his ass off at three in the morning?

> GIRL
>
> I seem to be out of cigarettes—I only smoke American.

> SCYLLA
> *(with a sigh)*
> Lucky for you I'm chauvinistic. *(He holds out a pack. As she reaches for it...)* Keep. *(She does.)*

> GIRL
> *(the preliminaries over)*
> You are Scylla?

> SCYLLA
>
> I better be after all that.

> GIRL
>
> I am instructed to say your price is too high.

> SCYLLA
> *(looking at her—She is staring too intently at him now.)*
> Are you also instructed to negotiate?

> GIRL
> *(eyes frozen on him)*
> Of course.

> SCYLLA
>
> Well then for chrissakes, make a counter offer, that's what negotiating *is*.

GIRL

Of course.

Only now she can't keep her eyes from flicking a little and the GIRL *is suddenly terrified and*

CUT TO

SCYLLA, *watching her, wondering what the hell's going on and then he knows, he knows, he's under some kind of attack and*

CUT TO

A WIRE COMING IN AROUND HIS THROAT, *and he barely manages to get his hand up in time, but then the wire starts pulling tighter, tighter, and as his hand begins to bleed—*

FREEZE ON SCYLLA BEING GARROTED.

Come out of it with a tight close up of something scary—the glass eye we saw in the darkness of the broken house before. Now we see the face.

Now we hear dialogue—the same as a few moments before: we've gone back in time, and are doubling back into the present.

SCYLLA (off-screen)

Who the hell else do you think would be sitting here freezing his ass off at three in the morning.

GIRL

I seem to be out of cigarettes—I only smoke American.

Now we pull back still further to see where CHEN *has been, and it's that deep bush area behind* SCYLLA'S *bench. Not a leaf stirred then. As he stands, nothing stirs now. The man is incredible, he lives in silence.*

SCYLLA (off-screen)

Lucky for you I'm chauvinistic. *(pause)* Keep.

GIRL (off-screen)

You are Scylla?

SCYLLA (off-screen)

I better be after all that.

CHEN *begins moving forward. He holds a wood stick in each hand, the sticks connected by a wire. He is an athlete and moves like one. His arms are loose, ready. Ahead of him, we can see* SCYLLA, *his back to us.*

> GIRL

I am instructed to say your price is too high.

CHEN keeps moving, bringing his wire weapon a little higher. He makes absolutely no sound.

> SCYLLA

Are you also instructed to negotiate?

> GIRL

Of course.

CHEN'S arms are high. He is two steps behind SCYLLA. He takes one of them.

> SCYLLA

Well then for chrissakes, make a counter offer, that's what negotiating is.

> GIRL
> (panicked)

Of course.

CUT TO

CHEN moving like the wind and he's got the garroting weapon around Scylla's throat and his body is balanced and as he pulls the wire tighter,

CUT TO

SCYLLA, gasping, blood pouring from his hand, blinking, dazed—

CUT TO

THE GIRL, standing, grabbing out a gun, moving across the walk toward the battle and

CUT TO

CHEN, bringing the wire through Scylla's flesh and he's small and SCYLLA'S big but when you have surprise, that doesn't matter so much, and it doesn't matter now until Scylla suddenly gives a wild shoulder throw and Chen is sailing across and slamming into THE GIRL and stunned, but so is Scylla and for a moment, no one moves because the girl is out of it, unconscious and then at the same moment Scylla and Chen both see her gun and they go for it and Chen gets there first but Scylla kicks it into the grassy darkness out of sight and then they're up and circling and no blows are struck, nothing, but the panting and the circling and Scylla's right hand is useless, and he keeps it behind him but that's the way Chen circles, toward the right, because he knows there's nothing Scylla can do with it so when he makes his final move, it's toward Scylla's right, and he walks right into Scylla's right hand blow, and the blow slashes at the side of Chen's neck and then as it hits there come two screams: Chen's final one of death, Scylla's of terrible pain as his hand spurts like a fountain.

CUT TO

A PHONE BOOTH BY THE PARK.

SCYLLA is finishing dialing, his right hand bound in a handkerchief, still bleeding badly.

> KAVANAUGH (off-screen)
Division. Kavanaugh.

> SCYLLA
Scylla.

> KAVANAUGH (off-screen)
Yes, Scylla.

> SCYLLA
Get removals.

> KAVANAUGH (off-screen)
How many dead?

> SCYLLA
Two. Between the Albert Memorial and Lancaster Walk.

> KAVANAUGH (off-screen)
I'll alert them. And you?

> SCYLLA
Hand.

> KAVANAUGH (off-screen)
I'll alert the clinic. (*He clicks off and as he does—*)

CUT TO

A LARGE HYPODERMIC NEEDLE. Filled.

CUT TO

SCYLLA, seated on a table in an area enclosed by a white curtain. A DOCTOR TYPE holds the hypo.

> SCYLLA
> (*kind of embarrassed*)
I'm afraid of needles.

THE DOCTOR puts the hypo down, takes Scylla's wounded hand which has been cleansed, picks up the proper equipment, makes the first stitch as we watch. SCYLLA watches too, and to our surprise and his, he winces.

> **SCYLLA**
> Hey? *(The Doctor looks at him.)* I guess I'm not that afraid.

THE DOCTOR takes the hypo, prepares to make an injection to numb the pain as THE COMMANDER enters, goes to SCYLLA. This next goes low and fast.

> **COMMANDER**
> Kavanaugh called me about this—*(indicates the hand)*—and I apologize about lunch; maybe you're not so paranoid. *(The Doctor works. Scylla looks away.)* I spent some time calling the States. Kaspar Szell was killed in Manhattan, accident with an oil truck.

CUT TO

SCYLLA, very much surprised. He looks at THE COMMANDER.

> **COMMANDER**
> Is that going to change much?

> **SCYLLA**
> *(There is a pause.)*
> Only everything...

THE DOCTOR continues to stitch.

HOLD. Then—

CUT TO

LIBRARY STACKS. EVENING.

A line of cubicles, many of them occupied, some not.

CUT TO

BABE, in a cubicle, the desk piled high with books. He is deeply engrossed in his work, writing furiously on a pad of lined yellow legal paper. He flips a page, continues writing as—

> **WOMAN'S VOICE** (off-screen)
> You are in my cubicle—*(Babe doesn't notice. The Voice gets louder, the accent vaguely foreign.)*—I was given 18 V, please move—

BABE
(desperately trying to finish a sentence)
This is 18 T. Bug out, lady. *(and as he looks up—)*

CUT TO

ELSA. *She stands there, arms full of books, a stunner. She turns, goes two cubicles farther on, puts down her stuff.*

CUT TO

BABE *staring after her. He tries to go back to his own work, gets nowhere.*

CUT TO

ELSA, *and now she is deeply engrossed in her work. She has a few books around her, is taking notes.*

BABE'S VOICE (off-screen)
It was an understandable mistake—

ELSA
(looks up)
What?

CUT TO

BABE AND ELSA.

BABE
T and V sound a lot alike, I wouldn't want you feeling silly.

ELSA
I don't feel silly. *(She looks at him like he might be some nut.)*

BABE
(tries a smile)
I'm Babe Levy.

ELSA
That is your problem, and I'm sure you'll be able to conquer it. *(She returns to her note-taking.)*

BABE
(muttering as he goes back to his cubicle)
The Balkan Phyllis Diller for chrissakes.

CUT TO

ELSA, later. She stretches, takes cigarettes and a lighter, stands, leaves the cubicle area. As soon as she's gone, BABE hurries to her cubicle, goes through her books. They're mostly medical stuff and they have her name and address neatly printed in ink on the inside cover. Babe glances around, takes the least impressive-looking book at the bottom of the pile and as he goes back to his own cubicle, he keeps it with him.

CUT TO

COLUMBIA AT NIGHT.

BABE runs along, carrying a bunch of books. His necktie flies out to one side as he goes along, reaches a corner, turns and

CUT TO

BABE, running, running through the Autumn evening.

CUT TO

ELSA, standing in the doorway of her apartment building. It's old and semi-run-down and BABE is hurrying along the corridor toward her. She is smoking, inhaling deeply as he approaches.

> BABE
> Sorry to bother you, Miss Opel, but one of your books must have fallen in your cubicle earlier and I happened to spot it—*(hands it over)*—just thought it might be important.

> ELSA
> That's very kind. *(starting to go inside)* Good night.

> BABE
> 'Night. Your name and address are on the inside—"Elsa Opel" and where you live—in case you were curious how I found you, Miss Opel.

> ELSA
> I wasn't. Good night.

> BABE
> 'Night.

> ELSA
> You keep saying that but you also don't leave.

> BABE
> I twisted my ankle on the way over, I was giving it a rest.

> ELSA

You weren't limping just now.

> BABE

I'm the worst when it comes to lying.

> ELSA
> *(curious)*

Did you take my book? *(Babe nods.)* Are you embarrassed? Is that why you're perspiring?

> BABE

No, it's 'cause I ran here, I run a lot. I'm gonna be a marathon man.

> ELSA

Well, Mr. Levy, I hope it was worth your exertions.

> BABE

It will be if you'll go out with me—what're you studying, medicine?

> ELSA

Nursing. Why do you want to see me?

> BABE

Probably because you're so pretty.

> ELSA
> *(sort of sad)*

If I am, it just happened, I didn't work for it.

> BABE

Well, Jesus, lady, I can't very well rave on about how intelligent you are, you might be a real dummy—my God, what kind of a nurse smokes? But I'm willing to give you a break. I'm smart as a whip, I'll learn all about tourniquets and we can have some real soul-searching discussions.

> ELSA
> *(And now she just breaks out laughing.)*

All right, all right, enough, I'll see you again. *(Then, strangely, she reaches out, touches his cheek.)* But it won't come to anything...

HOLD A MOMENT, then—

CUT TO

ELSA *later, alone in her apartment, small, furnished looking. She is talking on the phone, smoking, inhaling deeply.*

ELSA

He is terribly naive, terribly sweet. *(listens)* Yes, Erhard, I'm quite sure he finds me attractive. *(pause)* How long do I have? *(pause)* I would think it possible, yes. With any luck at all, in a week he'll love me.

HOLD ON—

ELSA. She hangs up, smokes in silence. The deep sadness that was around her before is still there.

CUT TO

BABE, seated at his desk in his apartment, writing a letter. We COME IN WITH VOICE-OVER SOUND until we see BABE'S FACE.

BABE
(He's written this much, we can see it.)
Doc, first the good news. Her name is Elsa Opel, she's my age, Swiss, a nurse, and not much more attractive than Grace Kelly. *(We see his face— it's swollen and that comes as a surprise. He's clearly been through something.)*

CUT TO

BABE AND ELSA walking down a West Side street in front of a movie theatre. The theatre is a shambles, and it's obviously gone forever. On the marquee is the sign: "Closed Temporarily."

Now BABE AND ELSA are eating in a Cuban restaurant. The window of the place has been broken and plastic has been taped over the break. It flaps. No one else is in the place—it looks like a disaster area.

BABE (off-screen)
I took her to all the chic places that us beautiful people go to; she'd never been, but I'm getting bored with them myself.

BABE AND ELSA are walking along Broadway at night. A crowd has gathered around two drunks trying to have a fight. But they're so far gone they can't really hit each other and just sort of swing and fall down from their own momentum. The crowd is enjoying it; no one moves to stop them, including a policeman who stands, watching, entertained like the rest.

BABE (off-screen)
Naturally, she was all over me from the very beginning—

We see BABE AND ELSA now by her front door. Babe wouldn't mind going in with her. No way. She shakes his hand firmly, goes inside and closes the door. He mouths something, probably "shit," and scuffs his way back down the corridor alone.

BABE AND ELSA are standing by a bus stop. So are a lot of other people. Cabs go by, all of them empty. A limousine passes. Someone throws a rock at it. The bus arrives. It is filled. No matter, as soon as it opens its doors, everyone tries to jam on.

BABE AND ELSA approach a museum, stop as they reach the entrance. The place is closed. A sign in front says "Closed Mondays." Added to that has been the words "through Thursdays." The place is only open weekends now.

BABE AND ELSA are by her front door again. Again they shake hands and she goes inside without him.

> **BABE** (off-screen)
> —but having been a sex symbol for so many years, her passion for me left me unmoved. It was not until I realized it was my soul she was after did I succumb. We are now, the both of us, deeply smitten.

We see BABE AND ELSA sitting on a rock in Central Park. It's really too dark to be sitting there but they don't move, just sit close, quietly watching the night.

This next goes quickly now.

ELSA shivers, stands, stretches, and as BABE starts to rise, TWO FIGURES appear from the night, one of them A LIMPER, small, the other A MAMMOTH. THE LIMPER goes for Elsa, backhands her hard across the mouth and as she falls, Babe starts for her, only the Mammoth blocks him, creams him, and as Babe goes down, the Mammoth is on him, pounding blow after blow into the middle of Babe's back, hitting at the base of the spine. All of this is sudden and shocking.

Again and again the blows from THE MAMMOTH, almost in slow motion now, all getting nightmarish, as if it's still going on, still is a part of Babe's mind.

> **BABE** (off-screen)
> The bad news is, we got mugged.

THE MAMMOTH IS STILL POUNDING AT BABE. In the background, THE LIMPER has ELSA down, is grabbing for her purse.

The motion is slower now, the impact dreadful.

> **BABE** (off-screen)
> We stayed too late in the Park, it was my fault, I knew better. This Limper and a Mammoth appeared and Doc, I COULDN'T DO ANYTHING!

THE MUGGING will not stop. THE MAMMOTH is tearing at Babe's wallet now, takes the money, throws the rest down. Then he and THE LIMPER are gone.

BABE tries crawling to ELSA. He's in pain. But he forces himself and as he does—

BABE AND ELSA are by a water fountain. She is crying and he can't make her stop. His face is bloody, starting to swell. He takes out a handkerchief, dabs at her face. She's shaking from what happened, really scared.

> **BABE** (off-screen)
> I couldn't help my one true woman. If I could have found those two guys, Doc, I mean this, if I could I would have killed them. I never knew I had all that inside me before.

Now BABE is alone, walking toward his brownstone. THE PUERTO RICANS are, as always, on their stoop, watching.

> **BABE** (off-screen)
> There's a bunch of delinquents a few buildings down, and when I run, they mock me but this time I figured maybe I'd get some respect, what with the blood and all. And you know what happened? When I passed, they looked at me, and the smartest of them, this kid Melendez, he looked at me and said, "Hey, Creep, who beat you up, a midget or a girl?"

And now the PUERTO RICANS are laughing.

> **BABE** (off-screen)
> Other than love and violence, nothing new in Magic Town.—Babe.

We see BABE in his apartment now, finishing the letter. He stands, moves across the room, bent over like an old man. He is in pain...

HOLD ON THE LETTER until suddenly—

CUT TO

TIGHTSHOT: BABE.

He is staring at the camera until from off to one side there begin A SERIES OF BRIGHT LIGHT EXPLOSIONS, pop, pop, pop. His head turns, looks toward the brightness, then quickly turns his head away.

> **BABE**
> Can't they stop that?

> **IRISH VOICE** (off-screen)
> They have their job to do, it won't take long.

The flashes continue. BABE looks about to come apart.

IRISH VOICE (off-screen)

Go on about the mugging, why don't you.

BABE
(blinks)

Why was I telling about it at all?

IRISH VOICE (off-screen)

Don't you remember me asking if there had been other crimes recently?

BABE
(looks front)

You think there's some connection? *(headshake)* There's none. Nothing involves me. *(louder)* Understand something, will you—*(big)*—I—don't—know—what's—happening. *(suddenly—)*

CUT TO

An ARMED GUARD. *We know that he's armed because we can see the rifle and bayonet in his swarthy arms. How we're sure he's a guard is a little more difficult, since he is not in a uniform. But he wears a bullet belt, has a tough sweating face. There is an insect buzz, steady and irritating and as the tough guard raises his hand—*

PULL BACK TO REVEAL

AN UNTRAVELED RUTTED ROAD.

Jungle all around. Ahead, an open truck comes toward the GUARD. *A* SWARTHY MAN *drives the truck; beside him sits a bull-shouldered* WOMAN *wearing a dark shawl.*

CUT TO

THE TOUGH GUARD; he gestures for the truck to proceed, and we follow it as it slowly turns into a long driveway and there, at the end of it, is a lone blue house. It is large and clearly the establishment of someone with money. But it is also surrounded by jungle, the heat is oppressive, the insect sound continuous. Now—

CUT TO

A SIDE DOOR OF THE HOUSE *as the* SWARTHY MAN *opens it and allows the bull-shouldered* WOMAN *inside.*

CUT TO

AN ENORMOUS PILE OF BEAUTIFUL SHIRTS. They are, or were once, of the finest quality. The BULL-SHOULDERED WOMAN *is ironing, her shawl over a chair now. Behind her, a few shirts, already finished, hang on hangers, immaculate. She works in the dining room of the house and it is really remarkably well appointed. Someone clearly has more than a passing acquaintance with civilization.*

Now the camera begins slowly to move and explore the house. Music is playing—Britten's "Fantasy for Oboe and Strings." The living room is filled with the sound. And lovely furniture, not primitive like the jungle outside. This looks almost elegant, perhaps French, probably antique. The music continues to play, the camera to move.

There are books, many books, in many languages. Paintings on the walls, all obviously by the same artist and these are kind of child-like: lovely little people, animals, children.

Outside the windows, insects are trapped in netting. Those still alive struggle to escape.

The room, incredibly, is air-conditioned. As we pass the machines, their hum momentarily intrudes on the music.

Where are we?—that's what we've got to be thinking; who lives here?

We continue on, as now a metallic sound begins. We're leaving the main room starting toward the bedroom.

Another air-conditioner—everything seems to be working wonderfully in this primitive area, inside at least. In New York and Europe, everything was malfunctioning, but wherever the hell we are now, inside, all goes well.

The METALLIC SOUND *is louder. Beneath the air conditioner now, a newspaper flutters lightly from the breeze. We don't see clearly, but it may have been open to photos of the cars crashing into the oil truck and the terrible flames.*

Now AN EASEL *and a half-completed painting. The same style as in the living room. Charming, almost professional in skill. Whoever lives here has painted them.*

CUT TO

SOMETHING BEAUTIFUL, ALL SNOWY AND WHITE, *and it takes us a moment to realize that we're in a bathroom, looking at a sink, and the snowy white stuff is hair.*

The metallic sound goes on a moment longer, and more beautiful white hair almost floats into the sink. Now the metallic sound stops, a pair of scissors appears, being placed down on the edge of the sink.

TILT UP TO

A MIRROR AND THE FACE OF A MAN REFLECTED IN IT. *He is probably close to sixty, but he doesn't look it. He has incredible eyes, extraordinarily bright. He reaches down, takes up a large straight razor. Leaning toward the mirror, his bright eyes concentrating completely, he begins to shave himself bald.*

CUT TO

THE SWARTHY DRIVER AND THE LAUNDRESS, leaving for the day, getting back into the truck.

CUT TO

THE TOUGH GUARD standing in the road. As the truck draws close, a look of astonishment hits his face and as he starts nervously to salute—

ZOOM TO

THE SWARTHY DRIVER AND THE LAUNDRESS WITH THE SHAWL. Only it isn't the laundress. It's the BALD MAN sitting there, eyes flicking from side to side; you get the impression that he misses nothing. His eyes never stop, as the following terse dialogue takes place in Spanish, subtitled.

> SWARTHY DRIVER
>
> What shall I tell the laundress?

> BALD MAN
>
> Nothing. Just that I shall be back in three days. She is my guest.

> SWARTHY DRIVER
>
> And if she wants to return to her village?

> BALD MAN
>
> Use all your charm. She must be handled with great care. *(The incredible eyes keep flicking, this way, that, alert always.)* I have not had shirts as crisp since '45.

Now, from the primitive jungle area and the rutted road —

CUT TO

THE SKYLINE OF MANHATTAN and a 747 roaring in for a landing.

CUT TO

CUSTOMS,

—and the airport is a disaster area.

> LOUDSPEAKER
>
> We're really sorry about the baggage handlers' strike, folks, but if you'll just have patience like you've been doing, it'll all be straightened out soon.

There is not the least sign of patience on anyone's face. VACATIONERS mill around angrily; a group of GERMAN TOURISTS jabber at each other in their native tongue.

THE BALD MAN is there, dressed in a business suit now. He looks, possibly, nervous. He has his bag and is heading toward customs when a burst of laughter explodes behind him and he whirls, surprised. Then he turns back, consciously stops, gets control, then heads toward the customs inspectors as we

CUT TO

THE BALD MAN, done with customs, moving slowly out into the main greeting area and his eyes are flicking again, looking for somebody and

CUT TO

A CROWD OF PEOPLE, many of them waving. The BALD MAN still looks around. None of them were waving for him. He hesitates, then starts to walk.

CUT TO

THE AIRPORT LOBBY,

—as the BALD MAN enters, puts his bag down. Now quickly —

CUT TO

THE LIMPER AND THE MAMMOTH WHO MUGGED BABE AND ELSA in the Park. They hurry forward to THE BALD MAN. He waits until they reach him. The big man takes his suitcase.

BALD MAN

Good evening, Erhard. *(Erhard, the Limper, nods.)*

HOLD ON THE THREE MEN

—as they move into the night. We don't know exactly what's going on yet, but clearly the clans are gathering—

CUT TO

BABE, in his room, alone, asleep. From somewhere, a sound. His eyes flutter. Again, a sound. BABE'S eyes are open now and he's taut, lying still.

CUT TO

THE ROOM.

Deep shadow. Hard to make out anything. But maybe there is something and maybe it is moving and

CUT TO

BABE, reaching out, silently takes the flashlight from his bedtable and as he flicks it on—

> **BABE**
> *(very Cagney)*
> I got a gun, you make a move, I'll blow your ass to Shanghai.

CUT TO

THE ROOM, as he flashes the light around the walls, and we get quick glimpses of runners and fathers and suddenly, and it comes as a clockstopper, a human face is caught in the light—SCYLLA.

> **SCYLLA**
> Don't kill me, Babe. *(He flicks on the light switch.)*

BABE, tumbling out of bed, really excited—

> **BABE**
> Aw, hey, Doc, shit, great.

> **DOC**
> *(For he is Scylla, smiling now.)*
> Articulate as always, I see. *(And he shuts the door, picks up an overnight Gucci bag and a plastic bag with bottles.)*

CUT TO

DOC. And if he seems a little different than when he was SCYLLA, he should, because his movements are different, more fastidious. He also seems somehow smaller, but that's maybe because he's dressed differently, super Ivy League. He could very well be the dilettante Babe described him as being. Now he glances around Babe's book-strewn room.

> **DOC**
> You've really done wonders fixing up the place.

> **BABE**
> It's not finished quite—my decorator's so goddam unreliable.

> **DOC**
> *(taking red wine bottles out of the plastic bag, examining them with care)*
> Listen, not many guys will tackle a job this size—*(whirling on his kid brother)*—Jesus, Babe, how can you live in an armpit like this?—*(shakes his head)*—hopeless.

CUT TO

THE KITCHEN AREA, as DOC starts opening a bottle of wine. From across the room, BABE watches.

DOC

This is a '71 Moulin-a-vent and I know you're going to be startled at its power—

BABE

You really think so, huh? *(He's already making his eyes heavy with boredom.)*

DOC

Yes. Usually, a Beaujolais hasn't the size one associates with most Burgundy—

BABE

...no kidding...*(And now an experimental snore escapes him.)*

DOC
(pulling the cork)

But being the king of Beaujolais, a great Moulin-a-vent sometimes can be full of surprises.

BABE
(snoring full out now)

...is this ever interesting...

DOC
(laughs)

You're a boor and a turd. *(pours)* Here. *(gives Babe a glass)* And I apologize for making any remarks about your hovel, listen, it's a crazy world, any way you can skin it, it's your business. *(swirls his wine, sips)* I was just reading today about three young Californians—you won't believe this, but these guys have sunk their life savings into an invention *(thinks a minute)*—oh yeah, I remember the name, they call it a br-oooo-mmm. *(And now BABE breaks out laughing.)* It's like a long stick with hay tied to one end; these guys actually claim you can clean things with their br-oooo-mmm, floors and stuff, just by sweeping.

BABE
(drinks)

Never catch on.

CUT TO

DOC AND BABE. For a moment they're quiet and, if it isn't clear by now, it should be— they may harass each other constantly, but they care for each other. A lot.

DOC goes to his Gucci bag, zips it open, starts to unpack.

DOC

Listen, I got your latest epistle and among other tidbits, you described a creature named Irmgard who, if you are to be believed, may be the first female in the history of the world to be even more desirable than Annette Funicello.

BABE
(breaking up)

Just screw, huh?

DOC

Okay if I take you and Etta to dinner?

BABE

If you promise not to eat with your fingers.

DOC
(tone change)

Hey? *(Babe hears it, waits.)* I didn't like the mugging part so much. How about coming down to D.C. with me? I'll set you up some place decent, you know I've got the bread.

BABE

Thanks.

He means "no thanks" and DOC reads him correctly. He stops unpacking for a moment, glances at the books piled all over BABE'S desk.

DOC

What's all this—? More crap for your thesis?

BABE

Delicately put.

DOC
(Suddenly it's not jokey anymore.)

Why don't you just once face facts? *(ticks them off)* McCarthy destroyed Dad, Dad became a drunk, Dad killed himself. *(indicates the books)* Nothing in here is gonna change that.

BABE

Go back to talking about wine, you were less boring.

DOC
(hesitates, then quietly)

Babe, do you think Dad would want you to throw your life away like this?

BABE

You telling me to turn into a businessman hustler like you?

CUT TO

Doc: *Close Up.*

DOC
(big)

My life' s thrown away already, don't you understand that?

BABE looks at his brother, surprised.

BABE

Hard times in the oil business?

DOC

Babe, I'm the best in my business—you know how I know?—because everybody thinks it's true. *(pauses again)* Everybody but me. I'm past it, and I know it, but sooner or later, it'11 be common knowledge. *(touches his heart)* There's nobody home here anymore.

BABE

Boy, something's sure got to you.

DOC
(nods)

You have. Living in this place, trying to clear a dead man—*(looks at Babe)*—you probably still got the gun, don't you?

BABE nods, opens his bottom desk drawer, takes it out. DOC keeps his distance from it.

DOC

Why for Chrissakes do you keep it?

BABE
(He holds the gun.)

Maybe McCarthy's alive, they lie a lot in Washington, haven't you noticed?

DOC
(shakes his head)

I'll tell you, for a liberal pacifist, you've got some sense of vengeance. *(pointing to the desk)* Put it back, huh? *(as Babe does)* Is Helga sadistic too— what do you do for entertainment if there isn't a vampire movie in town?

CUT TO

BABE, sprawling in a chair, the serious moment, whatever brought it about, is passed.

BABE

You're trying to bait me, you bastard, because before you called her Irmgard and I didn't correct you and then you called her Etta and I let that go too, and just now it came out Helga. Well, that's not gonna get a rise out of me either, but it's Elsa. Elsa. Not Ella or Ilse or Leila or Lola.

DOC

Sorry, I'm punchy from the traveling I've been doing, I won't get Olga wrong again, I promise.

BABE

Olga is close but Olga is wrong, and I know this is hard for a guy like you who couldn't master toilet training until he was into his teens, but we'll stay with it until you get it right.

DOC

Ursula?

BABE

Close, but not quite, not Ursula or Vida, Vera, Venetia. or Vanessa—Elsa!!!

DOC

Elsa, Elsa, okay, her I got—*(looks at Babe)*—but who the hell are you?

He holds out the bottle, BABE holds out his glass. DOC pours as we

CUT TO

A TAXI pulling up to Lutece. ELSA gets out; BABE, in a suit, follows. ELSA waits while he pays. She looks just gorgeous. But as she stares at the restaurant sign, she's nervous as hell.

CUT TO

INSIDE THE RESTAURANT.

—and DOC, sniffing a wine cork. He sits at a center table. He is perfectly attired in a grey Brooks Brothers type suit. BABE AND ELSA are seated; introductions are clearly over. BABE looks around; it's a very impressive place.

At a nearby table sit TWO MEN, one of them grey-haired and clearly rich; the other considerably younger and clearly handsome. Probably they are homosexual, but nothing in their behavior indicates it. They are eating in silence; the older man says something, we don't ever hear what. The younger one ignores it. The older one takes a long pull on his drink. All of this barely catches our attention, it's just a background texture, and all that's happening is two guys are probably having some kind of argument. All of the other tables are full, and no one looks remotely impoverished.

> **DOC**
> I had the wine opened earlier, to give it a chance to breathe—*(to Babe)*—you start yawning, you're in big trouble—*(to Elsa)*—I thought a white Burgundy to start, than a red for the main course, the rack of lamb here is generally excellent. And if I may, I'd like to recommend the truffle *en croute* to start —*(to Babe again)*—whenever you get hungry, give a whistle, I'll send a waiter out for your Big Mac—

BABE laughs, ELSA too, and in the midst of this, the lights suddenly almost go totally out in the restaurant.

Almost on cue, a WAITER leaps forward, explaining—

> **WAITER**
> It is nothing, another brown out, we are prepared...

He puts a candle on the table, lights it, smiles.

> **WAITER**
> ...much more romantic this way...

All over the restaurant, waiters can be seen lighting candles, and it is more romantic. Everyone looks better by candlelight, no one more than ELSA. DOC looks at her, leans toward BABE whispering intentionally loud so she can hear.

> **DOC**
> She's not half the dog you wrote she was.

It's a compliment, ELSA acknowledges it as such. DOC nods for the waiter to pour wine. As the waiter obeys—

> **DOC**
> You know, the great Chablis are almost green-eyed. Of all the wines in all the world, they're the ones that most resemble diamonds—

He raises his glass, looks at her. She hesitates, then lifts hers. They look at each other closely for a long moment.

BABE watches them. Nods. They're hitting it off...

CUT TO

A GLORIOUS CROWN RACK OF LAMB. A HEADWAITER type is finishing up carving it and it looks good enough to be illegal. ELSA is served, DOC too. BABE'S plate is put down and

Elsa takes a bite. Doc still looks like he's having a helluva time and Elsa isn't miserable either, but Babe is all different. He reaches for some red wine, pours himself a glass full.

> **DOC**
> *(to Elsa)*

Good?

> **ELSA**
> *(nods)*

Delicious; but you must never ever show me the bill.

> **DOC**
> *(smiles, shrugs)*

Forget about it—I'm coming more and more to believe that the only money I have is the money I've spent.

And now he is running his fingers across the skin of her arm, just barely grazing it, and he's looking at her eyes in candlelight and she doesn't pull her arm away, looks right back at him.

> **DOC**

'Course the secret is you've got to spend it on special items, quality merchandise.

His hand never stops touching her skin. They keep watching each other and Babe is watching them, drinking his wine and there's no way he can hide that he's hurting inside.

> **DOC**
> *(smiling at Babe now)*

Some lady.

BABE manages a nod, that's about all. DOC turns to ELSA again. Throughout this, they are constantly touching, and the throb of sexuality is never spoken, always evident.

> **DOC**

Miss home? Bet you do. *(Elsa nods.)* What d'ya miss exactly? The people, the country, skiing?

> **ELSA**

I suppose all.

> **DOC**

I don't know Switzerland, wherabouts you from?

> **ELSA**

A tiny place, Lake Constance—

> DOC

I never heard of—*(stops, surprised)*—hey, wait a sec', wait a sec' *(shakes his head)*—is that incredible? See, there's this ski freak works in the office, and that's his favorite spot, in all the world, Lake Constance is, 'cause it's near Mount Rosa, am I right or am I right?

> ELSA
> *(nods)*

One hundred percent.

> DOC

Want to make that two hundred percent?

> ELSA

All right; why?

> DOC

I'm making all this up. There isn't any ski freak and there isn't any Mount Rosa next to any Lake Constance, am I right or am I right?

BABE stares at DOC, then ELSA; they aren't touching anymore but whatever was going on between them before, this that's happening now is worse—

> DOC

I've done too much business in Switzerland, I know the way they talk, you're not Swiss, what are you?

> ELSA

Can't you guess?

> DOC

Sure, German, and you're no twenty-five, either; thirty, thirty-five, maybe?

> ELSA
> *(fighting for control)*

Anything else?

> DOC

Yeah. How much longer are your work papers good for?

> ELSA
> *(almost a whisper)*

Why do you humiliate me?

> DOC

No reason, except that a lot of foreigners like to marry a lot of Americans and then, when it's all nice and legal here, a lot of the marriages don't work out.

> ELSA

Ask me if I'm trapping Babe—

> DOC

—no reason to. You haven't told the truth yet, why start now? *(as Elsa shoves her chair back, runs from the room—)*

BABE, starting up, heading after her, only DOC reaches over with one of his big hands, holds BABE back, and it's all been quiet and civilized up until now, but no more—now voices start to raise and the other diners start to watch.

> DOC

Let her go—

> BABE
> *(whirling)*

Why, because *you* say so?

> DOC

—you're goddam right—you'll thank me some day—this was for your own good—

> BABE

Bullshit it was!

> DOC

—I could tell from your letter she was phony—Jesus, Babe, people just don't fall all over each other like that—they don't—

BABE rips free, takes off.

> DOC
> *(calling after him)*

Not unless somebody wants something...

BABE tears through the restaurant and is gone.

DOC sits alone now. He's still elegant and handsome in his Brooks Brothers suit, just like he was at the start of the scene. Only now there is murder in his eyes. He picks up a wine glass, holds it, almost subconsciously twirls the liquid slowly around.

Behind him, the TWO MEN *at the next table have clearly made up whatever was bothering them. The* OLDER ONE *holds up his wine glass, the* YOUNGER ONE *takes his, their glasses barely touch. From the angle we see this,* DOC *in front, the other two close behind, all three men might almost be sitting together at one and the same table. Hold on the men and their wine...*

CUT TO

BABE, *running out of Lutece, stopping on the sidewalk, looking one way, then the other. No Elsa. He sees a cab, races for it as we*

CUT TO

BABE, *running down* THE CORRIDOR *to Elsa's door, wildly upset, pounding on it, pauses, pounds again. Nothing inside.*

BABE

It's me—*(no reply)*—it's okay, everything's okay—*(silence)*

He takes a piece of paper from his wallet, scrawls the words "Call me," shoves it into the crack of the door.

OUTSIDE ELSA'S BUILDING, BABE *comes fast. He hesitates, touches a tooth in the front of his mouth. He half winces, it hurts like hell.*

BABE
(suddenly bellowing)

Goddammit!

And with that he breaks into a wild run, tie flapping, arms pumping, going like crazy.

CUT TO

AN OPEN PLAZA BY A NEW SKYSCRAPER.

It is on the second floor (the actual location is at Greenwich and Liberty) and there is a vast expanse of stone, stone tables and benches, with the skyscraper itself set back. This is on the second floor—the main entrance to the building is on this floor—and there is a long circular stone staircase leading to the open plaza. The stairs are outlined in a darker stone, and make a strong geometrical design leading down to the street.

It is night, and the BALD MAN *walks nervously across the plaza.* ERHARD, *the* LIMPER, *sits at one of the stone tables.*

BALD MAN

You ordered Scylla to be prompt.

It was not a question, but ERHARD *nods yes. The* BALD MAN *grunts, moves around the plaza. Across the street is a large block that has been razed in expectation of another skyscraper, only it never got built. Just a few stores are left facing the plaza, small, neighborhood places.*

One has a sign, "Closing soon, all sales final" but inside, it is already empty and deserted. The few stores that are left are heavily barred; the BALD MAN *looks at them.*

> **BALD MAN**
> *(gesturing)*
> The land of plenty. *(pacing)* They were always so sure God was on their side. I think now they are not so positive.

He continues his nervous angry walking; the area is deserted. Nothing moves. The BALD MAN *keeps pacing, his footsteps echoing in the night. He turns, stops, and as he does, the footsteps sound continues. Drawing close.*

The BALD MAN *hurries to the geometrical staircase. The footsteps are very loud.*

Then SCYLLA *appears, coming up, dressed as he was for dinner at Lutece.*

The LIMPER *rises, afraid, moves a few steps back.*

The BALD MAN *goes straight to* SCYLLA *and without any salutation of any kind, they set right in. FAST.*

> **BALD MAN**
> You toy with me, you keep me waiting, I am not one to be mocked and your behavior, may I tell you, is very irritating—

> **SCYLLA**
> —don't you give me any shit about my behavior after what you've been pulling—

> **BALD MAN**
> —I have done nothing—

> **SCYLLA**
> —you hired Chen to kill me—

> **BALD MAN**
> —never—

> **SCYLLA**
> —don't lie, I don't blame you for it—*(big)*—but I goddam well blame you for involving my brother—

BALD MAN

—it was nothing—

SCYLLA

—it was a violation—*(anger building)*—we do not involve family—we never involve family—

BALD MAN

—think of it as a warning, nothing more—*(and on those words—)*

CUT TO

SCYLLA, *as he suddenly backhands the* BALD MAN *across the face, hard, and the* BALD MAN *half cries out in shock and surprise, grabbing a bench for balance, then rising, moving away from Scylla.*

SCYLLA
(quietly)
—think of that as a warning, nothing more—

The BALD MAN *is almost panting as he touches his face where Scylla hit him, trying to regain control. Scylla closes in.* ERHARD, *eyes wide, watches.*

BALD MAN

...you would...you would like to fight, wouldn't you? You would like to unleash your hands and let them destroy me...

SCYLLA

Oh yes...

BALD MAN
(exploding)
It—will—not—happen—*(quieter)*—I am much too old and far too smart to enter such a losing battle—but we must talk. Truthfully. Are you to be trusted?

SCYLLA
(simply)

No.

BALD MAN

Was that the truth or are you toying with me again?

SCYLLA

I know why you're here and that sooner or later you're going to the bank—

> BALD MAN

—perhaps I have already been to the bank—

> SCYLLA

—if you had, you wouldn't be meeting with me now.

> BALD MAN

What else do you know?

> SCYLLA

That you're panicked about being robbed once you leave the bank—

> BALD MAN

—Who would do such a thing?

> SCYLLA

Obviously you think I would.

> BALD MAN

Am I right or wrong? Can I trust you?

> SCYLLA

You never could, you only had to—

And probably he means to go on, certainly his tone indicates as much. But he stops talking as suddenly, the BALD MAN'S knife begins to rearrange SCYLLA'S insides. It's a strange looking weapon from the flash we see of it, pointed like a hypo at the point, one side sharp but building almost triangularly and as the knife goes into SCYLLA'S stomach up to the hilt,

CUT TO

The BALD MAN, using both hands now, bringing the weapon upwards, starting it on its journey through SCYLLA'S body and

CUT TO

SCYLLA, and he can only gasp, stunned, as his hands drop limply to his sides and

CUT TO

The BALD MAN, spreading his legs for better leverage, greater power, as he continues his butchering in silence and

CUT TO

SCYLLA, starting to spurt, his eyes beginning to roll up into his head and

CUT TO

ERHARD, *biting on the edge of his hand, as he stares in silence and*

CUT TO

The BALD MAN *going about his business and* SCYLLA *is damn near torn in two now as we*

CUT TO

SCYLLA, *starting to fall and as he does,*

CUT TO

The BALD MAN, *expertly pulling his weapon free, stepping to one side as* SCYLLA *slides down.*

CUT TO

SCYLLA, *motionless, the blood spreading out on both sides of him as he lies head down, arms sprawled out wide.*

CUT TO

The BALD MAN, *staring, for a moment, at his victim. He gestures for* ERHARD *and the two of them half walk-half run toward the stairs. They look around.* ERHARD *is still stunned over what's happened; the* BALD MAN *isn't all that calm either. They start down the lovely geometrical stairs and blend into darkness. Soon only footsteps remain.*

CUT TO

SCYLLA *lying there, his blood spreading even more.*

CUT TO

SCYLLA'S GREAT HANDS. HOLD ON THEM. KEEP HOLDING. *Finally, one of the fingers, slowly, feebly, begins to move—*

CUT TO

BABE, ALONE IN HIS ROOM, *suitcoat and tie off, white shirt still on, pacing like a mad-man. He circles and circles the phone, and we can see objects behind him: runners and fathers and Burgundy bottles. We can occasionally hear the old building giving a creak, but our attention, as his, is mainly on the phone and when it rings, he's on it, before the first ring has ended.*

                              BABE
                             (a burst)
        It didn't happen—nothing happened—

> ELSA (off-screen)

—he never asked if I loved you—

> BABE

—it-didn't-take-place—

> ELSA (off-screen)
> *(big)*

—but it did! *(and on her sound—)*

CUT TO

ELSA, *alone in her room, sitting on the bed, smoking; drained and upset.*

> ELSA
> *(softer)*

If we ignored it, it would only fester. *(inhaling deep, talking fast)* I lied about my age because I am a woman, we are allowed to do that, and I lied about the Swiss because I was a child when Hitler died, but many Jews still think all Germans planned the blitzkrieg.

> BABE (off-screen)

Well I don't, so—

> ELSA

—there is more—I've been married and divorced, he did not ask me that but it is true. I smiled at him and let him touch me because it was important, he was your brother, he had to like me—*(inhaling deeply again)*—you are upset about my marriage, your silence tells that.

CUT TO

BABE, *and he is, kind of.*

> BABE

Why should I be? You were probably a kid and he was some jock, only you, being practically an infant didn't realize he was also a moron and when you did, you ended it, right?—what was he, probably a shot-putter, you krauts are big on the weight events, can we get together tomorrow? *(before she can reply)* Hey, Elsa, if you're German, do you grunt in German?—I mean, an American shotput goon, he goes 'oof' when he lets fly, do your guys go 'ach' or what? *(He has her laughing now.)* Tomorrow?

CUT TO

ELSA, *laughing harder.*

ELSA

Tomorrow. *(and as she hangs up—)*

CUT TO

ELSA'S BED, as she falls back and her laughter continues until her eyes fill with sudden tears and then she is weeping, and we didn't expect it and she didn't either, but now she is crying, the sobs loud and wrenching, pathetic, out of control.

CUT TO

BABE, standing happily by the phone; he starts to walk again, throwing an occasional punch of triumph at the ceiling, stopping only when DOC'S voice is heard—

DOC (off-screen)
(soft)

...Babe...

CUT TO

BABE: EXTREME CLOSE UP, and all the triumph is gone from his face as we

CUT TO

DOC IN THE DOORWAY, arms across himself, and

DOC
(one final scream)

BABE!!! *(And he tries taking a step or two forward, reaches out for his kid brother, and as his stomach starts to slip away—)*

CUT TO

BABE streaking across the room and, as DOC begins his fall, BABE'S there, grabbing him, holding him, taking him down gently and the two of them reach the floor, bathed in blood; the blood keeps coming and coming and BABE is rocking his brother now, cradling him almost as if he were a child who needed sleep and

HOLD...

HOLD AND PULL BACK.

We're above them now, watching as BABE continues his rocking, bending down close and maybe DOC is trying to whisper or maybe he isn't, it's impossible to tell. DOC really ought to be dead, but his eyes don't close, not all the way, and he looks up at BABE, who keeps rocking, rocking, and the blood continues to pour, but the blood isn't important, you can always get more blood, it's brothers that are hard to find—

CUT TO

TIGHTSHOT: BABE.

He is sitting as before, only now there is a commotion over where the flashbulbs had been and as BABE turns to see

CAMERA SLOWLY FOR THE FIRST TIME SHIFTS TO TAKE IN EVERYTHING.

We're in BABE's room. The MAN he's been talking to is a uniformed POLICEMAN with a small pad and pencil. DOC's body is covered with a sheet—

—and THE COMMANDER, the man we met in Europe, is coming quickly through the door. As he enters, he looks serious, efficient and very much the kind of guy you want on your side when trouble erupts. The air of the hero, in other words, clings to him still.

THE COMMANDER moves to DOC's body, kneels, pulls the sheet half off, stares quietly down. For a long moment, he simply studies DOC's face. They worked together; it's an emotional moment.

There are several police standing off to one side, plus one man clearly not with them, a CREW-CUTTED YOUNGER MAN who goes to THE COMMANDER, leans over, talks softly.

> **CREW CUT**
> Whoever did it must have ambushed him, Commander.

> **COMMANDER**
> That, or he knew them.

He replaces the sheet, stands, indicates the POLICE.

> **COMMANDER**
> They can all leave now.

> **CREW CUT**
> *(nods)*
> I'll bring up the ambulance men.

BABE sits watching it all; whatever's going on, he doesn't understand it a bit. THE POLICEMAN WITH THE IRISH ACCENT rises, goes to THE COMMANDER.

> **POLICEMAN**
> We'll be moving on then.

THE COMMANDER nods, gives a smile. He has a marvelous smile, quick and dazzling. He stares across at BABE, still moist with his brother's blood. THE COMMANDER hesitates—it's an awkward time, the boy looks whipped. He glances down at the body under the sheet, then crosses to BABE, starts talking quietly, as the police depart, leaving the two of them alone.

COMMANDER

I'm sorry to intrude, I know how close you were to your brother—

BABE
(suddenly exploding)
—you do, huh?—you know that, do you?—how the hell do you know anything about anything?!!

COMMANDER

I was just trying to ease into things, I'm sorry. Let's start over. *(holds out his hand)* My name's Peter Janeway, but my friends call me "Janey".

BABE doesn't shake. JANEWAY sighs, looks around the room, sees DOC'S bottles of red wine.

As he crosses to the wine, the CREW CUT hurries back into the room, followed by TWO MEN in white hospital clothes who carry a stretcher.

They go to DOC'S covered body, shift it to the stretcher. They are between BABE in his chair and JANEWAY across the room with the wine bottle. The CREW CUT looks at Janeway. After a moment, JANEWAY nods.

CUT TO

DOC'S BODY RISING. He is being lifted, of course, but we don't see the AMBULANCE MEN, just DOC with the sheet over him as he is elevated.

CUT TO

BABE IN HIS CHAIR, silently watching DOC.

CUT TO

DOC'S BODY, as now, slowly, it starts to move away.

CUT TO

JANEWAY, staring after DOC'S BODY. His attention is riveted on it. Finally he forces his attention to getting the Burgundy open. Then he quits and looks back at the body again.

CUT TO

BABE in the silence, drained, watching as his brother goes.

CUT TO

DOC'S BODY. It is by the doorway now.

JANEWAY, angrily pulling on the cork, ripping it out of the neck of the bottle and

CUT TO

DOC'S BODY, going, going—

CUT TO

BABE looking at it all. The CREW CUT *shuts the door behind him. Doc is gone.* BABE *and* JANEWAY *are alone again.* JANEWAY *brings the bottle and two glasses, starts toward* BABE. *He stops, glances at the floor. There is a dark stain on the tattered rug.* DOC'S BLOOD.

JANEWAY

I'm looking for a motive. *(He sits by* BABE, *pours wine.)* I'm just as anxious as you are to find whoever did it, believe me.

BABE

Bullshit—Doc was my brother, my father practically, he brought me up, and I never once heard your name, so I'm probably a little more anxious, wouldn't you agree?

JANEWAY
(after a pause)

Well, of course. *(He drinks.)* I think it may have been political, considering what your brother did. And of course, your father.

BABE

What about my father?

JANEWAY

He was H.V. Levy, for chrissakes—

BABE

—and he was innocent—*(passionately)*—my father was a great liberal historian and the Democrats wanted him in Washington so he was there when McCarthy hit—McCarthy was a Nazi, a fucking Nazi and he never offered legal support for one single charge—but he still destroyed innocent people with his Communist witchhunts. He destroyed my father, made him a joke, killed his ego and his reputation but it's all gonna come out fine, once I get my dissertation published—you'll see, every goddam one of you'll see—I'm clearing my father with truth.

JANEWAY looks at Babe a moment. Then, gently—

JANEWAY

I hope it all works out for you, Babe—*(sips his wine)*—but I'm still looking for a motive. Start with tonight, give me everything, all the details.

BABE

Okay. I was home. My brother died. You came.

> JANEWAY

That's everything?

> BABE
> *(nods)*

I'm a demon on details.

> JANEWAY

You mean you want me to do some explaining first, is that it?

BABE nods again. JANEWAY stands, swirls the wine, sniffs it.

> JANEWAY

Doc was not, I'm afraid, in the oil business.

> BABE

You just can't survive without bullshit, can you?

> JANEWAY

All right, follow me now—Doc lived in Washington; what's Washington the center of?

> BABE

Government.

> JANEWAY

Correct, and have you the least notion how much each branch of government hates its competitors? The Army hates the Navy and they both hate the Air Force. The same is true in our line; the F.B.I. hates the C.I.A. and they both loathe the Secret Service—constant squabbling and whining and the whining gets loudest when you reach the edges of their powers. Between those edges are crevices. *(He drinks some wine.)* We live in the crevices.

BABE hesitates—it doesn't sound like bullshit any more.

> BABE

Who're...you?

> JANEWAY

The Division.

> BABE

What do you do?

> JANEWAY

Provide.

> BABE

Provide what?

> JANEWAY

Anything.

> BABE

That's kind of vague.

> JANEWAY

Yes, isn't it.

> BABE

When you say "anything," you don't mean "anything;" I mean, not bad things.

CUT TO

DOC'S SUITCASE *in the corner.* JANEWAY *goes to it, puts it on* BABE'S *desk, opens it. For this next, he is packing* DOC'S *clothes.*

> JANEWAY

Do you know who Scylla was?

> BABE

'Course, but Scylla wasn't a "who," Scylla was a "what," a giant rock.

> JANEWAY

Scylla was your brother's code name, and he wasn't just a Provider, he was the best Provider. He only drank Scotch, except with you it was always wine; there wasn't a weapon he hadn't mastered, except with you he always pretended to panic at a BB pistol. We were...*(hesitates)*...very close for many years, and believe me, I know whereof I speak.

JANEWAY *looks at Babe a moment, then rubs his eyes.*

> JANEWAY

Look, I doubt that either of us are at our best just now, let's pick it up tomorrow, all right? *(BABE agrees.)* Just one last thing—obviously Doc was desperate to get here at the end. Do you remember anything he might have said?

> BABE

Nothing to remember—just my name twice, that's all.

> JANEWAY
> *(finishes packing)*

Now as to the matter of your safety—

BABE

—my what?

JANEWAY
(his back to Babe)

I'm just guessing that whoever killed Doc might also want a little chat with you. *(pause)* You still there?

BABE finishes his wine, pours himself another glass. JANEWAY turns, watches him.

JANEWAY

No one would have risked trying to kill Scylla if some situation weren't coming to a head. They must have assumed he knew something, and since he lived here when he was in town and since he died here, they also might assume you know something too. People do, it's known, say strange things when they're dying.

BABE

But I'm ignorant.

JANEWAY

How can they know, that? *(Babe has no answer.)* Now I'm staying just across the Park at the Carlyle—

BABE
(stunned)

You're leaving me here?

JANEWAY
(calmly)

I'd like to use you as possible bait, yes. *(looks at Babe)* You object?

BABE

I'm not all that wild about being left alone—

JANEWAY
(interrupting)

—no one said you'd be alone. You're under surveillance right now; two New York undercover cops are alternating watching the building and they'll stay at it 'til dawn, when I have four of my best men taking over. Just get your beauty sleep tonight, and tomorrow we'll talk in detail.

BABE
(glances at his drawer where the gun is)

You think they'll come tonight?

JANEWAY

No. But I wish they would. I would like whoever did this very much. *(finishes his Burgundy)*

BABE

Why can't you take me with you, though?

CUT TO

JANEWAY: CLOSE UP. And the man is under strain.

JANEWAY

I can, but if they're watching, they'll see, and they won't expose themselves. And if I stay here with you and they're watching, they'll have seen me come in and they won't expose themselves. If you want to come with me, come with me. If you want me to hide you in D.C., I'll keep you out of sight 'til whatever this is is over. *(moved)* Whatever you want, I'll do— if you've got better notions, tell me, anything you want, please, for God's sake, tell me.

CUT TO

BABE. It's a big decision. He stares again at the desk drawer holding the gun. He's about to speak, stops. Then his eye sees something and we

CUT TO

DOC'S BLOOD. The stain still moist.

CUT TO

BABE. He rivets his attention on DOC'S BLOOD, then glances again at the drawer, then back a final time to the blood. His mind's made up now.

BABE

You got your bait, Mr. Janeway...

HOLD ON THE TWO OF THEM. Then—

CUT TO

BABE IN THE BATHTUB. His pajamas are tossed on a hook. The door is half open.

BABE lies still in the water, staring at the wall. Sometimes he blinks. He half closes his eyes. The ancient building creaks. He opens his eyes a moment, then closes them again and as they shut, he hears his father's voice, coming to him through memory: "All the way, Babe..."

And now we see a bunch of images, starting with one we've seen before, his father holding out his arms and BABE *is a kid and he's running. And now there's* DOC, *smiling, pouring red wine into a glass, swirling, inhaling, studying the color and now here's* DOC *again, an arm around* BABE *as they walk into a fancy restaurant and* DOC *is saying, "Whatever you want you can have, it's all on expenses, thank God for the oil business," and then the building creaks again.*

BABE *opens his eyes. This creak sounded different, more like a click maybe, so he glances out toward the room, and maybe it does look a little darker, as if a light's been clicked off, but then again, maybe it's only imagination.* BABE *can see his desk where his gun rests in the bottom drawer.*

He closes his eyes again and suddenly McCarthy is gesturing and BABE'S FATHER *is trying to raise his hand, make a point, but McCarthy goes on and on and now we see that* BABE *is watching a tv program . He calls out proudly, "Doc—Daddy's on television."*

BABE *in the tub shakes his head. No bad memories now. Enough has happened without bad memories and as he sinks into reverie we see* DOC *laughing and then* BABE *is into his* FATHER'S ARMS, *and his father takes him and tosses him high and Babe shrieks with joy and* HIS FATHER *laughs and here's* DOC *laughing again. It's all happiness now.*

BABE *lies there in the tub. He reaches for a bar of soap, stops, whispers—*

BABE
...Jesus, I'm the last of them...

And in reply comes one of the most terrifying things that can happen—other people are whispering, just beyond the door, in his room, out of sight, and this now, this isn't imagination and suddenly

CUT TO

THE BATHROOM DOOR *as* BABE, *out of the tub, slams it shut, locks it.*

CUT TO

BABE, *he stands there, breathing hard, eyes wide and*

CUT TO

THE DOOR. *From beyond now, a different sound: "Click." A pause. Then again: "Click."*

CUT TO

BABE, *in his pajama bottoms now, putting on his tops. He stands by the door, ear pressed against it, listening. But there is nothing. No sound at all. You can see it in his face, the question of was it real or was it nerves. The dead silence continues.* BABE *begins to relax. He reaches out toward the lock, decides against it. He reaches toward a book, decides against that too. He stands there in total silence and just as he has about got his nerves conquered, a new and different sound starts—"scratch, scratch" and as BABE stares—*

CUT TO

THE BOTTOM HINGE OF THE BATHROOM DOOR. *Someone is starting to pull and twist it and*

CUT TO

BABE, *and under the door it's dark outside in the room now, but it sure as hell wasn't when he started to bathe and it isn't a matter of "if" anymore, it's a matter of "who."*

BABE
(tentatively)

Help. *(louder now)* Anybody.

CUT TO

THE BATHROOM DOOR, *as the bottom hinge is being pulled out now, sliding up and away and there are three hinges on the door and now the middle one is starting to move and*

CUT TO

BABE, *whirling, opening his bathroom cabinet, looking for something, anything, but he's only got an electric razor and Q-Tips and toothpaste and*

CUT TO

THE MIDDLE HINGE, *sliding out now and as the top hinge begins to get jostled—*

CUT TO

BABE, *hollering louder than before—*

BABE

Get the cops—*(huge)*—THE POLICE!—

CUT TO

THE DOOR *and now from beyond, someone has turned on his record player and Schubert is playing the Quintet in C Major, and maybe it's the single most beautiful piece of chamber music ever written. But it sure doesn't sound that way now because it's turned up all the way so that it's blasting like hell and covering Babe's cries, and as the third and last hinge starts to slide,*

CUT TO

BABE, *and he's doing not what you expect, because his actions don't match his words; what he's saying is more pleas for assistance but what he's doing is moving to the door, his hand on the knob as the third hinge continues to move and when it's out the door will be freed and* BABE *goes right on shouting—*

BABE

Help!—somebody save me for Jesus sakes—please somebody—ANY-BODY SAVE ME—DO SOMETHING—PLEEESE! *(and as his shouting builds—)*

CUT TO

THE LAST HINGE, *sliding free, and the second it is—*

CUT TO

BABE, AS HE YANKS THE DOOR IN WITH EVERYTHING HE HAS *and the move comes as a surprise to whoever's out there and as the door is freed we can see whoever's out there and it's the* LIMPER *who mugged Elsa, and* BABE *shoulders him and goes into a move toward the desk where the gun is and*

CUT TO

THE MAMMOTH, *moving from the darkness and* BABE *is candy, because before he can even try for the desk drawer* THE MAMMOTH *has him and with terrible power, shoves him down and before* BABE *can rise* THE MAMMOTH *is on him and he lifts* BABE *and throws him toward the light of the bathroom and the music is still blaring and*

CUT TO

BABE, *crashing down, stunned, trying to move, but* THE MAMMOTH *forces him back and into the tub. The music abruptly dies as* BABE'S *head goes under water.*

CUT TO

THE MAMMOTH, *and Christ, he's holding Babe under and* BABE'S *doing what he can and he finally does get his head above the water and as he does the music is blaring but then he's being forced back under and again there is quiet and*

CUT TO

THE LIT BATHROOM, *as seen from the dark bedroom. We can only make out* THE MAMMOTH *and from time to time, there is the blast of music and we know that means Babe has gotten a breath of air but those moments are few and brief, the silences longer.*

CUT TO

THE RECORD PLAYER. *Now the music is being turned back down by* THE LIMPER *to a lovely quiet level. There is nothing now but the glorious sound of the Schubert. It could not be more beautiful. Then the machine is turned off. No sound. Nothing at all until we*

CUT TO

A WINDOWLESS ROOM.

BABE is semi-conscious, wearing pajamas, damp. He sits in a chair, the chair is in a win-dowless room. BABE blinks, tries to get a better look at the place, but he's expertly bound to the chair. The room seems unusually bright. There is a sink, a table, it all seems clean.

There come SOUNDS from behind him and THE LIMPER and THE MAMMOTH walk around the chair. THE MAMMOTH carries an armload of clean white towels, beautifully folded.

> **LIMPER (ERHARD)**
> Give me. *(He puts the towels on the table as we—)*

CUT TO

The BALD MAN moving toward the chair, carrying a rolled up towel in one hand. He indi-cates that he wants a lamp brought closer. THE LIMPER hurriedly obeys, the BALD MAN turns quickly, washes his hands. As he does—

> **BALD MAN**
> *(quietly)*

Is it safe?

> **BABE**
> *(He wasn't ready for the question.)*

Huh?

> **BALD MAN**

Is it safe?

> **BABE**

Is what safe?

> **BALD MAN**
> *(His tone never changes; gently, patiently)*

Is it safe?

> **BABE**

I don't know what you mean.

> **BALD MAN**

Is it safe?

> **BABE**

I can't tell you if something's safe or not unless I know specifically what you're asking about.

BALD MAN
(His hands are clean now; Erhard hands him a towel.)
Is it safe?

BABE
(rattled)
Tell—me—what—the—"it"—refers—to.

BALD MAN
(softly as ever)
Is it safe?

BABE
Yes, it's very safe—it's so safe you wouldn't believe it. There; now you know.

BALD MAN
Is it safe?

BABE
No, it isn't safe. Very dangerous, be careful.

For a moment the BALD MAN stares down at Babe. There is a terrible intelligence working inside. Now a nod. Just one, that's all, and as he unwraps the towel he brought in, we see the contents: dental tools.

CUT TO

ERHARD, bringing the lamp closer still and, as THE MAMMOTH suddenly forces BABE'S mouth open with his powerful hands—

CUT TO

The BALD MAN. He selects an angled mirror and a spoon excavator, not sharp, and leans forward toward Babe. He is perspiring lightly and without a word, THE LIMPER takes a towel, dabs the BALD MAN'S forehead dry. The BALD MAN is concentrating totally on his work, and he is extraordinarily skilled.

CUT TO

BABE, helpless, while the BALD MAN gently taps and probes. His hands move expertly here, there. BABE is perspiring terribly. There is no sound in the room other than breathing. The BALD MAN switches from the rounded spoon excavator to a new tool, needle-pointed. BABE cannot stop sweating. The BALD MAN shakes his head almost sadly.

BALD MAN
You should take better care of your teeth, there is a bad cavity here, is it safe?

BABE

Look, I told you before and I'm telling you now—

But that's all he has time for because the BALD MAN *suddenly shoves the needle pointed tool up into the cavity and*

CUT TO

BABE, *beginning to scream, but* THE MAMMOTH *cups his big hands over* BABE'S *mouth, muffling the sound. When the scream is done, he takes his hands away. Now the* BALD MAN *has picked up a small bottle, opened it, poured some liquid on his finger. He brings the finger closer and closer to the cavity—*

BABE

—don't—please Jesus don't—I swear—

Now the finger is on the cavity and at first BABE *starts to wince but then after a moment he begins to almost lick at the finger, getting as much of the liquid as he can, as if he were a starving puppy and the* BALD MAN *was feeding him milk.*

The BALD MAN *watches, not taking his finger away.*

BALD MAN

Is it not remarkable? Simple oil of cloves and how amazing the results.

He pours some more on his finger, rubs it soothingly across Babe's cavity.

BALD MAN

Life can be, if only we allow it, so simple. *(holding up the bottle)* Relief. *(holding up the explorer tool)* Discomfort. *(looking at Babe)* Choose.

BABE

I can't satisfy...what you want...because...because...*(And now his tone changes.)* ...aw no...no...*(and on those words—)*

CUT TO

THE EXPLORER TOOL *moving toward the cavity.*

BABE'S VOICE (off-screen)

...if I knew I'd tell...Christ...wouldn't I tell...

CUT TO

The BALD MAN, *his eyes expressionless, thrusting it home. There is the start of a scream and now the eyes look almost sad. The scream continues, builds, abruptly stops and*

CUT TO

BABE IN THE CHAIR, *head slumped forward, semi-conscious, not moving.*

CUT TO

THE BALD MAN AND THE OTHERS.

THE LIMPER
(to the Bald Man)

You think he knows?

BALD MAN

Of course he knows, but he's being very stubborn. *(to the Mammoth)* Karl—take him to the spare room and bring him around.

CUT TO

THE BALD MAN IN CLOSE UP. *There is a pause. Then, almost sad—*

BALD MAN

Next time I may really have to hurt him.

CUT TO

BABE'S BODY *hitting a bare mattress hard; before he can sit, KARL is shoving smelling salts into his face and BABE reels back, coughing. KARL sits on the edge of the bed.*

KARL

Take this !

CUT TO

THE OIL OF CLOVES BOTTLE *as BABE grasps it, pours some on his index finger, rubs it desperately against his open tooth. KARL takes the bottle back, waits as BABE rubs, blinks, looks around. We're in a bare room, nothing on the walls. Just the bed in a corner, that's all. Half groggy, BABE rubs and rubs to make the pain go away and*

CUT TO

THE ROOM.

From Babe's point of view—it's all fuzzy and frightening.

BABE

...more...

KARL *nods, but instead of oil of cloves he shoves the smelling salts into BABE'S face again and Babe reels down flat in surprise, coughing; the place is still fuzzy to him, bad dreamlike, only now it's going into fantasy, because in his stunned state, he almost imagines he sees JANEWAY moving silently through the door, Indian quiet.*

CUT TO

THE DOORWAY, *and thank Jesus, it is* JANEWAY *and*

CUT TO

BABE, *quickly looking away, staring up at* KARL.

> **BABE**
> ...please... for the pain...*(Karl gives Babe the oil of cloves; Babe takes it, risks a glance toward the door—)*

CUT TO

JANEWAY, *and maybe the guy really is an Indian as he moves in silence closer, closer, and now there's a knife in his right hand, long and sharp and deadly, and* BABE *rubs the oil of cloves against his tooth, not looking up until we*

CUT TO

KARL, *turning, seeing* JANEWAY. *Karl jumps up, his huge hands moving to defend himself as we*

CUT TO

JANEWAY AND THE GUY IS A STREAK. *He moves inside* KARL'S *arms, and in one motion he throws his left arm around the Karl's throat, spins him halfway, lifts him slightly using his left hip for leverage and then as his right hand, the knife hand starts to move.*

CUT TO

BABE *on the bed, staring into* KARL'S *face as the sound of* JANEWAY'S *thrust hits home and Karl's eyes bulge, glaze, and he makes one pathetic cry as we*

CUT TO

KARL *falling forward across the bed and as he lands the knife handle is visible in his back, dead opposite where his heart would be and* BABE *stares but only for a moment as* JANEWAY *grabs him roughly, yanks him the hell up and out of the room and*

CUT TO

THE HALL OUTSIDE *and it's a railroad type flat, one long corridor and* JANEWAY *is pulling* BABE *along. When they reach the stairs,* THE LIMPER *appears at the end of the hall and he's got a pistol aimed and ready, but* JANEWAY *shoves* BABE *out of the line of fire on the stairs and*

CUT TO

BABE ON THE STAIRS, *watching as* JANEWAY *goes into a roll and now he's got a gun too and he's firing again and again, and from where* THE LIMPER *was, there is the sound of a dying cry and then* JANEWAY *is on the stairs with* BABE *and they take them as fast as* BABE *can and when they hit the street it's dark and* BABE *is stunned by the night air but nothing's going to stop* JANEWAY, *and he pulls Babe along saying "goddammit come on" and then they're at Janeway's car and he throws the door open, shoves Babe in the back—*

JANEWAY

Get in and get down and stay there—

JANEWAY jumps in, slams the door, starts the car and—

CUT TO

JANEWAY'S CAR, pulling off, burning rubber.

The street is bleak and deserted. It's the factory area in the west Fifties.

CUT TO

INSIDE THE CAR.

JANEWAY drives, BABE *is on the floor of the back seat, out of sight.*

JANEWAY

Okay, it's all starting to come together—that big guy was Franz Karl, a human pimple. The guy I shot was Peter Erhard, more acne. They lived in that house alone, they were cousins, and they both worked for Christian Szell.

BABE

Who?

JANEWAY
(taking a corner on two wheels)

Szell, for God's sake—he ran the experimental block at Auschwitz—he just might be the most wanted Nazi left alive and the reason he's alive is because he's smarter than anybody—the White Angel he was known as— *der weisse Engel*—on account of he had this incredible head of beautiful white hair.

CUT TO

JANEWAY'S CAR rocketing through the night, heading into another turn, and as the tires start to scream—

CUT TO

INSIDE THE CAR.

> JANEWAY

Word got around Auschwitz that if you paid Szell enough, he'd arrange escape, and he did let a few Jews out, to make the story seem real. Szell started on gold, naturally, but then he moved up to diamonds. Diamonds for freedom, that was his deal. He saw the end early on, and he got his father to America; the old man stayed here and so did they.

> BABE

They?

> JANEWAY

Szell's diamonds. He only kept enough to get to South America. He wanted his fortune here because, if he ever got caught, the diamonds would be safe and he could buy his way free. Whenever he needed money, his old man took some diamonds from a bank vault, Erhard got them to Washington and from there they went to London to an antiques guy who sold them for top dollar. Then a courier took the money down to Szell in Paraguay. It all worked until Szell's father died in a car crash—only the alternate can get into the box and that's Szell—I think he's in Paraguay right now, trying to figure if it's safe for him to come to America.

> BABE

Before, you said 'naturally' he started with gold. Why naturally?

> JANEWAY

He knocked it out of the Jews' teeth before he burned them—Szell was a dentist—

> BABE
> *(head up now)*

He's not coming to America, Mr. Janeway, he's already here. It was a dentist nearly killed me.

CUT TO

JANEWAY, tension rising.

> JANEWAY

Get back down—(BABE *does.*)—go on———

> BABE

—he just kept asking, "is it safe, is it safe," over and over and—

> JANEWAY

—did he have white hair?—

                              BABE
—no, he was bald but—

                            JANEWAY
                          (cutting in)
—but that doesn't mean shit, he could have shaved it off—*(pounding the steering wheel)*—he's here—the bastard's here and afraid to make his move—because once he gets his diamonds and leaves that bank, anyone can rob him. He can't very well go to the cops and complain.

                              BABE
Why is he after me?

                            JANEWAY
Because Doc was the guy who got the diamonds to London, and Szell must think he said something to you before he died—

JANEWAY drives even faster. The tires scream again.

                              BABE
Doc worked for Szell?

                            JANEWAY
We dealt with Szell because he ratted on other Nazis, so when there'd be raids after him, he'd get advance word. Don't try moralizing it, it has to be done. And there's one thing you have to do, Babe. For me.

                              BABE
Name it.

                            JANEWAY
Stop protecting your brother! Somehow he stayed alive long enough to see you, there has to be a reason—now for Christ's sake—what did he tell you?!

CUT TO

BABE: CLOSE UP.

                              BABE
—nothing—

CUT TO

JANEWAY: CLOSE UP.

                            JANEWAY
Shit ! *(And as he slams on the brakes—)*

CUT TO

ERHARD AND KARL, alive and waiting in the shadows of the building we saw them in; we're back where we started and as the car halts, they move toward it.

JANEWAY
I couldn't make him talk—he's Szell's now.

BABE'S head appears and he sees them and even before they are on him he is screaming—

BABE
—you killed them—

ERHARD AND KARL drag him from the car. In the darkness, JANEWAY watches. Nothing crosses his handsome face, no emotion at all.

CUT TO

BABE, back in the chair. ERHARD AND KARL have finished strapping him down. They quickly leave as JANEWAY looks at the boy.

BABE
(quietly)
You were some buddies, weren't you, you and Doc.

JANEWAY
We were never as friendly as he thought or as he hoped, let's put it that way—*(and now the smile is back)*—all yours.

This last was to SZELL who enters. He carries a wrapped towel.

JANEWAY LEAVES. BABE AND SZELL are alone. SZELL places the towel beside the chair, unwraps it. It contains sharp dental tools. He then turns, begins to fastidiously wash and wash his hands. BABE'S eyes are riveted on the sharp tools. His breathing already is starting to get just the least bit faster.

SZELL
So you are Scylla's brother. *(BABE says nothing; SZELL continues to wash.)* Would you like to know how you were taken in? The guns had blanks, the knife a retractable blade. Hardly original, but effective enough, wouldn't you agree?

BABE says nothing yet. SZELL takes a towel, dries his hands with care. He sits beside Babe, a reassuring smile. There is nothing in SZELL'S manner that indicates anything unpleasant. But Babe's fear is a physical thing, and as we watch, it grows. If anything, SZELL is fatherly here, interested, gentle, caring.

> SZELL

I am told you are a schoolboy...brilliant, yes?

He takes a towel, dabs Babe's sweating forehead dry.

> SZELL

The ventilation in here is dreadful, I'm sorry. *(looks at Babe)* You are an historian and I am a part of history; I would think you would find me interesting, and frankly, I'm disappointed in your silence.

And with that, he glances toward the tools and the instant he does—

> BABE

Why do you have so little accent? German's very hard to lose.

> SZELL
> *(smiles)*

I had alexia as a child, a disease in which—

> BABE

—it's where you can't understand written speech.

> SZELL
> *(impressed)*

Highest marks. At any rate, my handwriting is childish still, but I am fanatical about spoken language, accents, rhythms.

Babe's fear keeps growing even though Szell's tone is never hostile.

> SZELL

I envy you your schooldays—enjoy them fully—it's the last time in your life no one expects anything of you. *(straightens a strap)* More comfortable?

> BABE

You weren't so interested in my comfort before.

> SZELL

I behaved terribly—but I had to be sure what you knew. You see, I am quite positive your brother planned to rob me when I left the bank with my diamonds.

He lights a cigarette, offers to let Babe have an inhale.

> BABE

I don't smoke.

SZELL

At my age, it matters less. *(He puts a hand on Babe's shoulder, almost a family kind of touch.)* I envy you your women—I was, don't laugh, quite handsome once, and women—oh Babe, they used to swarm sometimes near me and I could pick the fairest, I still believe a young bosom is God's greatest creation. *(looks at Babe, smiles)* Scylla was planning the robbery, wasn't he?

BABE
(The question came as a surprise.)

I've—there's nothing I know—

SZELL nods, bends down, opens a case, takes out a curled up extension cord, begins unwinding it. And now the panic is wild in BABE.

BABE

What's—that for?

SZELL
(placid)

Do you know the value of diamonds? I don't—oh, I did once, but in today's market, how rich am I or am I rich at all—I haven't the least notion.

He plugs the cord into an outlet, goes back to the case, takes out something that looks like it might be a nail. (In reality, it's a diamond stone, but we don't know that yet.)

SZELL

Tomorrow, I must go to the diamond center and get some kind of knowledge so I will be better able to estimate my worth.

He has been looking at the nail under the light.

BABE

What are you going to do?

SZELL

That depends, as it always has, on you, because your brother was a wonderful courier, and I paid him willingly, but always small amounts. Now we have quantum jumped and I need to know: did he plan to rob me and if he did, was it to be alone, and if not, who were the others, and finally, since he is dead, did the plan die with him? Tell me those things now.

BABE
(struggling)

Christ, I would if I knew—

> SZELL

Your brother was incredibly strong—strength is an inherited trait—he died in your arms—he traveled great distances to reach you—there had to be a reason and you will tell it to me.

> BABE

I—don't—know—anything—

As urbane and smooth as Babe is not, SZELL kneels by the case.

> SZELL

You really should have taken better care of your teeth. *(reassuring)* Oh, don't worry, I'm not going to touch the cavity again, that nerve was already dying, a freshly-cut nerve is infinitely more sensitive.

> BABE

—you're not going to cut a nerve?

> SZELL
> *(nods)*

A live one, yes. I'll just drill into a healthy tooth until I reach the pulp— *(explaining)*—where the nerve fibers reside—

And with that he pulls out a portable hand drill, inserts the diamond stone, turns the drill on, off, on, off—

> SZELL
> *(calling)*

Karl!

As KARL immediately enters, goes into position as before.

> SZELL

We're both intellectuals, so we are both familiar with iron maidens in medieval times and testicle shock in the twentieth century, but they're unsatisfactory, you see, they have no build to them. But once we reach the pulp, well, you'll see.

And he turns the drill on, nods to KARL and we

CUT TO

Karl, using all his enormous power and BABE is helpless, as we

CUT TO

SZELL, concentrating on his work, drilling into the front tooth in the upper part of BABE'S mouth and

CUT TO

THE DRILL: CLOSE UP; *the sound is not nice.*

CUT TO

BABE dazed, but he's surviving it, his eyes on the ceiling.

CUT TO

SZELL, working. Then he flicks the drill off.

> **SZELL**
> *(to Babe)*
> You are strong. Many people would have already begun breaking. *(to Karl)* Let him rest—we are at the pulp.

KARL lets go for a moment and SZELL plays with the drill, giving it little staccato bursts of sounds, on, off, on again and this time he leaves it on as we

CUT TO

KARL, holding BABE who is trying to somehow squirm loose but it's impossible. SZELL starts to work—

CUT TO

JANEWAY AND ERHARD pacing in the hall, smoking, no talk; BABE'S scream starts, goes on and on, they continue their silent pacing until we

CUT TO

KARL IN CLOSE UP, and his face is contorted because what's happening is very bad, something he has never come in contact with before and it bothers even him and

CUT TO

SZELL, his understanding eyes as placid as ever. In a moment, he turns off the drill and now, at last

CUT TO

BABE in torment, but he will not cry. His head slumps; SZELL watches.

> **SZELL**
> Well?

> **BABE**
> How...how can...you do...

>   SZELL
> Shall I tell you one old Jew's answer? He said: "We were not, for them,
> the same."

>   BABE
> ...kill me...

>   SZELL
>   (always gentle and kind)
> A Jew cannot die when he will, only when we will (and as Karl pulls Babe's
> head back—)

CUT TO

THE VIEW OF THE CEILING *as seen from* BABE'S *point of view and two sounds start, the one the drill, the other from* BABE'S *throat, anguished, and the drill continues but after a moment,* BABE'S *sound begins to soften and as it does, the ceiling begins to be less clear. The drill sound goes on and on. Babe is almost quiet now. The ceiling is growing fuzzy.*

CUT TO

SZELL'S INCREDIBLE EYES IN CLOSE UP. *They seem so sympathetic. But the drilling sound goes on.*

CUT TO

THE CEILING, *and we can tell Babe is starting to experience momentary black outs now—it dims, gets bright, darkens. There is nothing coming from Babe any more.*

CUT TO

JANEWAY AND ERHARD *listening outside the door. There is only the drill. The drill will not stop. Then...silence. No more drill. Then the voice of Szell is calling out "Erhard!" and as they throw the door open—*

CUT TO

>   SZELL
> He knew nothing—if he had known he would have told—get rid of
> him—

ERHARD AND KARL *unstrap* BABE *who cannot move and is less than conscious in the chair.*

>   KARL
> Kill him you mean?

>   ERHARD
>   (making sure)
> How would you like it to happen?

SZELL

Do once something right without me!

And he storms from the room, gesturing for JANEWAY to follow, and as they go—

CUT TO

THE STAIRS *leading down to the street, only this time it's not JANEWAY taking Babe to safety, now it's KARL AND ERHARD, taking him to die.*

Silence except for their footsteps on the flight of stairs.

KARL *controls* BABE, *half dragging him, half forcing Babe to hold to the wooden banister. Babe can't go under his own power, but he's at least not totally helpless. ERHARD goes on ahead, opens the door to the street—*

KARL *comes out with Babe and as the night air hits them, BABE blinks a little, coming slowly through pain to some sense of consciousness.*

KARL

My car.

He gestures. They move in silence to a near corner, turn.

Darkness. Across, a few stores, vaguely lit, gated and locked.

Silence. They continue on through the night. ERHARD limps ahead a few steps. KARL continues with his burden of BABE, dragging him along. BABE can make his feet move now, he stumbles, stumbles again, manages to remain upright.

In a doorway, sudden movement, then a moan. ERHARD spins toward the sound. KARL keeps right on going with Babe.

KARL
(gesturing toward the doorway)

Nothing, a drunk.

ERHARD nods, slows his limping pace a little, coming back closer to the protection of Karl's size.

Ahead of them now: a CAR. They reach it. Stop. From behind them, another moan from the nightmared drunk. This time Erhard doesn't react to the sound.

Silence again. ERHARD takes BABE, as KARL reaches into a pocket, brings out a key ring, carefully makes sure he selects the proper one which he does, and—

CUT TO

BABE *shoving suddenly against ERHARD with whatever strength is left to him, and it isn't much, but* ERHARD *didn't expect it and it surprises him; he stumbles back and* BABE *begins feebly running down the dark street and*

CUT TO

KARL, *looking up from the lock, seeing what's happened, crying "Fool" at Erhard, and angrily goes to retrieve Babe.*

But it isn't that easy because BABE *had a little head start and it's night, and you can stumble so you have to watch it at least a little and sure, Karl is big, really big, with a massive chest and shoulders and hands that could twig-snap a neck—*

—but BABE *can run.*

Or he could once. Now he can only kind of weakly make his way along, doggedly forcing one leg after the other down the miserable street.

KARL *hurries after him, closing.*

BABE *goes a little faster. Not a lot, nothing terrific, but he's summoning whatever he's got and for a moment it helps because he opens a little distance on* KARL.

But only for a moment. Again KARL *starts to close.*

CUT TO

BABE, *and behind him there's the sound of Karl's footsteps and he hurts; he's been through a lot and the pain's all over his face but then—*

QUICK CUT TO

BABE'S *cap. The running cap. And now we pull back to see the photos of* NURMI AND BIKILA. *They are staring, both of them straight out and*

CUT TO

BABE *staring straight ahead and then quick cut back to the faces of the legends, and for a moment they almost seem to be watching each other through time and space,* NURMI AND BIKILA AND BABE, *staring dead at each other—*

—and now BABE *picks up the pace! Really picks it up. We know what his mind's full of and he's still feeble compared to what he once was, but* KARL *isn't any marathon man, he's great in the chest and shoulders, but not much for distance and it's just starting to show—*

—he's beginning slightly to labor.

BABE *increases his lead.*

KARL *is having increasing trouble breathing.*

BABE glances back, turns again and runs dead into a drunk who has appeared startling-ly from the darkness—BABE lets out a cry, the drunk holds on, holds on, BABE struggles, twists, finally pushes off, starts to gasp and run again, but his lead is gone.

Up ahead is 12th Avenue and the West Side Highway. But it's a long way, more than half a block, too far—

KARL is closing.

BABE stumbles, KARL stumbles, they keep on and on.

KARL has never been this close.

A police siren screams through the dreadful night, up ahead, out of sight, on 12th Avenue. The sound, already loud, grows louder, louder, and now, up at the head of the street the police car turns and heads toward us, the lights blinding, the siren starting to deafen—

KARL hesitates, nervous.

BABE runs toward his salvation, arms wide, straight into the approaching lights.

The siren is painful now.

KARL looks around, stopped, undecided, trying to catch his breath—

BABE continues his flight toward the police car—

—only it isn't a police car, it's an ambulance tearing through the night and it swerves one way, then the other around BABE, and then he's alone in the night again with KARL behind him.

KARL starts to run.

Only BABE has never stopped, and KARL looks far ahead in the darkness and BABE is going faster than before and he's farther ahead than before and KARL takes a few more strides, before suddenly coming to a stop and turning, calling out "Help!" into the night and as he does—

CUT TO

JANEWAY, leaving the house where Szell is, starting toward his car as the ambulance careens past and he's at his car and halfway in when suddenly on the night air KARL'S WORD echoes and JANEWAY isn't the kind of guy who hesitates a lot, he moves, and he's sprinting toward the corner before we expect it and one thing is clear the minute you see him in operation and it's this—JANEWAY is a guy who can run.

CUT TO

THE WEST SIDE HIGHWAY

—empty and lit by street lamps and HOLD FOR A MOMENT *until we* PULL BACK AND DOWN *and maybe a quarter of a block from it now comes* BABE *running and he's beaten them,* ERHARD AND KARL; *it's all over and he's a winner but he doesn't slow his pace, just keeps doggedly on and for a moment we hold on him and there is a sound, a footstep sound, and it's coming like crazy and* BABE *doesn't pay it much mind at first, just goes his own way but now the sound is louder, if anything, faster, and as* BABE *turns and looks down the dark block—*

CUT TO

THE BLOCK *behind him and there's not much to be made out except the sound is coming still faster and*

CUT TO

BABE, *trying to go faster now too, it hurts, he's in pain but he fights it, and now maybe it's an eighth of a block to 12th Avenue and the Highway, but it seems to be endless getting there and again* BABE *risks a look behind and*

CUT TO

JANEWAY, *racing like a ghost out of the darkness and*

CUT TO

BABE; *and* JANEWAY *is just tearing his lead to pieces so he tucks his head down, pumps his arms, gives with everything he has but* JANEWAY *won't break. Whatever the lead was, it's less.*

BABE *glances back, sees* JANEWAY *roaring on, turns and now—*

QUICK CUT AGAIN—*the same one as before—the running cap, the staring Nurmi, the great Bikila—it spurred Babe on once and now as we watch him run we can see it's working again, he's going faster, faster than ever before and as he glances back—*

JANEWAY *won't break. Whatever the lead was, it's less. And now* JANEWAY *takes out his pistol, grips it tightly in his right hand but as he raises it, he's got a problem, because he's running so fast and so hard that there's no foundation for the weapon, no way to hold it steady, and what he has to do to make it steady is slow down, but as he starts to do that another problem hits him—*BABE *begins to pull away again and* JANEWAY *holds the gun, keeps it ready, but he's not close enough to use it, not yet and*

BABE *is almost at the corner, and he's anguished, but if you're a marathon man, you understand pain, so he guts it out, keeps his pace—*

—but JANEWAY *is too fast, just too fast, and now he's coming closer than he's ever been—*

BABE *reaches the corner of 12th Avenue, hesitates only an instant before starting toward the inclined entrance to the Highway and as he starts for it, he has thoughts again, but not like before, not like the bathtub; happy family thoughts don't mean a thing now, now it's only pain that will keep you company and* BABE *sees his father staggering and drunk and looking like hell, trying to walk, stumbling, a wreck, and now he sees* SZELL *leaning forward with the drill and now there's* DOC'S *blood, the spot on the floor and here comes the sound of the shot and now the blood puddle from behind the bed where his father lay out of sight and dead—*

—and now comes the most painful of all, DOC *dying, falling, arms out wide in* BABE'S *apartment, and now here it comes again,* DOC *dying, and again it comes, remorselessly, over and over, the dread image keeps repeating like the nightmare it was and suddenly*

CUT TO

BABE: CLOSE UP; *and you can tell it in his eyes, he isn't going to lose this race, if it kills him, he's going to win, and it doesn't matter what* JANEWAY *tries or doesn't try, no one's going to catch* BABE *now and he's really tearing up the night and as* JANEWAY'S *footsteps start to lessen—*

CUT TO

JANEWAY *watching in a wild fury as* BABE *pulls away and it's over and he's lost and he screams out "Shit, Shit, son of a bitch" and fires and fires his pistol but the shots aren't even close and suddenly he whirls,* JANEWAY *does, hollering out with everything he has, "Get the car!"*

And BABE *keeps right on running, toward the incline and up and behind him, there's* JANEWAY *screaming again, "Bring the goddam car!" but nothing* Janeway *can do can matter;* BABE'S *a marathon man and tonight no one can outrun him and he races along the highway with the city vaguely visible behind him and it's not until he hears the roar of a car motor that he stops, suddenly looks back—*

—now from below a car stops, a door opens and slams shut, the motor comes again, louder—

—and BABE *realizes he's trapped.*

The car is louder still.

BABE *stands there a moment more, then takes off, because there's a low fence that divides the highway and the downtown incline is just across and as the sound of the car motor starts to deafen,* BABE *crosses over the fence, tears fast toward the downtown exit as we*

CUT TO

THE UPTOWN ENTRANCE *and for a moment there's nothing but then* KARL'S *car appears, gunned out full, rocketing into view up along the highway and, as they pass by,*

PULL BACK TO REVEAL

BABE, *alone in the shadows of the downtown incline, and hold on him a moment, crouched there like an animal—*

ZOOM TO

Someone we've never seen before, but it's a night doorman and there's a startled look on his face and now we see why, because outside in the night, pounding against the locked glass door of the apartment building is BABE, *and he's calling out loud, only we can barely hear him through the thick door, the word, "...Bies...en...thal..." as the doorman stares.*

Now, from that instant of sudden and unexpected confusion—

CUT TO

A TASTEFUL, PRECISELY DECORATED LIBRARY.

Bound sets of books. Framed prints. An antique desk with a cut glass decanter on it. BIESENTHAL *is heard talking as we see the room, and* BABE *gives an occasional answering sound.*

> BIESENTHAL (off-screen)
> You're simply not being logical, Levy, refusing to talk specifics. How am I to help without a knowledge of what's involved? *(answering sound from Babe)* Why did you come here then? Simply for the money and the clothes?

Another answering sound from BABE *as we see them.* BIESENTHAL, *in a Liberty print robe carries in a tray with coffee cups and a steaming carafe of coffee, sets it down on the table by the couch.*

BABE, *dressed in clothes now that come close enough to fitting, is in a constant state of motion. He paces, turns, paces, clearly distraught; God only knows where his mind is. A raincoat is draped across the couch and* BABE *goes to it, picks it up, changes his mind.*

> BABE
> *(abruptly)*
> Lemme use your phone?—I gotta call my girl—I gotta get away—

> BIESENTHAL
> That's not logical either, if you're going to use the phone, call the police. *(headshake from Babe)* If you want, I'll call them for you—

BABE
(sudden)

No!

BIESENTHAL

Why not?

BABE
(Starts to talk, stops; he can't get his brain working properly.)

I'm not so sure—*(stops, starts over)*—I don't think—*(another pause)*—I'm not all that interested in justice right now.

BIESENTHAL
(nods, pours)

Fine. What are you interested in?

BABE
(starts to talk; then a violent head shake)

Don't know. *(He takes the cup of coffee from Biesenthal and—)*

CUT TO

BABE as the steaming coffee hits his tooth and he cries out loud in sudden blinding pain, and he puts the cup down hard, moves to BIESENTHAL, talking loud, riding emotionally on remembered suffering—

BABE

I do know—I'm goddam sure what I'm interested in and it's blood—

BIESENTHAL

—how do you imagine your father would react to a statement like that?

BABE

I never *knew* my father—you did, that's why I'm here, for you to tell me—I want to know what he'd say—

BIESENTHAL

—emotions betray—that's what he'd tell you, and you'd better learn it now. If we don't use reason, we're back with the wolves—

BABE

—that's where I've been all night—

BIESENTHAL

—and look at you! Hear me now—logic's all you have or I have or your father had—

BABE

Did him a lot of good, didn't it? *(He stares coldly at Biesenthal as we—)*

CUT TO

BABE, *getting out of a cab in the night. It's 95th and Columbus, his corner, and dark, all the street lights having long since been broken. He moves quietly but quickly toward his apartment house, then suddenly stops dead as we*

CUT TO

A CAR *parked not far from Babe's building.* TWO MEN *sit inside it. We can't tell who.*

CUT TO

BABE, *heart pounding, breath held, he moves forward.*

CUT TO

THE CAR, *the* ANGLE MOVING *as* BABE MOVES *and slowly we can make out the two men and it's* ERHARD AND KARL *and*

CUT TO

BABE, *whirling up the steps of the nearest building, then silently he's in the little foyer, looking at the names listed by the buzzers. Constantly glancing around to see if* KARL AND ERHARD *have moved, he pushes a buzzer, then again. No reply. A third time and he keeps his thumb on it until suddenly the silence is broken by a woman screaming in Spanish—*

BABE
(whispering)
Mrs. Melendez—I need your son, your...*(He can't find the word for a moment.)*..hijo...*(She screams louder and—)*

CUT TO

ERHARD AND KARL, *sitting in the car, glancing around.*

CUT TO

BABE, *in the tiny foyer, going flat against the wall.*

BABE
(his voice a little louder—It's dangerous and he knows it.)
Hijo—get me your *hijo*—

But she hangs up. BABE *pushes again, mashing his finger against the button. Now a different voice screams out at him—it is* MELENDEZ—

> MELENDEZ (off-screen)

I'll cut your goddam finger off you don't let go—

> BABE

—Melendez, listen—it's me—

> MELENDEZ (off-screen)

—one more time I'm coming with a butcher knife, you got it?

> BABE
> *(the loudest yet)*

Melendez, don't you recognize me?

> MELENDEZ (off-screen)

—who's this?—

CUT TO

BABE. He hesitates. Then, hating himself, he says it.

> BABE

The creep.

> MELENDEZ (off-screen)
> *(after a pause)*

Creepy? *(There comes a click, the door opens.)*

CUT TO

MELENDEZ in underwear shorts, standing on the first floor as BABE enters, hurries to him.

> MELENDEZ

Ain't it past your bedtime, Creepy? *(He starts to laugh.)*

> BABE

I don't need your shit.

> MELENDEZ
> *(stops laughing)*

What you after?

> BABE

I want you to rob my apartment. I need my gun. *(Melendez looks at him funny.)* Right now or it's no deal. Take as many with you as you can, and if any of you have weapons, bring them too.

> MELENDEZ

You kidding, who don't have a weapon? *(pause)* Why?

> BABE

Some people are after me. If I go, they'll get me; they won't be as anxious to mess with you.

> MELENDEZ

What's in it for me?

> BABE

TV, hi-fi, books, anything you want.

> MELENDEZ

What's the catch?

> BABE

The catch is it's dangerous.

> MELENDEZ
> *(smiles)*

That's not the catch, that's the fun...

CUT TO

ERHARD AND KARL SEATED IN THE CAR.

ERHARD suddenly hears a sound, whirls, sees half a dozen PEOPLE quietly coming down the steps of Melendez's building. ERHARD watches nervously; KARL is placid.

> ERHARD

What is that?

> KARL
> *(shrugs)*

Spicks.

CUT TO

THE GANG. We can see now it's MELENDEZ AND THE OTHERS. They move quickly along the sidewalk, move silently to Babe's building, enter fast.

CUT TO

KARL AND ERHARD watching.

> ERHARD
> *(upset)*

They went inside.

KARL

So?

ERHARD

Shouldn't we do something?

KARL

Why? Janeway said to stay and watch. Well, I'm watching.

ERHARD

I still think—

KARL
(interrupting—big)

—they probably live in that building—all of them in one room along with half a dozen others. You want to do something, do it, but without me.

ERHARD, cowed, says nothing, does not move.

CUT TO

THE DOOR TO BABE'S APARTMENT.

Closed tight. HOLD FOR A MOMENT, *then*

PULL BACK TO REVEAL

The darkness of the next stairway. JANEWAY *waits. Now a sound starts. Footsteps from below. Quick and rising.*

CUT TO

JANEWAY, *out of the shadows. He has his gun, listens, confused. The footsteps grow louder. He leans over the stairs, looks down—*

CUT TO

THE VIEW DOWN.

It's one of those buildings where you can't see who's coming. But the footsteps continue to rise.

CUT TO

JANEWAY, *back into the darkness again, waiting. The sounds are very loud now, rising, rising, and then the* GANG *appears and as* MELENDEZ *immediately starts to work on* BABE'S LOCK—

CUT TO

THE DARKNESS where JANEWAY lurks. Long beat. Then he's out into view, gun ready.

JANEWAY
(And his voice has never been harder.)

All of you, move—right now—

CUT TO

MELENDEZ AND THE GANG. THE GANG spins toward JANEWAY. All but MELENDEZ. He continues to jimmy the door. Then, verrry slowly, he finally turns, looks dead at Janeway.

MELENDEZ

Blow it out your ass, motherfucker.

CUT TO

JANEWAY, and it's not the kind of answer he's used to receiving. He hesitates with his gun a moment and

CUT TO

THE GANG. They have guns too, Saturday night specials. Then the door to BABE'S apartment opens and THE GANG slips inside.

The moment they're gone, JANEWAY takes off down the stairs, two at a time and gone.

CUT TO

THE AREA NEAR KAUFMANN'S PHARMACY.

It's still dark but getting closer to dawn. There is a line of people huddled by a lit but locked shop—it's a bakery, they're waiting for bread. Papers blow along the street. Then as ELSA'S car comes into view BABE dashes out from Kaufmann's, gets in.

They embrace. ELSA begins to drive as BABE opens a small bottle of liquid, rubs it on his tooth.

BABE
(watching her)

Oil of cloves.

ELSA
(curious)

For what?

BABE

Tooth acting up.

ELSA
(nods)

Rest. (BABE'S *head goes on her shoulder.*)

BABE

Where we going?

ELSA

You said you needed to hide. When you phoned, you said you had to get away.

BABE

You got a spot?

ELSA
(smiles)

Let it come as a surprise...(*on the word* "surprise"—)

DISSOLVE TO

A JEWEL OF A LAKE.

Quiet, rural. Surrounded by summer houses, all of them shuttered and boarded away. One single small road surrounds the water. It all seems deserted, almost dead, as ELSA'S car appears, begins the drive around.

Inside the car, BABE is looking around, staring at the place as ELSA drives. Her voice is unchanged, she seems pleased with herself almost, but her hands are gripping the wheel tighter than maybe might be necessary.

ELSA

Amazing? So close to the city, yet so quiet. (*Babe nods.*) In the summer, it is not so quiet—this friend who owns here tells me so. But after the Labor Day, there is only activity on the weekends. On days like now, nothing.

Ahead is a not unusual house. Small, a decent front porch, not much else to say about it. ELSA pulls into the driveway, stops the car, kills the motor. They get out.

ELSA

I'm sure this is right—the key will be in the drainpipe.

BABE

Szell's?

ELSA
(didn't quite hear)

Szells?

> BABE

Oh come on.

> ELSA

You're very tired; better I get the key. *(She starts up toward the house.)*

> BABE
> *(calling after her)*

What did you do for Szell?

> ELSA

I hope the key is where it's supposed to be—

> BABE

Where's Janeway?

> ELSA
> *(at the drainpipe now)*

—I would feel such a fool if I'd gotten it wrong—

> BABE

—when are they all getting here? *(And his voice is building.)*

> ELSA
> *(louder too)*

—it isn't charming any more—stop it—

> BABE

—WHAT DID YOU DO FOR HIM?!—

> ELSA

—stop it I told you—

> BABE

—NOBODY'S STOPPING, NOW GODDAMMIT TELL ME, WHEN ARE THEY DUE?

CUT TO

BABE: *CLOSE UP. And he's scary now.*

CUT TO

ELSA, *starting to get frightened.*

> ELSA

...soon...

> BABE
> *(looks at her)*

Good. *(nods)* Right.

> ELSA

How did you know I was involved?

> BABE

I didn't, 'til now.

And with that he takes his father's gun out of his raincoat pocket. ELSA sees it and if she was frightened before, it's only getting worse now. BABE gestures with the gun toward the house.

> BABE

Whose place?

> ELSA

It was—it belonged to Szell's father, it reminded him somehow of home—*(and as she twists around, glances back at—)*

THE NARROW ROAD AROUND THE LAKE. Empty.

CUT TO

BABE AND ELSA, moving up the porch steps.

> BABE
> *(pointing to the front door)*

Unlock it—

> ELSA
> *(suddenly)*

—we have still time—I can get you out of here—

> BABE

—why worry about me?—

> ELSA

It is me that I worry about—

BABE takes the key, unlocks the door, throws it open. Inside, nothing moves. He glances back down the road.

CUT TO

THE ROAD. Still empty.

CUT TO

BABE AND ELSA ON THE PORCH.

> **BABE**
> What's keeping them—

> **ELSA**
> *(panicked)*
> —they had to be sure there were no police following—

> **BABE**
> —no police—*(looks at her)*—God, you're pretty; what were you, Szell's mistress?

> **ELSA**
> It does not matter, we should leave here, that alone matters—

> **BABE**
> —too late—*(and as he points—)*

CUT TO

THE ROAD AROUND THE LAKE. In the distance now, a car.

CUT TO

BABE AND ELSA watching it come.

> **BABE**
> Wasn't he a little old for you?

> **ELSA**
> *(staring at the car, quiet now)*
> I was a courier, nothing more. I took the money from an antiques dealer in London into Paraguay.

THE CAR, driving very slowly, is closer now, in no hurry.

> **BABE**
> *(riveted on it)*
> Glamour job, sounds like—excitement, easy hours, lots of travel—

But now he's starting to unravel around the edges. The minute the car appeared, he began to go, and now, as it keeps on coming, his nerves are beginning to betray him. The car keeps moving, slow and steady, always getting closer. BABE grips his gun tighter, his body getting rigid. When he speaks, it's hard to keep his voice even.

> **BABE**
> Here comes your boss now. *(Elsa nods.)*

CUT TO

BABE. He moves a few steps away, behind her, watching the car which is closer. He gets out some more oil of cloves, rubs it against the tooth. The car is almost to the driveway. It's hard to breathe.

> **BABE**
> *(whispered)*
> ...please...don't think too much...

CUT TO

THE CAR, *pulling in behind* ELSA'S CAR.

CUT TO

BABE, and suddenly he whirls, throws the bottle, smashes it against the side of the house and as the bottle hits the wall—

CUT TO

ELSA surprised, whirling, staring at the broken glass and the liquid rolling down the side of the house and

CUT TO

BABE: CLOSE UP, *inhaling sharply now, deeply, sucking the morning air against the open nerve, and Christ it hurts, but he keeps on and on, the sharp inhaled bursts the only sound.*

CUT TO

THE CAR. *It stops.* KARL *gets out.* ERHARD *gets out.* JANEWAY *gets out. They close the car door.*

CUT TO

BABE on the porch, stunned, grabbing ELSA—

> **BABE**
> Where is he?—where's Szell?

> **ELSA**
> I know nothing—

> **JANEWAY'S VOICE** (off-screen)
> Lovely morning.

CUT TO

THE THREE MEN, *starting casually up toward the porch.*

CUT TO

BABE *with* ELSA, *watching.*

> **ELSA**
> *(calling out)*

He has a pistol.

> **JANEWAY**

Can't be too safe nowadays, I suppose. *(And the dazzling smile flashes. They continue their approach.)*

> **BABE**
> *(sharp)*

Stop!

CUT TO

JANEWAY, ERHARD AND KARL. JANEWAY *immediately halts,* ERHARD *a moment later.* KARL *hesitates, finally obeys.*

CUT TO

BABE, *and in the silence he stands there. The unravelling has gone beyond his edges now and he can't stop it.*

CUT TO

JANEWAY AND THE OTHERS, *looking to the porch.* JANEWAY *is serene.* KARL *isn't, glances around.*

> **JANEWAY**

We're awaiting further instructions—do we take three giant steps or what?

CUT TO

BABE *watching them.*

> **BABE**

Tell Karl not to get upset—cops should be here in less than five minutes—

> **ELSA**

—he said there were no police—

BABE

—and I was telling the truth. *(beat)* Probably.

CUT TO

THE THREE MEN, *and now* ERHARD *is starting to glance around.*

CUT TO

BABE *looking at them. He keeps his voice as casual as he can.*

BABE

I haven't got my watch with me, anybody have the correct time?

JANEWAY

I don't believe the police are coming.

BABE

Neither do I. *(And he gives a dazzling smile back to Janeway. Another beat.)* Of course I could be wrong.

CUT TO

JANEWAY, *and now he's staring around, back along the empty road. He looks at Babe, hesitates; then—*

JANEWAY

All right, how much do you want, and can we for Chrissakes talk terms inside?

CUT TO

BABE, *standing close to* ELSA, *gun ready. After a pause, he nods, starts moving into the house, pulling Elsa with him.*

The room we enter is a living room and feels tremendously German. On a small table is a faded picture of a man—it's Szell when he was young, his hair already a glorious white. He looks to be in his mid-twenties, a faint smile on his face; he wears lederhosen. On the wall are stuffed dead birds. And framed mounted butterflies, which are pretty enough but there's something about them that reminds us of the trapped dead insects in the netting outside Szell's house in South America.

The silence is long and deadly. BABE *backs until he reaches a corner of the room.* ELSA *is in front of him.* JANEWAY *enters, then* ERHARD. *Finally, still looking back nervously,* KARL.

JANEWAY

You realize, of course, that I'm only authorized to go to certain limits—

                            BABE
—oh, cut the bullshit, there are no terms—

                          JANEWAY
Then why did you let us get close?

CUT TO

TIGHT CLOSE UP: BABE

                            BABE
Because you're all in my killing range now.

CUT TO

THE ROOM.

                          JANEWAY
                          (serene)
No, I'm sorry, you're just not good casting for the part.

                            BABE
                (gun raised toward Janeway)
I'm a crack shot—*(But his voice wasn't quite under control.)*

                          JANEWAY
—taken target practice, have you? A wizard at hitting paper? It's not the
same with flesh; it's different when you smash bone, and I somehow
doubt you're an old hand at that.

CUT TO

*BABE, and Janeway's right, and as BABE tries pushing himself deeper into the corner of
the room, his control is going, it's leaving him and he can't do a thing about it and*

CUT TO

JANEWAY, watching him.

                          JANEWAY
If there were police, you wouldn't be panicking—

                            BABE
—they're coming—

                          JANEWAY
—we'll just wait here for them then—

CUT TO

BABE, pulling the air against his bare nerve again, drawing the pain toward him, using it, trying to anyway, anything not to fold, not here, not now—

CUT TO

JANEWAY watching.

> **JANEWAY**
> We'll all wait, and we won't do a thing, will we, Erhard, because we don't have to, do we, Karl? And Elsa, why don't you move a bit? I think the boy could use more breathing room and—*(suddenly shouting)*—No!

CUT TO

KARL making his move, going for Babe with his big hands and as he's almost there as his fingers reach for BABE'S THROAT—

CUT TO

BABE, firing, and the sound explodes and ELSA is screaming and

CUT TO

KARL, careening into the wall, his face splattered and as he falls

CUT TO

BABE, moving from his corner now as ERHARD has his gun and BABE squeezes off a shot, another, and ERHARD shrieks and reaches for the remains of his face and

CUT TO

JANEWAY, going into his roll, gun half out, starting to point it and

CUT TO

BABE, and he's graceful now, and the gun works like it's part of him and he fires and JANEWAY is hit in the arm and BABE fires again and again and the noise is tremendous as JANEWAY crumples, his gun skittering across the room and ELSA races for it, she's got the angle over BABE and she's damn near there but that isn't good enough as he shoulders her into the wall and grabs up Janeway's gun and points it dead into her face and

> **ELSA**
> No—Jesus—

> **BABE**
> —where's Szell?—what bank?

> **ELSA**
> I don't know—

> BABE
>
> —you lying bitch you do, and you're going to tell me—

> ELSA
>
> —you'll kill me if I tell you—

> BABE
>
> —you're fucking right I'm going to kill you but you're still going to tell me!! (*And maybe he would have gone on but—*)

CUT TO

JANEWAY, shot to hell. Only his hands still work, and he's pulling at BABE, and you wouldn't think he'd have much strength, not the way he looks, but he continues to pull and across the room ERHARD is moving too, crawling slowly, forcing his crippled body toward his gun and BABE fires at ERHARD, fires at JANEWAY and the noise hurts and ELSA is screaming as, finally, BABE starts to fall—

PAN TO

The picture of Szell, the faded, faintly smiling young Szell, and it's as if someone had thrown a handful of blood across it. HOLD on the frame. The blood begins to slide down the glass as in the faded photo, young Szell, eyes bright, continues to smile.

HOLD ON YOUNG SZELL.

Then, gradually, DISSOLVE to SZELL as he is today, now, bald and looking at something, and that same kind of bemused smile is on his face as was in the picture.

We don't know what he's looking at or where he is. There is no sound.

Now we see what he's looking at, but not quite enough to be sure what it is. Still no sound.

Now PULL BACK AND BACK AND BACK AND AS WE DO—

Sound starts; street noise, chit-chat and car horns, loud, starting to get louder and louder and then we reveal—

We've been looking at salamis! A whole storefront, lining the row of a deli window like sentries and as the noise hits a peak—

CUT TO

47TH STREET

—and there isn't anyplace like it in the world! It's the diamond center of America, 47th between Fifth and Sixth, and it's jammed with diamond store after diamond store and literally hundreds of arcades inside other stores and the street is crammed with traffic, the sidewalks with people, all kinds, shapes, colors—there's blacks walking along and a lot of

Spanish types trying to get through but most of all what 47th Street is full of is Jews, young, old, very old, some bearded, some snazzily dressed, some in their black caps and robes, and there's delicatessens and watch shops and noise and bustle and groups standing around arguing and selling and telling stories and if there's one thing about 47th Street, you better believe it's alive, the decibel count always high, and every time the cars get stalled and horns start honking, well, naturally, everyone on the sidewalk has to start talking LOUDER *to make his point clear and that's what it's like now,* LOUD, *and it's also* HOT *and in the midst of all this wonderful chaos—*

CUT TO

CHRISTIAN SZELL wandering along the sidewalk, taking it all in. He carries a briefcase, is obviously enjoying himself, an amused expression very evident. And if the scene at the lake was BABE *in Germany, then this one coming is* SZELL *amongst the Jews. He passes stores with names like the Diamond Exchange and the Jewelry Exchange and the Jeweler's Exchange and the Diamond Center and the Diamond Tower and the Diamond Gallery and the Diamond Horseshoe and there are hot dog stands doing business as he goes by, mustard and kraut getting slapped on wieners as expertly as a surgeon might cauterize a wound and* SZELL *shakes his head at it all, the wild masses of people pushing and hawking their wares, shopping, hustling for a better deal. Then he turns, and as he does—*

CUT TO

A CLEARLY HIGH END STORE.

It is softly lit, and, for want of a better word, tasteful. SZELL *moves across the sidewalk, tries the door. It is locked. A buzzer has a* PUSH *sign above it.* SZELL *pushes, there is an answering* BUZZ, *and as the door opens—*

CUT TO

INSIDE THE STORE

—AND A BOUNCY LITTLE SALESMAN moving around the counter to SZELL, *all smiles.*

> **SZELL**
> I'd like to see a three-carat diamond—

> **BOUNCY SALESMAN**
> *(before Szell can finish)*
> —why?

> **SZELL**
> *(surprised)*
> Be-cuss—*(He stops—it's more German sounding than we're used to hearing him.)*

> BOUNCY SALESMAN

If all you want is just to see a three-carat job, go window-shop, but if you're the kind of man who wants to buy, if you want the best, the creme de la creme, the choicest rock on the block, then we can do business.

> SZELL

I was interested in—

> BOUNCY SALESMAN
> *(again before Szell can finish—*
> *It shocks Szell; he's not used to being interrupted.)*

—but before anything else there's gotta be trust, so what I'll do is I'll get a three-carat stone and I'll take it to this independent appraiser I know — *(gesturing above)*—one flight up—*(moving in)*—and if he doesn't swear that I'm practically giving the stone away, well—*(shrugs)*—I'll just have to get a new brother-in-law, that's all. *(And he laughs.)*

> SZELL
> *(He isn't laughing.)*

Can't you just tell me what it's worth?

> BOUNCY SALESMAN

—wait—wait—wait just one second—first you come traipsing in here asking to see, now all you're interested in is price. *(passionately)* I'm no high pressure artist, I sell value—

> SZELL
> *(whirling, starting out)*

You never answer me—*(and as he opens the door—)*

CUT TO

47TH STREET again as SZELL angrily storms out, slams the door behind him, moves back into the heat and the crowds.

CUT TO

SZELL, slowing down, getting control back. It's an effort of will and concentration, but he makes the anger leave him, the almost placid quality returns to his features, and as he walks on—

CUT TO

MUCH THE CLASSIEST SHOP WE'VE SEEN.

TWO SALESMEN are inside, one of them on the phone. SZELL approaches, pushes the buzzer by the PUSH sign, waits for the answering BUZZ, goes into the store. It is really very lovely. ONE MAN, *a fat man in a short-sleeved shirt is busy on the phone, the* OTHER, *a well dressed man with a* PENCIL MUSTACHE *smiles at Szell.*

> PENCIL MUSTACHE

Yes sir.

> SZELL
> *(going British)*

I'm rather interested in the cost of, say, a three-carat diamond.

> PENCIL MUSTACHE

That depends on the quality of the stone, sir.

> SZELL

I'd only want gem quality, the very best—you see, my wife and I, our 35th is coming up, but the diamond anniversary isn't 'til the 60th, and I rather doubt we'll be around that long. *(He holds up a hand.)* Just something perhaps the size of my little fingernail.

> PENCIL MUSTACHE
> *(smiles)*

You're talking at least six carats, sir, more probably.

> SZELL

Would that be prohibitive, do you think?

> PENCIL MUSTACHE

Fifteen thousand.

> SZELL
> *(Nods—he had hoped for twice that.)*

Fifteen.

> PENCIL MUSTACHE

Per carat, naturally.

> SZELL
> *(Thrilled—he cannot keep it from his eyes.)*

Naturally.

> MAN'S VOICE (off-screen)

I know you.

CUT TO

THE FAT SALESMAN IN THE SHORT-SLEEVED SHIRT. *Off the phone now, staring. He rubs his hand across his mouth; the tattoo from the concentration camp is visible on his arm and*

CUT TO

SZELL, and there isn't any thrill left in his eyes. It's what he's always dreaded most and now it's happening and as the FAT SALESMAN approaches, blocking Szell's path to the door, SZELL bursts into a big smile.

> SZELL
> *(terribly British now)*
>
> Oh I do hope so, I quite love surprises.

> FAT SALESMAN
> *(to his partner)*
>
> I remember this guy from someplace.

> SZELL
> *(shaking hands with the Fat Salesman)*
>
> Christopher Hesse, how do you do. *(now with the Pencil Mustache)* Christopher Hesse, how do you do. Perhaps you've been to our antiques shop in London, the missus and mine.

> FAT SALESMAN
>
> It wasn't London.

> SZELL
>
> We've been there since the Thirties, you see, Hitler, you see, we're Jewish, we were among the fortunate, we got out and our shop is quite trendy now, but it wasn't achieved without struggle.

> PENCIL MUSTACHE
>
> I always wanted to visit London.

> SZELL
>
> Oh do come. And pay us a visit. Hesse of Islington. Promise now. *(Pencil Mustache nods; to the Fat Man)* You too.

> FAT SALESMAN
> *(the suspicion gone)*
>
> Sure, sure.

> SZELL
> *(starting for the door)*
>
> And I appreciate your time. I fear ninety thousand is a bit steep for me— our shop isn't that trendy. Ta-ta. *(He waves, smiles, goes and—)*

CUT TO

THE TWO SALESMEN, smiling back, waving and

CUT TO

SZELL on the pavement again, out of their sight. The effort has been tremendous, he leans briefly against a building, wipes the perspiration from his face, takes a deep breath, starts walking again toward Sixth Avenue, faster than before. Traffic is heavier, going in fits and starts, and there is horn-blowing and the sidewalks seem fuller too, and there is a lot of talk and a lot of salesmen and hot dog vendors hawking and Spanish and black guys, many of them with portable radios blasting away, move on by as SZELL continues toward Sixth Avenue, the heat oppressive now, perspiration visible on his forehead. He flicks it away, moves on, unmindful of the masses or the radios with all their songs about "love" and "angel" and the people with portables keep walking so the love songs disappear but the word "ANGEL" doesn't, and as we realize this

CUT TO

SZELL, the perspiration heavier now, because it isn't "angel" that he's hearing, it's "ENGEL" and then it isn't even that, it's "der Engel, der Engel" repeated over and over and as it begins to build into a scream, SZELL tries to stare straight ahead but now the words are louder and now it's "der weisse Engel" and again, louder and louder, "DER WEISSE ENGEL!" and SZELL whirls and as he does,

ZOOM TO

AN ANCIENT OLD CRONE, BENT AND TREMBLING, ACROSS THE STREET. She holds out one trembling hand pointing it dead at SZELL, standing there crying out with whatever strength is left to her—

CRONE
Der weisse Engel—Szell—Szell—!!!!

CUT TO

SZELL—it takes everything he has not to break into a wild panicked run. But he doesn't. He turns away from the screaming crone, takes up his pace again, heading as before toward Sixth Avenue, as the word "SZELL" continues to be hurled into the steaming air and

CUT TO

A BUNCH OF YOUNG JEWISH GUYS, moving along, ignoring it all, whatever it is and

CUT TO

A SPANISH KID WITH HIS PORTABLE, and some Spanish tune is blaring away, he couldn't care less either and

CUT TO

TWO SUCCESSFUL LOOKING BLACK MEN, *early thirties, very conservatively attired; they glance around in the direction of the screaming, look back at each other, shrug; what the hell, New York is full of crazies and*

CUT TO

SZELL, *bathed in sweat now, but under control, not bolting, making his steady way but then*

CUT TO

AN OLD MAN WITH A BEARD. *He hesitates, listens, looks around—*

> **OLD BEARDED MAN**
> Szell?—Szell is here?—*(and as he stares—)*

CUT TO

ANOTHER OLD MAN, *turning around too.*

> **OLD MAN**
> *(louder now)*
> —where is Szell?—*(and as he looks around—)*

CUT TO

A GIANT OF A WOMAN WITH A DEEP, DEEP VOICE.

> **GIANTESS**
> He is dead—Szell is dead—*(little pause)*—everyone is dead—

CUT TO

THE CRONE, *still screaming, still pointing her fingers, her gnarled trembling hand following* SZELL'S *movement—*

> **CRONE**
> *(louder still)*
> —nein—NEIN—*(huge)* Der weisse Engel ist hier!!!

CUT TO

SZELL, *still making his way through the crowd, staring ahead, as behind him now, 47th Street is starting to explode.*

CUT TO

A BUNCH OF WINDOWS ON THE SECOND FLOOR. People are sticking their heads out, looking down, trying to locate the focus of what the hell's going on and

CUT TO

SHOP DOORS OPENING, owners coming out, glancing around and

CUT TO

THE TRAFFIC still moving jumpily as always, but now, suddenly, the honking lessens and drivers are shouting to passengers asking what is it and

CUT TO

THE SIDEWALK, and the flow of bodies is different, they don't swirl and eddy in quite the same way as before; something odd is going on and they know it, they just don't know exactly what yet and

CUT TO

SZELL, walking, walking through the heat of 47th Street, staring as before, straight ahead and

CUT TO

THE CRONE ACROSS THE STREET, tracking SZELL moving on her side of the street, pointing at him, dead at him and crying out.

CRONE
He is getting away—SEE? SEE?—(gesturing now)—someone stop der weisse Engel!—

CUT TO

SZELL, and now at last he can see the traffic moving quickly up Sixth Avenue and he allows himself just the least bit to pick up the pace and

CUT TO

A SKINNY LADY standing in her doorway as SZELL passes.

SKINNY LADY
What's all the tumuling?

SZELL
(a Jewish shrug)
Crazy peoples. (The skinny lady smiles.)

CUT TO

THE CRONE; she's hysterical now, watching helpless as Szell moves on and without warning she hobbles into the street and the traffic—

CRONE
I will stop him—*(And as she moves—)*

CUT TO

SZELL, daring a glance across at her as she gestures to cars to stop and get out of her ancient way and

CUT TO

THE CRONE, moving slowly but steadily and she's in the midst of traffic now and

CUT TO

SZELL, looking away from her, picking up his pace again and

CUT TO

THE CRONE, and my God, she's almost into a run as she does her best to dodge the traffic and her best is plenty good enough until there is a screech of brakes and a car tries desperately to stop, and it does, but not in time, as he strikes the crone, not hard, not a death blow, but enough to send her helpless to the middle of the street, unhurt but out of the race and

CUT TO

THE DRIVER OF THE CAR, racing out, going to the CRONE, trying to help her up and

CUT TO

THE CRONE, heartsick, beyond tears—

CRONE
FOOL—FOOL—WHO WILL STOP HIM NOW?

CUT TO

SIXTH AVENUE.

The traffic is moving freely. There are a ton of empty cabs.

CUT TO

SZELL nearing the corner. He passes a subway entrance. Beyond that there is one of those large one yard high round cement structures in which pathetic trees are planted and there's a pathetic tree in this one, maybe all of six feet high and two inches wide at the trunk, skinny as hell, just the reverse of the FAT SALESMAN *from the second shop who suddenly whirls* SZELL *and*

FAT SALESMAN
I knew you weren't English you murdering son of a bitch—

CUT TO

SZELL'S ARM *already into its swipe and as the* FAT SALESMAN *spins him* SZELL'S *thick cutter is already in his hand and, as the* TWO MEN *come face to face,* SZELL'S KNIFE *has already split the Fat Man's throat like a fire splits a sausage and as the* FAT MAN *makes a feeble grab toward his jugular—*

CUT TO

SZELL, *starting to cry out for help as the* FAT MAN *lurches forward and* SZELL *continues calling out as he lays the* FAT MAN *face down across the cement pot that holds the tree—*

SZELL
There's a sick man here—there's a man needs help here—there's a man here needs a doctor, get a doctor—

CUT TO

THE FAT MAN *dying, his blood draining into the dirt that supports the feeble tree and*

CUT TO

A CROWD, *gathering quickly, moving in, looking at the* FAT MAN, *at each other, not knowing which way to go or what to do and*

CUT TO

A CAB AS SZELL *extracts himself from the crowd, signals for the cab to stop and as it does—*

CUT TO

SZELL, *getting in, closing the door and*

CUT TO

THE CROWD *around the dead man, and if the street was exploding before, now it's going really crazy with screams and whistles and shrieks and tears and the noise builds and builds and for just a moment in the mob, the* CRONE *is visible again, pointing toward the taxi but then she is gone, the crowd has swelled, there's nothing anyone can do as we*

CUT TO

SZELL, *settled comfortably in the back seat of the cab. He has his handkerchief out and his empty briefcase open, so that the lid blocks the driver from seeing what he's doing, and what he's doing is wiping the blood from the blade of his cutter, then strapping it securely in place on his right forearm; he fastidiously goes about his business, leaving the noise and blood of 47th Street far behind—and from that noise—*

CUT TO

THE QUIET OF THE SAFE DEPOSIT VAULT AREA OF A BANK.

THE SAME GUARD *we saw with Szell's father is inserting a key into a safe deposit box.* SZELL *stands by, hands him another key. As the* GUARD *continues to work—*

CUT TO

THE BOX *being carried by the* GUARD *into a small private room.* SZELL *follows. The* GUARD *puts the box down, leaves.* SZELL *waits, checks that no one is lingering outside, then sits by the box. His hands are not as steady as he might like them. He makes a decisive move, throws the box wide open.*

CUT TO

THE BOX, *and inside are a large number of draw-string cloth bags, like kids use to carry marbles.*

CUT TO

SZELL, *grabbing the top bag, managing to pull the strings open, and as he pours out the contents,*

CUT TO

THE BOX, *as a bunch of diamonds rattle out against the metal box and the sound is louder than expected and*

CUT TO

SZELL, *covering the diamonds, heart pounding, staring at the door of the room. But nothing happens, no one comes. He takes his hand away, and we are looking at a bunch of diamonds the size of your little fingernail, maybe fifty or seventy-five of them, maybe more, it's hard to tell accurately. As* SZELL *grabs for the next bag—*

CUT TO

THE BOX *as another bunch of diamonds spill into view, some of these also the size of your little fingernail, some of them just a bit larger and*

CUT TO

ANOTHER BUNCH OF DIAMONDS *and these are thumbnail-sized now, and maybe there are a hundred of them and*

CUT TO

THE BOX, *as another full bag of diamonds spills across the bottom and there are hands full of them now, dazzling against the darkness of the box and* SZELL, *suddenly unable to contain himself, cries out loud with joy and*

CUT TO

SZELL, *amazed, as in his hands now he holds giant diamonds, incredible things, one of them the size of a baby's fist.*

> GUARD'S VOICE (off-screen)
> You call?—everything all right?

> SZELL
> *(throat dry)*
> ...all iss...*(He rubs the diamond with his fingertips.)*...wunderbar...*(Now, as he starts putting the stones into the briefcase—)*

CUT TO

SZELL, *leaving the safe deposit area, doing what he can to maintain his dignity and*

CUT TO

SZELL, *starting up the stairs that lead to the main floor of the bank, and his attitude is damn near jaunty and then he reaches the main room and crosses it cheerily but he may be the one cheery person in view, because all around him is an air of panic. AN OLD WOMAN, with a black shawl, stands licking her thumb, counting out a few dollar bills that she's gotten from a teller; her hands tremble as she counts, she's that old and that poor. Beyond her is A YOUNGISH COUPLE and they're bickering because there's no money left and he blames her for clothes and she blames him for liquor and* SZELL *moves on, past a bank officer at his desk who is shaking his head at a* SMALL MAN *who sits in a chair, maybe trying for a loan or an extension of a loan but in any case, the answer is "no" and another bank officer is spreading his hands, palms down, another "no" to another customer because there's no money, there's just no money, times are hard, and through it all,* SZELL *makes his way, polite and smiling, and finally he gets across the floor and as he does we*

CUT TO

THE SIDEWALK.

Bathed in sunlight, SZELL *leaves the bank, moves to the curb, starts to hail a cab as* BABE *moves up behind him.*

> BABE

It isn't safe.

CUT TO

SZELL, whirling, and for a moment he almost bolts, but the figure standing before him with his right hand in his raincoat pocket is not going to be that easy to escape.

It's the same person Szell had in his chair not too many hours before. Only it isn't, that was someone you could handle. Before him now stands a genuine adversary.

> SZELL

What—*(quieter)*—what happens now? *(BABE moves his right arm from his raincoat and the second the gun is visible.)* Please—there are things you don't know, I have items in my possession you must see, terms can be made—

> BABE
> *(gun hidden again; tonelessly)*

Where do you want to die?

> SZELL
> *(stares wildly around, sees the Park, points)*

—the park—we can talk there—it is quiet there—please—*(BABE nods, SZELL turns and we—)*

CUT TO

BABE AND SZELL, moving along 91st Street, SZELL leading.

> BABE

Faster.

> SZELL

You must hear me—you are young—you are very smart, but not yet wise—

> BABE

You killed my brother.

> SZELL

That is a lie, I was not even present.

> BABE

Janeway told me.

> SZELL

It had to be done, I had to do it, there was no choice.

> BABE
> *(implacable)*

Janeway didn't tell me anything. So don't worry about me, all right? I'm fucking wise.

CUT TO

BABE AND SZELL *in the park, moving quickly. They are crossing a children's playground near Fifth Avenue and the place is jammed with little children, all of them rich—you can tell it because there are uniformed nannies all over and the carriages are all enormous and expensive and there is a lot of high-pitched shouting and some kids are swinging and some are climbing and some are playing games, tag and cowboys and Indians, and as* BABE AND SZELL *move past, several kids shoot at them and a couple of others fire imaginary bows and arrows and the nannies don't much like people in their kingdom, they watch without pleasure as* BABE AND SZELL *move by and now*

CUT TO

BABE AND SZELL, *deeper into the park, the playground behind them.* SZELL *is growing wild.*

> SZELL

Killing me accomplishes nothing.

> BABE

Not for you.

> SZELL

Nothing!

> BABE

Faster!!

SZELL *shifts his briefcase into his left hand. He touches his right arm. His killing blade is ready—*

CUT TO

THE RESERVOIR

—and people running. More than the last time we saw the place. Up ahead is an incredible looking building, ancient and built of dark stone, like something from another world.

> BABE

Here. Show me.

> SZELL

No. No. Here is too crowded. *(upset and louder)* What you will see will change your life, but private. It must be private.

BABE points to the building and we

CUT TO

THE OLD STONE EDIFICE.

The door's open as they enter and, my God, it is from another world. A latticed floor over water and an incredible winding staircase that must be a hundred years old, and it goes down and down and it's where they control the reservoir flow, but it's somehow terrible, terrible and moist and frightening.

MAINTENANCE MAN
(suddenly appearing)

Sorry, but you can't—*(And he stops dead; Babe has brought out the gun.)*

BABE
(quietly)

We won't be long.

THE GUY takes off.

CUT TO

SZELL, dropping to his knees by the stairs, his hands trembling as he puts down his brief-case. Behind him now are strange lights, dim, and dripping water, and brick over a century old and feet thick and who knows what concentration camps looked like inside, but this could have been one.

CUT TO

BABE, starting to point the gun at SZELL'S HEAD and

SZELL
(crying out)

Christ—one request—just that you come beside me and look—one final wish, you must grant that—

CUT TO

SZELL, in a frenzy as BABE cocks the pistol. He puts his hands to the briefcase, opens it, the case away from Babe.

SZELL

—look—look here—you must look, I am begging—

BABE

I don't want your begging, I don't want your diamonds, I just want you dead—*(and then)*—Jesus—

CUT TO

THE FORTUNE *as* SZELL *turns the briefcase. It's the first time we've seen it all—before in the bank was just a portion. And it's awesome—the case is damn near overflowing and* BABE *is drawn to the fortune, he can't help it; he moves closer, closer and as he does*

CUT TO

SZELL, *on his knees, talking all the while as his right arm moves slightly away from his body.*

SZELL
You see? So many millions for us both—you must not pass up such a chance—I was right, do you understand?

CUT TO

THE FORTUNE *and even in a blackout it would dazzle and—my God, how many millions of dollars must there be in the briefcase, a hundred, two hundred, more?*

CUT TO

BABE, *and there's really never ever been a sight like it and transfixed, he kneels near Szell by the diamonds and*

CUT TO

SZELL, *his right hand in motion, the knife already sliding into killing position and as he starts his swipe, a gunshot explodes and* SZELL *staggers back a moment, and for a moment, he cannot believe what has happened as we*

CUT TO

BABE, *very calm, the gun in his hand, ready to fire again. He's a long way now from the distraught kid we met early on.*

SZELL'S *disbelief has given way to something else: he doesn't know what it is he's facing but it scares him. He is starting to bleed badly now from his chest but he makes another swipe with his cutter but too slow, too slow and too late, as* BABE *fires again, again, the sound echoing off the ancient walls.*

SZELL *starts to topple backward down the long winding stairs. Over he goes, over and over, his body spinning and flipping and then it crashes into a banister halfway down.*

From the top, curious, BABE *watches in silence.*

SZELL *grabs the banister, pulls himself to his feet, slowly, but he makes it, and then he takes a step back up toward Babe, then a second step, and you just know that somehow this man is going to make it all the way back up to the top and just as that knowledge is certain,* SZELL *does something completely unexpected— he dies. Just like that. His body sags, his eyes glaze and darken and then he is falling again, all the way down this time, over the banister and through space and we hear him collide with the wet concrete floor far below. We hear him because we don't see him—from Babe's position, Szell is out of sight.*

BABE *stands motionless, looking down. And as he watches, far below, a blood puddle begins, spreading as he stares, just as the blood puddle happened when he found his father. The puddle grows and finally* BABE *moves around so that he can see the body.*

SZELL, *in blood, lies dead.*

BABE *watches a moment more. Then he lifts his father's gun, looks at it for awhile. Finally he opens his hand and the gun starts to fall toward Szell's still body and, while the gun is in the air—*

CUT TO

Something else that's also in the air. For a moment we're not sure what it is but then it hits and skips and we realize it's stones being thrown across water.

PULL BACK TO REVEAL

BABE, *and he's standing on a little dock at the rear of the old building, and those aren't stones he's skipping across the reservoir, those are* SZELL'S DIAMONDS, *because the briefcase is at Babe's feet and, as he reaches down for another handful,*

CUT TO

THE BRIEFCASE. *It's almost empty now.* BABE *begins to throw again. For a moment we think the sun is causing him to blink but then we know it isn't that—it's this: at last the boy is crying. It's over, everything is over, and he's the last of the line on this beautiful day with the diamonds skimming across the water.*

Behind him now, the MAINTENANCE MAN FROM THE BUILDING *is visible with a* YOUNG COP, *running toward the building. As they come, they pass* A BUNCH OF JOGGERS *who are all grouped along*

THE FENCE, *watching* BABE. *The fence is thick and rusty—it might be used at a prison, and all the joggers grip it and their fingers are bent through the holes and for a moment, they might be prisoners too.*

BABE *is crying harder now, his face covered with tears. The diamonds are almost gone.*

THE JOGGERS *continue to stare, hunched, watching him through the thick fence. All over the world, people have held to fences like this, in prisons, concentration camps, ghettos.*

Holding tight and staring, staring—

BABE stands weeping in the brightness.

Birds fly across the water. The sun is dazzling. The diamonds catch the light as they skim across the water. When they hit they make ripples.

The ripples widen, widen. Tears, diamonds, flashing sun, staring eyes, fingers gripping fences. The ripples continue to enlarge, touching us all.

FINAL FADE OUT.

THE END

THE PRINCESS BRIDE

DIRECTOR	ROB REINER
PRODUCERS	ANDREW SCHEINMAN
	ROB REINER
CINEMATOGRAPHER	ADRIAN BIDDLE
EDITOR	ROBERT LEIGHTON
PRODUCTION DESIGNER	NORMAN GARWOOD
MUSIC	MARK KNOPFLER
SCREENPLAY	WILLIAM GOLDMAN
	(FROM HIS NOVEL)

Here is how the novel *The Princess Bride* happened.

I loved telling stories to my daughters. When they were small, I would go into their room and stories would just be there. Anyone who knows me knows that I don't think much of what I do is very terrific, but my God, I was wonderful those early evenings. Stuff just came. I knew that, because the girls would sneak out and tell their mother and she would say to me, "Write it down, write it down," and I told her I didn't need to, I was on such a hot streak I knew I'd remember.

All gone, of course, and of all the stuff I've done over almost 40 years of storytelling, more than anything I wish I had those moments back. Doesn't matter, really. Woulda shoulda coulda. At any rate, I was on my way to Magic Town around 1970, and I said to them both, to Jenny, then seven, and Susanna, then four, "I'll write you a story, what do you most want it to be about?" And one of them said "princesses" and the other one said "brides."

"Then that will be the title," I told them. And so it has remained.

The first snippets are gone. A couple of pages maybe, maybe a little more, sent from the Beverly Hills Hotel to home. Since it was to be then a kid's saga, the early names were silly names: Buttercup, Humperdinck. I'm sure those pages weren't much. I have never been able to write in Southern California.

(My fault, of course. I find it just too, well, wunderful. There was a time, before the recent madness, when people actually thought of L.A. as being that— wunderful. Wandering now, I suppose nothing has surprised me more than Los Angeles becoming a place people left. For the first half century of my life, it was, he said in as cornball a way as he could muster, the American dream. Walls closing in? Just drive to the western ocean, you'll be fine. For me, abrasiveness helps, so I have always written in New York.)

Anyway, the early pages disappeared. As did the notion of writing something for my ladies. And least consciously. I don't understand the creative process. Actually, I make more than a concerted effort not to understand it. I don't know what it is or how it works, but I am terrifed that one green morning it will decide to not work anymore, so I have always given it as wide a bypass as possible.

There is a story of Olivier after a particularly remarkable performance of Othello. Maggie Smith, his Desdemona, knocked on his dressing room door as she was on her way out of the theatre and saw him staring at the wall, holding a tumbler of whisky. She told him his work that night was magic. And he said in, I suspect, tears and despair, "I know it was...and I don't know how I did it."

This relates to me in but one way: *The Princess Bride* is the only novel of mine that I really like. And I don't know how I did it. I remember doing the first chapter about how Buttercup became the most beautiful woman in the world. And the second chapter, which is a rather unflattering intro of Prince Humperdinck, the animal killer in his Zoo of Death.

But then I went dry.

The nightmare of all of us who put words on paper. I stormed around the city, wild with ineptitude, because, you see, all these moments had happened in my head—the sword fight on the Cliffs of Insanity, for example, Inigo and his quest for the six-fingered man , for example, Fezzik and his rhymes—but I didn't know how to get to them, had no way to string them together. And I could feel the window of creativity starting to close. We move on, we move on, it's ok, we'll find other stories left to tell.

But I didn't want to tell other stories, don't you see, I wanted to tell *this* one. And I couldn't find a way. I suppose the most desperate I have ever been was when I was twenty-four and done with grad school and done with the Army and about to become a cursed copywriter in some ad agency in Chicago, when I wrote my first novel, *The Temple of Gold*, in three weeks and it was a couple of hundred pages long and I had never written anything more than thirty and I remember thinking, when I was on page 75 or 100 or 150, "I don't know where I am, all I know is I've never been here before." And the book got published and suddenly I was what I always dreamt of but never thought I'd be, a writer.

Then I got the idea that the whole thing was an abridgement of another longer book. That made *The Princess Bride* possible. My book would be an abidgement of an earlier book, written by S. Morgenstern. And Morgenstern's book would be one my father had read to him by his father when he was sick (in the movie it's the grandfather reading it to me), and my father only read me the good parts because he didn't want to bore me.

Which meant I could jump wherever I wanted. I was free. So I did the opening chapter which explains how I got sick and my father started reading to me to pass the time—

—and then I started to fly.

Ross Macdonald, whom I admired greatly but never got to meet, wrote that it was a "joyous and releasing book" and I treasured those words because that was how I felt while I was writing. Since I had no idea where I was, I kept bringing chunks home to my then wife—I ordinarily never show anybody anything until it's done—and asking was it ok? did it make sense? and all she ever said was keep writing, keep writing, and I did.

For the only time, I was happy with what I was doing. You can't know what that means if most of your life you're stuck in your pit, locked forever within your own limitations, unable to tap the wonderful stuff that lurks there in your head but flattens out whenever it comes near paper.

The most startling creative moment of my life happened here. I remember going to my office and Westley was in the Zoo of Death (the Pit of Despair in the movies—budgetary reasons) and he was being tormented by the evil Count Rugen who got his Ph.D. in pain (or would have, but doctorates didn't exist then; this was after education but before educators realized the real money was in diplomas) and Westley is strapped in The Machine and Prince Humperdinck roars down and turns it all the way up and Inigo and Fezzik are on the way to the rescue and the Deathscream begins and they track it and as I was going to work that morning I kind of wondered how I was going to get Westley out of it. I sat at my desk and had coffee and read the papers and fiddled awhile. And then I realized I wasn't going to get him out of it. And I wrote these words: Westley lay dead by The Machine.

I think I must have looked at them for a long time. Westley lay dead by The Machine. You see, he was perfect and beautiful but it hadn't made him conceited and he understood suffering and was no stranger to love, no stranger to pain, and the words were still there.

Westley lay dead by The Machine...

You killed him, I thought. You killed Westley. How could you do such a thing? And I stared at the words and I stared at the words and then I lost it, began to cry , and I was alone, you see, no one could help me get out of where I was and I didn't know where I was, I just knew I had never been there before and I was helpless, and even now more than twenty years after I can still truly feel the shocking heat of my tears, and I pushed away from my desk and made it to the bathroom and ran water on my face and I looked up and there in the mirror this red-faced and wracked person was staring back at me and who in the world were we and how were we going to survive?

I tell you that because I guess I want you to know, because although I don't think it is a good life, writing, not in so far as having relationships with other people, having loves, all that emotional stuff we all long for, or say we long for, still, there are worthwhile times. And if you were to ask me the high point of my creative life I would say there was only the one, and it was that day when Westley and I were joined.

The rest of the book went the way it's supposed to but never does. Hiram Haydn, my editor, loved it, but more than that, I loved it. After it was done I got very sick, was hospitalized, thought I was going to die.

*

Here is how the movie *The Princess Bride* happened.

The Greenlight Guy at Fox liked the book. (Note: these Premiere 100 types Out There have these different titles—Vice President in charge of this, Executive in charge of that, on and on. All salad. In movies, there is but one power, that of being able to greenlight any picture. Each studio has a grand total of one. Understand, most of us alive in the Continental United States can greenlight a picture. A movie can cost five thousand dollars. That is an affordable sum for a lot of us. Five grand to be, at least for a little, a mogul. Now, what kind of picture will you get? You will not have car crashes. You will not enjoy the services of Mr. Schwarzenegger. You had best employ a bunch of amateurs or one-take actors. It may not be what sets hearts aflutter on Saturday Night in Westwood. But, if you can purchase enough film stock, it will be a movie. That's our movie. At each major studio there is a guy who can greenlight any movie, and today, "any movie" can mean up to one hundred million dollars. Well, those other executives at that studio, regardless of their title, they are only oil slicks.)

As I was saying, the Greenlight Guy at Fox liked the book.

I was in.

Problem: He was not remotely sure if it was a movie. So an odd deal was struck. They would buy the book and I would write a screenplay, but they would not buy that unless they decided to make the movie. In other words, we each had half of the pie.

I wrote the screenplay. The GG at Fox liked it but wasn't 100% convinced yet that it was a movie. So he sent me to London to meet with Richard Lester who was just coming off a considerable success with *The Three Musketeers.* Lester, most famous for the Beatles pictures, is a brilliant man, a Philadelphian who lives in England.

We met, he had some suggestions, I did them, he liked what I did, but better than that, the only man of true import in the whole matter, the GG at Fox, liked what I did.

Home and dry.

Problem: the GG at Fox was fired.

Here is what happens when that happens: The old GG is stripped of his epaulets and his ability of get into Morton's on Monday nights and off he goes, rich—he had a deal in place for when this happened—but humiliated.

And the new GG takes the throne with but one rule set firmly writ in stone: nothing his predecessor had in motion must ever get made. Why? Say it gets made. Say it's a hit. Who gets the credit? The old GG. So when the new GG, who can now get into Morton's on Mondays, has to run the gauntlet there, he knows all his peers are sniggering, "That asshole, it wasn't his picture."

Death.

So *The Princess Bride* was buried, conceivably forever.

Of course, I was upset by this, but I was too frantic to give it the weight it deserved. Because, you see, there had been a reaction to my sickness and it was this: I was 42 years old, had zero money in the bank, and a wife and two kids I had to provide for. So I provided. Movies and books and rewrites of books and endless rewrites of movies and it was all honorable work, I wasn't throwing a bag over its head and doing it for Old Glory. I cared. (There are no rules to writing but if there were, caring would be up there. Or, as we intellectuals are fond of saying, you had better give a shit.)

But none of it meant to me what *The Princess Bride* did. And I finally realized that I had let control of it go. Fox had the book. So what if I had the screenplay, they could commission another. They could change anything they wanted. So I did something of which I am genuinely proud. I bought the book back from the studio, with my own money. I think they were suspicious I had a deal or some plan. I didn't. I just didn't want some fuckhead destroying what I had come to realize was the best thing I would ever write.

After a good bit of negotiating, it was again mine. I was the only fuckhead who could destroy it now.

I read recently about the fine Jack Finney novel *Time and Again* which has taken close to twenty years and still hasn't made it to the screen. *The Princess Bride* didn't take that long, but not a lot less either. I didn't keep notes, so this is from memory. Understand, in order for someone to make a movie, you need two things, passion and money. A lot of people, it turned out, loved *The Princess Bride*. I know of at least two different GG's who loved it. Who shook hands with me on the deal. Who wanted to make it more than any other movie.

Who each got fired the weekend before they were going to set things in motion. Believe this: one studio (a small one) *closed* the weekend before they were going to set things in motion. The screenplay began to get a certain reputation —one article listed it among the best that had never been shot.

The truth is, that after a decade and more, I thought it would never happen. Every time there was interest, I kept waiting for the other shoe to come clunking down and it always did. But events had been put in motion a decade before that eventually would be my salvation.

When *Butch Cassidy and the Sundance Kid* was done, I took myself out of the movie business for awhile. (We are back in the late Sixties now.) I wanted to try something I had never done, non-fiction. I got a very silly idea from listening to some very disturbed acquaintances talking of the pluses and minuses of their mental institutions. "The Hatches" was what I decided to write, a magazine-length piece based on the premise that mental institutions might send out brochures as if they were colleges and universities. "Our manic-depressive department is known world wide." I decided to visit them and talk about the entrance requirements, class size, size of student body, quality of food, like that. I realized before I had gone much further that the piece was dead if Menninger's didn't cooperate. I dropped the idea. I have never liked being at anyone's mercy.

I fiddled for awhile, wondering what I could investigate where I knew someone would always talk. And I decided on Broadway. I had been a failed playwright already, had three plays on by the time I was thirty, hated it—it was just too brutal. Unlike a movie or a novel, where there is often a year between when you finish and when the public is allowed in, on Broadway it's immediate—you are often still rewriting as Opening Night comes thundering down. Your scar tissue never gets a chance to heal. Agony.

So I knew a lot about the theatre, had a lot of friends and acquaintances who worked that side of the streeet, had done my graduate work in theatre. Plus, the theatrical world is so filled with envy, hatred, and bile. I knew someone would always tell me what was going on. If the producer or writer wouldn't talk to me, well, I could get to stage managers.

So I wrote a book about Broadway called *The Season*. In the course of a year I went hundreds of times, both in New York and out of town, saw everything at least once. But the show I saw most was a terrific comedy called *Something Different*.

By Carl Reiner.

He was terribly helpful to me and I liked him a lot. When the book was done I sent him a copy. And a few years later when *The Princess Bride* was done, I sent him the novel. And one day he gave it to his eldest son. "Here's something," he said to his boy Robert one day. "I think you'll like this."

Fortunately for all concerned, Carl was right. Rob was years away from being a director at that point. He was starring in the number one TV show of the decade, "All in the Family," created and produced by Norman Lear. Ten years later, Rob was a director and had formed a little company with his friend and producer Andy Scheinman. Reiner had directed *This is Spinal Tap*, had just finished a rough cut of his second movie, *The Sure Thing*. They were sitting around one day wondering what to do next, when Rob remembered the book, talked about it, reread it, got excited.

Eventually we met and the movie happened. But in between there was a lot of frustration because the movie that established him as a commercial director, *Stand By Me*, had yet to happen. But he can be magnificently stubborn and eventually, Norman Lear got us the money. I was grateful then, still am, always will be.

We had our first script reading in a hotel in London. Rob and Andy were there. Cary Elwes and Robin Wright were there, Westley and Buttercup. Chris Sarandon and Chris Guest, the villains, Humperdinck and Count Rugen. Wally Shawn, the evil genius Vizzini. Mandy Patinkin, who played Inigo, was very much there. And sitting by himself, quietly—he always tried to sit quietly—was Andre the Giant who was Fezzik.

Not your ordinary Hadassah group.

Sitting suavely in a corner was *moi*. Two of the major figures of my time in the entertainment business—Elia Kazan and George Roy Hill—both said the same thing to me in interviews: that by the first cast reading, the crucial work was done. If you had gotten the script to work and cast it properly, then you had a chance for something of quality. But if you had not, it didn't matter how skillful the rest of the process was, you were dead in the water.

This probably sounds like madness to the uninitiated, and it should, but it is very much true. The reason it sounds like madness is this: *Premiere Magazine* isn't around when the script is being prepared. *E.T.* isn't around for casting. They are only around during the shooting of a flick, which is the least important part of the making of any movie. Shooting is just the factory putting together the car. (Post production, editing and scoring, is waaaay more important.)

But shooting is all we know—from those awful articles in magazines or on the tube that purport to be on the inside but are only only only bullshit. The movie company knows who is watching and they behave accordingly. Stars do not misbehave when the enemy is about. Directors do not admit their terrors when the enemy is about. Writers, to give us our due, are not even there when the enemy is about. (And when I am forced to be there, and the enemy is about, I lie. "Oh, this is an amazing shoot, it's just been a dream." "I don't know where Dusty (or Barbra or Sly or Eddie or fill in your own blank) gets this bad rap about being hard to work with, he's (she's) been a dream here." So it goes.

Sitting suavely in a corner, wrote he, doubling back, was *moi*. And I was terrified. Not only is that my natural state when I am around actors, this was almost a decade and a half from when I first scaled the Cliffs of Insanity. Most of the people I knew of. The others I had heard read. But there were two who were essentially new to me.

Robin Wright, our Buttercup, was new to everybody, except the faithful watchers of the soap *Santa Barbara*. A California kid of maybe 20, she was neither experienced nor trained. She was being asked to be first a farmgirl, unspoiled and in love, then a princess, regal and emotionally dead, all this, by the way, with an English accent. (It turns out she has a brilliant ear.) It also was important that she be the most beautiful woman in the world, and of course that is all a matter of personal taste. There is no single most beautiful woman. Except looking at Robin that London morning, watching her as she sat there with no makeup, she sure had one hell of a case. We started the reading then and this is what I thought when we were done—

—I thought she was going to be the biggest lady star in the world.

Hasn't happened. I don't know her, have seen her once in five years, we have no friends in common. Still, I think I know why. *She doesn't want it.*

To be a star, yes, you have to have talent, my God, do you ever have to be lucky, but riding alongside is this: desire. One so consuming that you are willing to piss away everything else in life. Stars have no friends, they have business acquaintances and serfs. They can only fake love on screen.

But they get the good table at Spago.

And if that is your heart's desire, and it is a lot of people's heart's desire, get rid of everything personal that might hinder you and good luck. I promise to stare as you go by.

Wright has been in a few movies, and her work is always fine. But I think what she wants is to spend a little time on the occasional job, and to spend a lot of time with her family. She had not been in a big commercial success until *Forrest Gump*. She was almost in one earlier. She was to be the lead opposite Kevin Costner in *Robin Hood*. But she had to drop out because she was having a baby.

I remember, when I read that, thinking this: Barbra Streisand does not get pregnant at such a time....

A. R. Roussimoff was the other new kid on the block that rehearsal morning. Actually, he was not precisely new to any of us, he was just new as an actor because, as Andre the Giant, he was the most famous wrestler in the world. I had become convinced that if there ever was to be a movie, he should be Fezzik, the strongest man. I had become a lunatic Andre fan, would go to the Garden to watch him entertain the masses.

Andre was always still. When he entered a room he would look for a place in a corner and go there. A man with a great and good heart, I suspect he had grown weary of the strange ways humans reacted to him. They either took to him immediately as we all did, or they panicked.

Andre came from France and his voice came from the basement so he was not always a thrill to understand. When Reiner gave him the part, he also gave him a tape with his part recorded on it. Reiner, a wonderful actor, had done the line readings himself. He hoped Andre would take the time to memorize his role. Which in point of fact he had. But his readings that morning, to be honest, had a certain rote quality to them.

After the script was read, Reiner broke some scenes down and had the actors work on them. One such occasion involved Andre and Cary Elwes, rehearsing their talking fight scene. They stood in front of us and went through it very slowly and said the words, and it was cool in the room as Andre began to perspire. We are not talking a little schwitz here. As we watched we were all stunned to see Andre's shirt become, suddenly, sopping. We kept watching. In a few moments more, the shirt was dry. You turn your head away—soaked. It was simply the first physical manifestion of how different giants were from the rest of us. There was never any odor to the perspiring. It just became a part of the day: "Oh, Andre's wet again."

It was a beautiful afternoon when we broke for lunch, and we found a nearby bistro with outside tables. It was perfect except the chairs were far too small for Andre—the width was for normal people, the arms far too close. There was a table inside that had a bench and someone suggested we eat there. Except Andre wouldn't hear of it. So we sat outside and I can still see him pulling the arms of the chair wide apart, managing to squeeze in, then watching the arms all but snapping back into place where they pinioned him for the remainder of the meal. He ate very little. And the utensils were like baby toys, dwarfed by his hands.

After lunch we rehearsed again, and now Andre was working with our Inigo, Mandy Patinkin. They were doing one of their scenes and Mandy was trying to get some information out of Andre and Andre was giving one of his slow, rote memory readings, and Mandy as Inigo tried to get Fezzik to go faster. And Andre gave back one of his slow, rote memory readings. And they went back and tried it again, and again Mandy as Inigo asked Andre as Fezzik to go faster— Andre came back at the same speed as before—

—which was when Mandy went, "Faster Fezzik"—and slapped Andre hard in the face.

I still see Andre's eyes go wide. I don't think he had been slapped outside a ring since he was little. And he looked at Mandy and it was all so sudden and there was a brief pause.

And Andre started speaking faster. He just rose to the occasion and gave it more pace and energy and you could almost see his mind going, "Oh, this is how you do it outside the ring, let's try it for awhile." And in truth, it was the beginning of the happiest period of his life.

It was my happiest movie experience too. I am almost never around the set mainly because it is so boring. Now, the producer Andy Scheinman and I would arrive late morning and stay through dailies. There were the standard tensions caused by weather, budget and ego—all movie sets are plagued by weather, budget and ego—but beyond that, the shoot went wonderfully well. Post production was difficult for the same reason the whole project was difficult, why so many bright and talented men wanted to make it and ultimately failed—just what was the movie? Was it a comedy? Fingers crossed, yes. Action flick? Fingers crossed again. Spoof? I don't do spoofs but a lot of people thought it was. Romance? Believe it.

We were in dangerous terrain—because whenever you mix genres in a movie, that's where you end up. I remember George Hill calling me in despair the night after the first *Butch Cassidy* sneak. Because the audience hadn't liked it? The reverse. They had loved it—they just thought it was so funny. And George was convinced that the balance had to be right, because if it was too funny, the shootout at the end wouldn't be moving. And if it was too dour, the whole beginning third, the fun and games part, would just lie there. So he set out the next morning going through the flick and taking out laughs until he got the balance right.

Reiner fought that same battle, and eventually, as had Hill, won. When we started having sneaks, the audience loved us. The test scores were sensational, among the top results of that year. Fabulous. We were flying. And we should have been.

I was talking once to a famous critic's darling director and he said this: "People talk about movies in three parts, preparing, shooting and post production. That's wrong. There are really only two parts: the making of the movie and the selling of the movie." I'm not sure he wasn't right.

The studio did not know how to sell us. (No criticism intended here. Heartbreak, sure, but everybody was behind the movie.) But what the hell was it? They never figured it out. Our trailer—one of the more crucial selling tools—was so confusing it was pulled from theatres, something I had never heard of before. The ad campaign was changed and changed again. We had nothing to sell us, no stars. The book, successful, was a cult success, no King, no Grisham.

We came out and were a mild hit. A double, to use their terminology. (A home run today is over 100 million in box office gross. Although your children will live to see the day when that's a flop.) Audiences loved us once we got them in. They just didn't see any reason to come. When we came out on cassette, word of mouth had caught up with us and we were the hit we should have been in theatres.

It had been a difficult wait, a decade and a half. I started writing something for my kids when the Seventies started. It's the Nineties now and your kids can see it. When you say that, smile.

Andre died in early '93. I hadn't seen him but once, I think, since the movie was done, but I was terribly upset. I spoke to Rob, Andy, Billy Crystal, all the same. We told Andre stories, made ourselves feel better. We were shocked, you see, but not surprised. Andre, who was turning forty when the movie was made, knew it was coming soon. Here is what I wrote when I heard the news.

REQUIEM FOR A HEAVYWEIGHT

PARIS. Jan. 30 (AP)—The professional wrestler, Andre Rene Roussimoff, a native of France who was known to fans as Andre the Giant, died this week, apparently of a heart attack. He was 46.

He was handsome once. I remember a photo he showed me, taken at a beach with some friends. Dark, good looking kid, maybe seventeen. Big sure—he said he was around six foot eight then and weighed 275—but that was before the disorder really kicked in. Acromegaly. Something goes haywire with the growth hormones. He was working as a furniture mover during the day, taking wrestling lessons at night, sleeping when he could.

At twenty-five, he topped out, but I don't think he ever actually knew his size. I met him in England when he was playing the rhyme-loving Fezzik in *The Princess Bride*. This was in the summer of '86 and Andre's publicity listed him at seven foot five, 550 pounds. Close enough. All he was sure of was that he'd had pneumonia a little while earlier and had lost 100 pounds in three weeks in the hospital.

Gone now at 46, he was the most popular figure on any movie set I've ever been on.

He was very strong. I was talking to an actor who was shooting a movie in Mexico. What you had to know about Andre was that if he asked you to dinner, he paid, but when you asked him, he also paid. This actor, after several free meals, invited Andre to dinner and, late in the meal, snuck into the kitchen to give his credit card to the maitre d'. As he was about to do this, he felt himself being lifted up in the air. The actor, it so happens, was Arnold Schwarzenegger who remembers, "When he had me up in the air, he turned me so I was facing him, and he said, 'I pay.' Then he carried me back to my table where he set me down in my chair like a little boy. Oh yes, Andre was very strong."

When Arnold Schwarzenegger tells me someone is very strong, I'll go along with it.

Andre once invited Schwarzenegger to a wrestling arena in Mexico where he was performing in front of 25,000 screaming fans, and, after he'd pinned his opponent, he gestured for Schwarzenegger to come into the ring.

So through the noise, Schwarzenegger climbs up. Andre says, "Take off your shirt, they are all crazy for you to take off your shirt. I speak Spanish." So Schwarzenegger, embarrassed, does what Andre tells him. Off comes his jacket, his shirt, his undershirt, and he begins striking poses. And then Andre goes to the locker room while Schwarzenegger goes back to his friends.

And it had all been a practical joke. God knows what the crowd was screaming, but it wasn't for Schwarzenegger to strip and pose. "Nobody gave a shit if I took my shirt off or not, but I fell for it. Andre could do that to you."

Andre never knew what reaction he might cause in people. Sometimes children and grown-ups would see him and be terrified. Sometimes children would see him, shriek with glee, and begin clambering all over him as if the greatest toy imaginable had just been given them. And he would sit, immobile, as they roamed around him. Sometimes he'd put a hand out, palm up, and they'd sit there, for what they hoped would be forever.

Andre would never come out and say that wrestling might not be legit. He fought 300 plus times a year for about 20 years, and all he ever admitted was that he didn't like being in the ring with someone he thought might be on drugs. When he was in his prime, men who weighed 250 or 300 pounds would hurl themselves on him from the top rope and he would catch them and not budge.

But even seven years ago his body was beginning to betray him. There is a scene at the end of *The Princess Bride* where Robin Wright jumped out of a castle window, and Andre was to catch her at the bottom.

The shot was set up for Robin to be lifted just above camera range and then dropped into Andre's arms. Maybe a foot. Maybe two. But not much and Robin was never that heavy.

The first take, she was dropped and he caught her—and gasped, suddenly white like paper, and almost fell to his knees. His back was bad. And getting worse, and soon there would be surgery.

Andre once said to Billy Crystal, "We do not live long, the big and the small."

Alas.

CAST LIST

CARY ELWES	WESTLEY
ROBIN WRIGHT	BUTTERCUP
MANDY PATINKIN	INIGO
CHRIS SARANDON	PRINCE HUMPERDINCK
CHRISTOPHER GUEST	COUNT RUGEN
WALLACE SHAWN	VIZZINI
ANDRE THE GIANT	FEZZIK
FRED SAVAGE	THE KID
PETER FALK	THE GRANDFATHER
PETER COOK	IMPRESSIVE CLERGYMAN
CAROL KANE	VALERIE
MEL SMITH	ALBINO
BILLY CRYSTAL	MIRACLE MAX

FADE IN ON

A VIDEO GAME ON A COMPUTER SCREEN.

The game is in progress. As a sick coughing sound is heard

CUT TO

THIS KID

lying in bed, coughing. Pale, one sick cookie. Maybe he's seven or eight or nine. He holds a remote in one hand, presses it, and the video game moves a little bit. Then he's hit by another spasm of coughing, puts the remote down.

His room is monochromatic, greys and blues, mildly high-tech. We're in the present day and this is a middle class house, somewhere in the suburbs.

CUT TO

THE KID'S MOTHER as she enters, goes to him, fluffs his pillows, kisses him, and briefly feels his forehead. She's worried, it doesn't show. During this --

> MOTHER
> You feeling any better?

> THE KID
> A little bit.

> MOTHER
> Guess what.

> THE KID
> What?

> MOTHER
> Your grandfather's here.

> THE KID
> *(not overjoyed)*
> Mom, can't you tell him that I'm sick?

> MOTHER
> You *are* sick, that's why he's here.

> THE KID
> He'll pinch my cheek. I hate that.

> MOTHER
> Maybe he won't.

THE KID shoots her an "I'm sure" look, as we

CUT TO

THE KID'S GRANDFATHER bursting into the room. Kind of rumpled. But the eyes are right. He has a wrapped package tucked under one arm as he immediately goes to The Kid, pinches his cheek.

> **GRANDFATHER**
>
> Hey! How's the sickie? Heh?

THE KID gives his MOTHER an "I told you so" look. THE MOTHER ignores it, beats a retreat.

> **MOTHER**
>
> I think I'll leave you two pals. *(And she is gone. There's an uncomfortable silence, then—)*

> **GRANDFATHER**
>
> I brought you a special present.

> **THE KID**
>
> What is it?

> **GRANDFATHER**
>
> Open it up.

THE KID does. He does his best to smile.

> **THE KID**
>
> A book?

> **GRANDFATHER**
>
> That's right. When I was your age, television was called books. And this is a special book. It was the book my father used to read to me when I was sick, and I used to read it to your father. And today, I'm gonna read it to you.

> **THE KID**
>
> Has it got any sports in it?

CUT TO

THE GRANDFATHER. Suddenly passionate.

> **GRANDFATHER**
>
> Are you kidding? Fencing. Fighting. Torture. Revenge. Giants. Monsters. Chases. Escapes. True love. Miracles.

CUT TO

THE TWO OF THEM as the GRANDFATHER sits in a chair by the bed.

THE KID
(manages a shrug)
It doesn't sound too bad. I'll try and stay awake.

GRANDFATHER
Oh. Well, thank you very much. It's very nice of you. Your vote of confidence is overwhelming. All right. *(Book open now, he begins to read.)* The Princess Bride, by S. Morgenstern. Chapter One. Buttercup was raised on a small farm in the country of Florin.

DISSOLVE TO

The story he's reading about, as the monochromatic look of the bedroom is replaced by the dazzling color of the English countryside.

GRANDFATHER (off-screen)
Her favorite pastimes were riding her horse and tormenting the farm boy that worked there. His name was Westley, but she never called him that. *(To The Kid)* Isn't that a wonderful beginning?

THE KID (off-screen)
(doing his best)
Yeah. It's really good.

GRANDFATHER (off-screen)
(reading)
Nothing gave Buttercup as much pleasure as ordering Westley around.

CUT TO

BUTTERCUP'S FARM. DAY.

BUTTERCUP is standing, holding the reins of her horse, while in the background, WESTLEY, in the stable doorway, looks at her.

BUTTERCUP is in her late teens; doesn't care much about clothes and she hates brushing her long hair, so she isn't as attractive as she might be, but she's still probably the most beautiful woman in the world.

BUTTERCUP
Farm boy. Polish my horse's saddle. I want to see my face shining in it by morning.

> WESTLEY
> *(quietly, watching her)*

As you wish.

WESTLEY is perhaps half a dozen years older than Buttercup. And maybe as handsome as she is beautiful. He gazes at her as she walks away.

> GRANDFATHER (off-screen)

"As you wish" was all he ever said to her.

DISSOLVE TO

WESTLEY, outside, chopping wood. BUTTERCUP drops two large buckets near him.

> BUTTERCUP

Farm Boy. Fill these with water—*(a beat)*—please.

> WESTLEY

As you wish.

She leaves; his eyes stay on her. She stops, turns—he manages to look away as now her eyes stay on him.

> GRANDFATHER (off-screen)

That day, she was amazed to discover that when he was saying, "As you wish," what he meant was, "I love you."

DISSOLVE TO

BUTTERCUP IN THE KITCHEN. DUSK.

WESTLEY enters with an armload of firewood.

> GRANDFATHER (off-screen)

And even more amazing was the day she realized she truly loved him back.

> BUTTERCUP
> *(pointing to a pitcher that she could reach herself)*

Farm Boy, fetch me that pitcher.

He gets it, hands it to her; they are standing very close to each other gazing into each other's eyes.

> WESTLEY

As you wish. *(Now he turns, moves outside.)*

DISSOLVE TO

WESTLEY AND BUTTERCUP, outside his tiny hovel in the red glow of sunset. They are locked in a passionate kiss.

THE KID (off-screen)

—hold it, hold it—

CUT TO

THE KID'S ROOM.

THE KID

What is this? Are you trying to trick me?—Where's the sports?—Is this a kissing book?

GRANDFATHER

—wait, just wait—

THE KID

—well, when does it get good?

GRANDFATHER

Keep your shirt on. Let me read. *(reading again)* Westley had no money for marriage. So he packed his few belongings and left the farm to seek his fortune across the sea.

CUT TO

WESTLEY AND BUTTERCUP.

They stand near the gate to the farm, locked in an embrace.

GRANDFATHER (off-screen)
(reading)

It was a very emotional time for Buttercup—

THE KID (off-screen)
(groaning)

I don't be-leeve this.

BUTTERCUP

I fear I'll never see you again.

WESTLEY

Of course you will.

BUTTERCUP

But what if something happens to you?

> WESTLEY

Hear this now: I will come for you.

> BUTTERCUP

But how can you be sure?

> WESTLEY

This is true love. You think this happens every day?

He smiles at her, she smiles too, throws her arms so tightly around him. They kiss. Then as WESTLEY walks away, BUTTERCUP watches him go.

> GRANDFATHER (off-screen)
> (*reading*)

Westley didn't reach his destination. His ship was attacked by the Dread Pirate Roberts, who never left captives alive. When Buttercup got the news that Westley was murdered—

> THE KID (off-screen)
> (*perking up just a little*)

—murdered by pirates is good—

CUT TO

CLOSE UP: BUTTERCUP, staring out the window of her room.

> GRANDFATHER (off-screen)

She went into her room and shut the door. And for days, she neither slept nor ate.

> BUTTERCUP
> (*no emotion at all in her voice*)

I will never love again.

HOLD ON HER FACE, perfect and perfectly sad.

DISSOLVE TO

FLORIN CASTLE. DAY.

The main courtyard of Florin replete with townspeople, livestock, and a bustling market-place.

> GRANDFATHER (off-screen)
> (*reading*)

Five years later, the main square of Florin City was filled as never before to hear the announcement of the great Prince Humperdinck's bride-to-be.

CUT TO

PRINCE HUMPERDINCK, a man of incredible power and bearing, standing in his royal robes on a castle balcony. Three others standing behind him: an OLD COUPLE with crowns, the aging KING AND QUEEN, and a dark bearded man who seems the Prince's match in strength: this is COUNT RUGEN.

HUMPERDINCK
(raises his hands, starts to speak)
My people...a month from now, our country will have its 500th anniversary. On that sundown, I shall marry a lady who was once a commoner like yourselves—*(pause)*— but perhaps you will not find her common now. Would you like to meet her?

And the answering YESSSS booms like summer thunder.

CUT TO

A giant staircase leading to the CROWD and as a FIGURE just begins to become visible,

CUT TO

THE CROWD, as they see the FIGURE. (We haven't yet.) And if there is such a thing as collective action, then this CROWD, collectively, holds its breath.

CUT TO

THE STAIRCASE, as the figure appears in the archway. It is BUTTERCUP. And she is resplendent.

HUMPERDINCK
My people...the Princess Buttercup!!

She descends the stairs and starts to move amongst the people.

CUT TO

THE CROWD, and they do a very strange thing: with no instruction at all, they suddenly go to their knees. Great waves of people kneeling and—

CUT TO

BUTTERCUP, terribly moved. She stands immobile among her SUBJECTS, blinking back tears. HOLD on her beauty for a moment.

GRANDFATHER (off-screen)
Buttercup's emptiness consumed her. Although the law of the land gave Humperdinck the right to choose his bride, she did not love him.

CUT TO

WOODLANDS

—and BUTTERCUP, *barreling along, controlling her horse easily.*

> **GRANDFATHER** (off-screen)
> Despite Humperdinck's reassurance that she would grow to love him, the only joy she found was in her daily ride.

CUT TO

A WOODED GLEN, CLOSE TO SUNDOWN.

Lovely, quiet, deserted. BUTTERCUP *suddenly reins in.*

> **VOICE**
> A word, my lady?

CUT TO

THREE MEN, *standing close together in the path. Beyond them can be seen the waters of Florin Channel. The* THREE MEN *are not your everyday commuter types. Standing in front is a tiny man with the most angelic face. He is Sicilian and his name is* VIZZINI. *Beside him is a Spaniard, erect and taut as a blade of steel. His name is* INIGO MONTOYA. *Beside him is a giant. His name is* FEZZIK.

> **VIZZINI**
> We are but poor, lost circus performers. Is there a village nearby?

> **BUTTERCUP**
> There is nothing nearby; not for miles.

> **VIZZINI**
> Then there will be no one to hear you scream—

He nods to the giant, FEZZIK, *who merely reaches over, touches a nerve on* BUTTERCUP'S *neck, and the start of a scream is all she manages—unconsciousness comes that fast. As she starts to fall—*

CUT TO

A TINY ISOLATED SPOT AT THE EDGE OF FLORIN CHANNEL.

A sailboat is moored. It's dusk now, shadows are long.

INIGO, *the Spaniard, busies himself getting the boat ready.*

CUT TO

The giant FEZZIK *carries* BUTTERCUP, *unconscious, on board.*

VIZZINI *rips some tiny pieces of fabric from an army jacket and tucks them along the saddle of Buttercup's horse. There is about the entire operation a sense of tremendous skill and precision.*

> INIGO
>
> What is that you're ripping?

> VIZZINI
> *(not stopping or turning)*
> It's fabric from the uniform of an Army officer of Guilder.

> FEZZIK
>
> Who's Guilder?

> VIZZINI
> *(pointing straight out)*
> The country across the sea. The sworn enemy of Florin. *(slaps the horse's rump)* Go!

The horse takes off. They start for the boat.

> VIZZINI
>
> Once the horse reaches the castle, the fabric will make the Prince suspect the Guilderians have abducted his love. When he finds her body dead on the Guilder frontier, his suspicions will be totally confirmed.

> FEZZIK
>
> You never said anything about killing anyone.

VIZZINI *hops onto the boat.*

> VIZZINI
>
> I've hired you to help me start a war. That's a prestigious line of work with a long and glorious tradition.

> FEZZIK
>
> I just don't think it's right, killing an innocent girl.

> VIZZINI
> *(whirling on Fezzik)*
> Am I going mad or did the word "think" escape your lips? You were not hired for your brains, you hippopotamic land mass.

> INIGO
>
> I agree with Fezzik.

CUT TO

CLOSE UP: VIZZINI, *in a fury.*

VIZZINI
(We only thought he was in a fury—now he's really getting mad.)
Oh. The sot has spoken. What happens to her is not truly your con-
cern—I will kill her—*(louder)* And remember this—never forget this—

CUT TO

INIGO AND FEZZIK, *as* VIZZINI *advances on them. Nothing shows on Inigo's face, but* FEZZIK *is panicked by* VIZZINI.

VIZZINI
(to Inigo)
— when I found you, you were so slobbering drunk you couldn't buy
brandy—*(now to Fezzik, who retreats as much as he can while Vizzini
advances.)*—and you—friendless, brainless, helpless, hopeless—Do you
want me to send you back to where you were, unemployed in Greenland?

VIZZINI *glares at him, then turns, leaves them.*

During this, INIGO *has gone close to* FEZZIK *who is very distressed at the insults he's just received. As Inigo casts off:*

INIGO
(softly)
That Vizzini, he can *fuss. (a slight emphasis on the last word)*

FEZZIK
(looking at Inigo)
... fuss ... fuss...*(Suddenly, he's got it again, emphasis on the last word.)* I think
he likes to scream at us.

INIGO
Probably he means no harm.

FEZZIK
He's really very short on charm.

INIGO
(proudly)
Oh, you've a great gift for rhyme.

FEZZIK
Yes, some of the time. *(He starts to smile.)*

                              VIZZINI
                         (whirling on them)
   Enough of that.

As they sail off, we hear their voices as the boat recedes.

                              INIGO
   Fezzik, are there rocks ahead?

                              FEZZIK
   If there are, we'll all be dead.

                              VIZZINI
   No more rhymes now, I mean it.

                              FEZZIK
   Anybody want a peanut?

As VIZZINI screams we

DISSOLVE TO

THE SAILBOAT RACING ACROSS THE DARK WATERS.

INIGO is at the helm, FEZZIK stands near the body of the princess—whose eyelids flutter slightly—or do they? VIZZINI sits motionless. The waves are higher, there are only occasional flashes of moon slanting down between clouds.

                              VIZZINI
                           (to Inigo)
   We'll reach the Cliffs by dawn.

INIGO nods, glances back.

                              VIZZINI
   Why are you doing that?

                              INIGO
   Making sure nobody's following us.

                              VIZZINI
   That would be inconceivable.

                              BUTTERCUP
Despite what you think, you will be caught. And when you are, the Prince will see you all hanged.

VIZZINI turns a cold eye on the PRINCESS.

VIZZINI

Of all the necks on this boat, Highness, the one you should be worrying about is your own.

INIGO keeps staring behind them.

VIZZINI

Stop doing that. We can all relax, it's almost over—

INIGO

You're sure nobody's following us?

VIZZINI

As I told you, it would be absolutely, totally, and in all other ways, inconceivable. No one in Guilder knows what we've done. And no one in Florin could have gotten here so fast. Out of curiosity, why do you ask?

INIGO

No reason. It's only, I just happened to look behind us, and something is there.

VIZZINI

What?

And suddenly the THREE whirl, stare back and as they do—

CUT TO

THE DARKNESS BEHIND THEM. *It's hard to see; the moon is behind clouds now. But the wind whistles. And the waves pound. And suddenly it's all gone ominous.*

CUT TO

INIGO, FEZZIK AND VIZZINI *squinting back, trying desperately to see. At this moment, they are all holding their breaths.*

CUT TO

THE DARKNESS BEHIND THEM. *And there's still nothing to be seen. It's still ominous. Only now it's eerie too.*

Then—

The moon slips through and—

INIGO *was right—something is very much there. A sailboat. Black. With a great billowing sail. Black. It's a good distance behind them, but it's coming like hell, closing the gap.*

CUT TO

INIGO, FEZZIK AND VIZZINI *staring at the other boat.*

                        VIZZINI
            (explaining with as much logic as he can muster)
Probably some local fisherman out for a pleasure cruise at night through
eel-infested waters.

And now as a sound comes from their boat they turn as we—

CUT TO

BUTTERCUP, *diving into the water, starting to swim away.*

CUT TO

THE BOAT, *and* VIZZINI *screaming.*

                        VIZZINI
    Go in, get after her!

                        INIGO
    I don't swim.

                        FEZZIK
            (to the unasked question)
    I only dog paddle.

                        VIZZINI
    Veer left. Left. Left!

CUT TO

BUTTERCUP, *still close to the boat, switching from a crawl to a silent breast stroke. The
wind dies and as it does, something new is heard: a not-too-distant high-pitched shrieking sound.* BUTTERCUP *stops suddenly, treads water.*

CUT TO

THE BOAT.

                        VIZZINI
Do you know what that sound is, Highness? Those are the Shrieking
Eels—if you doubt me, just wait. They always grow louder when they're
about to feed on human flesh.

CUT TO

BUTTERCUP, *treading water, still not far from the boat. The shrieking sounds are getting
louder. And more terrifying.* BUTTERCUP *stays silent.*

CUT TO

THE BOAT.

> **VIZZINI**
> If you swim back now, I promise, no harm will come to you. I doubt you will get such an offer from the Eels.

CUT TO

BUTTERCUP, and she's a gutsy girl. The shrieking sound is louder still, but she doesn't make a sound. Behind her now, something dark and gigantic slithers past.

She's scared, sure, petrified, who wouldn't be, but she makes no reply—

—and now a SHRIEKING EEL has zeroed in on her—

—and now she sees it, a short distance away, circling, starting to close—

—and BUTTERCUP is frozen, trying not to make a movement of any kind—

—and the EEL slithers closer, closer—

— and BUTTERCUP knows it now, there's nothing she can do, it's over, all over—

—and now the EEL opens its mouth wide, and it's never made such a noise, and as its great jaws are about to clamp down—

> **GRANDFATHER** (off-screen)
> She doesn't get eaten by the Eels at this time.

And the second we hear him:

CUT TO

THE SICK KID'S ROOM.

THE KID looks the same, pale and weak, but maybe he's gripping the sheets a little too tightly with his hands.

> **THE KID**
> What?

> **GRANDFATHER**
> The Eel doesn't get her. I'm explaining to you because you looked nervous.

> **THE KID**
> Well, I wasn't nervous.

His GRANDFATHER says nothing, just waits.

THE KID

Well, maybe I was a little bit concerned. But that's not the same thing.

GRANDFATHER

Because I can stop now if you want.

THE KID

No. You could read a little bit more...if you want.

(He grips the sheets again, as the GRANDFATHER picks up the book.)

GRANDFATHER
(reading)

"Do you know what that sound is, Highness?"

CUT TO

VIZZINI. We're back in the boat.

VIZZINI

Those are the Shrieking Eels.

THE KID (off-screen)

We're past that, Grandpa.

CUT TO

THE SICK KID'S ROOM.

THE KID

You read it already.

GRANDFATHER

Oh. Oh my goodness, I did. I'm sorry. Beg your pardon.

CUT TO

BUTTERCUP, treading water.

GRANDFATHER (off-screen)

All right, all right, let's see. Uh, she was in the water, the Eel was coming after her. She was frightened. The Eel started to charge her. And then —

And we're back where we were at the last moment we saw her, BUTTERCUP FROZEN, THE SHRIEKING EEL, jaws wide, about to clamp down as we —

CUT TO

A GIANT ARM, *pounding the Eel unconscious in one move, then easily lifting* BUTTERCUP.

PULL BACK TO REVEAL

The BOAT AND FEZZIK, BUTTERCUP *being deposited on the deck.*

VIZZINI
Put her down. Just put her down.

CUT TO

INIGO, *pointing behind them.*

INIGO
I think he's getting closer.

VIZZINI, *tying* BUTTERCUP'S HANDS.

VIZZINI
He's no concern of ours. Sail on! *(to Buttercup)* I suppose you think you're brave, don't you?

BUTTERCUP
(staring deep at him)
Only compared to some.

DISSOLVE TO

The BOAT AT DAWN, *being followed closely by the black sailboat, which we can see for the first time is being sailed by a* MAN IN BLACK, *and his boat almost seems to be flying.*

INIGO
Look! He's right on top of us. I wonder if he is using the same wind we are using.

VIZZINI
Whoever he is, he's too late—*(pointing ahead of them)*—see? *(big)* The Cliffs of Insanity.

And once he's said the name,

CUT TO

THE CLIFFS OF INSANITY AT DAWN.

They rise straight up, sheer from the water, impossibly high.

CUT TO

The TWO SAILBOATS *in a wild race for the Cliffs and the* MAN IN BLACK *is closing faster than ever, but not fast enough, the lead was too great to overcome, and as* INIGO *sails with great precision straight at the Cliffs —*

CUT TO

THE BOAT *being pursued.*

VIZZINI
Hurry up. Move the thing! Um...that other thing. Move it! *(staring back now)* We're safe—only Fezzik is strong enough to go up our way—he'll have to sail around for hours 'til he finds a harbor.

There is much activity going on, all of it swift, expert, economical. FEZZIK *reaches up along the Cliff face, grabs a jutting rock, reaches behind it. Suddenly there is a thick rope in his hands. He drops back to the boat, gives the rope a freeing swing and*

CUT TO

THE CLIFFS. *The rope goes all the way to the top.*

CUT TO

INIGO *hurrying to* FEZZIK. *He straps a harness to him, then lifts* BUTTERCUP *and* VIZZINI *in the harness. Finally, he himself gets in the harness. All three are strapped to* FEZZIK *like papooses.*

And he starts to ascend the rope, carrying them all along with him as he goes.

CUT TO

The MAN IN BLACK, *sailing in toward the Cliffs of Insanity, watching as* FEZZIK *rises swiftly through the first moments of dawn.*

CUT TO

THE TOP OF THE CLIFFS, LOOKING DOWN.

FEZZIK'S GROUP *is only faintly visible far below. This is the first time we've gotten the real vertigo feeling and it's a gasper.*

CUT TO

FEZZIK CLIMBING ON. BUTTERCUP *is almost out of her mind with fear.*

CUT TO

THE ENTIRE LENGTH OF THE CLIFFS. FEZZIK *is moving right along; however high they are, he's already over a third of the way done.*

CUT TO

The MAN IN BLACK, *leaping from his ship to the rope, starting to climb. He's impossibly far behind, but the way he goes you'd think he didn't know that because he is flying up the rope, hand over hand like lightning.*

CUT TO

VIZZINI AND THE OTHERS.

> **INIGO**
> *(looking down)*
> He's climbing the rope. And he's gaining on us.

> **VIZZINI**
> Inconceivable!

He prods FEZZIK, *who nods, increases his pace.*

CUT TO

The MAN IN BLACK, *roaring up the rope, and*

CUT TO

LONG SHOT—THE CLIFFS

—and the MAN IN BLACK *is cutting deeply into Fezzik's lead.*

CUT TO

VIZZINI AND THE OTHERS.

> **VIZZINI**
> *(shrieking)*
> Faster!

> **FEZZIK**
> I thought I was going faster.

> **VIZZINI**
> You were supposed to be this colossus. You were this great, legendary thing. And yet he gains.

> **FEZZIK**
> Well, I'm carrying three people. And he's got only himself.

> **VIZZINI**
> *(cutting through)*
> — I do not accept excuses. *(shaking his head)* I'm just going to have to find myself a new giant, that's all.

FEZZIK
(hurt)

Don't say that, Vizzini. Please.

And his arms begin moving much more slowly.

CUT TO

The MAN IN BLACK. *His arms still work as before. If anything, he has speeded up. Fezzik's lead is smaller and smaller.*

CUT TO

THE VIEW FROM THE TOP OF THE CLIFFS.

Maybe a hundred feet for FEZZIK *to go. Maybe more.*

CUT TO

VIZZINI AND THE OTHERS, *and it's getting too close now.*

VIZZINI

Did I make it clear that your job is at stake?

CUT TO

The MAN IN BLACK, *less than a hundred feet behind them. And gaining.*

CUT TO

THE CLIFF TOP AS FEZZIK MAKES IT!

VIZZINI *leaps off and takes out a knife, begins to cut the rope which is tied around a great rock while* INIGO *helps the* PRINCESS *to her feet and* FEZZIK *just stands around, waiting for someone to tell him to do something. Nearby are some stone ruins. Once they might have been a fort, now they kind of resemble Stonehenge.*

CUT TO

The MAN IN BLACK, *75 feet from the top now, maybe less—maybe only 50—and his pace is as dazzling as before, and*

CUT TO

VIZZINI, *cutting through the last of the rope and*

CUT TO

THE ROPE, *slithering across the ground and out of sight toward the Channel, like some great serpent at last going home.*

CUT TO

FEZZIK, *standing with* INIGO AND BUTTERCUP *by the cliff edge.*

FEZZIK
(to Inigo—impressed)
He has very good arms.

CUT TO

The MAN IN BLACK, *hanging suspended hundreds of feet in the air, holding to the jagged rocks, desperately trying to cling to life.*

CUT TO

VIZZINI, *stunned, turning to the* OTHERS, *looking down.*

VIZZINI
He didn't fall? Inconceivable!!

INIGO
(whirling on Vizzini)
You keep using that word—I do not think it means what you think it means. *(looks down again)* My God! He's climbing.

CUT TO

The MAN IN BLACK, *and so he is. Verrrry slowly, he is picking his way upwards, sometimes a foot at a time, sometimes an inch.*

CUT TO

The GROUP AT THE TOP, *staring down.*

VIZZINI
Whoever he is, he's obviously seen us with the Princess, and must therefore die. *(to Fezzik)* You, carry her. *(to Inigo)* We'll head straight for the Guilder frontier. Catch up when he's dead. If he falls, fine. If not, the sword.

INIGO *nods.*

INIGO
I want to duel him left-handed.

VIZZINI
You know what a hurry we're in.

> INIGO

Well, it's the only way I can be satisfied. If I use my right—tch—over too quickly.

> VIZZINI
> *(turns abruptly, starts off-screen)*

Oh, have it your way.

CUT TO

The MAN IN BLACK, *still creeping his way upward.*

CUT TO

FEZZIK, *who goes to* INIGO.

> FEZZIK

You be careful. *(Gravely)*—people in masks cannot be trusted.

> VIZZINI
> *(calling out)*

I'm waiting!

FEZZIK *nods, hurries after Vizzini.*

CUT TO

INIGO. *He watches them depart, then turns, peers down over the Cliffs. He watches a moment, then paces, shaking his hands loose. He practices a few of his honed fencing skills. He is a taut and nervous fellow, and has never been one for waiting around.*

CUT TO

The MAN IN BLACK, *climbing on. He must be six inches closer to the top than when last we saw him.* INIGO IS WATCHING.

CUT TO

INIGO, *walking away. Finally he goes back to cliff edge, starts to talk. It's instant death if the* MAN IN BLACK *falls, but neither gives that possibility much credence. This is our two heroes meeting. They don't know it yet; but that's what it is.*

> INIGO
> *(hollering down)*

Hello there.

The MAN IN BLACK *glances up, kind of grunts.*

                              INIGO

Slow going?

                         MAN IN BLACK

Look, I don't mean to be rude, but this is not as easy as it looks. So I'd
appreciate it if you wouldn't distract me.

                              INIGO

Sorry.

                         MAN IN BLACK

Thank you.

*INIGO steps away, draws his sword, loosens up with a few perfect thrusts. Then resheathes
and looks eagerly over the edge again.*

                              INIGO

I do not suppose you could speed things up?

                         MAN IN BLACK
                          (with some heat)

If you're in such a hurry, you could lower a rope, or a tree branch, or find
something useful to do.

                              INIGO

I could do that. In fact, I've got some rope up here. But I do not think
that you will accept my help, since I am only waiting around to kill you.

                         MAN IN BLACK

That does put a damper on our relationship. *(He finds another hold a few
inches higher.)*

                              INIGO

But I promise I will not kill you until you reach the top.

                         MAN IN BLACK

That's very comforting. But I'm afraid you'll just have to wait.

                              INIGO

I hate waiting. I could give you my word as a Spaniard.

                         MAN IN BLACK

No good. I've known too many Spaniards.

And he just hangs there in space, resting, gathering his strength.

                              INIGO

You don't know any way you'll trust me?

> **MAN IN BLACK**
>
> Nothing comes to mind.

And on these words, CAMERA ZOOMS *into a* CLOSE UP *of* INIGO. *He raises his right hand high, his eyes blaze, and his voice takes on a tone we have not heard before.*

> **INIGO**
>
> I swear on the soul of my father, Domingo Montoya, you will reach the top alive.

CUT TO

The MAN IN BLACK. *There is a pause. Then, quietly:*

> **MAN IN BLACK**
>
> Throw me the rope.

CUT TO

INIGO. *He dashes to the giant rock the rope was originally tied to.*

CUT TO

The MAN IN BLACK *as his grip loosens a moment, trying to cling to the side of the cliff.*

CUT TO

INIGO, *now with a small coil of rope, hurries back to the edge and hurls it over—*

CUT TO

THE ROPE. *It hangs close to the* MAN IN BLACK. *He releases the rocks, grabs the rope, hangs helplessly in space a moment, then looks up at* INIGO *and—*

CUT TO

INIGO, *straining, forcing his body away from the cliff edge and—*

CUT TO

The MAN IN BLACK *rising through the early morning light, slowly, steadily, and as the cliff top at last comes within reach—*

CUT TO

INIGO, *watching as the* MAN IN BLACK *crawls to safety, then looks to* INIGO.

> **MAN IN BLACK**
>
> Thank you. *(pulling his sword)*

INIGO

We'll wait until you're ready.

MAN IN BLACK

Again. Thank you.

The MAN IN BLACK *sits to rest on the boulder that once held the rope. He tugs off his leather boots and is amazed to see several large rocks tumble out. The* MAN IN BLACK *wears gloves.* INIGO *stares at them.*

INIGO

I do not mean to pry, but you don't by any chance happen to have six fingers on your right hand?

He glances up—the question clearly baffles him.

MAN IN BLACK

Do you always begin conversations this way?

INIGO

My father was slaughtered by a six-fingered man. He was a great sword-maker, my father. And when the six-fingered man appeared and requested a special sword, my father took the job. He slaved a year before he was done.

He hands his sword to the MAN IN BLACK.

MAN IN BLACK
(fondling it—impressed)

I have never seen its equal.

CUT TO

CLOSE UP: INIGO. *Even now, this still brings pain.*

INIGO

The six-fingered man returned and demanded it, but at one-tenth his promised price. My father refused. Without a word, the six-fingered man slashed him through the heart. I loved my father, so, naturally, challenged his murderer to a duel...I failed...the six-fingered man did leave me alive with the six-fingered sword, but he gave me these. *(He touches his scars.)*

CUT TO

The MAN IN BLACK, *looking up at* INIGO.

MAN IN BLACK

How old were you?

> INIGO

I was eleven years old. When I was strong enough, I dedicated my life to the study of fencing. So the next time we meet, I will not fail. I will go up to the six-fingered man and say, "Hello, my name is Inigo Montoya. You killed my father. Prepare to die."

> MAN IN BLACK

You've done nothing but study swordplay?

> INIGO

More pursuit than study lately. You see, I cannot find him. It's been twenty years now. I am starting to lose confidence. I just work for Vizzini to pay the bills. There's not a lot of money in revenge.

> MAN IN BLACK
> *(handing back the great sword, starting to rise)*

Well, I certainly hope you find him, someday.

> INIGO

You are ready, then?

> MAN IN BLACK

Whether I am or not, you've been more than fair.

> INIGO

You seem a decent fellow. I hate to kill you.

> MAN IN BLACK
> *(walking away a few paces, unsheathing his sword)*

You seem a decent fellow. I hate to die.

> INIGO

Begin!

And on that word—

CUT TO

THE TWO OF THEM. *And what we are starting now is one of the two greatest swordfights in modern movies (the other one happens later on), and right from the beginning it looks different.*

Because they aren't close to each other—none of the swords-crossing "en garde" garbage. No. What we have here is two men, two athletes, and they look to be too far away to damage each other, but each time one makes even the tiniest feint, the other counters, and there is silence, and as they start to circle—

CUT TO

THE SIX-FINGERED SWORD, *feinting here, feinting there and—*

CUT TO

The TWO MEN, *finished teasing, begin to duel in earnest.*

Their swords cross, then again, again, and the sound comes so fast it's almost continual. INIGO *presses on, the* MAN IN BLACK *retreating up a rocky incline.*

> INIGO
> *(thrilled)*
> You're using Bonetti's defense against me, ah?

> MAN IN BLACK
> I thought it fitting, considering the rocky terrain—

> INIGO
> Naturally, you must expect me to attack with Capo Ferro—

And he shifts his style now.

> MAN IN BLACK
> *(coping as best he can)*
> —naturally—*(suddenly shifting again)*—but I find Thibault cancels out Capo Ferro, don't you?

The MAN IN BLACK *is now perched at the edge of the elevated castle ruin. No where to go, he jumps to the sand.* INIGO *stares down at him.*

> INIGO
> Unless the enemy has studied his Agrippa—

And now, with the grace of an Olympian, INIGO *flies off the perch, somersaults clean over the* MAN IN BLACK'S *head, and lands facing his opponent.*

> INIGO
> —which I have.

The TWO MEN *are almost flying across the rocky terrain, never losing balance, never coming close to stumbling; the battle rages with incredible finesse, first one and then the other gaining the advantage, and by now, it's clear that this isn't just two athletes going at it, it's a lot more that that. This is two legendary swashbucklers and they're in their prime, it's Burt Lancaster in* The Crimson Pirate *battling Errol Flynn in* Robin Hood *and then, incredibly, the action begins going even faster than before as we*

CUT TO

INIGO. And behind him now, drawing closer all the time, is the deadly edge of the Cliffs of Insanity. INIGO fights and ducks and feints and slashes and it all works, but not for long, as gradually the MAN IN BLACK keeps the advantage, keeps forcing INIGO back, closer and closer to death.

>   **INIGO**
>   *(happy as a clam)*
> You are wonderful!

>   **MAN IN BLACK**
> Thank you—I've worked hard to become so.

The Cliff edge is very close now. INIGO is continually being forced toward it.

>   **INIGO**
> I admit it—you are better than I am.

>   **MAN IN BLACK**
> Then why are you smiling?

Inches from defeat, INIGO is, in fact, all smiles.

>   **INIGO**
> Because I know something you don't know.

>   **MAN IN BLACK**
> And what is that?

>   **INIGO**
> I am not left-handed.

And he throws the six-fingered sword into his right hand and immediately, the tide of battle turns.

CUT TO

The MAN IN BLACK, stunned, doing everything he can to keep INIGO by the Cliff edge. But no use. Slowly at first, he begins to retreat. Now faster. INIGO is in control and the MAN IN BLACK is desperate.

CUT TO

INIGO. And the six-fingered sword is all but invisible now, as he increases his attack, then suddenly switches styles again.

CUT TO

A ROCKY STAIRCASE leading to a turret-shaped plateau, and the MAN IN BLACK is retreating like mad up the steps and he can't stop INIGO—nothing can stop INIGO—and in a frenzy the MAN IN BLACK makes every feint, tries every thrust, lets go with all he has left. But he fails. Everything fails. He tries one or two final desperate moves but they are nothing.

> **MAN IN BLACK**
> You're amazing!

> **INIGO**
> I ought to be after twenty years.

And now the MAN IN BLACK is smashed into a stone pillar, pinned there under the six-fingered sword.

> **MAN IN BLACK**
> *(hollering it out)*
> There's something I ought to tell you.

> **INIGO**
> Tell me.

> **MAN IN BLACK**
> I am not left-handed either.

And now he changes hands, and at last, the battle is fully joined.

CUT TO

INIGO. *And to his amazement, he is being forced back down the steps. He tries one style, another, but it all comes down to the same thing—the MAN IN BLACK seems to be in control. And before INIGO knows it, the six-fingered sword is knocked clear out of his hand.*

INIGO *retreats, dives from the stairs to a moss-covered bar suspended over the archway. He swings out, lands, and scrambles to his sword and we*

CUT TO

The MAN IN BLACK who watches INIGO, then casually tosses his sword to the landing where it sticks in perfectly. Then the MAN IN BLACK copies INIGO. Not copies exactly, improves. He dives to the bar, swings completely over it like a circus performer and dismounts with a 9.7 backflip.

CUT TO

INIGO, *staring in awe.*

INIGO

Who are you?!

MAN IN BLACK

No one of consequence.

INIGO

I must know.

MAN IN BLACK

Get used to disappointment.

INIGO

Okay.

CUT TO

INIGO, *moving like lightning, and he thrusts forward, slashes, darts back, all in almost a single movement and—*

CUT TO

The MAN IN BLACK. *Dodging, blocking, and again he thrusts forward, faster even than before, and again he slashes but—*

CUT TO

INIGO. *And there is never a move anyone makes he doesn't remember, and this time he blocks the slash, slashes out himself with the six-fingered sword.*

On it goes, back and forth across the rocky terrain, INIGO'S *feet moving with the grace and speed of a great improvisational dancer.*

CUT TO

THE SIX-FINGERED SWORD *as it is knocked free, arching up into the air, and—*

CUT TO

INIGO *catching it again. And something terrible is written behind his eyes: he has given his all, done everything man can do, tried every style, made every maneuver, but it wasn't enough, and on his face for all to see is the realization that he,* INIGO MONTOYA *of Spain, is going to lose.*

CUT TO

The MAN IN BLACK, *moving in for the end now, blocking everything, muzzling everything and*

CUT TO

THE SIX-FINGERED SWORD, sent flying from INIGO'S grip. He stands helpless only a moment. Then he drops to his knees, bows his head, shuts his eyes.

INIGO

Kill me quickly.

MAN IN BLACK

I would as soon destroy a stained glass window as an artist like yourself. However, since I can't have you following me either—

And he clunks Inigo's head with his heavy sword handle. INIGO pitches forward unconscious.

MAN IN BLACK

Please understand, I hold you in the highest respect.

He grabs his scabbard and takes off after the Princess and we

CUT TO

CLOSE UP: VIZZINI.

VIZZINI

Inconceivable!

PULL BACK TO REVEAL

VIZZINI, staring down from a narrow mountain path, as far below the MAN IN BLACK can be seen running. FEZZIK, carrying the PRINCESS, stands alongside. It's a little later in the morning.

VIZZINI

Give her to me. *(grabs Buttercup starts off)* Catch up with us quickly.

FEZZIK
(starting to panic)

What do I do?

VIZZINI

Finish him, finish him. Your way.

FEZZIK

Oh, good, my way. Thank you, Vizzini. *(little pause)* Which way is my way?

CUT TO

A COUPLE OF ROCKS.

Nothing gigantic. Vizzini points to them. There is a large boulder nearby.

VIZZINI

Pick up one of those rocks, get behind the boulder, and in a few minutes, the Man in Black will come running around the bend. The minute his head is in view, hit it with the rock!

As Vizzini and Buttercup hurry away.

FEZZIK
(little frown; softly)
My way's not very sportsmanlike.

He grabs one of the rocks and plods behind the boulder and we—

DISSOLVE TO

The Man in Black, racing up the mountain trail. Ahead is a bend in the trail. He sees it, slows. Then he stops, listening.

Satisfied by the silence, he starts forward again and as he rounds the bend—a rock flies INTO FRAME, shattering on a boulder inches in front of him.

CUT TO

Fezzik. He moves into the mountain path. He has picked up another rock and holds it lightly.

FEZZIK

I did that on purpose. I don't have to miss.

MAN IN BLACK

I believe you—So what happens now?

FEZZIK

We face each other as God intended. Sportsmanlike. No tricks, no weapons, skill against skill alone.

MAN IN BLACK

You mean, you'll put down your rock and I'll put down my sword, and we'll try to kill each other like civilized people?

FEZZIK
(gently)
I could kill you now.

He gets set to throw, but the Man in Black shakes his head, takes off his sword and scabbard, begins the approach toward the Giant.

MAN IN BLACK

Frankly, I think the odds are slightly in your favor at hand fighting.

FEZZIK

It's not my fault being the biggest and the strongest. I don't even exercise.

He flips the rock away.

CUT TO

THE MOUNTAIN PATH AND THE TWO MEN. The MAN IN BLACK is not now and has never been a shrimp. But it's like he wasn't even there, FEZZIK towers over him so much.

There is a moment's pause, and then the MAN IN BLACK dives at FEZZIK'S chest, slams him several tremendous blows in the stomach, twists his arm severely, slips skillfully into a beautifully applied bear hug, and in general makes any number of terrific wrestling moves.

FEZZIK just stands there, kind of taking in the scenery. Finally the MAN IN BLACK pushes himself away, stares up at the GIANT.

MAN IN BLACK

Look, are you just fiddling around with me or what?

FEZZIK

I just want you to feel you're doing well. I hate for people to die embarrassed.

They get set to begin again. Then suddenly—

CUT TO

FEZZIK, as he jumps forward with stunning speed for anyone his size and reaches for the MAN IN BLACK who drops to his knees, spins loose, and slips between the GIANT'S legs.

FEZZIK

You're quick.

MAN IN BLACK

And a good thing too.

FEZZIK
(getting set for another onslaught)

Why do you wear a mask? Were you burned by acid, or something like that?

MAN IN BLACK
Oh no. It's just that they're terribly comfortable. I think everyone will be wearing them in the future.

FEZZIK considers this a moment, then attacks, and if he moved quickly last time, this time he is blinding and as the MAN IN BLACK slips down to avoid the charge, FEZZIK moves right with him, only instead of twisting free and jumping to his feet, this time the MAN IN BLACK jumps for FEZZIK'S back and in a moment he is riding him, and his arms have FEZZIK'S throat, locked across FEZZIK'S windpipe, one in front, one behind. The MAN IN BLACK begins to squeeze. Tighter.

FEZZIK
(standing, talking as he does so)
I just figured out why you give me so much trouble.

CUT TO

FEZZIK, as he charges toward a huge rock that lines the path, and just as he reaches it he spins his giant body so that the entire weight of the charge is taken by the MAN IN BLACK.

CUT TO

The MAN IN BLACK. And the power of the charge is terrible, the pain enormous, but he clings to his grip at FEZZIK'S windpipe.

MAN IN BLACK
(his arms never leave Fezzik's throat)
Why is that, do you think?

FEZZIK
(his voice just beginning to get a little strained)
Well, I haven't fought just one person for so long. I've been specializing in groups. Battling gangs for local charities, that kind of thing.

CUT TO

ANOTHER HUGE ROCK ON THE OTHER SIDE OF THE PATH. Again FEZZIK charges, slower this time, but still a charge, and again he spins and creams the MAN IN BLACK against the rough boulder.

CUT TO

The MAN IN BLACK. And the punishment is terrible, and for a moment it seems as if he is going to let go of Fezzik's windpipe and crumble, but he doesn't, he holds on.

MAN IN BLACK
Why should that make such a difference?

FEZZIK

Well...(*And now his voice is definitely growing weaker.*)...you see, you use different moves when you're fighting half a dozen people than when you only have to be worried about one.

Again FEZZIK *slams the* MAN IN BLACK *against a boulder, only this time his power has diminished and* FEZZIK *starts to slowly collapse.*

CUT TO

FEZZIK. *And there isn't much breath coming.*

CUT TO

The MAN IN BLACK, *holding his grip as* FEZZIK *tries to stand, halfway makes it, but there is no air. Back to his knees he falls, holds there for a moment, and pitches down to all fours. The* MAN IN BLACK *increases the pressure.* FEZZIK *tries to crawl. But there is just no air. No air.* FEZZIK *goes to earth and lies still.*

CUT TO

FEZZIK, *as the* MAN IN BLACK *turns him over, puts his ear to Fezzik's heart. It beats. The* MAN IN BLACK *stands.*

MAN IN BLACK

I don't envy you the headache you will have when you awake. But, in the meantime, rest well...and dream of large women.

And he nimbly scoops up his sword with his foot, catches it and as he dashes off up along the mountain path—

CUT TO

PRINCE HUMPERDINCK, *as he slips his boot into a footprint in the sand.*

COUNT RUGEN *mounted, watches. Behind him, half a dozen armed* WARRIORS, *also mounted. A* GREAT WHITE HORSE *waits riderless in front.* HUMPERDINCK *is all over the rocky ground, and maybe he isn't the best hunter in the world. Then again, maybe he is. Because, as he begins to put his feet into strange positions, we realize that what he is doing is miming the fencers.*

HUMPERDINCK

There was a mighty duel—it ranged all over. They were both masters.

RUGEN

Who won? How did it end?

HUMPERDINCK
(*looking down in the position where Inigo fell unconscious*)
The loser ran off alone. (*points in the direction Vizzini and Fezzik took*) The winner followed those footprints toward Guilder!

RUGEN
Shall we track them both?

HUMPERDINCK
The loser is nothing.— Only the Princess matters—(*to the armed warriors*)— clearly this was all planned by warriors of Guilder. We must be ready for whatever lies ahead.

RUGEN
Could this be a trap?

HUMPERDINCK
(*vaulting onto his horse*)
I always think everything could be a trap—Which is why I'm still alive.

And he gallops off—

CUT TO

The MAN IN BLACK, *cresting the peak of the mountain.*

CUT TO

CLOSE-UP ON *a knife pointed at a throat—*PULL BACK TO REVEAL VIZZINI *munching on an apple, holding the knife to* BUTTERCUP'S THROAT. *She is blindfolded.*

A PICNIC SPREAD *is laid out. A tablecloth, two goblets and between them, a small leather wine container. And some cheese and a couple of apples. The picnic is set on a lovely spot, high on the edge of a mountain path with a view all the way back to the sea.*

The MAN IN BLACK *comes running around the path, sees* VIZZINI, *slows. The* TWO MEN *study each other. Then—*

VIZZINI
So, it is down to you. And it is down to me.

The MAN IN BLACK *nods and comes nearer—*

VIZZINI
If you wish her dead, by all means keep moving forward.

And he pushes his long knife harder against Buttercup's unprotected throat.

> MAN IN BLACK

Let me explain—

> VIZZINI

—there's nothing to explain. You're trying to kidnap what I've rightfully stolen.

> MAN IN BLACK

Perhaps an arrangement can be reached.

> VIZZINI

There will be no arrangement—*(deliberate)—and you're killing her!*

CUT TO

BUTTERCUP'S THROAT, *as* VIZZINI *jabs with his long knife.* BUTTERCUP *gasps against the pain.*

CUT TO

The MAN IN BLACK, *stopping fast.*

> MAN IN BLACK

But if there can be no arrangement, then we are at an impasse.

> VIZZINI

I'm afraid so—I can't compete with you physically. And you're no match for my brains.

> MAN IN BLACK

You're that smart?

> VIZZINI

Let me put it this way: have you ever heard of Plato, Aristotle, Socrates?

> MAN IN BLACK

Yes.

> VIZZINI

Morons.

> MAN IN BLACK

Really? In that case, I challenge you to a battle of wits.

> VIZZINI

For the Princess?

The MAN IN BLACK *nods.*

VIZZINI

To the death?

Another nod.

VIZZINI

I accept.

MAN IN BLACK

Good. Then pour the wine.

As VIZZINI fills the goblets with the dark red liquid, the MAN IN BLACK pulls a small packet from his clothing, handing it to VIZZINI.

MAN IN BLACK

Inhale this, but do not touch.

VIZZINI
(doing it)

I smell nothing.

MAN IN BLACK
(taking the packet back)

What you do not smell is called iocane powder. It is odorless, tasteless, dissolves instantly in liquid, and is among the more deadlier poisons known to man.

VIZZINI

Hmm.

CUT TO

VIZZINI, watching excitedly as the MAN IN BLACK takes the goblets, turns his back. A moment later, he turns again, faces VIZZINI, drops the iocane packet. It is now empty.

The MAN IN BLACK rotates the goblets in a little shell game maneuver then puts one glass in front of VIZZINI, the other in front of himself.

MAN IN BLACK

All right: where is the poison? The battle of wits has begun. It ends when you decide and we both drink, and find out who is right and who is dead.

VIZZINI

But it's so simple. All I have to do is divine from what I know of you. Are you the sort of man who would put the poison into his own goblet, or his enemy's?

He studies the MAN IN BLACK now.

VIZZINI

Now, a clever man would put the poison into his own goblet, because he would know that only a great fool would reach for what he was given. I'm not a great fool, so I can clearly not choose the wine in front of you. But you must have known I was not a great fool; you would have counted on it, so I can clearly not choose the wine in front of me.

MAN IN BLACK
(And now there's a trace of nervousness beginning.)
You've made your decision then7

VIZZINI

Not remotely. Because iocane comes from Australia, as everyone knows. And Australia is entirely peopled with criminals. And criminals are used to having people not trust them, as you are not trusted by me. So I can clearly not choose the wine in front of you.

MAN IN BLACK
Truly, you have a dizzying intellect.

VIZZINI
Wait till I get going! Where was I?

MAN IN BLACK
Australia.

VIZZINI

Yes—Australia, and you must have suspected I would have known the powder's origin, so I can clearly not choose the wine in front of me.

MAN IN BLACK
(very nervous)
You're just stalling now.

VIZZINI
(cackling)
You'd like to think that, wouldn't you? *(stares at the Man in Black)* You've beaten my giant, which means you're exceptionally strong. So, you could have put the poison in your own goblet, trusting on your strength to save you. So I can clearly not choose the wine in front of you. But, you've also bested my Spaniard which means you must have studied. And in studying, you must have learned that man is mortal so you would have put the poison as far from yourself as possible, so I can clearly not choose the wine in front of me.

As VIZZINI's pleasure has been growing throughout, the MAN IN BLACK's has been fast disappearing.

MAN IN BLACK

You're trying to trick me into giving away something—it won't work—

VIZZINI
(*triumphant*)

It has worked—you've given everything away—I know where the poison is.

MAN IN BLACK
(*fool's courage*)

Then make your choice.

VIZZINI

I will. And I choose—

And suddenly he stops, points at something behind the MAN IN BLACK.

VIZZINI

— what in the world can that be?

CUT TO

The MAN IN BLACK, *turning around, looking.*

MAN IN BLACK

What? Where? I don't see anything.

CUT TO

VIZZINI, *busily switching the goblets while the* MAN IN BLACK *has his head turned.*

VIZZINI

Oh, well, I—I could have sworn I saw something. No matter.

The MAN IN BLACK *turns to face him again.* VIZZINI *starts to laugh.*

MAN IN BLACK

What's so funny?

VIZZINI

I'll tell you in a minute. First, let's drink—me from my glass, and you from yours.

And he picks up his goblet. The MAN IN BLACK *picks up the one in front of him. As they both start to drink,* VIZZINI *hesitates a moment.*

Then, allowing the MAN IN BLACK *to drink first, he swallows his wine.*

MAN IN BLACK

You guessed wrong.

VIZZINI
(roaring with laughter)
You only think I guessed wrong—*(louder now)*—that's what's so funny! I switched glasses when your back was turned. You fool.

CUT TO

The MAN IN BLACK. There's nothing he can say. He just sits there.

CUT TO

VIZZINI, watching him.

VIZZINI
You fell victim to one of the classic blunders. The most famous is "Never get involved in a land war in Asia." But only slightly less well known is this: "Never go in against a Sicilian when death is on the line."

He laughs and roars and cackles and whoops and is in all ways quite cheery until he falls over dead.

CUT TO

The MAN IN BLACK, stepping past the corpse, taking the blindfold and bindings off BUTTERCUP, who notices VIZZINI lying dead.

The MAN IN BLACK pulls her to her feet.

BUTTERCUP

Who are you?

MAN IN BLACK
I am no one to be trifled with, that is all you ever need know.

He starts to lead her off the mountain path into untraveled terrain.

BUTTERCUP
(a final glance back toward Vizzini)
To think—all that time it was your cup that was poisoned.

MAN IN BLACK
They were both poisoned. I spent the last few years building up an immunity to iocane powder.

And with that, he takes off, dragging her behind him.

CUT TO

A MOUNTAIN PATH.

It's where Fezzik fought the Man in Black. CAMERA PULLS BACK TO REVEAL *the* PRINCE, *kneeling, inspecting every grain of misplaced sand. The* OTHERS *wait behind him.*

> **HUMPERDINCK**
>
> Someone has beaten a giant! *(roaring)* There will be great suffering in Guilder if she dies.

He leaps onto his horse and they charge off.

CUT TO

A WILD STRETCH OF TERRAIN.

The MAN IN BLACK *comes running into view, still dragging* BUTTERCUP, *who sometimes stumbles, but he keeps forcing her along. Finally, when she is close to exhaustion, he lets go of her.*

> **MAN IN BLACK**
> *(his voice harsh now, carrying the promise of violence)*
> Catch your breath.

> **BUTTERCUP**
> If you'll release me...whatever you ask for ransom...you'll get it, I promise you...

> **MAN IN BLACK**
> And what is that worth, the promise of a woman? You're very funny, Highness.

> **BUTTERCUP**
> I was giving you a chance. No matter where you take me...there's no greater hunter than Prince Humperdinck. He could track a falcon on a cloudy day. He can find you.

> **MAN IN BLACK**
> You think your dearest love will save you?

> **BUTTERCUP**
> I never said he was my dearest love. And yes, he will save me. That I know.

> **MAN IN BLACK**
> You admit to me you do not love your fiance?

BUTTERCUP

He knows I do not love him.

MAN IN BLACK

"Are not capable of love" is what you mean.

BUTTERCUP

I have loved more deeply than a killer like yourself could ever dream.

And the MAN IN BLACK *cocks back a fist.* BUTTERCUP *flinches, but does not retreat.*

MAN IN BLACK

That was a warning, Highness. The next time, my hand flies on its own. For where I come from, there are penalties when a woman lies.

CUT TO

VIZZINI'S BODY. *The picnic is spread as before.*

CAMERA PULLS BACK TO REVEAL *the* PRINCE *kneeling by the body as the* OTHERS *ride up. The* PRINCE *grabs the empty poison packet, hands it to* RUGEN, *after first sniffing it himself.*

HUMPERDINCK

Iocane. I'd bet my life on it. *(gestures to the trail ahead)* And there are the Princess's footprints. She is alive...or was, an hour ago. If she is otherwise when I find her, I shall be very put out.

And as he vaults onto his horse and they all charge off—

CUT TO

BUTTERCUP, *being spun* INTO CAMERA VIEW, *falling heavily as the* MAN IN BLACK *releases her. We are at the edge of an almost sheer ravine. The drop is sharp and severe. Below, the ravine floor is flat, but getting there would not be half the fun.*

MAN IN BLACK

Rest, Highness.

BUTTERCUP
(stares at him)

I know who you are—your cruelty reveals everything.

The MAN IN BLACK *says nothing.*

BUTTERCUP

You're the Dread Pirate Roberts; admit it.

> MAN IN BLACK

With pride. What can I do for you?

> BUTTERCUP

You can die slowly cut into a thousand pieces.

> MAN IN BLACK

Hardly complimentary, Your Highness. Why loose your venom on me?

CLOSE-UP: BUTTERCUP, *quietly now.*

> BUTTERCUP

You killed my love.

CUT TO

The MAN IN BLACK, *watching her closely.*

> MAN IN BLACK

It's possible; I kill a lot of people. Who was this love of yours? Another Prince, like this one, ugly, rich, and scabby?

> BUTTERCUP

No. A farm boy. Poor. Poor and perfect, with eyes like the sea after a storm.

CUT TO

BUTTERCUP. *And probably, if she did not hate* ROBERTS *so, there would be tears.*

> BUTTERCUP

On the high seas, your ship attacked, and the Dread Pirate Roberts never takes prisoners.

> MAN IN BLACK
> (*explaining as a teacher might*)

I can't afford to make exceptions. Once word leaks out that a pirate has gone soft, people begin to disobey you, and then it's nothing but work, work, work, all the time.

> BUTTERCUP

You mock my pain.

> MAN IN BLACK

Life is pain, Highness. Anyone who says differently is selling something. I remember this farm boy of yours, I think. This would be, what, five years ago?

BUTTERCUP *nods.*

MAN IN BLACK

Does it bother you to hear?

BUTTERCUP

Nothing you can say will upset me.

MAN IN BLACK

He died well, that should please you. No bribe attempts or blubbering. He simply said, "Please. Please, I need to live." It was the "please" that caught my memory. I asked him what was so important for him. "True love," he replied. And then he spoke of a girl of surpassing beauty and faithfulness. I can only assume he meant you. You should bless me for destroying him before he found out what you really are.

BUTTERCUP

And what am I?

MAN IN BLACK

Faithfulness he talked of, madam. Your enduring faithfulness. Now, tell me truly. When you found out he was gone, did you get engaged to your prince that same hour, or did you wait a whole week out of respect for the dead?

BUTTERCUP

You mocked me once, never do it again—*I died that day!*

The MAN IN BLACK is about to reply as they stand there on the edge of the sheer ravine. But then something catches his attention and as he stares at it briefly,

CUT TO

HIS P.O.V.: The dust cloud caused by HUMPERDINCK'S HORSES is rising up into the sky.

CUT TO

BUTTERCUP, and while his attention is on the dust cloud, rising high, she pushes him with all the strength she has.

BUTTERCUP

You can die too, for all I care!!

CUT TO

The MAN IN BLACK, teetering on the ravine edge, for a moment, then he begins to fall. Down goes the MAN IN BLACK. Down, down, rolling, spinning, crashing always down toward the flat rock floor of the ravine.

CUT TO

BUTTERCUP, *staring transfixed at what she has wrought.*

There is a long pause. She stands there, alone, as from far below the words come to her, drifting on the wind—

MAN IN BLACK
...as...you...wish...

BUTTERCUP
Oh, my sweet Westley; what have I done?

And without a second thought or consideration of the dangers, she starts into the ravine. A moment later, she too is falling, spinning and twisting, crashing and torn, cartwheeling down toward what is left of her beloved.

CUT TO

THE DUST CLOUD, *rising.*

PULL BACK TO REVEAL

PRINCE HUMPERDINCK AND THE OTHERS *reining in at the spot where* Buttercup *promised ransom in exchange for her freedom. The* PRINCE *shakes his head.*

HUMPERDINCK
Disappeared. He must have seen us closing in, which might account for his panicking in error. Unless I'm wrong, and I am never wrong, they are headed dead into the fire swamp.

CUT TO

COUNT RUGEN. *The mere mention of the Fire Swamp makes him pale.*

CUT TO

THE RAVINE FLOOR.

TWO BODIES *lie a few feet apart, not moving. It is, of course,* BUTTERCUP AND WESTLEY. *They might be corpses. After a time,* WESTLEY *slowly forces his body into motion and as he does,*

CUT TO

BUTTERCUP, *bruised and torn, as* WESTLEY *crawls slowly toward her.*

WESTLEY
Can you move at all?

BUTTERCUP
(weakly stretching out an arm toward him)
Move? You're alive. If you want, I can fly.

WESTLEY
I told you, "I would always come for you." Why didn't you wait for me?

BUTTERCUP
Well...you were dead.

WESTLEY
Death cannot stop true love. All it can do is delay it for a while.

BUTTERCUP
I will never doubt again.

WESTLEY
There will never be a need.

And now, they begin to kiss; it's a tender kiss, tender and loving and gentle and—

THE KID (off-screen)
Oh no. No, please.

CUT TO

THE KID'S BEDROOM

GRANDFATHER
What is it? What's the matter?

THE KID
They're kissing again, do we have to hear the kissing part?

GRANDFATHER
Someday, you may not mind so much.

THE KID
Skip on to the Fire Swamp—that sounded good.

GRANDFATHER
Oh. You're sick, I'll humor you. *(He picks up the book again.)* So now, where were we here? Yeah, yeah, yeah. Ah. Oh. Okay. Westley and Buttercup raced along the ravine floor.

CUT TO

WESTLEY AND BUTTERCUP racing along the ravine floor. Westley glances up.

CUT TO

HUMPERDINCK *and his men perched on top of the cliff, looking down at* WESTLEY AND BUTTERCUP.

CUT TO

WESTLEY.

> **WESTLEY**
> Ha. Your pig fiance is too late. A few more steps and we'll be safe in the Fire Swamp.

CUT TO

BUTTERCUP, *and* WESTLEY *has tried to say it with Chevalier-like nonchalance, but she ain't buying.*

> **BUTTERCUP**
> We'll never survive.

> **WESTLEY**
> Nonsense—you're only saying that because no one ever has.

As they race off leaving HUMPERDINCK *and his men stranded, defeated—*

CUT TO

THE FIRE SWAMP.

And it really doesn't look any worse than any other moist, sulphurous, infernal horror you might run across. Great trees block the sun.

CUT TO

WESTLEY AND BUTTERCUP. BUTTERCUP *is clearly panicked and maybe* WESTLEY *is too, but he moves jauntily along, sword in hand.*

> **WESTLEY**
> It's not that bad. I'm not saying I'd like to build a summer home here, but the trees are actually quite lovely.

THE GIANT TREES, *thick and black-green, look ominous as hell and they shield all but intermittent stripes of sun.*

A GIANT SPURT OF FLAME *leaps up, preceded by a slight popping sound, and this particular spurt of flame misses* WESTLEY, *but* BUTTERCUP *is suddenly on fire; at least the lower half of her is and—*

CUT TO

WESTLEY, instantly forcing BUTTERCUP to sit, gathering her flaming hem in his hands, doing his best to suffocate the fire. This isn't all that easy and it causes him a bit of grief, but he does his best to sound as jaunty as before.

> WESTLEY
>
> Well now, that was an adventure.

He examines where the flames burst over her.

> WESTLEY
>
> Singed a bit, were you?

> BUTTERCUP
> *(She wasn't and she shakes her head "no.")*
>
> You?

He was, and he shakes his head "no." As he pulls her to her feet—

CUT TO

THE SWAMP FLOOR

—and as there's another popping sound,

CUT TO

WESTLEY grabbing BUTTERCUP, pulling her aside to safety as another great spurt of flame suddenly shoots up.

> WESTLEY
>
> Well, one thing I will say. The Fire Swamp certainly does keep you on your toes.

BUTTERCUP is frozen with fear. He takes her hand, gently leads her forward as we—

CUT TO

THE TWO OF THEM moving slowly along through a particularly dangerous part of the Fire Swamp.

It's later now, the sun slants down at a slightly different angle.

> WESTLEY
> *(happily)*
>
> This will all soon be but a happy memory because Roberts' ship "Revenge" is anchored at the far end. And I, as you know, am Roberts.

BUTTERCUP

But how is that possible, since he's been marauding twenty years and you only left me five years ago?

WESTLEY

I myself am often surprised at life's little quirks.

There is again a popping sound, then a huge spurt of flame. WESTLEY simply picks up BUTTERCUP as they walk along, moves her out of danger, puts her back down, goes right on talking without missing a beat.

WESTLEY

You see, what I told you before about saying "please" was true. It intrigued Roberts, as did my descriptions of your beauty.

CUT TO

SOME HIDEOUS VINES—they look like they could be flesh eating. WESTLEY takes his sword, slices a path for them to follow. The vines groan as they fall. He's been chatting away the entire time.

WESTLEY

Finally, Roberts decided something. He said, "All right, Westley, I've never had a valet. You can try it for tonight. I'll most likely kill you in the morning." Three years he said that. "Good night, Westley. Good work. Sleep well. I'll most likely kill you in the morning." It was a fine time for me. I was learning to fence, to fight, anything anyone would teach me. And Roberts and I eventually became friends. And then it happened.

BUTTERCUP

What?—go on—

WESTLEY picks her up, carrying her across some swampwater that is bridged by a narrow, rickety tree branch.

WESTLEY

Well, Roberts had grown so rich, he wanted to retire. So he took me to his cabin and told me his secret. "I am not the Dread Pirate Roberts," he said. "My name is Ryan. I inherited this ship from the previous Dread Pirate Roberts, just as you will inherit it from me. The man I inherited it from was not the real Dread Pirate Roberts, either. His name was Cummerbund. The real Roberts has been retired fifteen years and living like a king in Patagonia." Then he explained the name was the important thing for inspiring the necessary fear. You see, no one would surrender to the Dread Pirate Westley.

THE TWO OF THEM have by now crossed the pond.

WESTLEY

So we sailed ashore, took on an entirely new crew and he stayed aboard for awhile as first mate, all the time calling me Roberts. Once the crew believed, he left the ship and I have been Roberts ever since. Except, now that we're together, I shall retire and hand the name over to someone else. Is everything clear to you?

BUTTERCUP, *perplexed, is about to reply but the ground she steps on gives way—it's Lightning Sand—a great patch of it, and it has her—a cloud of powder rises and she sinks into the stuff crying Westley's name but then she is gone as we—*

CUT TO

WESTLEY *whirling, slashing at a U-shaped vine, hacks it in half—it's still connected to the tree. Then he grabs it, drops his sword, and, clutching the other end of the vine, he dives into the* LIGHTNING SAND *and there is another cloud of white powder, but it settles quickly.*

Now nothing can be seen. Nothing at all. Just the lightning sand, lovely and lethal.

HOLD ON THE LIGHTNING SAND—THEN—

An odd panting sound is heard now. The panting sound is suddenly very loud. And then a giant R.O.U.S. darts into view. The R.O.U.S.—a Rodent of Unusual Size—is probably no more than eighty pounds of bone and power. It sniffs around a bit then, as quickly as it has come, it goes.

CUT TO

THE LIGHTNING SAND, *as* WESTLEY, *lungs long past the bursting point, explodes out; he has* BUTTERCUP *across his shoulders and as he pulls to the edge of the lightning sand pit, using the vine—*

CUT TO

CLOSE UP—BUTTERCUP. *Her face is caked with the white powder. It is in her eyes, her ears, hair, mouth. She's still probably beautiful, but you have to look awfully hard to see it. As* WESTLEY *continues to pull them to safety—*

CUT TO

The R.O.U.S., high above them; it watches—

CUT TO

BUTTERCUP, *placed against a tree.* WESTLEY *is cleaning the lightning sand from her face. He hesitates, glances around and*

CUT TO

The R.O.U.S. on a much lower branch now. It stares down at WESTLEY.

WESTLEY *stares back up at the beast.* BUTTERCUP *is oblivious. Her eyes flutter. He continues to work on her as—*

BUTTERCUP
We'll never succeed—we may as well die here.

WESTLEY
No. No. We have already succeeded. (*He glances back again.*)

NOW THERE ARE TWO R.O.U.S.'S. *They have climbed into a nearby tree, stare hungrily down.*

CUT TO

WESTLEY, *picking her up. He puts an arm around her, starts to walk with her as he encouragingly goes on talking.*

WESTLEY
I mean, what are the three terrors of the Fire Swamp? One, the flame spurts. No problem. There's a popping sound preceding each, we can avoid that. Two, the Lightning Sand. But you were clever enough to discover what that looks like, so in the future we can avoid that too.

BUTTERCUP
Westley, what about the R.O.U.S.'s?

WESTLEY
Rodents of Unusual Size? I don't think they exist...

And as he says that, a R.O.U.S. comes flying at him from off-screen.

CUT TO

BUTTERCUP, *screaming and—*

WESTLEY, *pinned under the attacking R.O.U.S., trying to fend it off. Can't. The thing's teeth sink deep into his arm. He howls.*

WESTLEY *drives a fist into the beast's face, rolling it off. He reaches for his sword just a few feet away, but the R.O.U.S. is back atop him. It's a fierce battle, and just when we think Westley can't possibly win, he flips the ugly rodent clear.*

WESTLEY *scrambles for his sword. The R.O.U.S. stampedes on, changing its target, heading right for—*

BUTTERCUP, *and she's scared to death and—*

BUTTERCUP

Westley!

WESTLEY abandons his sword, reaching for the rodent, grabbing only a tail, wrestling with it. BUTTERCUP grabs a small branch, and using it as a club, beats the skull of the thing, doing pretty well, but the beast manages to snag her hem with its razor teeth, and she's pulled to the ground, and

CUT TO

WESTLEY, jumping onto its back, and the R.O.U.S. is all over him now, sinking needle teeth into Westley's shoulder.

CUT TO

WESTLEY, with death close at hand, as a popping sound start. He tries one desperate move, rolls into the sound—

CUT TO

A FLAME SPURT shooting skyward and—

CUT TO

WESTLEY, with the R.O.U.S. pinned under him, and as the beast bursts into flame, it lets go and WESTLEY rolls safely free, grabs his sword and exhaustedly stabs the R.O.U.S., which is trying to put itself out.

The R.O.U.S. collapses dead. WESTLEY stands motionless, exhausted. The danger has passed.

CUT TO

BUTTERCUP, relieved.

DISSOLVE TO

THE FAR EDGE OF THE FIRE SWAMP.

Beyond, a beach.

CUT TO

BUTTERCUP AND WESTLEY.

BUTTERCUP
(almost in disbelief)

We did it.

WESTLEY

Now, was that so terrible? *(And from somewhere they summon strength, pick up their pace, and as they reach the edge of the Fire Swamp—)*

CUT TO

Something we hadn't expected: HUMPERDINCK *on his horse,* RUGEN *beside him.* THREE WARRIORS, *armed and ready, are mounted in formation behind.* BUTTERCUP AND WESTLEY *are at the edge of the Fire Swamp, about to leave it. They stop.* BUTTERCUP *looks beyond exhaustion.* WESTLEY *looks worse.*

HUMPERDINCK

Surrender!

It's dusk. Behind Humperdinck are the waters of the bay.

CUT TO

WESTLEY AND BUTTERCUP, *staring out at the* OTHERS.

WESTLEY

You mean you wish to surrender to me? Very well, I accept.

HUMPERDINCK

I give you full marks for bravery—don't make yourself a fool.

WESTLEY

Ah, but how will you capture us? We know the secrets of the Fire Swamp. We can live there quite happily for some time. So, whenever you feel like dying, feel free to visit.

HUMPERDINCK

I tell you once again—surrender!

WESTLEY

It will not happen!

CUT TO

BUTTERCUP, *looking from one to the other; then something else catches her eye and we—*

CUT TO

AN ARMED WARRIOR, *in shadow, with a loaded crossbow aimed at* WESTLEY'S *heart.*

CUT TO

BUTTERCUP, *looking the other way—*

CUT TO

ANOTHER WARRIOR, crossbow aimed at WESTLEY.

> **HUMPERDINCK**
> *(roaring)*

For the last time—*SURRENDER!*

> **WESTLEY**
> *(roaring right back, bigger)*

DEATH FIRST!!

CUT TO

BUTTERCUP, frantically staring around, and now

CUT TO

A THIRD WARRIOR, crossbow stretched, ready to shoot; this one is hidden in a tree blocking any escape Westley might try.

> **BUTTERCUP**

Will you promise not to hurt him?

CUT TO

HUMPERDINCK, whirling to face her.

> **HUMPERDINCK**

What was that?

CUT TO

WESTLEY, whirling to face her.

> **WESTLEY**

What was that?

CUT TO

BUTTERCUP, talking to them both.

> **BUTTERCUP**

If we surrender, and I return with you, will you promise not to hurt this man?

> **HUMPERDINCK**
> *(right hand high)*

May I live a thousand years and never hunt again.

BUTTERCUP
(looks at Westley)

He is a sailor on the pirate ship "Revenge." Promise to return him to his ship.

HUMPERDINCK

I swear it will be done.

CUT TO

BUTTERCUP AND WESTLEY, *staring deep into each other's eyes.*

CUT TO

HUMPERDINCK AND RUGEN.

HUMPERDINCK

Once we're out of sight, take him back to Florin and throw him in the Pit of Despair.

RUGEN
(almost a smile)

I swear it will be done.

CUT TO

BUTTERCUP AND WESTLEY.

BUTTERCUP

I thought you were dead once, and it almost destroyed me. I could not bear it if you died again, not when I could save you.

WESTLEY *is dazed. Silent.*

BUTTERCUP *tries to speak again, can't and is swooped off her feet onto Humperdinck's horse, and off they go.*

CUT TO

WESTLEY, *staring after her.* RUGEN *watches as his* WARRIORS *bring* WESTLEY *to him.* THE COUNT *has a heavy sword and he holds it in his hand.*

RUGEN

Come, sir. We must get you to your ship.

WESTLEY

We are men of action. Lies do not become us.

RUGEN

Well spoken, sir—

WESTLEY is looking at him.

RUGEN

—what is it?

WESTLEY

You have six fingers on your right hand—someone was looking for you—

COUNT RUGEN clubs WESTLEY hard across the skull. WESTLEY starts to fall—the screen goes black.

FADE IN ON

THE PIT OF DESPAIR,

Dank and chill, underground and windowless, lit by flickering torches. Frightening. WESTLEY lies in the center of the cage, chained and helpless.

CUT TO

SOMETHING REALLY FRIGHTENING: *A BLOODLESS-LOOKING ALBINO. Dead pale, he silently enters the pit, carrying a tray of food and medication. He puts it down.*

WESTLEY

Where am I?

ALBINO
(He only whispers.)

The Pit of Despair.

He begins tending Westley's wounds. WESTLEY winces.

ALBINO

Don't even think—*(A hack, sputter, cough—now his voice seems normal again.)*—don't even think about trying to escape. The chains are far too thick. And don't dream of being rescued either. The only way in is secret. And only the Prince, the Count, and I know how to get in and out.

WESTLEY

Then I'm here till I die?

ALBINO
(working away)

Till they kill you. Yeah.

                              WESTLEY
Then why bother curing me?

                              ALBINO
The Prince and the Count always insist on everyone being healthy before
they're broken.

                              WESTLEY
So it's to be torture.

From the ALBINO: a nod.

                              WESTLEY
I can cope with torture.

From the ALBINO: a shake of the head.

                              WESTLEY
You don't believe me?

                              ALBINO
You survived the Fire Swamp. You must be very brave...*(little pause)*...but
nobody withstands The Machine.

He studies WESTLEY whose face is almost sad.

CUT TO

*BUTTERCUP, and her face is sad. Pallid, perhaps ill. She wanders down a corridor in
Florin Castle. As she moves unseeing past an intersecting corridor:*

CUT TO

PRINCE HUMPERDINCK AND COUNT RUGEN, watching her.

                              HUMPERDINCK
She's been like that ever since the Fire Swamp. *(looks at Rugen)* It's my
father's failing health that's upsetting her.

                              RUGEN
Of course.

As they move on,

CUT TO

FLORIN CASTLE AT NIGHT.

CAMERA HOLDS ON IT while we hear the GRANDFATHER'S voice reading.

GRANDFATHER (off-screen)

The King died that very night, and before the following dawn, Buttercup and Humperdinck were married.

CUT TO

MAIN SQUARE OF FLORIN CASTLE.

And if we thought it was packed before, we didn't know how many more could fit in this courtyard. HUMPERDINCK, RUGEN and the QUEEN stand high on the balcony.

GRANDFATHER (off-screen)

And at noon, she met her subjects again. This time as their Queen.

HUMPERDINCK

My father's final words were...

THE KID (off-screen)

— hold it. Hold it, Grandpa.

And the scene FREEZES, HUMPERDINCK caught in mid-sentence.

CUT TO

THE KID'S ROOM.

THE KID is half sitting now, not strong yet, but clearly stronger than when we first saw him.

THE KID

You read that wrong. She doesn't marry Humperdinck, she marries Westley. I'm just sure of it. After all that Westley did for her, if she does not marry him, it wouldn't be fair.

GRANDFATHER

Well, who says life is fair? Where is that written? Life isn't always fair.

THE KID

I'm telling you you're messing up the story, now get it right!

GRANDFATHER

Do you want me to go on with this?

THE KID

Yes.

GRANDFATHER

All right, then. No more interruptions. *(starts to read again)*...at noon, she met her subjects again. This time as their Queen.

And on these words,

CUT TO

PRINCE HUMPERDINCK.

> **HUMPERDINCK**
> My father's final words were "love her as I loved her, and there will be joy." I present to you your Queen. Queen Buttercup.

And on his words,

CUT TO

THE CROWD, *and it's gigantic.*

CUT TO

THE ARCHWAY *we saw before, as* BUTTERCUP *emerges.*

CUT TO

THE CROWD, *suddenly going to its knees, wave after wave of silent* KNEELING PEOPLE. *All of them down.*

CUT TO

BUTTERCUP, *touched as before, but then she seems stunned as we*

CUT TO

THE CROWD. SOMEONE *is* BOOING! *The* BOOING *gets louder as an* ANCIENT WOMAN *approaches* BUTTERCUP *through the crowd,* BOOING *every step of the way.*

> **BUTTERCUP**
> Why do you do this?

> **ANCIENT BOOER**
> Because you had love in your hands, and you gave it up.

> **BUTTERCUP**
> *(distraught)*
> But they would have killed Westley if I hadn't done it.

> **ANCIENT BOOER**
> Your true love lives and you marry another—*(to the crowd)*—True love saved her in the Fire Swamp, and she treated it like garbage. And that's what she is, the Queen of Refuse! So, bow down to her if you want. Bow to her. Bow to the Queen of Slime, the Queen of Filth, the Queen of Putrescence. Boo! Boo! Rubbish! Filth! Slime! Muck! Boo! Boo!

She advances on BUTTERCUP *now, who is more and more panicked.*

CLOSE-UP: THE ANCIENT BOOER. *Louder and louder and LOUDER she shrieks vituperation at* BUTTERCUP, *reaching out her old hands toward Buttercup's throat, and* BUTTERCUP *is as frightened now as Dorothy was when the Witch went after her in* The Wizard of Oz, *and suddenly,*

CUT TO

BUTTERCUP, *coming out of her nightmare, alone in her castle bedroom., as she frantically grabs a robe and starts to run.*

> GRANDFATHER (off-screen)
> *(still reading)*
It was ten days till the wedding. The King still lived, but Buttercup's nightmares were growing steadily worse.

> THE KID (off-screen)
See?—Didn't I tell you she'd never marry that rotten Humperdinck?

> GRANDFATHER (off-screen)
— yes, you're very smart. Shut—Up.

CUT TO

BUTTERCUP, *bursting into the Prince's chambers.* COUNT RUGEN *stands nearby.*

> BUTTERCUP
It comes to this: I love Westley. I always have. I know now I always will. If you tell me I must marry you in ten days, please believe I will be dead by morning.

CUT TO

PRINCE HUMPERDINCK. *Just stunned. Finally, softly, he begins to talk.*

> HUMPERDINCK
I could never cause you grief; consider our wedding off. *(to Rugen)* You returned this Westley to his ship?

> RUGEN
Yes.

> HUMPERDINCK
Then we will simply alert him. *(to Buttercup now)* Beloved, are you certain he still wants you? After all, it was you who did the leaving in the Fire Swamp. Not to mention that pirates are not known to be men of their words.

BUTTERCUP

My Westley will always come for me.

HUMPERDINCK

I suggest a deal. You write four copies of a letter. I'll send my four fastest ships. One in each direction. The Dread Pirate Roberts is always close to Florin this time of year. We'll run up the white flag and deliver your message. If Westley wants you, bless you both. If not...please consider me as an alternative to suicide. Are we agreed?

And she nods—

CUT TO

A VERY THICK GROVE OF TREES.

The trees are unusual in one respect: all of them are extraordinarily heavily knotted.

PULL BACK TO REVEAL

HUMPERDINCK AND RUGEN, *walking into the grove of trees.*

RUGEN

Your Princess is really a winning creature. A trifle simple, perhaps, but her appeal is undeniable.

HUMPERDINCK

Oh, I know. The people are quite taken with her. It's odd, but when I hired Vizzini to have her murdered on our engagement day, I thought that was clever. But it's going to be so much more moving when I strangle her on our wedding night. Once Guilder is blamed, the nation will be truly outraged. They'll demand we go to war.

They are deeper into the grove now. RUGEN is searching around.

RUGEN

Now, where is that secret knot? It's impossible to find. *(Finding the knot on the tree he hits it, and it opens, revealing a staircase leading underground.)* Are you coming down into the Pit? Westley's got his strength back. I am starting him on The Machine tonight.

HUMPERDINCK

Tyrone, you know how much I love watching you work. But, I've got my country's five hundredth anniversary to plan, my wedding to arrange, my wife to murder, and Guilder to frame for it. I'm swamped.

RUGEN

Get some rest—if you haven't got your health, you haven't got anything.

UGEN smiles and hurries down the stairs as.the tree slides back perfectly into place.

UT TO

AN ENORMOUS THING. We can't tell quite what it is or what it does, but somehow it is unsettling.

PULL BACK TO REVEAL

COUNT RUGEN, dragging WESTLEY up alongside the thing. Levers and wheels and wires, you name it, it's there.

RUGEN

Beautiful, isn't it? *(The Albino starts attaching suction cups to Westley.)* It took me half a lifetime to invent it. I'm sure you've discovered my deep and abiding interest in pain. At present I'm writing the definitive work on the subject. So I want you to be totally honest with me on how The Machine makes you feel.

CUT TO

A DIAL with numbers ranging from a low of "1" to a high of "50." RUGEN goes to it.

RUGEN

This being our first try, I'll use the lowest setting.

And he turns the dial to "1."

CUT TO

WESTLEY. He has suction cups on his head now, on his temple, on his heart, his hands and feet. He says nothing, keeps control of himself.

CUT TO

COUNT RUGEN, fiddling with his Machine a moment more. And then he opens the flood gate, water pours down the chute, turning the wheel, which in turn really gets The Machine going.

CUT TO

WESTLEY, and he's lying on the table, and he's only flesh and the chains are metal and thick, but such is his desperation it almost seems he might break them. A terrible sound comes from his throat, an incessant gasping. It keeps on coming as we finally

CUT TO

COUNT RUGEN. *He switches off The Machine, picks up a large notebook and pen, sits in a chair. The* NOISE *of The Machine subsides.* RUGEN *opens the book to a blank page.*

> **RUGEN**
> As you know, the concept of the suction pump is centuries old. Well, really, that's all this is. Except that instead of sucking water, I'm sucking life. I've just sucked one year of your life away. I might one day go as high as five, but I really don't know what that would do to you. So, let's just start with what we have. What did this do to you? Tell me. And remember, this is for posterity, so be honest—how do you feel?

AND NOW, AT LAST,

CUT TO

WESTLEY, *in anguish so deep it is dizzying. Helpless, he cries.*

COUNT RUGEN *watches the tears, then starts to write.*

> **RUGEN**
> Interesting.

CUT TO

HUMPERDINCK *in his quarters, swamped. Piles of papers are strewn all over. Now* YELLIN, *a pale, shifty, quick-eyed man appears in the doorway.*

> **HUMPERDINCK**
> Yellin.

> **YELLIN**
> *(bows, then kneels)*
> Sire.

> **HUMPERDINCK**
> As Chief Enforcer of all Florin, I trust you with this secret: killers from Guilder are infiltrating the Thieves' Forest and plan to murder my bride on our wedding night.

> **YELLIN**
> My spy network has heard no such news.

CUT TO

BUTTERCUP *entering.*

BUTTERCUP

Any word from Westley?

CUT TO

THE PRINCE AND YELLIN, *turning to her in the doorway.*

HUMPERDINCK

Too soon, my angel. Patience.

BUTTERCUP

He will come for me.

HUMPERDINCK

Of course.

As she glides out,

HUMPERDINCK

She will not be murdered. On the day of the wedding, I want the Thieves' Forest emptied and every inhabitant arrested.

YELLIN

Many of the thieves will resist. My regular enforcers will be inadequate.

HUMPERDINCK

Form a Brute Squad then. I want the Thieves' Forest emptied before I wed.

YELLIN

It won't be easy, Sire.

HUMPERDINCK
(alone, exhausted)

Try ruling the world sometime.

CUT TO

THE THIEVES' FOREST, DAY.

A lot of hollering is going on. The THIEVES *are being rounded up by the* BRUTE SQUAD, *a large group of large men.* YELLIN *stands on a wagon in the midst of all the scuffling.*

GRANDFATHER (off-screen)

The day of the wedding arrived. The Brute Squad had their hands full carrying out Humperdinck's orders.

> YELLIN
> *(to an unpleasant-looking assistant)*

Is everybody out?

> ASSISTANT BRUTE

Almost. There's a Spaniard giving us some trouble.

> YELLIN

Well, you give him some trouble. Move!

And his wagon starts, and as it does,

CUT TO

INIGO, drunk as a skunk, sprawled in front of a hovel, a bottle of brandy in one hand, the six-fingered sword in the other. He looks dreadful: unshaven, puffy-eyed, gaunt. But the way he brandishes the great sword in front of him would give anyone cause for worry.

> INIGO

I am waiting for you, Vizzini. You told me to go back to the beginning. So I have. This is where I am, and this is where I'll stay. I will not be moved.

He takes a long pull from his brandy bottle. He stops as the ASSISTANT BRUTE comes into view.

> ASSISTANT BRUTE

Ho there.

> INIGO

I do not budge. Keep your "Ho there." *(He waves his sword dangerously.)*

> ASSISTANT BRUTE

But the Prince gave orders—

> INIGO

— So did Vizzini—when a job went wrong, you went back to the beginning. And this is where we got the job. So it's the beginning, and I'm staying till Vizzini comes.

> ASSISTANT BRUTE
> *(gesturing off-screen)*

You! Brute! Come here.

> INIGO

—I—am—waiting—for—Vizzini—

> VOICE (off-screen)

You surely are a meanie.

NIGO feels a hand on his back. A huge hand. He compares it to his own smaller hand.

> FEZZIK

Hello.

> INIGO

It's you.

> FEZZIK

True!

And as the ASSISTANT BRUTE is just about to club Inigo's brains out, FEZZIK lets fly with a stupendous punch.

The ASSISTANT BRUTE takes the full force of the blow right in the chops. It's like he was shot from a cannon as he careens backwards out of sight across the street.

There is a pause. Then a crunching sound, as he clearly has come in contact with something hard and immobile.

FEZZIK puts INIGO down.

> FEZZIK

You don't look so good. *(after Inigo blasts air in protest)* You don't smell so good either.

> INIGO

Perhaps not. I feel fine.

> FEZZIK

Yeah?

And so FEZZIK puts INIGO down. That's when INIGO faints, and as he does,

CUT TO

AN EMPTY ALEHOUSE IN THE THIEVES' QUARTER.

INIGO sits slumped in a chair, while FEZZIK spoons him some stew.

> GRANDFATHER (off-screen)

Fezzik and Inigo were reunited. And as Fezzik nursed his inebriated friend back to health, he told Inigo of Vizzini's death and the existence of Count Rugen, the six-fingered man. Considering Inigo's lifelong search, he handled the news surprisingly well.

And he faints again into his stew.

CUT TO

TWO LARGE TUBS, one filled with steaming water, the other with water clearly of an icy nature. Without a word, FEZZIK stuffs INIGO'S HEAD into the icy water, then, after a reasonable amount of time, pulls him out, ducks him into the steaming stuff, and, a short time after that, puts him back in the cold again, then back in the hot—

> **GRANDFATHER** (off-screen)
> Fezzik took great care in reviving Inigo.

> **INIGO**
> *(up and going)*
> That's enough. That's enough! Where is this Rugen so I may kill him?

> **FEZZIK**
> He's with the Prince in the Castle. But the castle gate is guarded by thirty men.

> **INIGO**
> How many could you handle?

> **FEZZIK**
> I don't think more than ten.

> **INIGO**
> *(doing the math on his fingers)*
> That leaves twenty for me. At my best, I could never defeat that many. *(He sinks sadly down.)* I need Vizzini to plan. I have no gift for strategy.

> **FEZZIK**
> But Vizzini's dead.

CUT TO

THE TWO OF THEM. Silent and bereft. Then a wild look hits INIGO.

> **INIGO**
> No—not Vizzini—I need the Man in Black—

> **FEZZIK**
> — what?—

> **INIGO**
> —look, he bested you with strength, your greatness. He. bested me with steel. He must have out-thought Vizzini, and a man who can do that can plan my castle's onslaught any day. Let's go—

FEZZIK

—where?

INIGO

To find the Man in Black, obviously.

FEZZIK

But you don't know where he is.

INIGO

(He is possessed by demons now.)

Don't bother me with trifles; after twenty years, at last, my father's soul will be at peace.

CUT TO

CLOSE UP—INIGO.

INIGO

(big)

There will be blood tonight!!

CUT TO

PRINCE HUMPERDINCK'S CHAMBERS

—*strewn with maps, etc. YELLIN enters, and kneels.*

HUMPERDINCK

(sharpening his dagger)

Rise and report.

YELLIN

The Thieves' Forest is emptied. Thirty men guard the castle gate.

HUMPERDINCK

Double it. My Princess must be safe.

YELLIN

The gate has but one key, and I carry that.

He shows the key, dangling from a chain around his neck.

Just at that moment, BUTTERCUP enters.

HUMPERDINCK

Ah! My dulcet darling. Tonight we marry. Tomorrow morning, your men will escort us to Florin Channel where every ship in my armada waits to accompany us on our honeymoon.

BUTTERCUP

Every ship but your four fastest, you mean.

The PRINCE looks at her blankly for a moment.

BUTTERCUP

Every ship but the four you sent.

HUMPERDINCK

Yes. Yes, of course. Naturally, not those four.

YELLIN
(bows, exits)

Your Majesties.

CUT TO

BUTTERCUP, *staring at* HUMPERDINCK.

BUTTERCUP

You never sent the ships. Don't bother lying. It doesn't matter. Westley will come for me anyway.

HUMPERDINCK
(sharply)

You're a silly girl.

BUTTERCUP

Yes, I am a silly girl, for not having seen sooner that you were nothing but a coward with a heart full of fear.

HUMPERDINCK
(close to erupting; speaks very distinctly)
I—would—not—say—such things—if—I—were—you—

BUTTERCUP

Why not? You can't hurt me. Westley and I are joined by the bonds of love. And you cannot track that. Not with a thousand bloodhounds. And you cannot break it. Not with a thousand swords. And when I say you are a coward, that is only because you are the slimiest weakling ever to crawl the earth.

CUT TO

HUMPERDINCK *jumping at her, yanking her by the hair, starting to pull her along, out of control, his words indistinct.*

HUMPERDINCK
IWOULDNOTSAYSUCHTHINGSIFIWEREYOU!

CUT TO

A CORRIDOR OF THE CASTLE, as the PRINCE throws open the door to BUTTERCUP'S room, slams it shut, locks it, breaks into a wild run and—

CUT TO

WESTLEY in The Machine, but it's not on. COUNT RUGEN is adding more notes to his book. He looks up as the PRINCE suddenly comes down the steps, raging.

HUMPERDINCK
(at Westley)
You truly love each other, and so you might have been truly happy. Not one couple in a century has that chance, no matter what the storybooks say. And so I think no man in a century will suffer as greatly as you will.

And with that he whirls, turns on The Machine, grabs the lever and—

CUT TO

COUNT RUGEN calling out—

RUGEN
Not to fifty!!!

But it's too late as we—

CUT TO

PRINCE HUMPERDINCK, shoving the lever all the way up and

CUT TO

WESTLEY'S FACE. And there has never been such pain. The pain grows and grows and with it now, something else has started:

THE DEATH SCREAM. As THE DEATH SCREAM starts to rise—

CUT TO

OUTSIDE THE PIT OF DESPAIR as the SOUND moves along, LOUDER AND LOUDER, and—

CUT TO

YELLIN AND HIS SIXTY BRUTES. And they hear it, and a few of the BRUTES turn to each other in fear, and as the SCREAM builds—

CUT TO

BUTTERCUP IN HER ROOM. She hears the SOUND, doesn't know what it is, but her arms involuntarily go around her body to try to control the trembling, and the SCREAM still builds and—

CUT TO

ESTABLISHING SHOT ACROSS THE RIVER. There are many PEOPLE—it is the day of the country's 500th Anniversary—but all the PEOPLE stop as the SOUND hits them. A few CHILDREN pale, bolt toward their PARENTS and—

CUT TO

INIGO AND FEZZIK, trying to make their way through the jammed marketplace, which suddenly quiets as the fading sound comes through.

> **INIGO**
> *(instantly)*
> Fezzik, Fezzik, listen, do you hear?—That is the sound of ultimate suffering. My heart made that sound when Rugen slaughtered my father. The Man in Black makes it now.

> **FEZZIK**
> The Man in Black?

> **INIGO**
> His true love is marrying another tonight, so who else has cause for Ultimate Suffering? *(trying to push through)* Excuse me—

It's too crowded.

> **INIGO**
> — pardon me, it's important—

No one budges and the sound is fading faster.

> **INIGO**
> — Fezzik, please—

FEZZIK, gigantic and roaring.

> **FEZZIK**
> Everybody...MOVE ! !

And the CROWD begins to fall away, and he and INIGO start to track the FADING SOUND.

> **INIGO**
> Thank you.

CUT TO

A GROVE OF TREES NEAR THE PIT OF DESPAIR.

The ALBINO *appears wheeling a barrow.* INIGO'S SWORD *pushes at his chest.*

INIGO
Where is the Man in Black?

The ALBINO *shakes his head, says nothing.*

INIGO
You get there from this grove, yes? *(silence)* Fezzik, jog his memory.

And FEZZIK *crunches the* ALBINO *on the top of the head as if he had a hammer and was driving in a nail. The* ALBINO *drops without a sound.*

FEZZIK
(upset)
I'm sorry, Inigo. I didn't mean to jog him so hard. Inigo?

CUT TO

INIGO. *He kneels, the sword held tight between his hands. Eyes closed, he faces the grove of trees, starts to talk, his voice low and strange.*

INIGO
Father, I have failed you for twenty years. Now our misery can end. Somewhere...somewhere close by is a man who can help us. I cannot find him alone. I need you. I need you to guide my sword. Please.

And now he rises, eyes still closed.

INIGO
Guide my sword.

CUT TO

THE GROVE OF TREES *as* INIGO, *eyes shut tight, walks forward,* THE GREAT SWORD HELD IN HIS HANDS.

FEZZIK, *frightened, follows close behind.*

CUT TO

THE SECRET KNOT *that reveals the staircase.*

CUT TO

INIGO walking blind through the grove of trees. He moves to the Secret Knot, hesitates, then moves past it.

Then INIGO stops. For a long moment he stands frozen. Suddenly he whirls, eyes still closed, and the sword strikes home dead center into a knot and—

Nothing. He has failed.

In utter despair he collapses against the tree. Against a knot in the tree. Against THE KNOT in the tree. It slides away, revealing the staircase. FEZZIK AND INIGO look at each other, then start down.

CUT TO

WESTLEY, dead by The Machine. FEZZIK leans over him, listening for a heartbeat. Then he looks at INIGO, shakes his head.

FEZZIK

He's dead.

INIGO is in despair. For a moment, he just sags.

INIGO
(barely able to speak)

It just is not fair.

THE KID (off-screen)

— Grandpa, Grandpa—wait—

CUT TO

THE KID'S ROOM.

He is terribly excited and looks stronger than we've yet seen him.

THE KID

—wait—what did Fezzik mean, "He's dead?" I mean he didn't mean dead. *(The Grandfather says nothing, just sits there.)* Westley's only faking, right?

GRANDFATHER

You want me to read this or not?

CUT TO

THE KID: CLOSE UP.

THE KID

Who gets Humperdinck?

GRANDFATHER

I don't understand.

THE KID

Who kills Prince Humperdinck? At the end, somebody's got to do it.
Is it Inigo? Who?

GRANDFATHER

Nobody. Nobody kills him. He lives.

THE KID

You mean he wins? Jesus, Grandpa! What did you read me this thing for?

And he desperately fights for control.

GRANDFATHER

You know, you've been very sick and you're taking this story very seriously. I think we better stop now. *(starts to get up)*

THE KID

(shaking his head)

No! I'm okay. I'm okay—*(gestures toward the chair)*— sit down. All right?

GRANDFATHER

Okay. *(sitting and opening the book again)* All right, now, let's see. Where
were we? Oh yes. In the Pit of Despair.

CUT TO

*INIGO, in despair. (We're back in the Pit, the same shot as before.) For a moment, he just
sags.*

INIGO

Well, we Montoyas have never taken defeat easily. Come along, Fezzik.
Bring the body.

FEZZIK

The body?

INIGO

(not stopping)

Have you any money?

FEZZIK

I have a little.

INIGO

I just hope it's enough to buy a miracle, that's all.

As FEZZIK takes the corpse, follows INIGO up the stairs—

CUT TO

A HOVEL, DUSK.

INIGO, FEZZIK, WESTLEY approach the door. They knock. From inside the hovel a little man's voice is heard. If Mel Brooks' 2000 Year Old Man was really old, he'd resemble this GUY.

> **LITTLE OLD GUY** (off-screen)
>
> Go away!

INIGO pounds again.

> **MIRACLE MAX**
> *(opening a small window in the door)*
>
> What? What?

> **INIGO**
>
> Are you the Miracle Max who worked for the King all those years?

> **MIRACLE MAX**
>
> The King's stinking son fired me. And thank you so much for bringing up such a painful subject. While you're at it, why don't you give me a nice paper cut and pour lemon juice on it? We're closed!

He shuts the window. They rap on the door.

> **MIRACLE MAX**
> *(opening the window)*
>
> Beat it or I'll call the Brute Squad.

> **FEZZIK**
>
> I'm on the Brute Squad.

> **MIRACLE MAX**
> *(looking at the Giant)*
>
> You *are* the Brute Squad.

> **INIGO**
>
> We need a miracle. It's very important.

> **MIRACLE MAX**
>
> Look, I'm retired. And besides, why would you want someone the King's stinking son fired? I might kill whoever you wanted me to miracle.

> **INIGO**
>
> He's already dead.

> MIRACLE MAX
> *(for the first time, interested)*

He is, eh? I'll take a look. Bring him in.

He unlocks the door and lets them in.

CUT TO

INIGO AND FEZZIK, hurrying inside. FEZZIK carries WESTLEY who is just starting to stiffen up a little. He lays WESTLEY down across a bench by the fireplace. MAX picks Westley's arm up and lets it drop limp.

> MIRACLE MAX

I've seen worse.

He studies WESTLEY a moment, checking here, checking there.

> INIGO

Sir. Sir.

> MIRACLE MAX

Hah?

> INIGO

We're really in a terrible rush.

> MIRACLE MAX
> *(He takes nothing from nobody.)*

Don't rush me, sonny. You rush a miracle man, you get rotten miracles. You got money?

> INIGO

Sixty-five.

> MIRACLE MAX

Sheesh! I never worked for so little, except once, and that was a very noble cause.

> INIGO

This is noble, sir. *(pointing to Westley)* His wife is crippled. His children are on the brink of starvation.

> MIRACLE MAX

Are you a rotten liar.

> INIGO

I need him to help avenge my father, murdered these twenty years.

MIRACLE MAX
Your first story was better. *(looking around)* Where's that bellows? *(spots it)* He probably owes you money, huh? Well, I'll ask him.

He goes to get a huge bellows.

INIGO
(stupefied)
He's dead. He can't talk.

MIRACLE MAX
Look who knows so much. Well, it just so happens that your friend here is only mostly dead. There's a big difference between mostly dead and all dead. Please open his mouth.

INIGO does. MAX inserts the bellows in WESTLEY'S MOUTH and starts to pump.

MIRACLE MAX
Now, mostly dead is slightly alive. Now, all dead...well, with all dead, there's usually only one thing that you can do.

INIGO
What's that?

He stops pumping.

MIRACLE MAX
Go through his clothes and look for loose change.

He starts pumping again.

MIRACLE MAX
(to Westley)
Hey! Hello in there. Hey! What's so important? What you got here that's worth living for?

And he presses lightly on WESTLEY'S CHEST.

WESTLEY
...tr...oooo....luv....

Everybody stares at WESTLEY lying there on the bench.

INIGO
True love. You heard him. You could not ask for a more noble cause than that.

MIRACLE MAX

Sonny, true love is the greatest thing in the world. Except for a nice MLT, a mutton, lettuce and tomato sandwich, where the mutton is nice and lean and the tomato is ripe. They're so perky, I love that. But that's not what he said. He distinctly said "to blave." And, as we all know, "to blave" means "to bluff." So you're probably playing cards, and he cheated—

A WOMAN'S VOICE

— Liar—LIAR—LI-A-A-AR—

VALERIE, an ancient fury, storms out of a back room and toward MAX.

MIRACLE MAX

—get back, witch—

VALERIE

I'm not a witch, I'm your wife. But after what you just said, I'm not even sure I want to be that anymore.

MIRACLE MAX

You never had it so good.

VALERIE

"True love." He said, "true love," Max. My God—

MIRACLE MAX
(retreating)

Don't say another word, Valerie.

VALERIE
(turning to Inigo and Fezzik)

He's afraid. Ever since Prince Humperdinck fired him, his confidence is shattered.

MIRACLE MAX

Why'd you say that name—you promised me that you would never say that name—

VALERIE
(pursuing him now)

What, Humperdinck? Humperdinck. Humperdinck. Ooo-ooo, Humperdinck—

MIRACLE MAX
(holding his hands over his ears)

I'm not listening.

> VALERIE

A life expiring and you don't have the decency to say why you won't help—

> MIRACLE MAX

Nobody's hearing nothing!

> VALERIE

Humperdinck. Humperdinck! Humperdinck!

> INIGO

—But this is Buttercup's true love—If you heal him, he will stop Humperdinck's wedding.

> VALERIE

Humperdinck. Humperdinck—

> MIRACLE MAX
> *(to Valerie)*

Shut up—*(now to Inigo)* Wait. Wait. I make him better, Humperdinck suffers?

> INIGO

—Humiliations galore!

> MIRACLE MAX

That is a noble cause. Give me the sixty-five, I'm on the job.

And as VALERIE shrieks excitedly we

CUT TO

THIS LUMP. *It is somewhat smaller than a tennis ball.*

PULL BACK TO REVEAL MAX AND VALERIE, *exhausted, looking at the lump with beatific pleasure, as VALERIE, cooking utensil in hand, covers the thing with what looks like chocolate. INIGO AND FEZZIK stare at the thing too, but more dubiously.*

> INIGO
> *(a little appalled)*

That's a miracle pill? *(Max nods.)*

> VALERIE
> *(finishing)*

The chocolate coating makes it go down easier. But you have to wait fifteen minutes for full potency. And you shouldn't go swimming after, for at least, what?

                          MIRACLE MAX
An hour.

                          VALERIE
Yeah, an hour.

                          MIRACLE MAX
A good hour. Yeah.

INIGO accepts the pill as FEZZIK takes WESTLEY, who is stiff as a board now.

                          INIGO
               (heading out the door, Fezzik close behind)
Thank you for everything.

                          MIRACLE MAX
Okay.

                          VALERIE
               (waving after them)
Bye-bye, boys.

                          MIRACLE MAX
Have fun storming the castle.

                          VALERIE
               (to Max)
Think it'll work?

                          MIRACLE MAX
It would take a miracle. Bye!

                          VALERIE
Bye.

And as they wave, trying to look happy we—

CUT TO

FEZZIK, INIGO, WESTLEY, on the top of the outer wall of the castle. They look down to the front gate of the castle. The sixty BRUTES are visible.

FEZZIK is thunderstruck by how many Brutes there are. Upset, he turns to INIGO, who is concentrating unsuccessfully, trying to prop WESTLEY against the wall.

                          FEZZIK
Inigo—there's more than thirty—

> INIGO
> *(absolutely unfazed)*
> What's the difference? *(indicating the half-dead Westley)* We've got him—
> Help me here. We'll have to force feed him.

> FEZZIK
> Has it been fifteen minutes?

> INIGO
> We can't wait—the wedding's in half an hour and we must strike in the
> hustle and the bustle beforehand.

During this, FEZZIK, using all his strength, has managed to get WESTLEY into a right-angled sitting postion, while INIGO brings out the miracle pill.

> INIGO
> Tilt his head back. Open his mouth.

> FEZZIK
> *(following orders)*
> How long do we have to wait before we know if the miracle works?

CUT TO

INIGO. Pill in hand, he drops it into Westley's mouth.

> INIGO
> Your guess is as good as mine—

> WESTLEY
> I'll beat you both apart. I'll take you both together.

> FEZZIK
> I guess not very long.

INIGO AND FEZZIK REACT. WESTLEY is the only one not amazed.

> WESTLEY
> Why won't my arms move?

He sits there, immobile, like a ventriloquist's dummy.

> FEZZIK
> You've been mostly dead all day.

> INIGO
> We had Miracle Max make a pill to bring you back.

WESTLEY

Who are you?—Are we enemies? Why am I on this wall?—Where's Buttercup?—

INIGO

Let me explain—*(pauses very briefly)*—No, there is too much. Let me sum up. Buttercup is marrying Humperdinck in a little less than half an hour, so all we have to do is get in, break up the wedding, steal the Princess, make our escape after I kill Count Rugen.

WESTLEY

That doesn't leave much time for dilly dallying.

He is watching his fingers, one of which twitches now.

FEZZIK

You've just wiggled your finger. That's wonderful.

WESTLEY

I've always been a quick healer. *(to Inigo)* What are our liabilities?

INIGO

There is but one working castle gate.

FEZZIK helps INIGO raise WESTLEY just high enough so he can see for himself.

INIGO

And it is guarded by sixty men.

WESTLEY

And our assets?

INIGO

Your brains, Fezzik's strength, my steel.

CUT TO

WESTLEY, absolutely stunned.

WESTLEY

That's it? Impossible. If I had a month to plan, maybe I could come up with something. But this...

He shakes his head from side to side.

CUT TO

INIGO AND FEZZIK.

FEZZIK
(*trying to be cheery*)
You just shook your head—that doesn't make you happy?

WESTLEY
My brains, his steel, and your strength against sixty men, and you think a little head jiggle is supposed to make me happy? I mean, if we only had a wheelbarrow, that would be something.

INIGO
Where did we put that wheelbarrow the Albino had?

FEZZIK
Over the Albino, I think.

WESTLEY
Well, why didn't you list that among our assets in the first place? What I wouldn't give for a holocaust cloak.

INIGO
There we cannot help you.

FEZZIK
(*pulling one out*)
Will this do?

INIGO
(*to Fezzik—surprised*)
Where did you get that?

FEZZIK
At Miracle Max's. It fit so nice, he said I could keep it.

WESTLEY
All right, all right. Come on, help me up.

INIGO AND FEZZIK do.

WESTLEY
Now, I'll need a sword eventually.

INIGO
Why? You can't even lift one.

WESTLEY
True, but that's hardly common knowledge, is it? (*And his head tilts limply back. Fezzik sets it upright for him.*) Thank you. Now, there may be problems once we're inside.

INIGO

I'll say—how do I find the Count?—Once I do, how do I find you again?—Once I find you again, how do we escape?—

FEZZIK
(sharply)

Don't pester him, he's had a hard day.

INIGO
(nods)

Right, right, sorry.

CUT TO

A SHOT OF THE THREE OF THEM IN PROFILE. They move along the wall in silence for a time. Then these words come to us on the wind—

FEZZIK

Inigo.

INIGO

What?

FEZZIK

...I hope we win...

CUT TO

BUTTERCUP, in her bridal gown, and she's incredible. It's not just her beauty; there's a tranquility about her now.

PULL BACK TO REVEAL

THE PRINCE, fastening a pearl necklace around her.

HUMPERDINCK

You don't seem excited, my little muffin.

BUTTERCUP

Should I be?

HUMPERDINCK

Brides often are, I'm told.

BUTTERCUP
(gently, confidently)

I do not marry tonight.

CUT TO

BUTTERCUP. *And she couldn't seem more serene.*

                          BUTTERCUP
     My Westley will save me.

CUT TO

HER WESTLEY *looking down on the gate with* INIGO AND FEZZIK.

CUT TO

THE MAIN GATE OF THE CASTLE

—and YELLIN, *standing there, flanked by his* SIXTY BRUTES.

CUT TO

WESTLEY AND INIGO AND FEZZIK, *looking out at the* ENEMY. *This is it.* INIGO AND FEZZIK *shake hands.*

WESTLEY *can't even do that, but after a bit of rocking back and forth, he manages to get enough momentum to catapult his arm over and onto his friend's.*

CUT TO

AN ABSOLUTELY GEM-LIKE LITTLE CHAPEL.

PULL BACK TO REVEAL

THE MOST INTELLIGENT LOOKING, THE MOST IMPRESSIVE APPEARING CLERGYMAN IMAGINABLE. BUTTERCUP AND HUMPERDINCK *kneel before the* CLERGYMAN. *Behind them sit the mumbling old* KING AND QUEEN. *Standing in the back is* COUNT RUGEN.

FOUR GUARDS *are in position flanking the chapel door.*

                    IMPRESSIVE CLERGYMAN
                (clears his throat, begins to speak)
     Mawidge...mawidge is what bwings us togewer today...

He has an impediment that would stop a clock.

                    IMPRESSIVE CLERGYMAN
     Mawidge, the bwessed awwangement, that dweam wiffim a dweam...

And now, from outside the castle, there begins to come a commotion. And then—

                    YELLIN (off-screen)
     Stand your ground, men. Stand your ground.

CUT TO

THE BRUTES AND YELLIN, by the gate, for it is indeed they who are making the commotion, frightened, pointing—

YELLIN

Stand your ground.

CUT TO

THEIR P.O.V.: And it is a bit unnerving—a GIANT seems to be floating toward them out of the darkness, a GIANT in a strange cloak, and with a voice that would crumble walls.

FEZZIK

I AM THE DREAD PIRATE ROBERTS. THERE WILL BE NO SURVIVORS.

CUT TO

FEZZIK, and he seems to be floating because he's standing in the wheelbarrow, as INIGO, hidden behind him, busts a gut by pushing it and supporting WESTLEY.

INIGO

Now?

WESTLEY

Not yet.

CUT TO

THE GIANT FLOATING CLOSER.

FEZZIK

MY MEN ARE HERE, AND I AM HERE, BUT SOON YOU WILL NOT BE HERE—

CUT TO

YELLIN, keeping the BRUTES in position, or trying to, shouting orders, instructions and as yet the BRUTES hold. Now—

CUT TO

INIGO AND WESTLEY. INIGO struggles bravely under their combined weight—

INIGO

Now?

WESTLEY

Light him.

CUT TO

THE BRUTES, as the GIANT bursts suddenly, happily into flames.

> **FEZZIK**
> *(roaring)*
> THE DREAD PIRATE ROBERTS TAKES NO SURVIVORS. ALL
> YOUR WORST NIGHTMARES ARE ABOUT TO COME TRUE.

CUT TO

THE CHAPEL, where THE IMPRESSIVE CLERGYMAN plods on.

> **IMPRESSIVE CLERGYMAN**
> ...Ven wuv, twoo wuv, wiw fowwow you fowever...

CUT TO

PRINCE HUMPERDINCK, turning quickly, giving a sharp nod to COUNT RUGEN who immediately takes off out of the chapel with the FOUR GUARDS as we

CUT TO

FEZZIK, flaming and scary as hell.

> **FEZZIK**
> THE DREAD PIRATE ROBERTS IS HERE FOR YOUR SOULS!

CUT TO

YELLIN, as suddenly the BRUTES just scream and take off in wild panic—

> **YELLIN**
> Stay where you are. I said stay where you are!

CUT TO

INSIDE THE CHAPEL.

> **IMPRESSIVE CLERGYMAN**
> ...so tweasuwe your wuv...

> **HUMPERDINCK**
> Skip to the end.

> **IMPRESSIVE CLERGYMAN**
> Have you the wing?

As HUMPERDINCK whips out the ring—the screams are very loud outside.

> **BUTTERCUP**
> Here comes my Westley now.

CUT TO

FEZZIK, *as he pulls off the holocaust cloak.*

WESTLEY
Fezzik, the portcullis.

And FEZZIK *rushes forward, grabbing the portcullis, which is indeed closing quickly.* FEZZIK *grabs the gate: and swings the tonnage back upward.* YELLIN *just watches in fear.*

CUT TO

THE CHAPEL, *as* HUMPERDINCK *shoves the ring on* BUTTERCUP'S *finger.*

HUMPERDINCK
Your Westley is dead.

BUTTERCUP *only smiles, shakes her head.*

HUMPERDINCK
I killed him myself.

BUTTERCUP
(never more serene)
Then why is there fear behind your eyes?

CUT TO

PRINCE HUMPERDINCK. *And she's right. It's there.*

CUT TO

YELLIN, *pressed against the main gate.* WESTLEY, INIGO *and* FEZZIK *close in.*

WESTLEY
Give us the gate key.

YELLIN
(every ounce of honesty he's got)
I have no gate key.

INIGO
Fezzik, tear his arms off.

FEZZIK *steps toward him.*

YELLIN
Oh, you mean this gate key.

And he whips it out, hands it to FEZZIK.

CUT TO

HUMPERDINCK AND BUTTERCUP AND THE IMPRESSIVE CLERGYMAN.

> **IMPRESSIVE CLERGYMAN**
> And do you, Pwincess Buwwercwup...

> **HUMPERDINCK**
> Man and wife—say *man* and *wife*...

> **IMPRESSIVE CLERGYMAN**
> Man and wife.

> **HUMPERDINCK**
> *(whirling to the King and Queen)*
> Escort the bride to the Honeymoon Suite—I'll be there shortly.

And as he dashes off—

CUT TO

BUTTERCUP, *standing there. Dazed.*

> **BUTTERCUP**
> He didn't come.

CUT TO

COUNT RUGEN AND HIS FOUR WARRIORS, *racing through the castle, and as they reach a complex intersection of several corridors,* RUGEN *stops, incredulous, as we*

CUT TO

WESTLEY, INIGO AND FEZZIK, *moving toward them. Actually* FEZZIK *is dragging* WESTLEY, *who is, in turn, dragging* YELLIN'S *sword like a stiff dog leash—*WESTLEY *simply hasn't the strength to raise it.*

CUT TO

COUNT RUGEN, *as the confrontation is about to start.*

> **RUGEN**
> Kill the dark one and the giant, but leave the third for questioning.

And as his WARRIORS *attack—*

INIGO *goes wild, and maybe the* WARRIORS *are good, maybe they're even better than that—but they never get a chance to show it because this is something now, this is* INIGO *gone mad and the six-fingered sword has never flashed faster and the* FOURTH WARRIOR *is dead before the* FIRST ONE *has even hit the floor. There is a.pause. Then—*

> **INIGO**
> *(to Rugen, evenly and soft)*
> Hello. My name is Inigo Montoya. You killed my father. Prepare to die.

CUT TO

COUNT RUGEN. *For a moment he just stands there, sword in hand. Then he does a most unexpected thing: he turns and runs the hell away.*

CUT TO

INIGO, *momentarily surprised, then taking off after him, leaving* WESTLEY *and* FEZZIK *to exchange curious looks and* RUGEN, *running through a half-open heavy wooden door, shutting it and locking it just as* INIGO *throws himself against it. He tries again. No kind of chance.*

> **INIGO**
> *(calling out)*
> Fezzik, I need you—

CUT TO

FEZZIK WITH WESTLEY, *who is still unable to walk under his own power. He calls back—*

> **FEZZIK**
> *(indicating Westley)*
> I can't leave him alone.

CUT TO

INIGO, *desperately pounding at the heavy door.*

> **INIGO**
> He's getting away from me, Fezzik. Please. Fezzik!

CUT TO

FEZZIK AND WESTLEY.

> **FEZZIK**
> *(to Westley)*
> I'll be right back.

And he props WESTLEY *up against a large suit of armour and takes off toward the intersection where* INIGO'S *voice came from—*

CUT TO

INIGO, still hammering the door. FEZZIK approaches, gestures for him to stop, and with one mighty swipe of his mighty hands the door crumbles—

                        INIGO
    Thank you—

And INIGO flies through as FEZZIK heads back to WESTLEY.

CUT TO

BUTTERCUP WALKING WITH THE KING AND QUEEN. The QUEEN, more sprightly, is several paces ahead.

                        KING
                (can hardly be understood)
    Strange wedding.

                        QUEEN
    Yes. A very strange wedding. Come along.

BUTTERCUP gently stops the KING and places a kiss on his forehead. He's very surprised and pleased.

                        KING
    What was that for?

                        BUTTERCUP
    Because you've always been so kind to me. And I won't be seeing you
    again since I'm killing myself once we reach the Honeymoon Suite.

                        KING
            (Smiling away—his hearing isn't what it once was.)
    Won't that be nice? *(calling out to the Queen)* She kissed me...

And on those words—

CUT TO

COUNT RUGEN. And he's running, dashing through corridors and as he glances back—

CUT TO

INIGO, behind him, coming like a streak and—

CUT TO

THE INTERSECTION, with the large suit of armour, and FEZZIK gaping, staring at all those choices, trying to piece together the puzzle of the missing Westley.

CUT TO

COUNT RUGEN, flashing out of one room, down a staircase, picking up his pace. He pulls out a deadly looking dagger, with a sharp point and a triangular shaped blade, and sprints on and—

CUT TO

INIGO, closing the gap, closer, closer and he's down the stairs and heading into a dining hall and—

CUT TO

COUNT RUGEN, throwing the dagger—

CUT TO

INIGO, trying like hell to get out of the way, but no, and it sticks deep into his stomach, and he hurtles back helplessly against the wall of the room, his eyes glazed, blood coming from his wound.

The room is going white on him.

> **INIGO**
> ...Sorry, Father...I tried...I tried...

CUT TO

COUNT RUGEN, looking across the room at INIGO. He stares at INIGO'S face, and then touches his own cheeks, as memory comes.

> **RUGEN**
> You must be that little Spanish brat I taught a lesson to all those years ago. It's simply incredible. Have you been chasing me your whole life only to fail now? I think that's the worst thing I ever heard. How marvelous.

INIGO sinks.

CUT TO

BUTTERCUP, shutting the door of the Honeymoon Suite, crossing quietly to the far wall where she sits at a table, opens a jeweled box. and takes out a very deadly looking dagger. She seems very much at peace as she touches the knife to her bosom.

> **WESTLEY**
> There's a shortage of perfect breasts in this world. It would be a pity to damage yours.

And BUTTERCUP whirls as we—

CUT TO

WESTLEY, lying on the bed. YELLIN'S SWORD is beside him. His voice sounds just fine, but he does not move.

BUTTERCUP leaps to the bed, covering him with kisses. WESTLEY is helpless.

> **BUTTERCUP**
> Oh, Westley, darling. *(more kisses)* Westley, why won't you hold me?

> **WESTLEY**
> *(gently)*
> Gently.

> **BUTTERCUP**
> At a time like this that's all you can think to say? "Gently?"

> **WESTLEY**
> *(not so gently)*
> Gently!!

And she lets go, thumping his head against the headboard and

CUT TO

COUNT RUGEN, looking very much surprised.

> **RUGEN**
> Good heavens. Are you still trying to win?

PULL BACK TO REVEAL

INIGO, struggling feebly, pulling the dagger from his stomach. Holding the wound with his left hand.

RUGEN is pushing off from the table, sword in hand, moving in to kill INIGO.

> **RUGEN**
> You've got an overdeveloped sense of vengeance. It's going to get you into trouble some day.

INIGO watches the COUNT approach, and the COUNT flicks his sword at INIGO'S HEART, and there's not much Inigo can do, just kind of vaguely parry the thrust with the six-fingered sword and COUNT RUGEN'S blade sinks deeply into Inigo's left shoulder.

INIGO doesn't seem to feel it, his other agonies are so much worse.

CUT TO

HE COUNT, *stepping back, going for the heart again.*

UT TO

INIGO. *And as this blow comes he's trying to use the wall for support in forcing himself to is feet, and it's not a roaring success of an attempt, but he does at least make some rogress, and again he manages to parry the thrust, as this time Rugen's sword runs rough his right arm. Again,* INIGO *doesn't seem to mind, doesn't even feel it.*

UT TO

OUNT RUGEN, stepping back for just a moment, watching as INIGO *continues to inch his ay to his feet and then, just before the* COUNT *is about to strike again,* INIGO *manages little flick of his own and* RUGEN *hadn't expected it, and he jumps back, makes a little nvoluntary cry of surprise and*

UT TO

INIGO, *slowly pushing away from the wall.*

> **INIGO**
> *(all but audible)*
> Hello. My name is Inigo Montoya, you killed my father; prepare to die.

UT TO

COUNT RUGEN, *suddenly going into a fierce attack, striking with great power and precision for he is a master swordsman, and he forces* INIGO *easily back, drives him easily into he wall. But he does not penetrate Inigo's defense. None of the Count's blows get home. As the* COUNT *steps back a moment—*

UT TO

INIGO, *pushing slowly off from the wall again.*

> **INIGO**
> *(a little louder)*
> Hello. My name is Inigo Montoya, you killed my father, prepare to die.

UT TO

THE COUNT. *And again he attacks, slashing with wondrous skill. But none of his blows get through and, slowly,* INIGO, *again moves forward.*

> **INIGO**
> *(a little louder still)*
> Hello. My name is Inigo Montoya. You killed my father. Prepare to die.

RUGEN

Stop saying that!

CUT TO

COUNT RUGEN, *retreating more quickly around the table.*

INIGO *drives for the Count's left shoulder now, thrusts home where the Count had gotten him. Then another move and his blade enters the Count's right shoulder, the same spot* INIGO *was wounded.*

INIGO
(all he's got)
HELLO! MY NAME IS INIGO MONTOYA. YOU KILLED MY FATHER. PREPARE TO DIE.

RUGEN

No—

INIGO

—offer me money—

And now the six-fingered sword strikes and there is a slash bleeding along one of RUGEN'S *cheeks.*

RUGEN

—yes—

INIGO

—power too—promise me that—

The great sword flashes again, and now there is a parallel slash bleeding on RUGEN'S *other cheek.*

RUGEN

—all that I have and more please—

INIGO

—offer me everything I ask for—

RUGEN

—anything you want—

INIGO
(roaring)
I WANT MY FATHER BACK, YOU SON-OF-A-BITCH!

And on that—

CUT TO

INIGO, *and almost too fast for the eye to follow, the sword strikes one final time and—*

CUT TO

COUNT RUGEN, *crying out in fear and panic as the sword hits home dead center and—*

CUT TO

INIGO AND RUGEN, *the sword clear through the* COUNT. *They are almost frozen like that for a moment. Then* INIGO *withdraws his sword and as the* COUNT *pitches down—*

CUT TO

RUGEN, *lying dead. His skin is ashen and the blood still pours from the parallel cuts on his cheeks and his eyes are bulging wide, full of fear.*

CUT TO

INIGO, *staring at Rugen. And now* INIGO *does something we have never seen him do before: he smiles.* HOLD FOR JUST A MOMENT *on Inigo smiling, then—*

CUT TO

INSIDE THE HONEYMOON SUITE.

WESTLEY *lies as before, not a muscle has moved, his head is still on the headboard,* YELLIN'S SWORD *at his side.* BUTTERCUP *is alongside the bed; her eyes never leave his face.*

BUTTERCUP

Oh, Westley, will you ever forgive me?

WESTLEY

What hideous sin have you committed lately?

BUTTERCUP

I got married. I didn't want to. It all happened so fast.

WESTLEY

It never happened.

BUTTERCUP

What?

WESTLEY

It never happened.

BUTTERCUP

But it did. I was there. This old man said, "Man and wife."

WESTLEY

Did you say, "I do"?

BUTTERCUP

Well, no, we sort of skipped that part.

WESTLEY

Then you're not married—if you didn't say it, you didn't do it—*(a pause)*—wouldn't you agree, Your Highness?

CUT TO

HUMPERDINCK, *entering the room, staring at them. He pulls out his sword.*

HUMPERDINCK

A technicality that will shortly be remedied. But first things first. To the death.

WESTLEY

No. *(a little pause)* To the pain.

HUMPERDINCK
(about to charge, stops short)

I don't think I'm quite familiar with that phrase.

WESTLEY

I'll explain. And I'll use small words so that you'll be sure to understand, you wart-hog-faced buffoon.

HUMPERDINCK

That may be the first time in my life a man has dared insult me.

CUT TO

WESTLEY, *lying there comfortably, his words quiet at first.*

WESTLEY

It won't be the last. To the pain means the first thing you lose will be your feet, below the ankles, then your hands at the wrists, next your nose.

CUT TO

HUMPERDINCK, *gripping his sword, watching.*

HUMPERDINCK

—and then my tongue, I suppose. I killed you too quickly the last time, a mistake I don't mean to duplicate tonight.

WESTLEY

I wasn't finished—the next thing you lose will be your left eye, followed by your right—

HUMPERDINCK
(takes step forward)
—and then my ears, I understand. Let's get on with it—

CUT TO

CLOSE UP: WESTLEY. HUGE.

WESTLEY

Wrong! Your ears you keep, and I'll tell you why—

CUT TO

HUMPERDINCK. And now he stops, and the look that was in his eyes at the wedding, that look of fear, is starting to return.

WESTLEY

—so that every shriek of every child at seeing your hideousness will be yours to cherish—every babe that weeps at your approach, every woman who cries out, "Dear God, what is that thing?" will echo in your perfect ears. That is what "to the pain" means. It means I leave you in anguish, wallowing in freakish misery forever.

CUT TO

HUMPERDINCK, doing his best to hide the fear that keeps building inside him.

HUMPERDINCK

I think you're bluffing—

CUT TO

WESTLEY, lying there, staring at him.

WESTLEY

It's possible, pig—I might be bluffing—it's conceivable, you *miserable vomitous mass*, that I'm only lying here because I lack the strength to stand—then again, perhaps I have the strength after all.

And now, slowly, WESTLEY begins to move. His body turns, his feet go to the floor, he starts to stand—

CUT TO

HUMPERDINCK, staring, eyes wide.

CUT TO

WESTLEY. And now he is standing, sword in fighting position.

WESTLEY
—DROP YOUR SWORD!

CUT TO

PRINCE HUMPERDINCK, and he's so panicked he doesn't know whether to pee or wind his watch. He throws his sword to the floor.

WESTLEY
(To Humperdinck)
Have a seat.

CUT TO

WESTLEY, speaking to BUTTERCUP as HUMPERDINCK sits.

WESTLEY
Tie him up. Make it as tight as you like.

And as she sets to work—

CUT TO

INIGO, entering, looking around.

INIGO
Where's Fezzik?

WESTLEY
I thought he was with you.

INIGO
No.

WESTLEY
In that case—*(And his balance betrays him.)*

INIGO
(to Buttercup)
Help him.

> **BUTTERCUP**

Why does Westley need helping?

> **INIGO**

Because he has no strength—

CUT TO

HUMPERDINCK, and now he starts wrestling mightily with his bonds.

> **HUMPERDINCK**

I knew it! I knew you were bluffing! I knew he was bluffing.

> **INIGO**
> *(staring at the Prince)*

Shall I dispatch him for you?

> **WESTLEY**
> *(considers this, then)*

Thank you, but no—whatever happens to us, I want him to live a long life alone with his cowardice.

> **FEZZIK** (off-screen)

Inigo! Inigo, where are you?

They look at each other, then move to the balcony, and

CUT TO

FEZZIK, leading FOUR GREAT WHITE HORSES. He glances up, sees them on the balcony.

> **FEZZIK**

Ah, there you are. Inigo, I saw the Prince's stables, and there they were, four white horses. And I thought, there are four of us, if we ever find the lady—hello, lady—so I took them with me, in case we ever bumped into each other. *(considers things a moment)* I guess we just did.

CUT TO

INIGO AND WESTLEY AND BUTTERCUP, looking down at FEZZIK.

> **INIGO**

Fezzik, you did something right.

> **FEZZIK**

Don't worry—I won't let it go to my head.

And as he holds out his great arms,

CUT TO

SOMETHING UNEXPECTED AND VERY LOVELY: BUTTERCUP *floating through the air.*
What's happening, of course, is that she's jumping from the balcony so FEZZIK *can catch*
her. But her fall is in slow motion so you might think she was flying.

WESTLEY AND INIGO, *watching as* FEZZIK *catches Buttercup.*

INIGO
You know, it's very strange—I have been in the revenge business so long,
now that it's over, I don't know what to do with the rest of my life.

WESTLEY
(as Inigo gets him ready for his jump)
Have you ever considered piracy? You'd make a wonderful Dread Pirate
Roberts.

Now from that—

CUT TO

THE FOUR GLORIOUS WHITE HORSES WITH THEIR FOUR RIDERS, *triumphantly racing*
through the night—

CUT TO

BUTTERCUP AND WESTLEY, *and at last their trials are done. They stop.*

GRANDFATHER (off-screen)
They rode to freedom. And as dawn arose, Westley and Buttercup knew
they were safe. A wave of love swept over them. And as they reached for
each other...

As BUTTERCUP AND WESTLEY *begin their ultimate kiss—*

CUT TO

THE KID'S BEDROOM.

THE GRANDFATHER *stops reading.*

THE KID
What? What?

GRANDFATHER
No, it's kissing again. You don't want to hear it.

THE KID

I don't mind so much. *(He gestures for his Grandfather to read.)*

GRANDFATHER

Okay.

CUT TO

BUTTERCUP AND WESTLEY.

GRANDFATHER (off-screen)

Since the invention of the kiss, there have been five kisses that were rated the most passionate, the most pure. This one left them all behind. The end.

CUT TO

THE KID'S ROOM.

THE GRANDFATHER *snaps the book closed.*

GRANDFATHER

Now I think you ought to go to sleep.

THE KID

Okay.

GRANDFATHER
(standing, readying to leave)

Okay. Okay. Okay. All right. So long.

THE KID

Grandpa? *(The Old Man stops, turns.)* Maybe you could come over and read it again to me tomorrow.

GRANDFATHER
(There is a pause; then—)

As you wish...

And his smile is enough. As THE GRANDFATHER *steps out the door,*

FINAL FADE OUT.

THE END

MISERY

DIRECTOR	ROB REINER
PRODUCERS	ANDREW SCHEINMAN
	ROB REINER
CINEMATOGRAPHER	BARRY SONNENFELD
EDITOR	ROBERT LEIGHTON
PRODUCTION DESIGNER	NORMAN GARWOOD
MUSIC	MARC SHAIMAN
SCREENPLAY	WILLIAM GOLDMAN
	(FROM THE NOVEL
	MISERY
	BY STEPHEN KING)

Misery came about like this.

I got a call from Rob Reiner saying he was interested in this book by Stephen King and would I read it. He became interested when Andy Scheinman, Reiner's producer and now a director on his own (*Little Big League*), read it on a plane and wondered who owned the movie rights. The book had been published for a while, was a number one novel, standard for King.

They found out it hadn't been sold—not for any lack of offers but because King wouldn't sell it. He has disliked most of the movies made from his work and didn't want this one, perhaps his favorite, Hollywooded up.

Reiner called him and they talked. Now, one of the movies made from his fiction that King did like was *Stand By Me*, which Reiner directed. The conversation ended with King saying sure, he would sell it, but he would have to be paid a lot of money and that Reiner would agree to either produce or direct it.

Reiner, who had no intention of directing, agreed. He would produce. He called me. I read *Misery*. I had read enough of King to know this: Of all the phee-noms that have appeared in the past decades, King is the stylist. If he ever chooses to leave the world that has made him the most successful writer in memory, he won't break a sweat. The man can write anything. He is that gifted.

Misery is about a famous author who has a terrible car crash during a blizzard. He is rescued by a nurse. Who turns out to be his number one fan. Who also turns out to be very crazy. And who keeps him prisoner in her out-of-the-way Colorado home. It all ends badly for them both (worse for her). I was having a fine old time reading it. I'm a novelist too, so I identified with Paul Sheldon who was not just trapped with a nut, but also trapped by his own fear of losing success. And Annie Wilkes, the nurse/prison guard, is one of King's best creations.

When I do an adaptation, I have to be kicked by the source material. One of the ways I work is to read that material again and again. And if I don't like it a lot going in, that becomes too awful. Half-way through, I wasn't sure I would write the movie, but I was enjoying the hell out of the novel.

Then on page 191 the hobbling scene began.

Paul Sheldon has managed to get out of the bedroom in his wheelchair. He has gotten back in time to have fooled Annie Wilkes. That was more than a little important to him, because Annie was not the kind of lady you wanted real mad at you. Except, secretly, she did know, and in the next fifteen pages, takes action.

I remember thinking, Jesus, what in the world will she do? Annie has a volcanic temper. What's in her head? She talks to Paul about his behavior, and then she eventually works her way around to the Kimberly diamond mines and asks him how he thinks they treat workers there who steal the merchandise. Paul says I don't know, kill them, I suppose. And Annie says, oh no, they hobble them.

And then, all for the need of love, she takes a propane torch and an ax and cuts his feet off: "Now you're hobbled," she tells him, when the deed is done.

I could not fucking believe it.

I mean, I knew she wasn't going to tickle him with a peacock feather, but I never dreamt such behavior was possible. And I knew I had to write the movie. That scene would linger in audiences' memories as I knew it would linger in mine.

The next half year or so are taken up with various versions, and I work with Reiner and Scheinman—the best I have ever known for a script. We finally have a version that they OK, and we go director-hunting. Our first choice is George Roy Hill and he says yesss. Nirvana...

Then Hill calls and says he is changing his mind. We all meet. And Hill, who has never in his life done anything like this, explains. "I was up all night. And I just could not hear myself saying 'action' on that scene. I just haven't got the sensibility to do that scene."

"What scene?" (I am in agony. I desperately want him to do it. He is tough, acerbic, brilliant, snarly, passionate.)

"The lopping scene."

What madness is this? What lopping scene?

"The scene where she lops his feet off."

"George, how can you be so wrong? (After *Butch Cassidy* and *Waldo Pepper*, we have been through a lot. The only way to survive with George is to give him shit right back.) "That is not a 'lopping' scene, that is a 'hobbling' scene. And it is great and it is the reason I took this movie, and she only does it out of love."

"Goldman, she lops his fucking feet off. And I can't direct that."

"It's the best scene in the movie when she hobbles him. It's a character scene, for chrissakes."

He would not budge. And of course, since it was the most important scene and the best scene, it had to stay. A sad, sad farewell. We were about to send the script to Barry Levinson when Rob said, "To hell with it, I'll direct it myself."

And so the lopping scene poll came into my life—because Hill has a brilliant movie mind, and you must pay attention. Rob had no problem directing the scene. But what if George was right? I, of course, scoffed. The hobbling scene was a character scene, unlike anything yet filmed, and it was great and was the reason I took the picture and it had to stay.

Still, we asked people. A poll was taken at Castle Rock, informally, of anyone who had read the script. 'And what do you think of the lopping scene?' Rob would keep me abreast in New York: "A good day for the hobblers today, three secretaries said leave it alone." That wasn't exactly verbatim but you get the idea.

Enter Warren Beatty. Beatty understands the workings of the town, I think, better than anyone. He has been a force for thirty-five years, has been in an amazing number of flops, and whenever his career seems a tad shaky, he produces a wonderful movie or directs a wonderful movie and is safe for another half decade.

Beatty was interested in playing Paul. Rob and Andy met with him a lot, and I spent a day there when the lopping scene came up. Beatty's point was this: he had no trouble losing his feet at the ankles. But know that, if you did it, the guy would be crippled for life and would be a loser.

I said nonsense, it was a great scene, a character scene, was the reason I took the movie and it had to stay as it was. Beatty had a confict with *Dick Tracy*, so casting continued. As did the lopping queries. I went on vacation as we were about to start and while I was gone, Rob and Andy wanted to take a final pass at the script and I was delighted. They wanted it shorter, tighter, tauter, and they are expert editors. When I got back, I read what they had done.

It was shorter, tighter,tauter—

—only the lopping scene was gone, replaced with what you saw in the movie: she breaks his ankles with a sledgehammer.

I scrreeeamed. I got on the phone with Rob and Andy and told them they had ruined the picture, that it was a great and memorable scene they had changed, it was the reason I had taken the job. I was incoherent (they are friends and expect that) but I made my point. They just wouldn't buy it. The lopping scene was gone, now and forever replaced by the ankle-breaking scene. I hated it, but there it was.

I am a wise and experienced hand at this stuff, and I know when I am right.

And you know what?

I was wrong. It became instantly clear when we screened the movie.

What they had done—it was exactly the same scene except for the punishment act—worked wonderfully and was absolutely horrific enough. If we had gone the way I wanted, it would have been too much. The audience would have hated Kathy and, in time, hated us.

If I had been in charge, *Misery* would have been this film you might have heard of but would never have gone to see. Because people who had seen it would have told you to ride clear. What makes a movie a hit is not the star and not the advertising but this: word of mouth. So in the movie business as in real life, we all need all the help we can get. And we need it every step of the way.

CASTING KATHY BATES

"I'm going to write the part for Kathy Bates."

"Oh good. She's great. We"ll use her."

I was the first speaker, Rob Reiner the second. And lives changed.

I had seen Kathy Bates for many years on Broadway. We had never met but I felt then what I do now: She is, simply one of the major actresses of our time. I'd seen her good heartedness in *Vanities* where she played a Texas cheerleader. I'd seen the madness when she played the suidical daughter in '*Night*,

Mother. (I had no sure sense that her talent would translate—a lot of great stage performers are less than great on film—Gielgud, Julie Harris, Kim Stanley will do as examples. But there is an old boxing expression that goes like this: *bury me with a puncher.*) And it was a moment in *Frankie and Johnny at the Clare de Lune* that made me know she was the lady I had to be buried with. She plays a waitress who has a fling with a cook, and at one point she is wearing a robe, and he wants to see her body.

The scene was staged so that he saw her naked body and the audience saw her face, and there was such panic in her eyes and at the same time, this wondrous *hope.* (Casting note: when Michelle Pfeiffer, who I think is a brilliant character actress, played the part in the movie, the same moment was there. But it didn't work for me because Pfeiffer is so loved by the camera that all I kept thinking was, why was she worrying when the worst that could happen would be a pubic hair maybe out of place.)

Anyway Kathy got the part.

It was really almost that simple because Reiner had seen her on Broadway and thought she was as gifted as I did. We could have had almost any actress in the world. Obviously it's a decent part—Kathy won the Oscar for it—but the main reason so many women were interested is there is almost *nothing* for women out there nowadays. Sad but very true. Rob had lunch with Bette Midler who would have been fine and would have helped open the picture. But she did not want to play someone so ugly and Rob realized she would be wrong for the part. *All* stars would be wrong for the part, he decided. Annie is this unknown creature who appears alone out of a storm. We know nothing about her. But stars bring history with them, and I believe, in this case, they would have been damaging.

Example: there is a scene where Annie asks Paul to burn his most recent book in manuscript. It is the one thing on earth he wants least to do and he says no. They argue but he is firm.

Fine, Annie says, I love you and I would never dream of asking you to do anything you didn't want to do. Forget it. I never asked. But—

—big but—

—while she is saying 'forget I ever asked,' what she is doing is walking around his bed flicking lighter fluid onto the sheets. She is threatening, in Annie's sweet, shy way, to fry him.

Rob and Andy and I talked so much about that scene. Was it enough? Did she have to do more? We decided to go with it. But my feeling is that even with as brilliant a performer as Streep in the part, it would not have worked because sitting out there in the dark, some part of us would have known that Meryl Streep wasn't really going to incinerate Jimmy Caan.

But no one knew who Kathy Bates was. And because of that, not to mention her skill, the scene held. One of the advantages to working with an independent like Castle Rock is that they have more freedom in casting. No way Mr. Disney or The Brothers Warner let us go with an unknown in the lead of what they hoped would be a hit movie. And you know what? If I had been the head of a large studio, I wouldn't have cast her either...

CASTING JIMMY CAAN

It was as simple and discouraging as this: no one would play the part.

We knew the role was less flashy. Had to be, the guy's in the sack most of the movie. We also knew he was under the control of the woman, something stars *hate*. But we also felt the movie was essentially what the Brits call a 'two-hander.' The Paul Sheldon part is not only the hero, he's in almost every scene. Wouldn't *anyone* say yes?

We went to William Hurt—

—didn't want to do it.

We rewrote it, went back to William Hurt—

—didn't want to do it yet again.

Kevin Kline—

—didn't want to do it.

Michael Douglas—

—met with Rob, didn't want to do it.

Harrison Ford—

—didn't want to do it.

Dustin Hoffman was called in London—

—liked Castle Rock, liked Rob, didn't want to do it.

Understand, this entire casting process took maybe six months, and we are well into it by now and this is where my respect for Mr. Reiner reached epic size. Because you must understand that well before this point, *all* the major studios would have had me in for rewrites or fired me, because they would have known the script stunk. It had to stink. Look at all those rejections.

Reiner simply got more and more bullheaded.

And secondly, he *needed* a famous face as Paul Sheldon, because Paul Sheldon was famous, just as Annie Wilkes was unknown. On he trudged.

DeNiro—

—didn't want to do it.

Pacino—

—didn't want to do it.

Dreyfuss—

—WANTED TO DO IT.

Yes, Lord.

You see, Rob and Richard Dreyfuss had gone to high school together. And more than that, Rob had offered *When Harry Met Sally* to Dreyfuss. Who said no. Biiiig mistake, as Jack Slater kept saying.

This time when Rob called him Dreyfuss said this: "Whatever it is, I'll do it." Rob was, of course, amazingly relieved. But he felt it was silly for Dreyfuss to take the part without first at least reading it. Rob gave him the script. Dreyfuss read it—oops—

—didn't want to do it.

Hackman would have been wonderful—

—didn't want to do it.

Well before this point, Mr. Redford was sent the script. He would have been extraordinary. He met with Rob. He felt the script would make a very commercial movie.

Long regretful pause—

—didn't want to do it.

How many is that? You count, it's too painful. Understand, this is not the order of submission. My memory is that William Hurt may have been first but his second rejection came well after a bunch of others had passed. Anyway, it is all a swamp to me now.

Enter Warren Beatty.

Kind of wanted to do it. Had a number of wonderful suggestions that helped close holes in the script. But there was this wee problem with *Dick Tracy*, which he was producing, directing and starring in and which conflicted. To this day, I don't think Warren Beatty has said no.

Andy one day mentioned Jimmy Caan. Who had been in the wilderness. Rob met with him, asked about his supposed drug problem. Caan replied that he was clean. "I will pee in a bottle for you," he said. "I will pee in a bottle every day."

He didn't have to.

The reason for the detailing above is because there is a lesson here. Two, actually. First is this: *we will never know.* Would Kevin Kline have made it a better flick? We will never know. Would any of the skilled performers listed? We will never know. They never played the part. They might have been better or worse, all that we can be sure of is that they would have been different. Jimmy Caan did play it and he was terrific.

One thing Caan brought to the party is that he is a very physical guy , he is like a shark, he has to keep moving, he cannot be still in a room. And playing Paul, month after month trapped in that bed drove him nuts. That pent-up energy you saw on screen was very real. And it was one of the main reasons, at least for me, the movie worked.

Second point. When we read about George Raft turning down *The Maltese Falcon* because he didn't trust one of the great directors of all time, John Huston, it seems like lunacy. (The movie also went on to make Mr. Bogart a star.) But Bogart was a nothing then, a small bald New York stage actor who was going nowhere. And Huston had never directed. The same is true when we read of all the people who were offered the lead in *East of Eden* or *On the Waterfront* or *Raiders of the Lost Ark.*

Careers are primarily about timing.

Paul Sheldon is an attractive, sensitive man in his forties, a writer of romance fiction. If you asked me what star best describes that guy I would answer with two words: Richard Gere.

Why didn't we go to him?

Wrong question.

The real question is this: how is it possible for us to spend six months looking for an actor for a part for which Richard Gere would have been perfect and never once, *not even one time mention his name*? That's how dead he was at the time we were looking. We were looking before *Internal Affairs* revived him and *Pretty Woman* put him back on top. We were looking in 1989, seven years since *An Officer and A Gentleman*. And in those seven years, these were his choices: *The Honorary Consul, Breathless, The Cotton Club, King David, No Mercy, Miles From Home.*

He was not just dead, he was forgotten. Happens to us all. God knows it happened to me. I was a leper for five years in the early Eighties. Phone didn't ring. There's a good and practical reason Hollywood likes Dracula pictures—it's potentially the story of all our lives...

THE AUTHOR SEES HIS CHILDREN

Misery was Stephen King's baby. He made it up. And we wanted very much that he like what we had done with it. He was in California and a screening was arraanged, hundreds of people, and he sat unnoticed in the middle of the audience. (King, in case anyone is interested, is amazingly unpretentious. And real smart.)

Anyway, the screening starts and we are pacing around in the back or sitting in corners, because this book meant a lot to him. Near the climax, Annie Wilkes is bringing some champagne into Paul Sheldon's room supposedly to celebrate, but as in the novel, she is going to kill him. She puts a gun into her apron.

Now, by total accident the person sitting next to King is involved with Castle Rock. And reported the following. As Annie takes the tray down to Paul's room, an edgy Stephen King is hunkered down in his seat, muttering to himself. And this is what he is saying: "Look out—don't trust her— she's got a gun in her ayy-pron..."

(He liked it fine. As did we all.)

CAST LIST

JAMES CAAN   PAUL SHELDON

KATHY BATES   ANNIE WILKES

RICHARD FARNSWORTH   BUSTER

FRANCES STERNHAGEN   VIRGINIA

LAUREN BACALL   MARCIA SINDELL

FADE IN ON

A SINGLE CIGARETTE. A MATCH. A HOTEL ICE BUCKET *that holds a bottle of champagne. The cigarette is unlit. The match is of the kitchen variety. The champagne, unopened, is Dom Perignon. There is only one sound at first: a strong* WIND—

—now another sound, sharper—a sudden burst of TYPING *as we*

PULL BACK TO REVEAL

PAUL SHELDON *typing at a table in his hotel suite. It's really a cabin that's part of a lodge. Not an ornate place. Western themed.*

He is framed by a window looking out at some gorgeous mountains. It's afternoon. The sky is grey. Snow is scattered along the ground. We're out west somewhere. The WIND *grows stronger—there could be a storm.*

PAUL *pays no attention to what's going on outside as he continues to type.*

He's the hero of what follows. Forty-two, he's got a good face, one with a certain mileage to it. We are not, in other words, looking at a virgin. He's been a novelist for eighteen years and for half that time, the most recent half, a remarkably successful one.

He pauses for a moment, intently, as if trying to stare a hole in the paper. Now his fingers fly, and there's another burst of TYPING. *He studies what he's written, then —*

CUT TO

THE PAPER, *as he rolls it out of the machine, puts it on the table, prints, in almost child-like letters, these words:*

THE END

CUT TO

A PILE OF MANUSCRIPT *at the rear of the table. He puts this last page on, gets it straight and in order, hoists it up, folds it to his chest, the entire manuscript—hundreds of pages.*

CUT TO

PAUL, *as he holds his book to him. He is, for just a brief moment, moved.*

CUT TO

A SUITCASE *across the room.* PAUL *goes to it, opens it and pulls something out from inside: a battered leather briefcase. Now he takes his manuscript, carefully opens the briefcase, gently puts the manuscript inside. He closes it, and the way he handles it, he might almost be handling a child. Now he crosses over, opens the champagne, pours himself a single glass, lights the one cigarette with the lone match—there is a distinct feeling of ritual about this. He inhales deeply, makes a toasting gesture, then drinks, smokes, smiles.*

HOLD BRIEFLY, *then—*

CUT TO

LODGE. DAY.

PAUL—*exiting his cabin. He stops, makes a snowball, throws it, hitting a sign.*

PAUL

Still got it.

He throws a suitcase into the trunk of his '65 MUSTANG *and, holding his leather case, he hops into the car and drives away.*

CUT TO

A SIGN *that reads "Silver Creek Lodge." Behind the sign is the hotel itself—old, desolate. Now the '65 Mustang comes out of the garage, guns ahead toward the sign. As "Shotgun" by Jr. Walker and the Allstars starts, he heads off into the mountains.*

CUT TO

THE SKY. *Gun-metal grey. The clouds seem pregnant with snow.*

CUT TO

PAUL, *driving the Mustang, the battered briefcase on the seat beside him.*

CUT TO

THE ROAD AHEAD. *Little dainty flakes of snow are suddenly visible.*

CUT TO

THE CAR, *going into a curve and*

CUT TO

PAUL, *driving, and as he comes out of the curve, a stunned look hits his face as we*

CUT TO

THE ROAD AHEAD—*and here it comes—a mountain storm; it's as if the top has been pulled off the sky and with no warning whatsoever, we're into a blizzard and*

CUT TO

THE MUSTANG, *slowing, driving deeper into the mountains.*

CUT TO

PAUL, *squinting ahead, windshield wipers on now.*

CUT TO

THE MUSTANG, *rounding another curve, losing traction—*

CUT TO

PAUL, *a skilled driver, bringing the car easily under control.*

CUT TO

THE ROAD. *Snow is piling up.*

CUT TO

PAUL *driving confidently, carefully. Now he reaches out, ejects the tape, expertly turns it over, pushes it in and, as the* MUSIC *continues, he hums along with it.*

CUT TO

THE SKY. *Only you can't see it.*

There's nothing to see but the unending snow, nothing to hear but the wind which keeps getting wilder.

CUT TO

THE ROAD. *Inches of snow on the ground now. This is desolate and dangerous.*

CUT TO

PAUL, *driving.*

CUT TO

THE SNOW. *Worse.*

CUT TO

THE ROAD, *curving sharply, dropping. A sign reads: "Curved Road, Next 13 Miles."*

CUT TO

THE MUSTANG, *coming into view, hitting the curve—no problem—no problem at all— and then suddenly, there is a very serious problem and as the car skids out of control—*

CUT TO

PAUL, *doing his best, fighting the conditions and just as it looks like he's got things going his way—*

CUT TO

THE ROAD, *swerving down and*

CUT TO

THE MUSTANG, *all traction gone and*

CUT TO

PAUL, *helpless and*

CUT TO

THE MUSTANG, *skidding, skidding and*

CUT TO

THE ROAD *as it drops more steeply away and the wind whips the snow across and*

CUT TO

THE MUSTANG *starting to spin and*

CUT TO

THE MOUNTAINSIDE *as the car skids off the road, careens down, slams into a tree, bounces off, flips, lands upside down, skids, stops finally, dead.*

HOLD ON THE CAR A MOMENT.

There is still the sound of the WIND, *and there is still the music coming from the tape, perhaps the only part of the car left undamaged, Nothing moves inside. There is only the* WIND *and the* TAPE. *The wind gets louder.*

CUT TO

THE WRECK *looked at from a distance. The* MUSIC *sounds are only faintly heard.*

CUT TO

THE AREA WHERE THE WRECK IS—AS SEEN FROM THE ROAD. *The car is barely visible as the snow begins to cover it.*

CUT TO

THE WRECK *from outside, and we're close to it now, with the snow coming down ever harder—already bits of the car are covered in white.*

CAMERA MOVES IN TO

PAUL. *He's inside and doing his best to fight it, but his consciousness is going. He tries to keep his eyes open but they're slits.*

Slowly, he manages to reach out with his left arm for his briefcase—

—and he clutches it to his battered body. The MUSIC *continues on.*

But PAUL *is far past listening. His eyes flutter, flutter again. Now they're starting to close.*

The man is dying.

Motionless, he still clutches the battered briefcase.

HOLD ON THE CASE. *Then—*

DISSOLVE TO

THE BRIEFCASE *in Paul's hands as he sits at a desk.*

SINDELL (off-screen)

What's that?

PULL BACK TO REVEAL

We are in New York City in the office of Paul's literary agent, MARCIA SINDELL. *The walls of the large room are absolutely crammed with book and movie posters, in English and all kinds of other languages, all of them featuring the character of* MISERY CHASTAIN *a perfectly beautiful woman.* Misery's Challenge, Misery's Triumph—*eight of them. All written by Paul Sheldon.*

CUT TO

PAUL, *lifting up the battered briefcase—maybe when new it cost two bucks, but he treats it like gold.*

PAUL

An old friend. I was rummaging through a closet and it was just sitting there. Like it was waiting for me.

CUT TO

SINDELL
(searching for a compliment)

It's...it's nice, Paul. It's got...character.

CUT TO

THE TWO OF THEM.

PAUL

When I wrote my first book, I used to carry it around in this while I was looking for a publisher. That was a good book, Marcia. I was a writer then.

SINDELL

You're still a writer.

PAUL

I haven't been a writer since I got into the Misery business—

SINDELL

(holding up the cover art of Misery's Child*)*

Not a bad business. This thing would still be growing, too. The first printing order on *Misery's Child* was the most ever—over a million.

PAUL

Marcia, please.

SINDELL

No, no. Misery Chastain put braces on your daughter's teeth and is putting her through college, bought you two houses and floor seats to the Knick games and what thanks does she get? You go and kill her.

PAUL

Marcia, you know I started "Misery" on a lark. Do I look like a guy who writes romance novels? Do I sound like Danielle Steel? It was a one-time shot and we got lucky. I never meant it to become my life. And if I hadn't gotten rid of her now, I'd have ended up writing her forever. *(touches his briefcase)* For the first time in fifteen years, I think I'm really onto something here.

SINDELL

I'm glad to hear that, Paul, I really am. But you have to know—when your fans find out that you killed off their favorite heroine, they're not going to say, "Ooh, good, Paul Sheldon can finally write what we've always wanted: an esoteric, semi-autobiographical character study."

PAUL

(passionately)

Marcia, why are you doing this to me? Don't you know I'm scared enough? Don't you think I remember how nobody gave a shit about my first books? You think I'm dying to go back to shouting in the wilderness? *(beat)* I'm doing this because I have to. *(Marcia is stopped.)* Now, I'm leaving for Colorado to try to finish this and I want your good thoughts— because if I can make it work...*(beat)* I might just have something that I want on my tombstone.

On the word "tombstone"

CUT TO

PAUL'S TOMBSTONE—*the upside down car with the blizzard coming gale-forced and his motionless body trapped inside the car.*

The WIND screams. PAUL'S EYES flutter, then close.

HOLD

KEEP HOLDING AS—

Suddenly there's a new sound as a crowbar SCRATCHES at the door—

— and now the door is ripped open as we

PULL BACK TO REVEAL

A BUNDLED-UP FIGURE gently beginning to pull PAUL and the case from the car. For a moment, it's hard to tell if it's a man or a woman—

— not to let the cat out of the bag or anything, but it is, very much, a woman. Her name is ANNIE WILKES and she is close to Paul's age. She is in many ways a remarkable creature. Strong, self-sufficient, passionate in her likes and dislikes, loves and hates.

CUT TO

PAUL AND ANNIE *as she cradles him in her arms. Once he's clear of the car, she lays him carefully in the snow.*

CUT TO

PAUL AND ANNIE: CLOSE UP. *She slowly brings her mouth down close to his. Then their lips touch as she forces air inside him.*

> **ANNIE**
> *(Their lips touch again. Then—)*
> You hear me—Breathe! *I said breathe!!!*

CUT TO

PAUL, *as he starts to breathe—*

—in a moment his eyes suddenly open wide, but he's in shock, the eyes see nothing—

CUT TO

ANNIE—*the moment she sees him come to life, she goes into action, lifting PAUL in a fireman's carry, starting the difficult climb back up the steep hill.*

As she moves away, she and Paul are obliterated by the white falling snow.

DISSOLVE TO

THE WHITE OF WHAT SEEMS LIKE A HOSPITAL. *Everything is bled of color. It's all vague—*

—we are looking at this from Paul's blurred vision.

And throughout this next sequence, there are these SOUNDS, *words really, but they make no sense.*

> "...no...worry ...
> ...be...fine...
> ... good care...you...
> ...I'm your number one fan..."

The first thing we see during this is something all white. It takes a moment before we realize it's a ceiling.

Now, a white wall.

An I.V. BOTTLE *is next, the medicine dripping down along a tube into* PAUL'S LEFT ARM. *The other arm is bandaged and in a sling.*

ANNIE *is standing beside the bed. She wears off-white and seems very much like a nurse. A good nurse. She has pills in her hands.*

CUT TO

PAUL. *Motionless, dead pale. He has a little beard now. Eyes barely open, he's shaking with fever.*

> **PAUL**
> *(hardly able to whisper)*
> ...where...am I...?

ANNIE *is quickly by his side.*

> **ANNIE**
> *(so gently)*
> Shhh...we're just outside Silver Creek.

> **PAUL**
> How long...?

> **ANNIE**
> You've been here two days. You're gonna be okay. *(relieved)* My name is Annie Wilkes and I'm—

> PAUL

—my number one fan...

And now the gibberish words make sense.

> ANNIE

That's right. I'm also a nurse. Here. *(now, as she brings the pills close)* Take these. *(She helps him to swallow, as Paul's eyes close.)*

DISSOLVE TO

AN EXTERIOR OF THE PLACE. It's a farmhouse—we're in a desolate area with mountains in the background.

THE HOUSE is set on a knoll so that Paul's room, although on the first floor, is ten feet off the ground.

CUT TO

PAUL, in the room. He's not on the I.V. anymore. His fever has broken. Annie enters, pills in her hand.

> ANNIE

Here.

> PAUL

What are they...?

> ANNIE

They're called Novril—they're for your pain. *(helps him take them)*

ANNIE applies a cool rag to his forehead.

> PAUL

Shouldn't I be in a hospital?

> ANNIE

The blizzard was too strong, I couldn't risk trying to get you there. I tried calling, but the phone lines are down.

PAUL tries to test his left arm.

> ANNIE
> *(Gently, her fingers go to his eyelids, close them.)*

Now you mustn't tire yourself. You've got to rest, you almost died.

CUT TO

ANNIE: CLOSE UP. Sometimes her face shows the most remarkable compassion. It does now.

HOLD ON IT briefly.

DISSOLVE TO

CLOSE UP ON PILLS IN ANNIE'S HAND.

> ANNIE (off-screen)
> Open wide.

CUT TO

PAUL'S ROOM.

He lies in bed. His fever is gone, but he's terribly weak.

CUT TO

ANNIE. As she lays the pills on PAUL'S TONGUE, she gives him a glass of water from the nearby bed table.

CUT TO

PAUL, swallowing eagerly.

CUT TO

ANNIE, watching him, sympathetically.

> ANNIE
> Your legs just sing grand opera when you move, don't they? *(Paul says nothing, but his pain is clear.)* It's not going to hurt forever, Paul, I promise you.

> PAUL
> Will I be able to walk?

> ANNIE
> Of course you will. And your arm will be fine, too. Your shoulder was dislocated pretty badly. It was a little stubborn, but I finally popped it back in. *(proudly)* But what I'm most proud of is the work I did on those legs. Considering what I had around the house, I don't think there's a doctor who could have done any better. *(And now suddenly she flicks off the blanket, uncovering his body.)*

CUT TO

PAUL, staring, stunned at the bottom half of his body as we

CUT TO

PAUL'S LEGS. *From the knees down he resembles an Egyptian mummy—she's splinted them with slim steel rods that look like the hacksawed remains of aluminum crutches and there's taping circling around.*

From the knees up they're all swollen and throbbing and horribly bruised and discolored.

CUT TO

PAUL, *lying back, stunned with disbelief.*

> **ANNIE**
> It's not nearly as bad as it looks. You have a compound fracture of the tibia in both legs, and the fibula in the left leg is fractured too. I could hear the bones moving, so it's best for your legs to remain immobile. And as soon as the roads open, I'll take you to a hospital—

CUT TO

ANNIE: CLOSE UP.

> **ANNIE**
> In the meantime, you've got a lot of recovering to do, and I consider it an honor that you'll do it in my home.

HOLD ON HER ECSTATIC FACE. Then—

CUT TO

MISERY'S PERFECT FACE. *We're back in* SINDELL's *office in New York. The office looks just the same, posters and many scripts all over. But she doesn't.*

She holds the phone and she is fidgety, insecure.

> **SINDELL**
> This is Marcia Sindell calling from New York City. I'd like to speak to the Silver Creek Chief of Police or the Sheriff.

> **MALE VOICE** (off-screen)
> Which one do you want?

> **SINDELL**
> Whichever one's not busy.

CUT TO

A SMALL OFFICE IN SILVER CREEK

...with a view of the mountains.

A MARVELOUS LOOKING MAN sits at a desk, by himself, holding the phone. In his sixties, he's still as bright, fast and sassy as he was half-a-lifetime ago. Never mind what his name is, everyone calls him BUSTER.

> **BUSTER**
> I'm pretty sure they're both not busy, Ms. Sindell, since they're both me. I also happen to be President of the Policeman's Benefit Association, Chairman of the Patrolman's Retirement Fund, and if you need a good fishing guide, you could do a lot worse; call me Buster, everybody does, what can I do for you?

CUT TO

SINDELL in her office. She pushes the speakerphone, gets up, paces; she's very hesitant when she speaks about Paul. Almost embarrassed—

> **SINDELL**
> I'm a literary agent, and I feel like a fool calling you, but I think one of my clients, Paul Sheldon, might be in some kind of trouble.

> **BUSTER**
> Paul Sheldon? You mean Paul Sheldon the writer?

> **SINDELL**
> Yes.

> **BUSTER**
> He's your client, huh?

> **SINDELL**
> Yes, he is.

CUT TO

BUSTER'S OFFICE.

He rolls a penny across the back of one hand—he's very good at it, doesn't even look while he does it.

> **BUSTER**
> People sure like those Misery books.

> **SINDELL**
> I'm sure you know Paul's been going to the Silver Creek Lodge for years to finish his books.

> **BUSTER**
> Yeah, I understand he's been up here the last six weeks.

SINDELL

Not quite. I just called, and they said he checked out five days ago. Isn't that a little strange?

BUSTER

I don't know. Does he always phone you when he checks out of hotels?

CUT TO

SINDELL, *really embarrassed now.*

SINDELL

No, no, of course not. It's just that his daughter hasn't heard from him, and when he's got a book coming out, he usually keeps in touch. So when there was no word from him...

BUSTER

You think he might be missing?

SINDELL
(shakes her head)

I hate that I made this call— tell me I'm being silly.

CUT TO

BUSTER. *He nods as a* WOMAN *enters, carrying lunch. It's his wife,* VIRGINIA. *She begins putting the food down on a table for the both of them.*

BUSTER

Just a little over-protective, maybe. *(beat)* Tell you what—nothing's been reported out here—*(He puts Paul Sheldon's name with a ? on a 3 x 5 card.)*— but I'll put his name through our system. *(He tacks the card to a bulletin board.)* And if anything turns up, I'll call you right away.

CUT TO

SINDELL. *She smiles; a genuine sense of relief.*

SINDELL

I appreciate that. Thanks a lot.

CUT TO

BUSTER.

BUSTER

G'bye, Ms. Sindell.

As he hangs up—

> VIRGINIA

We actually got a phone call. Busy morning.

> BUSTER
> (smiles)

Work, work, work. (gives her a hug) Virginia? When was that blizzard?

> VIRGINIA

Four or five days ago. Why?

CUT TO

BUSTER. The penny flies across the back of his hand now. He doesn't look at it, stares instead out the window at the mountains.

> BUSTER
> (a beat)

...no reason...

HOLD ON BUSTER for a moment.

CUT TO

PAUL' S ROOM.

> PAUL'S VOICE
> (soft)

I guess it was kind of a miracle...you finding me...

ANNIE's soft, sweet laughter is heard. She stands over him, finishing shaving him with a very sharp straight razor. She wears what we will come to know as her regular costume— plain wool skirts, grey cardigan sweaters.

> ANNIE

No, it wasn't a miracle at all...in a way, I was following you.

> PAUL

Following me?

ANNIE concentrates on shaving him with great care; she has wonderful, strong hands.

> ANNIE
> (explaining, normally)

Well, it wasn't any secret to me that you were staying at the Silver Creek, seeing as how I'm your number-one fan and all. Some nights I'd just tool on down there, sit outside and look up at the light in your cabin—(gently moves his head back, exposing his neck; this next is said with total sincerity, almost awe)—and I'd try to imagine what was going on in the room of the world's greatest writer.

> PAUL

Say that last part again, I didn't quite hear—

> ANNIE
> *(smiles)*

Don't move now—wouldn't want to hurt this neck—*(shaving away)* Well, the other afternoon I was on my way home, and there you were, leaving the Lodge, and I wondered why a literary genius would go for a drive when there was a big storm coming.

> PAUL

I didn't know it was going to be a big storm.

> ANNIE

Lucky for you, I did. *(pauses)* Lucky for me too. Because now you're alive and you can write more books. Oh, Paul, I've read everything of yours, but the *Misery* novels...

CUT TO

ANNIE: CLOSE UP

> ANNIE

I know them all by heart, Paul, all eight of them. I love them so.

CUT TO

PAUL, looking at her. There's something terribly touching about her now.

> PAUL

You're very kind...

> ANNIE

And you're very brilliant, and you must be a good man, or you could never have created such a wondrous, loving creature as Misery Chastain. *(runs her fingers over his cheek)* Like a baby. *(smiles)* All done. *(starts to dab away the last bits of soap)*

ANNIE starts cleaning up.

> PAUL

When do you think the phone lines'll be back up? I have to call my daughter, and I should call New York and let my agent know I'm breathing.

ANNIE

It shouldn't be too much longer. *(gently)* Once the roads are open, the lines'll be up in no time. If you give me their numbers, I'll keep trying them for you. *(suddenly almost embarrassed)* Could I ask you a favor? *(Paul nods.)* I noticed in your case there was a new Paul Sheldon book and... *(hesitant)* and I wondered if maybe... *(Her voice trails off.)*

PAUL

You want to read it?

ANNIE
(quietly)

If you wouldn't mind.

PAUL

I have a hard and fast rule about who can read my stuff at this early stage—only my editor, my agent, and anyone who saves me from freezing to death in a car wreck.

ANNIE
(genuinely thrilled)

You'll never realize what a rare treat you've given me.

CUT TO

PAUL. *His eyes close briefly, he grimaces.*

CUT TO

ANNIE, *watching him, concerned. She glances at her watch.*

ANNIE

Boy, it's like clockwork, the way your pain comes—I'll get you your Novril, Paul. Forgive me for prattling away and making you feel all oogy. *(She turns and goes out of the room.)*

CUT TO

PAUL, *watching her.*

ANNIE (off-screen)

What's your new book called?

PAUL

I don't have a title yet.

ANNIE (off-screen)

What's it about?

> PAUL
> *(fast)*

It's crazy, but I don't really know, I mean I haven't written anything but "Misery" for so long that—you read it you can tell me what *you* think it's about. Maybe you can come up with a title.

> ANNIE
> *(in the doorway)*

Oh, like I could do that?

CUT TO

THE MANAGER'S OFFICE AT THE SILVER CREEK LODGE.

Small, neat, one window—outside, snow covers all.

BUSTER AND LIBBY, THE MANAGER, are going over books and records. Libby is an old guy, walks with a cane.

> LIBBY

Nothing unusual about Mr. Sheldon's leaving, Buster—you can tell by the champagne.

> BUSTER

Maybe you can, Libby.

> LIBBY

No, see, he always ordered a bottle of Dom Perignon when he was ready to go. Then he'd pay up and be out the door.

> BUSTER

No long-distance phone calls, Federal Express packages—anything at all out of the ordinary?

> LIBBY
> *(head shake)*

I don't think Mr. Sheldon likes for things to be out of the ordinary. Considering who he is and all, famous and all, he doesn't have airs. Drives the same car out from New York each time—'65 Mustang—said it helps him think. He was always a good guest, never made a noise, never bothered a soul. Sure hope nothing happened to him.

> BUSTER

So do I...

> LIBBY

I'll bet that old Mustang's pulling into New York right now.

BUSTER

I'm sure you're right.

But you can tell he's not sure at all as we

CUT TO

A SPOON FILLED TO THE BRIM WITH BEEF BARLEY SOUP.

CUT TO

PAUL'S ROOM.

He lies in bed. Sun comes in the lone window. ANNIE sits on the bed, a large bowl of soup in her hands, feeding him.

ANNIE
(almost shy about this)
I know I'm only forty pages into your book, but...

She stops, fills the spoon up again.

PAUL

But what?

ANNIE

Nothing.

PAUL

No, what is it?

ANNIE

Oh, it's ridiculous, who am I to make a criticism to someone like you?

PAUL

I can take it, go ahead.

ANNIE

Well, it's brilliantly written, but then everything you write is brilliant.

PAUL

Pretty rough so far.

ANNIE
(a burst)
The swearing, Paul. *(beat)* There, I said it.

PAUL

The profanity bothers you?

> ANNIE

It has no nobility.

> PAUL

Well, these are slum kids, I was a slum kid, everybody talks like that.

CUT TO

ANNIE. *She holds the soup bowl in one hand, the muddy-colored beef barley soup close to spilling.*

> ANNIE

They do not. What do you think I say when I go to the feed store in town? "Now, Wally, give me a bag of that effing pigfeed and ten pounds of that bitchly cow-corn"—

PAUL *is amused by this.*

CUT TO

THE SOUP, *almost spilling as she gets more agitated.*

> ANNIE

—and in the bank do I tell Mrs. Bollinger, "Here's one big bastard of a check, give me some of your Christing money."

CUT TO

PAUL, *almost laughing as some soup hits the coverlet.*

> ANNIE
> *(seeing the spill, suddenly upset)*

There! Look there! See what you made me do!

CUT TO

PAUL—*his smile disappears.*

CUT TO

ANNIE, *and she is just totally embarrassed.*

> ANNIE

Oh, Paul, I'm sorry. I'm so sorry. Sometimes I get so worked up. Can you ever forgive me? Here...

She hands him his pills and starts to clean the soup off the coverlet. Then she makes the sweetest smile.

ANNIE

I love you, Paul. *(more embarrassed than ever)* Your mind. Your creativity—that's all I meant. *(Flustered, she turns away as we—)*

CUT TO

A ROAD IN THE MOUNTAINS. *Piles of snow all around but it's been ploughed enough so it's driveable.*

CUT TO

A CAR *coming into view. Up ahead is the road sign we've already seen: "Curved Road, Next 13 Miles."*

CUT TO

INSIDE THE CAR.

BUSTER AND HIS WIFE VIRGINIA: *Virginia is driving, while Buster intently studies the terrain. He reaches for a large thermos, pours some coffee, offers it to her. She shakes her head. He begins to sip it.*

VIRGINIA

This sure is fun. *(She puts her hand on his leg.)*

BUSTER
(removing it)

Virginia, when you're in this car, you're not my wife, you're my deputy.

VIRGINIA

Well, this deputy would rather be home under the covers with the Sheriff.

CUT TO

THE CAR. *Suddenly, it goes into a little icy spin—she fights it back under control.*

CUT TO

INSIDE THE CAR.

BUSTER
(suddenly)

Stop—stop right here.

VIRGINIA

What? What is it?

CUT TO

The car, skidding, slowing, stopping. Both of them get out, go to the edge of the road. Mountains of snow. Nothing much else visible. Then Buster points.

BUSTER
Look at that broken branch there...

CUT TO

Virginia, seeing it, unconvinced.

VIRGINIA
Could be the weight of the snow.

BUSTER
Could be—or a rotten branch or a mountain lion could have landed on it. Could be a lot of things. *(He steps off the road, starts down.)*

CUT TO

Virginia, watching him, worried—it's very slippery.

CUT TO

Buster, graceful, in great shape, navigating down easily.

CUT TO

The tree that the car ran into. Buster reaches it, studies it.

CUT TO

Virginia, staring out after him—she can't see him because the drop is both too steep and covered with trees and mounds of snow.

VIRGINIA
Anything down there?

BUSTER'S VOICE (off-screen)
Yeah. An enormous amount of snow.

CUT TO

Buster. He's moved away from the tree now, going toward where the Mustang is buried.

CUT TO

The mound of snow with the Mustang inside.

CUT TO

Buster, making his slow way closer to it, closer, staring around.

CUT TO

THE AREA. *Nothing to be seen—everything is covered with mountains of snow. You could have a house down there and not be able to see it. Just glaring white.*

CUT TO

BUSTER, *angry, frustrated, turning around and around and*

CUT TO

BUSTER *from another angle, from behind the mound with the Mustang inside— and out of his sight, glistening in the sun, a bit of the door protrudes. But, of course, Buster can't see it.*

HOLD ON BUSTER, *in a sour mood, staring around as the edge of the door continues to glisten.*

CUT TO

VIRGINIA, *on the road as Buster makes his way back up, still ticked.*

> **VIRGINIA**
> *(They move to the car.)*
> You really think Sheldon's out there?

> **BUSTER**
> Hope not— if he is, he's dead. Let's go to the newspaper office *(as they get in the car—)*

ANOTHER CAR DRIVING BY—*it's Annie in her Jeep—neither she nor Buster notice each other.*

CUT TO

PAUL'S ROOM.

The door opens and ANNIE *enters.*

> **ANNIE**
> Oh, I'm sorry. I didn't mean to wake you.

> **PAUL**
> It's fine.

PULL BACK TO REVEAL

Paul's eyes fluttering awake to see the hardback copy of his novel, Misery's Child, *in Annie's hands. She's never been more excited—*

> ANNIE

They had it at the store, Paul, there was a whole batch of them there. As soon as I saw it, I slammed my money down. I got the first copy.

> PAUL

Then the roads are open...

> ANNIE

The one to town is, but that's about it. I called the hospital and talked to the head orthopedic surgeon. I told him who you were and what had happened. He said as long as there's no infection, you're not in any danger, and as soon as the road to the hospital is open, they'll send an ambulance for you.

> PAUL

The phones are working?

> ANNIE

Well, mine's still out. But the ones in town were working just fine. I called that agent of yours. *(soft now)* Oh, Paul, I peeked at the very beginning. *(looks at him)* What a wonderful first page—just to read the name Misery Chastain...

> PAUL

My daughter must be going nuts.

> ANNIE

...it's like a visit from my oldest, dearest friend.

> PAUL

I was supposed to be home for her birthday three days ago.

> ANNIE

The agent said she would tell her you were okay. But I'm afraid you'll have to wait till tomorrow if you want to speak to her yourself.

She starts to leave, stops at the door.

> ANNIE
> *(She looks at him now with almost a look of wonderment.)*
> Oh, Paul, what a poet you are... *(as she leaves)*

DISSOLVE TO

PAUL, *watching as she enters, moves to him, carrying a tray.*

ANNIE

I made you my speciality—scrambled eggs a la Wilkes. And I'm on page 75.

PAUL

I guess that means it's okay.

ANNIE

No. No, it isn't, it's—*(halts)*—oh pooh, I can't think of any words. Would "great" be insulting?

PAUL

I can live with "great." *(He starts, with effort, to eat.)*

ANNIE
(as she turns, goes)
No, it's not just great, it's perfect, a perfect, perfect thing.

CUT TO

PAUL'S ROOM. MID-AFTERNOON.

ANNIE is clearing Paul's tray. She hands him his Novril; he quickly swallows them.

ANNIE

I'm up to page 185. I always get sad when I pass the halfway point. Will you do me a favor? I'd love it if you would autograph my copy. I already have your autograph on a picture, but it would mean so much to me to get it in person. I know you're right-handed, so don't worry if it's not so legible. I'll cherish it anyway.

As PAUL signs the book:

ANNIE

I don't mean to pry, but I've read in two magazines now where you were seeing this model who does those disgusting jeans commercials. And I said it can't be true. Paul Sheldon would never waste his time with a trampy woman like that.

PAUL

Well, you can't believe everything you read in magazines.

ANNIE

I knew it. I knew it wasn't true. Boy, how do they get away with printing stuff like that?

PAUL

You'd be amazed at what some people will believe.

He finishes the autograph, hands the book back to her.

> ANNIE
> Thank you so much.

> PAUL
> My pleasure.

DISSOLVE TO

THE WINDOW. LATE-AFTERNOON SUNLIGHT.

CUT TO

THE DOOR. It opens and guess what—a sow lumbers in.

CUT TO

PAUL, kind of stunned as this female pig skitters its way around the room, excited, confused, slipping and sliding.

CUT TO

ANNIE, all smiles and happiness, laughing in the doorway.

> ANNIE
> I thought it was time you two should meet. Paul, say hello to my favorite beast in all the world, my sow, Misery.

> PAUL
> Misery?

CUT TO

THE PIG, snorting around the room.

CUT TO

PAUL AND ANNIE, watching it.

> ANNIE
> Yes. I told you I was your number-one fan.

> PAUL
> I'm getting to believe you.

> ANNIE
> This farm was kind of dreary, what with just the few cows and chickens and me—*(happy)* But when I got Misery here, everything changed— she just makes me smile so.

PAUL

She's a fine...uh...pig is what she is...

ANNIE
(scooping up the pig, holding it tight as she stands by Paul)
I'm on page three-hundred now, Paul, and it's better than perfect—it's divine. What's the ceiling that dago painted?

PAUL

The Sistine Chapel?

ANNIE

Yeah, that and *Misery's Child*—those are the only two divine things ever in this world...

PAUL watches, as the pig skitters out of the room with ANNIE in pursuit, happily imitating the pig.

ANNIE

Woink! Whoink! Whuh—Whuh—WHOINK!

CUT TO

PAUL staring after them—what the hell was that?

CUT TO

THE WINDOW. DUSK.

ANNIE'S VOICE is heard softly.

ANNIE (off-screen)
When my husband left me...I wasn't prepared, it wasn't an easy time...

PULL BACK TO REVEAL

ANNIE, standing staring out the window, her back to the room.

In bed, PAUL is dealing with a bedpan, peeing.

ANNIE

For a while I thought I might go crazy.

PAUL

I know how that can be.

> ANNIE

I don't know about you, but what I did to get through it was I dove into work—days, nights—night shifts can be lonely at a hospital. I did a lot of reading. That was when I first discovered Misery. She made me so happy. She made me forget all my problems. *(She smiles now.)* 'Course, I suppose you had a little something to do with that too.

There is a peeing sound.

> PAUL

Yeah, well...

He is embarrassed.

> ANNIE
> *(She isn't.)*

I just kept reading them over and over. I know when I finish this one— and I've only got two chapters to go—I'll just turn right to the first page and start reading it again.

> PAUL

I'm...

> ANNIE
> *(She turns around, moves to the bed.)*

Done?

> PAUL

Yeah, thanks.

> ANNIE

No problem.

As she takes the bedpan...

> ANNIE

Don't get me wrong. I'm not against marriage per se. But it would take a pretty special guy to make me want to go down the aisle again.

> PAUL

Well, it's not something you should enter into lightly.

> ANNIE

It boils down to respect. People just don't respect the institution of marriage anymore. They have no sense of real commitment.

CUT TO

PAUL, *attempting to smile. There is not much he can say to this.*

ANNIE

I'd love to stay here and chat, but I'm right at the end and I gotta find out what happens.

PAUL

Well, I hope you like it.

ANNIE

Of course I'll like it. Misery's about to have her child. What's it gonna be, a boy or a girl? Ooh, don't tell me.

With that, she exits.

CUT TO

THE WINDOW. MOONLIGHT.

CUT TO

PAUL. *He's been dozing but now his eyes flutter awake as we*

CUT TO

THE DOOR. *It opens and* ANNIE *enters, comes to his bedside.*

CUT TO

PAUL. *Hard to see. He squints up as we*

CUT TO

ANNIE. CLOSE UP: *her face is ashen pale.*

ANNIE

You...you dirty bird. She can't be dead. Misery Chastain cannot be dead! How could you?

PAUL

Annie, in 1871, women often died in childbirth, but her spirit is the important thing, and Misery's spirit is still alive—

ANNIE
(screaming)
I DON'T WANT HER SPIRIT! I want HER! And you MURDERED her!

PAUL

I DIDN'T...

ANNIE

Then who did?

PAUL

No one—she just died—she slipped away, that's all.

ANNIE
(screaming)
She slipped away? She slipped away? She didn't just slip away. You did it.
You did it. You did it. You did it. You murdered my Misery.

And now she has lifted a chair—it's heavy but she's very strong—and she raises it and turns on Paul, and it's high above her head, and PAUL realizes that this might be it, she might shatter him with it, crunch his skull—and that's just what she seems she's about to do—and then she swings it, not against him but against the wall, and it shatters and she's panting from the effort as she turns on him again, her voice surprisingly soft.

ANNIE
I thought you were good, Paul, but you're not good, you're just another
lying old dirty birdie and I don't think I better be around you for awhile.
(She crosses to the door, then stops.) And don't even think about anybody
coming for you, not the doctors, not your agent, not your family—
because I never called them. Nobody knows you're here. And you better
hope nothing happens to me because if I die, you die.

CUT TO

PAUL, watching as she closes the door behind her. Then there is a RATTLE OF A KEY and the sound of the door to his room LOCKING.

CUT TO

ANNIE, getting in her Cherokee and gunning away.

CUT TO

THE ROOM.

PAUL lies still. He looks around the room and listens for sounds. All he hears are the SOUNDS OF A WINTER NIGHT in the mountains. After a few beats, he takes a deep breath and then begins his greatest effort of all: to force his body out of the bed, to make it move.

He's still weak from what he's endured, but that's not the main thing: it's the pain. Any attempt at movement and his legs scream. He sags back, lies there still a moment. Slowly he tries to maneuver his body off the bed. He rolls over onto his stomach, then tries to lower himself onto the floor by moving down head first. His good arm hits the floor, and he is able to hold himself up but, realizing there is no way to get out of bed without caus-

ng tremendous pain, he girds himself and flings himself out of bed and comes crashing to the floor.

The pain is excruciating. After he regains his composure, he slowly crawls toward the door.

He reaches up and tries the handle. It is, in fact, locked. He awkwardly tries to slam up against the door, but it is much too painful and to no avail. He crawls back over to the bed, realizes there's no way to climb back in, then grabs the blanket from the bed, wraps it around himself, and closes his eyes.

DISSOLVE TO

BUSTER'S OFFICE. DAY.

He sits alone at his desk on the telephone, staring at The Rocky Mountain Gazette, *spread in front of him.*

CUT TO

THE NEWSPAPER'S FRONT PAGE.

In a prominent spot on the top is what is most likely a book-jacket photo of Paul. Above the picture is the following: "HAVE YOU SEEN PAUL SHELDON?"

BUSTER is on the phone with Marcia Sindell.

BUSTER
No, Ms. Sindell, there's no point in coming up here now. Everything that can be done is... Yes, we're working closely with the state police, and the FBI has been informed. Right...Right...As soon as we know anything we'll let you know. No, it's no bother. Call anytime. Bye, Ms. Sindell.

VIRGINIA enters, carrying some files.

VIRGINIA
Here's the list of all Sheldon's credit charges. Nothing after the Silver Creek. *(With a glance at his dour face, she indicates the photo.)* Any calls?

BUSTER
Just from his agent.

CUT TO

BUSTER. His eyes flick up to her. An almost imperceptible shake of the head.

HOLD FOR A MOMENT, then—

FACES. They are distorted, and they come into view but briefly, then change into the next distorted face. All kinds—there is no order to them— young, oriental, female, male, pret-

ty, sad, black, not so pretty, happy, white, old— what we HEAR *is this:*

"...You've changed my life..."

"...I'm your number one fan..."

"...I'm a really big fan of yours..."

"...I'm your biggest fan..."

"...Don't ever stop writing those Misery books..."

"...I've read all your books, but the Miserys... well..."

"...I'm your number one fan..."

"...You've given me such pleasure..."

"...I feel like you're writing just for me..."

AND NOW, IT GETS KICKED UP IN SPEED AND ALL GOES FASTER, MANY TIMES OVERLAPPING.

"...I love you...I'm your number one fan...I'm your biggest fan...We love you...number one...love you...biggest...love you...number one...number one... you poor dear thing..."

This last was said by Annie, out of focus, and for a moment, she stays that way—

CUT TO

THE ROOM, AS IT SNAPS BACK INTO FOCUS—ANNIE *is standing by the bed. It is dusk.*

She wears a dark blue dress and a hat with a sprig of flowers. Her eyes are bright and vivacious—the fact is, this is the prettiest ANNIE WILKES *has ever looked.*

> ANNIE
> What are you doing on the floor? *(crossing to the bed)* It's my fault. If I'd had a proper hospital bed, this never would have happened. Here, let me help you back in. *(She lifts him back into the bed, which causes considerable pain.)* I know this hurts, but it'll only take a few seconds. There you go. Comfy?

> PAUL
> *(in pain)*
> Perfect.

> ANNIE
> You're such a kidder. I have a big surprise for you. But first there's something you must do.

PAUL

I don't suppose I could have a little snack while I wait for the surprise?

ANNIE

I'll get you everything you want, but you must listen first. Sometimes my thinking is a little muddy, I accept that. It's why I couldn't remember all those things they were asking me on the witness stand in Denver.

Now she turns, goes to the doorway, keeping on talking. She is never out of sight.

ANNIE

But this time I thought clearly. I asked God about you and God said, "I delivered him unto you so that you may show him the way."

PAUL

Show me the way?

ANNIE

Yes.

She exits and re-enters wheeling something toward his bed. It's a charcoal barbecue, the kind you use in summer for cooking hamburgers. She holds several items in her arms: a box of Diamond Blue Tip wooden matches, a can of lighter fluid. And most noticeably, Paul's manuscript.

CUT TO

ANNIE AND PAUL. He watches, mute, as she takes off the grill, puts the manuscript into the barbecue itself where the charcoal goes, spritzes it with lighter fluid. The grill is close enough to the bed for him to reach out and drop a match.

PAUL

When I mentioned a snack, I was thinking more along the lines of a cheese and crackers kind of thing.

CUT TO

ANNIE, looking at him.

ANNIE

Paul, this is no time for jokes. You must rid the world of this filth.

She hands him the box of kitchen matches.

PAUL

You want me to burn my book?

ANNIE
(She nods.)

Yes.

PAUL

You want me to burn my book?

ANNIE

I know this may be difficult for you, but it's for the best.

PAUL

This isn't difficult, my agent's made dozens of copies. There's gonna be an auction on this, and every publishing house in New York is reading it now. So if you want me to burn it, fine. You're not ridding the world of anything.

CUT TO

ANNIE, *watching him.*

ANNIE
(quietly)

Then light the match, Paul.

PAUL

No big deal.

ANNIE

So you've indicated. Do it.

CUT TO

THE MATCHES. PAUL'S HANDS *are starting to tremble now. He can't do it.*

ANNIE

I know this is the only copy, Paul. When you were twenty-four you wrote your first book and you didn't make a copy, because you didn't think anybody would take it seriously. But they did. And ever since you've never made any copies because you're superstitious—it's why you always come back to the Silver Creek Lodge. You told that story to Merv Griffin eleven years ago.

PAUL

You know, Annie, this book never would have survived without you. When it gets to New York, there will be a big auction, and whatever it brings we can split. *(pause)* God knows you're entitled to it.

ANNIE

Oh, Paul. This isn't about money. It's about decency and purity. It's about God's values.

PAUL

You're right. You're right. I don't know what I was thinking. I'll tell you what. It doesn't have to be published. Nobody ever has to see it. I'll just keep it for myself. No one will ever have to know it exists.

ANNIE

As long as it does exist, your mind won't ever be free. I think you should light the match, Paul.

There is a long silence. PAUL doesn't move.

ANNIE

Can't you see it's what God wants?

She's holding the can of lighter fluid in her hand as she speaks and absentmindedly flicks a few drops of the fluid on the bed.

ANNIE

You're so brilliant. I would think you'd certainly be able to see that. *(More drops fall on the bed.)* We're put on this earth to help people, Paul. Like I'm trying to help you.

PAUL watches as the fluid continues to drop on the bed.

ANNIE

Please help me help you.

CUT TO

PAUL. His hands shaking. Almost robot-like, he strikes one. It flames.

ANNIE

You're doing the right thing, Paul.

CUT TO

THE BARBECUE, as Paul's hand appears, drops the match on the fluid-soaked manuscript. For a moment—nothing—

—and then, KABOOM, the goddam thing practically explodes and

CUT TO

PAUL, staring, dazed, and as the flames leap higher,

CUT TO

ANNIE, *suddenly scared and startled at the heat and the size of the flames and the fu*
baking heat and

> ANNIE
> *(crying out)*

Goodness!

CUT TO

THE BARBECUE. *The sound is* LOUDER *as the flames leap up and now charred bits of pape*
begin floating upward and

CUT TO

ANNIE, *watching, as more bits of paper rise.*

> ANNIE

Goodness—Goodness—Oh, my gracious—*(And she starts trying to catch*
them.)

CUT TO

A PIECE OF BURNING PAPER *in midair, floating against the gauzy curtain, and for a*
moment it looks like the curtain will catch fire and

CUT TO

ANNIE, *panicked, racing out of the room, going "Goodness, heavens to Betsy"—*

CUT TO

THE BARBECUE, *and what's left of the book.*

CUT TO

PAUL, *and he cannot take his eyes off the disaster.*

CUT TO

ANNIE, *hurrying back in, carrying a big bucket, slopping water as she lifts the bucket.*

CUT TO

THE LAST *of the manuscript as the bucket of water is tossed onto it—there's hissing and*
steam and as the steam clears it all looks now like a log in a brackish pond.

> ANNIE

Well, isn't that an oogy mess?

s she starts to wheel the barbecue out, suddenly there is a new and different sound as we

JT TO

4UL, head turning toward the window.

JT TO

NNIE taking a step toward the window, stopping for a moment. The sound we're hear-
g is a motor. A HELICOPTER MOTOR. And it's getting louder. Annie goes to the window
w, looks toward the sky as we

UT TO

HELICOPTER flying along.

UT TO

NSIDE THE HELICOPTER.

USTER and a PILOT are in the machine. Buster has a pair of binoculars looped around
s neck, a map rumpled in his lap.

> BUSTER
> *(pointing out)*
> That's the Steadman place up there. *(The pilot nods. Buster points again.)*
> The only other place up here is the Wilkes farm.

nother nod. The PILOT points down. BUSTER stares through the binoculars.

VHAT HE SEES: ANNIE'S JEEP parked in front of her house.

UT TO

NSIDE THE HELICOPTER.

> BUSTER
> That's no '65 Mustang. *(shakes his head)* There's nothing else out this
> way—circle on back.

As the pilot starts to change direction

UT TO

NNIE at the window, watching, as the helicopter turns, starts off.

UT TO

PAUL, listening as the MOTOR sound recedes.

UT TO

ANNIE, staring out the window.

> **ANNIE**
> I do believe the winters are getting shorter and shorter every year. People say it has something to do with the ozone layer. What do you think?

> **PAUL**
> I don't know.

> **ANNIE**
> Yeah, well, it's a theory. Here's your Novril. *(She wheels the barbecue to the door, stops.)* How does tuna casserole sound for dinner?

> **PAUL**
> Great.

She exits. PAUL takes the two Novril, stares at them, then deliberately tucks them unde his mattress.

DISSOLVE TO

PAUL'S ROOM. NIGHT.

As PAUL is finishing the last of his tuna casserole. There are two Novrils on his tray. W hear strains of TV GAME SHOW THEME MUSIC. These sounds are not surprising. Pau has heard them before.

CUT TO

ANNIE'S ROOM. NIGHT.

It is much smaller than Paul's and filled with religious bric-a-brac, pictures of Pau Sheldon, and a TV on a portable stand. Annie lies in bed, with an open bag of Cheeto resting on her stomach and a big quart-sized plastic bottle of Coke on the nightstand. A she munches away, she is heavily engrossed in her favorite TV show, "The Lov Connection." As Chuck Woolery extracts the embarrassing details of a couple's romanti interlude, we

CUT TO

Paul faintly hearing the sounds of the TV. He has now finished eating. He takes the tw Novril from under the mattress. He then undoes the sheet, takes his fork and delicatel pokes a hole in the mattress, then stuffs all four pills back into the hole.

DISSOLVE TO

FARMHOUSE.

Coming up to dawn.

CUT TO

PAUL'S DOOR slowly opening.

CUT TO

PAUL, staring at the door.

CUT TO

WHEELS, seen from underneath the bed, being rolled around the foot of the bed. We realize PAUL is in a wheelchair with ANNIE pushing him.

> **ANNIE**
> See, isn't this nice?

> **PAUL**
> Great. I've always wanted to visit the other side of the room.

> **ANNIE**
> And look what I've got for you. An electric razor so you can shave yourself now.

> **PAUL**
> If I knew this was gonna be the surprise, you could've gotten me to burn all my books.

> **ANNIE**
> *(She hands him some Novril.)*
> Now don't josh. This is a very big day for you, Paul. Here. You just sit tight, and I'll set everything up.

ANNIE exits.

CUT TO

PAUL, quickly shoving the Novril into the mattress.

> **PAUL**
> Set what up?

> **ANNIE** (off-screen)
> That's the big surprise. Your new studio—after all, writers do need a place to work.

> **PAUL**
> Work? You mean, write? What in the world do you think I'd write?

> ANNIE

Oh, but Paul! *(flushed)* I don't think, I know! Now that you've gotten rid of that nasty manuscript, you can go back to doing what you're great at— *(beat)*—you're going to write a new novel—your greatest achievement ever—*Misery's Return.*

CUT TO

PAUL. Stunned.

> PAUL
> *(after a beat)*

Misery's Return?

> ANNIE

I know you didn't mean it when you killed her, and now you'll make it right.

CUT TO

ANNIE: CLOSE UP. In an almost religious fervor.

> ANNIE

Yes. It will be a book in my honor. For saving your life and nursing you back to health. I'll be the first one to read it. *(beat)* Oh, Paul, you're going to make me the envy of the whole world...

CUT TO

PAUL.

> PAUL

You just expect me to whip something off, that it?

> ANNIE
> *(nods)*

I expect nothing less than your masterpiece.

> PAUL

You do understand that this isn't the ordinary way books get written—I mean, some people might actually consider this an oddball situation.

She rolls him over to a table she has set up by the window.

> ANNIE

I have total confidence in your brilliance—besides, the view will inspire you.

CUT TO

THE WINDOW, *as the wheelchair approaches it.*

The sky is innocent of clouds. There's a green forest climbing the flank of the nearest mountain. A plot of open ground between the house and the mountain. A neat red barn where the livestock stay. A Jeep Cherokee, maybe five years old. A Fisher plow. And no neighbors in sight. This is a desolate place.

> ANNIE (off-screen)
> You just inhale that. I'll be right back.

CUT TO

PAUL, *staring out the window.*

> PAUL
> *(calling out)*
> I guess you don't get bothered by neighbors much.

> ANNIE (off-screen)
> Don't worry about that. You'll have total solitude so you can concentrate on your work.

> PAUL
> Great.

CUT TO

ANNIE *in the doorway, carrying reams of typing paper, pencils, pens and sharpener.*

CUT TO

PAUL, *watching her—it's all kind of amazing. She hands him a box of typing paper.*

> ANNIE
> I got you this expensive paper to type on.

CUT TO

PAUL, *looking at the paper. It's Corrasable Bond. An idea hits him; he masks it as best he can.*

> ANNIE
> *(putting the rest of the paper on the table)*
> And I got a great deal on this fifty-pound clunker—on account of it's missing an "n." I told the saleslady "n" was one of the letters in my favorite writer's name.

PAUL

It's two of the letters in my favorite nurse's name, Annie.

ANNIE
(embarrassed, blushing)
You—fooler...! *(turns, grabs up pens, pencils, paper)* Did I do good?

PAUL
(gesturing to the box of paper)
You did great, except there's just one little thing—I can't work with this paper. It's Corrasable Bond, it smudges. Maybe you could go back into town and bring me some white, long-grained mimeo.

ANNIE
But mine cost the most so I don't see how it can smudge.

PAUL
(quickly taking a sheet of paper, making a pencil mark on it)
C'mere, I'll show you.

As she approaches, he rubs his thumb over the pencil mark.

ANNIE
(looking at it)
Well, it does smudge after all—isn't that fascinating?

PAUL
I thought you'd be interested. I'd like you to be in on everything, Annie. Not just the finished book, but how it's written.

ANNIE
Thank you for thinking of me. *(She can be so charming when she wants.)* Anything else I can get while I'm in town? Any other crucial requirements that need satisfying? Would you like a tiny tape recorder? Or maybe a handmade set of writing slippers?

PAUL
No, just the paper will be fine.

ANNIE
(suddenly getting very agitated)
Are you sure? 'Cause if you want, I'll bring back the whole store for you.

PAUL
Annie, what's the matter?

ANNIE

What's the matter? I'll tell you what's the matter. I go out of my way for you. I do everything to try and make you happy. I feed you, I clean you, I dress you. And what thanks do I get? "You bought the wrong paper, Annie. I can't write on this paper, Annie." Well, I'll get your stupid paper, but you just better start showing me a little more appreciation around here, Mister Man.

With that, she throws the ream of paper in PAUL'S LAP, causing considerable pain.

CUT TO

THE DOOR as she slams it shut, locks it, stomps off and

CUT TO

THE WINDOW. Annie, in a parka, can be seen storming out in the direction where her Cherokee was parked. She gets in and drives off.

CUT TO

PAUL. He heaves a sigh, reaches out toward his tortured knees, then drops his head. He sees something.

CUT TO

A BOBBY PIN on the floor.

CUT TO

PAUL, as he moves toward the bobby pin. Or tries to. It's brutally hard for him. The chair moves half a foot. Stops. Paul strains again. Another half foot. Another.

CUT TO

The BOBBY PIN. The wheel chair is beside it now. PAUL reaches down for it. Can't make it. Tries again. Can't. He takes a deep breath, forces himself to bend, ignoring the pain. The bobby pin is in his hands.

CUT TO

PAUL, inserting the bobby pin into the keyhole, beginning to jimmy the lock.

CUT TO

THE LOCK—it makes a SOUND—something has caught.

CUT TO

PAUL, excited, trying to force the bobby pin and he's doing great—

—until it slips from his hands, falls to the floor again.

PAUL
(furious)

Shit...

CUT TO

THE BOBBY PIN. *Paul reaches for it. The pain has him. He reaches again, involuntarily cries out. But he grabs it, clutches it tight.*

CUT TO

THE KEYHOLE. *Paul is trying to jimmy the lock a second time.*

No luck.

CUT TO

PAUL. *In wild frustration.*

PAUL

You've written how to do this—*now do it!*

CUT TO

THE KEYHOLE. *There is a loud* CLICKING *sound.*

CUT TO

THE DOOR *as Paul turns the knob. The door opens a crack.*

PAUL
(amazed)

What do you know, it actually works.

CUT TO

PAUL, *trying to get out of the room—but it's a bitch because in order to get to the lock he had to move the wheelchair up to the door and in order to get out, he's got to maneuver it out of the way of the door and every turn of the chair's wheels is an effort for him. He works at it and works at it, but his energy is failing him. He's pale, perspiring. Finally he succeeds, barely forces his way into the hall.*

CUT TO

PAUL, *in the hallway outside. He looks around for a phone. Doesn't see one. He wheels himself over to the front door, tries it. It's locked from the outside.*

PAUL

What a surprise.

He looks off into the living room, and...

CUT TO

THE TELEPHONE.

CUT TO

PAUL, wheeling into the living room. Dark red predominates. It's a musty room. Over the mantel, a photograph of a six-year-old ANNIE, with her mother and father in front of the family car—a new 1952 Buick. These were happier times.

The windows have bars on them.

As PAUL begins to wheel as fast as he can toward the phone—

CUT TO

THE PHONE as PAUL at last grabs for it, gets it, punches the "operator" button—

PAUL

Operator...*(nothing)*...OPERATOR...*(wildly frustrated)*...Shit!

He shakes the phone. It's terribly light. He picks it up, turns it over—it's hollow, just a hell of a telephone. He stares at it for a long moment, shaking his head, the disappointment plain.

PAUL

You crazy bitch...

He puts the phone back on the table.

CUT TO

THE GENERAL STORE. DAY.

Annie exits the store, carrying new paper, hops into her Cherokee and drives off.

CUT TO

THE STUDY, as PAUL enters. He looks around.

It's stuffed with heavy, graceless furniture as well as lots of coffee tables covered with knickknacks. As he, with effort, wheels across it—

CUT TO

A shelf of BOOKS. PAUL SHELDON books. EVERY Paul Sheldon book.

CUT TO

PAUL, *pausing, looking at her collection. The only book on the shelf that isn't his is a large scrapbook. The title on the back reads "My Life."*

He glances back at the shelf as he forces his wheelchair across the study, and we

CUT TO

A SMALL TABLE *with little ceramic doodads on top. The wheelchair hits it, one of the doo-dads topples—it's a penguin, fragile looking, and as it's about to fall to the floor and shat-ter—*

CUT TO

PAUL, *grabbing for it, catching it, putting it back where it was. He continues his slow way across the room and*

CUT TO

THE HALLWAY.

Out in the hallway, on his way toward the kitchen, PAUL *notices a door to his right. He wheels over and surprisingly it opens. However, this is not a door to the outside of the house, only a storage pantry. He looks around—nothing but canned goods, potato chips, cereals and large plastic Coke containers, etc. Just as he is about to close the door, he notices an open cardboard box. He opens the flap and sees all kinds of prescription drugs. Among them are a couple of strips of Novril encapsulated in blisters. He grabs them and stuffs them into his sweatpants. Now he closes the pantry door and heads to the kitchen.*

CUT TO

THE KITCHEN.

As PAUL *approaches it. He starts to wheel his way in, but he has trouble.*

He backs up slightly, wheels forward again—

—but the door is too narrow for the chair to fit through. He pounds his fists on the chair arm, staring as we

CUT TO

THE BACK DOOR. *It's at the far end of the kitchen leading to the outside. It seems some-how less formidable than the front door did. The windows around the kitchen are barred.*

CUT TO

PAUL, *staring at the kitchen door—*

—then without warning, he makes his move, starting to lower himself out of the chair ently to the floor—

—only it doesn't work that way. It's too awkward, he doesn't have the strength to maneu-er properly—

—and his body tilts awkwardly out of the chair, slams hard against the hard floor.

CUT TO

PAUL, crying out in pain as he lands. He lies there for a moment. Little droplets of sweat are on his forehead now. He is hurting.

He closes his eyes, gathering strength—

—and then slowly, very slowly, inch by inch, he moves his body across the floor toward the kitchen door.

CUT TO

THE KITCHEN DOOR. It's still a long way away.

CUT TO

PAUL, ignoring his pain, his awkwardness, making his body move.

CUT TO

THE KITCHEN DOOR. Closer now.

CUT TO

PAUL, growing pale, but he won't stop, and now the door is just ahead of him, and with his good arm he reaches out and up and grabs the doorknob—

CUT TO

THE KITCHEN DOOR. Locked solid.

CUT TO

PAUL: CLOSE UP. The disappointment and anger is plain on his face. His arm drops. He lies still for a moment, panting from the effort. Then—

CUT TO

PAUL, and his eyes are wide for a moment. You can feel his wild excitement, as we

PULL BACK TO REVEAL

Sitting on the counter: A SET OF CARVING KNIVES sticking out of a slotted wooden block.

They seem to be out of reach, but that doesn't stop him. He starts to crawl over to the counter.

CUT TO

THE ROAD.

ANNIE is driving along in her Cherokee. She is heading home.

CUT TO

THE KITCHEN.

Now at the counter, PAUL tries to pull himself up with his one good arm, but even though he is able to chin himself up to the top of the counter, he is still unable to reach the knives. He makes a desperate attempt which sends him crashing to the floor.

As he starts to force his way up again—from outside there comes a sound—the motor of a car.

CUT TO

OUTSIDE ANNIE'S.

ANNIE, driving up to the house.

CUT TO

THE KITCHEN.

PAUL, throwing himself back to the floor, starting a wild crawl back across the kitchen toward the wheelchair and

CUT TO

OUTSIDE ANNIE'S.

ANNIE, getting out of her jeep and

CUT TO

KITCHEN.

PAUL, crawling, crawling and

CUT TO

OUTSIDE ANNIE'S.

ANNIE, walking around to the back of the Jeep and

CUT TO

KITCHEN.

PAUL, *scrambling wildly up into his wheelchair, starting to get it turned and*

CUT TO

ANNIE'S.

ANNIE, *opening the back of the Jeep and lifting out several rectangular boxes of paper and*

CUT TO

PAUL, *straightened out now, forcing the wheelchair to move, and now we're into a race, a crazed life-and-death race and the cuts go fast—*

—*and* ANNIE *closes the door of the car—*

—*and* PAUL *is suddenly stuck, there's no traction on the rug—*

—*now* ANNIE, *purchases in hand, starts away from the car for the house—*

—*and now* PAUL *is finally moving toward the bedroom.*

—*and* ANNIE *is moving swiftly toward the front door.*

—*She drops one of the packages of paper.*

CUT TO

PAUL, *still biting down, churning his arms with all the strength he has left.* PAUL'S ARMS, *aching, start to turn to rubber.*

CUT TO

ANNIE'S FEET, *walking quickly across the snow-covered area in front of the house and*

CUT TO

THE BEDROOM DOOR *as Paul gets through it, shuts it, and attacks the bedroom lock with the bobby pin and*

CUT TO

ANNIE, *unlocking the front door of the house and*

CUT TO

THE BEDROOM DOOR, *as it locks and*

CUT TO

THE FRONT DOOR, *unlocking and*

CUT TO

ANNIE balancing the bundles under her chin as she jiggles the key out of the front door lock and

CUT TO

PAUL, soaked.

> **ANNIE** (voice over)
> *(her voice from the hallway, close and growing closer)*
> Paul, I've got your paper.

CUT TO

PAUL. He wheels to exactly where he was when she left him. He at last allows himself a sigh of relief.

CUT TO

THE DOOR as the sound of a lock CLICKING is heard.

> **ANNIE** (voice over)
> Just the kind you asked for. *(and as the door opens—)*

CUT TO

PAUL—looking down. Paul's waistband—a half a dozen strips of Novril ominously stick out.

As the door swings open, he quickly covers the Novril with his hands.

CUT TO

ANNIE, in the doorway, a strange look on her face.

> **ANNIE**
> Paul, you're dripping with perspiration, your color is very hectic—what have you been doing?

> **PAUL**
> You know goddam well what I've been doing—I'VE BEEN SITTING HERE SUFFERING. I need my pills.

> **ANNIE**
> *(tenderly, as she starts toward him)*
> Poor dear...Let's get you back in bed and I'll get them for you.

PAUL
(exploding—a real child's tantrum)
I want my pills NOW!

ANNIE
It'll only take a second.

PAUL
I want my pain to go 'way, Annie—make it go 'way, please Annie—*(She looks at him—you can't tell if she's buying it or not.)*—please...

CUT TO

ANNIE. She stares a moment more, then turns, starts for the door.

ANNIE
(upset)
It just breaks my heart to see you like this...

CUT TO

PAUL watching, and the instant she is out the door in the hallway, he stuffs the Novril into his pants.

ANNIE (off-screen)
(coming closer)
I've done a lot of thinking on the drive...

CUT TO

ANNIE, entering the room, the Novril in her hand. She is genuinely contrite.

ANNIE
...and I'm absolutely convinced that the main reason I've never been more popular is because of my temper. You must be so mad at me. The truth now.

She hands him the pills. And rolls him over to the bed.

PAUL
Well, I don't hold grudges. After all, who doesn't let off a little steam once in a while.

CUT TO

PAUL putting the pills in his mouth, as she picks him up from the chair and puts him gently down in bed.

> ANNIE
> My genius needs his rest before he writes.

She hands him a pad and pencil.

> ANNIE
> Here, in case you think of any ideas.

> PAUL
> Yeah, well I wouldn't expect too much.

> ANNIE
> Don't be silly. You'll be brilliant. Think of me as your inspiration.

CUT TO

THE DOORWAY, as ANNIE starts to it.

> ANNIE
> I have faith in you...*(beat)*...my darling...

On that she turns—for the first time, a coquettish look comes to her face.

> ANNIE
> Catch this—*(She throws him a kiss—it's grotesque.)*—ummmm-wahhhh.

CUT TO

PAUL, summoning up all his courage, as he mimes catching it and forces a smile on. She waves, closes the door.

HOLD ON PAUL. The smile dies. He reaches in and pulls the two Novril capsules out of his mouth. Now—

CUT TO

THE SHADOW OF A HELICOPTER.

CUT TO

INSIDE THE HELICOPTER.

BUSTER AND PILOT flying along. Buster is all bundled up as he stares out, using the binoculars...

CUT TO

SOMETHING SHINY reflecting the sun.

HOLD AS IT ALMOST BLINDS US—we're looking at the part of Paul's Mustang that was revealed by the snow when Buster almost found the car.

> **BUSTER**
> *(to Pilot)*
> Walter, we could be skipping lunch today.

CUT TO

CRASH SITE.

Paul's car being hoisted by chains from the ground and, as it starts to rise up into the afternoon air...

PULL BACK TO REVEAL

THE AREA BY THE CAR—BUSTER is there and a bunch of STATE POLICEMEN and various MEDIA PEOPLE are there—Buster stands with the STATE POLICE CHIEF watching as the car is hoisted via derrick: the sound of the powerful MOTOR lifting the car is enormous and as the car keeps rising higher and higher and PEOPLE take pictures and stare and

CUT TO

The STATE POLICE CHIEF is addressing maybe a dozen REPORTERS. It's very cold. BUSTER stands slightly away from the group.

> **STATE POLICE CHIEF**
> The presumption must now be that Paul Sheldon is dead. We know he somehow crawled out of his car. But we have been unable to locate his body in the vicinity of the crash. We also know if anyone had found him, they would have taken him to an area hospital. His body is undoubtedly out there buried somewhere in the snow. We'll find him after the first thaw—unless the animals have gotten to him first. *(beat)* I'll take questions.

After the first sentence, a very cold and very unhappy BUSTER leaves the gathering.

CUT TO

PAUL'S CAR as Buster studies it, especially the area by the driver's side where there are still dents visible from Annie's crowbar.

VIRGINIA moves to him now. They exchange a glance, start walking together toward their car.

CUT TO

THE CHIEF, surrounded—people are asking questions, raising hands for attention, and as he answers them—

CUT TO

BUSTER *and* VIRGINIA, *close together, walking toward their car.*

> **VIRGINIA**
> You don't think he's dead, do you?

> **BUSTER**
> He might well be. But not the way they say. He didn't crawl out of that car by himself. You saw those dents on the door—someone pulled him out.

> **VIRGINIA**
> It was an old car—those dents could have been there forever.

> **BUSTER**
> There's two kinds of people that drive around in old cars: the ones that can't afford new ones, and the ones who wouldn't give 'em up for anything in the world. That second bunch don't drive around with twenty-five-year-old dents. *(as they drive off)*

CUT TO

PAUL'S ROOM. NIGHT.

PAUL *lies in bed listening to the strains of "The Love Connection," coming from upstairs As Chuck Woolery drones on, Paul is intently involved in folding a piece of paper from his pad. He is making a container of some sort. He finishes, then reaches down and grabs the Novril capsules that he has been stashing in the mattress.*

Carefully, he opens one and pours it into the palm of his hand. First he smells it—no odor—then he takes a tiny bit on a finger and tastes it—no taste. Then, he takes his paper container and empties the contents of all the pills into it, then places it under the mattress.

Now, what to do with the empty capsules. He thinks for a second, then—what the hell—he swallows them. He then places the packet back in the mattress.

CUT TO

THE TYPEWRITER. DAY.

The window is visible behind it. From this angle, it almost seems to be staring at PAUL, *broken "n" and all.* PAUL *tests his wounded arm. He's able to raise it a few inches, but that's it.*

CUT TO

OUTSIDE THE WINDOW.

ANNIE is visible heading for the barn, followed by MISERY, the pig. For a moment, she stops, turns to look back.

> **ANNIE**
> *(calling out)*
> Don't be nervous—*(beat)*—just remember, I'll treasure whatever you do.

Now, as she turns again, moves quickly away—

CUT TO

THE TYPEWRITER.

CUT TO

PAUL. *He rolls in a piece of paper, types briefly.*

CUT TO

WHAT HE'S WRITTEN, AND IT'S THIS:

> "Misery's Retur ."
> by Paul Sheldo
> for A   ie Wilkes

CUT TO

PAUL, *studying the paper. He takes it out, starts to roll in a new sheet.*

CUT TO

THE MACHINE *as the new sheet is rolled in.*

CUT TO

PAUL, *staring at the blank page. He takes a deep breath, glances outside, then back to the paper.*

CUT TO

THE BLANK PAGE.

CUT TO

PAUL, *and now there's a brief light behind his eyes and suddenly he types a burst, stares at what he's written.*

CUT TO

THE PAPER *and these words:* "fuckfuckfuckfuckfuck."

CUT TO

PAUL. *He closes his eyes briefly, mutters something, kind of nods, opens his eyes, grabs for another piece of paper, rolls it in and starts mechanically to type.*

DISSOLVE TO

A NEW PIECE OF PAPER *with the words "Chapter Two" and a half paragraph of writing as we*

PULL BACK TO REVEAL

PAUL WORKING *in his room.* ANNIE *enters, the first pages of manuscript in her hands. It's dusk.*

ANNIE

I'm sorry, Paul. This is all wrong, you'll have to do it over again.

PAUL
(totally stunned)
What? What happened to "I'll treasure whatever you do?"

ANNIE

Paul, it's not worthy of you. Throw it all out except for the part of naming that gravedigger after me. You can leave that in.

PAUL

I really value your criticism, but maybe you're being a little hasty here.

ANNIE

Paul, what you've written just isn't fair.

PAUL

—not fair?

ANNIE

That's right—when I was growing up in Bakersfield, my favorite thing in all the world was to go to the movies on Saturday afternoons for the chapter plays...

PAUL
(It just comes out.)
—cliff-hangers—

ANNIE
(suddenly angry)
I know that, Mister Man—they also call them serials. I'm not stupid, you know. *(And she's a child again.)*—Anyway, my favorite was Rocket Man, and once it was a no-brakes chapter, the bad guys stuck him in a car on a mountain road and knocked him out and...   *(MORE...)*

ANNIE (cont.)
welded the doors shut and tore out the brakes and started him to his
death and he woke up and tried to steer and tried to get out, but the car
went off a cliff before he could escape and it crashed and burned and —
I was so upset and excited and the next week you better believe I was first
in line and they always start with the end of the last week and there was
Rocket Man trying to get out, and here came the cliff and JUST BEFORE
the car went off he jumped free and all the kids cheered—*(standing up
now)*—but I didn't cheer, I stood right up and started shouting, "This isn't
what happened last week—have you all got amnesia?—THEY JUST
CHEATED US—THIS WASN'T FAIR—"

ANNIE: CLOSE UP. Still in her childhood reverie. Shouting:

ANNIE
"HE DIDN'T GET OUT OF THE COCADOODIE CAR!"

PAUL
They always cheated like that in cliff—*(stops himself)*—chapter plays.

ANNIE
But not you. Not with my Misery. Remember, Ian did ride for Dr. Cleary
at the end of the last book, but his horse fell jumping that fence and Ian
broke his shoulder and his ribs and lay there all night in the ditch so he
never reached the doctor, so there couldn't have been any "experimental
blood transfusion" that saved her life. Misery was buried in the ground at
the end, Paul, so you'll have to start there. *(As she goes—)*

PAUL
Look at this, I've got Lizzie Borden for an editor, here.

PAUL slumped, staring balefully at the typewriter.

DISSOLVE TO

OUTSIDE THE FARMHOUSE. NIGHT.

DISSOLVE TO

OUTSIDE THE FARMHOUSE. NEXT MORNING.

CUT TO

PAUL'S ROOM. DAY.

*PAUL is at the table. He takes the Novril off his breakfast tray, wheels over to the bed,
and stuffs them into the mattress. He hears FOOTSTEPS coming down the hall. He
smoothly wheels back to the table. A pause.*

ANNIE enters to remove the tray.

> **ANNIE**
> What's the matter, Paul? You haven't written a word.

> **PAUL**
> I can't write this anymore.

> **ANNIE**
> Don't be silly. Of course you can.

> **PAUL**
> I'm telling you, I can't.

> **ANNIE**
> You can—you have the "gotta"—

> **PAUL**
> The what?

> **ANNIE**
> The "gotta." Remember, you talked about it in *Playboy* magazine. You said there's a million things you can't do in this world: you can't hit a curve ball, you can't fix a leaky faucet or make a marriage work—but there's one thing you always have, and that's the power of the "gotta."

> **PAUL**
> I said that?

> **ANNIE**
> You said you can make it so they gotta turn the page. You know, "I 'gotta' know will she live," "I 'gotta' know will he catch the killer." "I gotta see how this chapter ends." You said it. I don't usually buy that magazine. I only got it, 'cause they were interviewing you.

CUT TO

PAUL: CLOSE UP. Blinking.

> **PAUL**
> *(quietly)*
> What about a bee...?

> **ANNIE**
> What?

> **PAUL**
> Nothing.

CUT TO

THE KEYBOARD *as the piece of paper slides in and the keys start to move. Annie stands there for a moment, then quietly backs out of the room.*

DISSOLVE TO

THE WINDOW. *It's late afternoon.*

PULL BACK TO REVEAL

PAUL *in the wheelchair watching as* ANNIE *finishes reading.*

> **PAUL**
> Well, is it fair? Should I keep going?

> **ANNIE**
> You better. Oh, Paul, when Ian realized that the reason they'd buried Misery alive was because the bee sting had put her in that temporary coma—

CUT TO

ANNIE, *in a fervor.*

> **ANNIE**
> —and when Gravedigger Wilkes remembered how thirty years earlier, the same thing had happened to Lady Evelyn-Hyde—*(hands clasped)*— and then old Dr. Cleary deduced that Misery must be Lady Evelyn-Hyde's long-lost daughter because of the rarity of deadly bee-stings—my heart just leapt.

CUT TO

PAUL, *watching her. It's as if he had nothing to do with anything she's read as she goes on.*

> **ANNIE**
> I've known from the very first book that Misery had to be born of nobility and I was right!

> **PAUL**
> *(mumbling to himself)*
> Yeah, yeah...

CUT TO

THE TWO OF THEM; *she touches the pages as if they were gold, rubbing gently with the tips of her fingers.*

> ANNIE

Oh, Paul, can I read each chapter when you finish? I can fill in the "n"s. *(Paul nods, and she's off again.)* Will she be her old self, now that Ian has dug her out, or will she have amnesia...?

> PAUL

...have to wait.

> ANNIE

Will she still love him with that special perfect love?

> PAUL

Have to wait.

> ANNIE
> *(pleading)*

Not even a hint? *(Paul shakes his head.)*

CUT TO

ANNIE, spinning around the room like a happy child.

> ANNIE

Misery's alive! Misery's alive. Oh, it's so romantic—this whole house is going to be filled with romance. I'm going to put on my Liberace records—*(stops, looks at Paul)*—you do like Liberace, don't you?

> PAUL
> *(quickly)*

Whenever he played Radio City, who do you think was right there in the front row?

> ANNIE

I'm going to play my records for you all day long—to inspire you—he's my all-time favorite. *(And with that, she starts to leave.)*

> PAUL

Annie?

She stops at the door.

> PAUL

Would you have dinner with me tonight?

She can't speak.

PAUL

To celebrate Misery's return. I couldn't have done it without you.

ANNIE

Oh, Paul. It would be an honor.

ANNIE dashes excitedly out of the room. PAUL wheels over to the bed, pulls the packet of Novril powder out from the mattress and stuffs it in his pants. The sound of Liberace playing "Tammy" with orchestra and chorus booms in from beyond the door.

PAUL

Jesus Christ.

CUT TO

BUSTER'S OFFICE. DUSK.

VIRGINIA is on the phone.

VIRGINIA
(into phone)

No, he's not here. I don't know where he went. He never tells me anything anymore. He's probably out having an affair somewhere. Wait a minute. I think I hear him coming.

BUSTER enters carrying a bagful of books.

VIRGINIA
(to Buster)

It's Jim Taylor. He wants to know who you've been having an affair with.

CUT TO

BUSTER. HE puts the bag down, shoots Virginia a look and grabs the phone. VIRGINIA looks in the bag.

BUSTER

Hey, Jim, what's doing? Uh-huh...uh-huh...Jim, we've been over this. If you're gonna have benches in front of your store, people are gonna sit on them. I don't like him either, but I'm not going to come over there and tell him to move. Give my best to Denise. Bye.

VIRGINIA
(looking through the books, all paperback Misery novels)

Well, whoever she is, she sure likes to read a lot.

BUSTER

Virginia, I'm flattered you think I got that much energy. I just figured if I can't find Paul Sheldon, at least I can find out what he wrote about.

> **VIRGINIA**
> What do you expect to find? A story about a guy who drove his car off a cliff in a snowstorm?

> **BUSTER**
> Now, you see, it's that kind of sarcasm that's given our marriage real spice.

CUT TO

STUDY. NIGHT.

PAUL is sitting at a table that Annie has set up with her best china and silverware. It is as romantic as Annie Wilkes gets. ANNIE enters, carrying a basket of rolls. She sits and serves Paul.

> **ANNIE**
> I hope you like it

> **PAUL**
> It looks wonderful. And so do you.

> **ANNIE**
> Oh...

They eat in awkward silence. Finally:

> **PAUL**
> I've never had meatloaf this good, what do you do to it?

> **ANNIE**
> My secret is I only use fresh tomatoes, never canned. And to give it that little extra zip, I mix in some Spam with the ground beef.

> **PAUL**
> Oh. *(pause)* You can't get this in a restaurant in New York.

After another pause:

> **PAUL**
> Annie, I think we should have a toast.

> **ANNIE**
> A toast?

> **PAUL**
> Yes, to Misery. Let me pour you some more wine.

Paul pours more of the Gallo wine, then raises his glass.

ANNIE

To Misery.

PAUL

Wait, let's do this right. Do you have any candles?

ANNIE

Oh, I don't know. I think so. I'll go look.

SHE exits into the kitchen. PAUL quickly pulls the packet filled with Novril powder from his pants. He empties it into her glass of wine, stuffs the empty packet back into his pants, talking the whole time:

PAUL

Did you study decorating, or do you just have a flair?

ANNIE (off-screen)

Oh, you. I just picked things up over the years.

PAUL

Well, it certainly says you.

ANNIE (off-screen)

You really think so?

PAUL

Absolutely. Listen, if you can't find any, it's okay. I just thought it might be nice.

ANNIE re-enters with a candle.

ANNIE

Are you kidding? If anyone ever told me that one day I'd be having a candlelit dinner with Paul Sheldon in my own house, I woulda checked both legs to see which one was being pulled. Will this do?

PAUL

It's perfect.

She places the candle on the table. With a slight tremor in her hand, she lights the candle. PAUL raises his glass.

PAUL

To Misery and to Annie Wilkes, who brought her back to life.

ANNIE raises her glass.

> ANNIE
>
> Oh, Paul, every time I think about it, I get goosebumps.

They clink glasses.

And with that, her emotions having gotten the best of her, she knocks over the candle. In trying to right the situation, she places her glass back down, and as she reaches for the candle, she knocks over her glass, spilling the wine.

> ANNIE
> *(wiping up the spilled wine with her napkin)*
>
> Oh, God, what have I done? I'm so sorry, Paul. I ruined your beautiful toast. Will you ever forgive me? Here, let me pour another one. *(She does.)* Can we pretend this never happened? To Misery?

> PAUL
>
> To Misery.

So they drink their wine.

CUT TO

OUTSIDE THE FARMHOUSE. DAY.

The snow, although still present, has melted somewhat. And starting now and continuing throughout is this: the sound of typing.

CUT TO

PAUL'S ROOM.

PAUL, working at his typewriter.

CUT TO

THE MANUSCRIPT. Growing.

CUT TO

ANNIE'S BEDROOM. DUSK.

ANNIE, in her room. Reading and loving it.

CUT TO

BUSTER'S DEN. NIGHT.

BUSTER sitting in his den reading a Misery novel by the fire. VIRGINIA brings him a cup of tea.

CUT TO

PAUL'S ROOM. DAY.

PAUL, the sling off, moving his injured arm. It's more mobile than before. Testing his strength, he uses his arm to remove the page and place it on the pile. He puts in another page and continues to type.

CUT TO

ANNIE, entering Paul's room, carrying a chapter. Handing him a cup of tea.

> **ANNIE**
> Paul, this is positively the best Misery you've ever written.

> **PAUL**
> I think you're right.

CUT TO

THE PILE OF PAPER. Bigger.

CUT TO

OUTSIDE THE BARN.

ANNIE, out by the barn. She stares in at the house. Framed in the window is PAUL, working. She smiles, enters the barn.

CUT TO

PAUL'S ROOM. NIGHT.

He stretches but only briefly, then back to his typing.

CUT TO

THE KITCHEN.

ANNIE, cooking happily away, reading a chapter.

CUT TO

PAUL'S ROOM.

PAUL, arm out of the sling. He manages to lift the typewriter once, sets it back down, puts the sling back on.

CUT TO

PAUL'S ROOM. LATER.

ANNIE, bringing a tray of food.

                    ANNIE
I think it's so wonderful that Misery would sacrifice her title to take up
the cause of her people. That's true nobility.

Paul hands her some new pages. As she exits,

CUT TO

BUSTER'S OFFICE.

BUSTER, in his office reading. He is alone.

CUT TO

ANNIE'S LIVING ROOM. NIGHT.

Annie is reading by the fire. Her pig Misery sits beside her, staring at the pages.

CUT TO

PAUL'S. DAY.

His fingers just fly, faster than he's ever typed and

CUT TO

PAUL'S. NIGHT.

PAUL, staring and

CUT TO

THE PILE, growing, growing and

CUT TO

PAUL'S FINGERS

CUT TO

PAUL'S ROOM.

PAUL, ripping open a new ream of paper...

CUT TO

PAUL'S ROOM. DUSK.

His lips move silently. He's not even aware of it as he nods and...

CUT TO

THE PAPER IN THE TYPEWRITER, line after line being written.

INTERCUT WITH

Paul's face at DAY, NIGHT, and DUSK in rapid succession, ending with

CUT TO

ANNIE'S FARMHOUSE. NIGHT.

Lightning! Giant deep rolls of THUNDER as RAIN begins...

CUT TO

TYPEWRITER being lifted out of frame, then back in, then out again.

CUT TO

PAUL'S ROOM. NIGHT.

The pile of manuscript has doubled. Maybe two hundred pages.

PAUL, with some effort, is pumping the typewriter up and down. Finally, he places it back down and puts his arm back in the sling.

CUT TO

PAUL, looking outside briefly.

CUT TO

THE RAIN. Worse. The SOUND hits the roof of the house, hits the window.

CUT TO

ANNIE, lumbering in—she's never looked like this: She's wearing her slippers and her pink quilted housecoat. Her eyes are without life. Her hair, loose and straggly, hangs around her face. Slowly, like a robot, she goes to PAUL, who looks silently up at her.

ANNIE

Here's your pills. *(She drops them on the table.)*

CUT TO

PAUL, as the pills hit his chest and bounce into his lap.

PAUL

Annie, what is it?

CUT TO

ANNIE.

> ANNIE
> (half turns away, turns back, gestures outside)
> The rain...sometimes it gives me the blues...

CUT TO

ANNIE: CLOSE UP. And suddenly it's as if she's been turned off, gone lifeless.

CUT TO

PAUL, staring at her. No sound but the rain.

CUT TO

ANNIE, seen straight on. No light in her eyes.

> ANNIE
> When you first came here, I only loved the writer part of Paul Sheldon. But now I know I love the rest of him too. As much as Misery loves Ian. (beat) I know you don't love me—don't say you do—you're a beautiful, brilliant, famous man of the world; and I'm...not a movie star type. You'll never know the fear of losing someone like you if you're someone like me.

> PAUL
> Why would you lose me?

> ANNIE
> The book is almost finished. Your legs are getting better. Soon you'll be able to walk. You'll be wanting to leave.

> PAUL
> Why would I want to leave? I like it here.

> ANNIE
> That's very kind of you, but I'll bet it's not altogether true.

> PAUL
> It is.

She slowly reaches into the pocket of her bathrobe and pulls out a .38 Special.

> ANNIE
> I have this gun, and sometimes I think about using it.

She is absentmindedly clicking the empty gun.

ANNIE

I better go now. I might put bullets in it.

Robot-like, she crosses to the door and leaves. As she closes and locks the door—

CUT TO

PAUL, stunned, listening, waiting—

—there is the sound of the front door closing—

—then footsteps on the outside walk—

—the sound of a car door opening and slamming shut.

Now comes the GUNNING *of the motor.*

CUT TO

THE WINDOW *as* ANNIE *drives by, hunched over the wheel. The* MOTOR *sound grows fainter, faint...*

CUT TO

BUSTER AND VIRGINIA'S BEDROOM. NIGHT.

BUSTER AND VIRGINIA are lying in bed. Buster is reading yet another Misery novel, Misery's Trial. Virginia is also reading.

BUSTER

"There is a justice higher than that of man. I will be judged by Him."

VIRGINIA

What?

BUSTER

They're hauling Misery into court.

VIRGINIA

That's nice.

BUSTER
(mutters under his breath)

"There is a justice higher than that of man—I will be judged by Him."

CUT TO

ANNIE'S KITCHEN.

The kitchen KNIVES on the counter.

CUT TO

PAUL, *now using both arms, forcing his body up toward them.*

This isn't easy, it was a bitch the first time he tried it, but nothing's going to stop him now. He's leaning against the cupboard, using it for balance—

—his balance starts to go but he won't let it as we

CUT TO

THE KNIVES, AS HIS HAND *grabs the largest one, a fat-handled sharp beauty and*

CUT TO

PAUL, *and you can sense the relief as he begins to lower himself to the floor.*

CUT TO

THE STUDY.

PAUL, *back in his wheelchair, knife in his lap, carefully opening drawers of little tables, looking inside. He closes them, moves on, unmindful of the rain. Now—*

CUT TO

THE SHELF OF PAUL SHELDON BOOKS. *As before—*

—except the "My Life" scrapbook is gone.

CUT TO

PAUL, *glancing around—*

—and there it is, on a coffee table in the living room. Also on the table is a roll of scotch tape, a pair of scissors, and a copy of Newsweek. *Paul wheels toward the table and the book, which is as big as a folio Shakespeare play and as thick as a family Bible.*

CUT TO

THE LIVING ROOM.

PAUL, *opening the book.*

CUT TO

THE FIRST PAGE OF THE BOOK, *as Paul opens it. It's a newspaper clipping as is almost all of what follows. A small article: simply a birth announcement for Anne Marie Wilkes.*

PAUL *turns the page. This headline reads: "Investment Banker Carl Wilkes Dies in Freak Fall."*

"USC Nursing Student Dies in Freak Fall." That's the headline on the next page.

Now: "Miss Wilkes is Nursing School Honors Graduate."

Paul turns the page.

Manchester, New Hampshire, Union Leader: *"Ernest Gonyar, 79, Dies After Long Illness."*

Now that phrase seems to be what catches our eye—"after long illness" is from the next article. "Long illness" from the one after that. Then, on the next page, a variation: "Short Illness."

Now we're in Pennsylvania: "New Hospital Staff Announced."

And here come those phrases again on page after page—"After Long Illness." "After Long Illness."

"After Long Illness."

CUT TO

PAUL, *transfixed; he keeps on turning the pages—the states keep changing, moving west. Pennsylvania to Minnesota, Minnesota to North Dakota. And always the clippings reporting deaths and deaths and—*

—and now we're in Colorado. "NEW HEAD MATERNITY NURSE NAMED." And now the dead are young and helpless; babies. More and more of them.

> PAUL
> *(stunned)*

Holy shit.

Then a headline which reads:

"HEAD MATERNITY NURSE QUESTIONED ON INFANT DEATHS"

Next page: *"MISS WILKES RELEASED."*

Next page: *"THREE MORE INFANTS DIE."*

Next page, at last: "DRAGON LADY ARRESTED."

Then a photo: the front page of the Rocky Mountain Gazette. *Annie on the courthouse steps. "DRAGON LADY CLAIMS INNOCENCE," under which there is a statement by Annie Wilkes.*

Paul turns quickly to the next page and a very large headline:
"DRAGON LADY FOUND NOT GUILTY"

PAUL *just sits there, shaking his head in bewilderment.*

CUT TO

THE BOOK, *as Paul turns the* LAST *page.*

CUT TO

PAUL, *stunned and now we find out why, as we*

CUT TO

THE PAGE IN THE BOOK. *It's an article from* Newsweek *magazine, a picture of Paul's car being hauled up out of the snow. Above it this caption: "Presumed Dead—Paul Sheldon."*

CUT TO

PAUL. *Slamming the book shut, putting it back on the coffee table, then quickly turning his wheelchair as we*

CUT TO

PAUL, *steering his wheelchair toward the front door. He tries to position himself for a surprise attack of* ANNIE, *but he can't find a way to get close enough. The wheelchair is too cumbersome. He looks around and decides to head back to his room. He is faced with the same problem there—so he struggles back into bed and, lying on his back, he rests the knife on his chest and stares up at the ceiling.*

DISSOLVE TO

PAUL'S WINDOW, *hours later. The rain has stopped.*

CUT TO

PAUL—*trying to stay awake. After a few beats, he hears something. It's the sound of a* CAR PULLING UP.

HEADLIGHTS *can be seen flashing through the window.* PAUL *grips the knife and hides it under the covers. The sound of a* CAR DOOR OPENING AND CLOSING, *then* FOOTSTEPS.

As the FRONT DOOR OPENS, PAUL *girds himself for attack. The* FRONT DOOR CLOSES, *then a couple of* FOOTSTEPS. *Then silence. Then the* FOOTSTEPS *continue down the hall and up the stairs.*

After a beat, we hear the TELEVISION. *Someone is explaining how you can buy millions of dollars of prime real estate with no money down.*

PAUL, *allowing himself to relax, slips the knife under the mattress. As the TV* DRONES ON, *Paul lies staring up at the ceiling.*

DISSOLVE TO

OUTSIDE THE FARMHOUSE. NIGHT.

We hear a clap of THUNDER *and once again the rain pours down.*

CUT TO

CLOSE UP: PAUL—eyes closed. There is another loud THUNDERCLAP *which causes Paul to stir and open his eyes.*

He turns his head and another CLAP OF THUNDER *is heard,* LIGHTNING *flashes and reveals* ANNIE *standing over his bed.*

Before he can react, she jabs a needle into his arm, pulls it out and starts out of the room.

PAUL tries to raise himself, but the power of the drug causes him to collapse, unconscious.

CUT TO

THE ROOM. EARLY MORNING.

It's stopped raining, PAUL *lies asleep. Now, surprisingly, we hear a* VOICE *we've never heard in the movie before—loud—for an instant we don't recognize the voice, then we do: It's* LIBERACE *talking to his audience on a record going, "Thank you, thank you, what a wonderful thing it is for me to be back with you in Paris..."* PAUL *stirs and awakens to discover that he is strapped to his bed. He can move his arms, but that's it.*

CUT TO

ANNIE, standing in the room, and she looks very together; her eyes are bright. Too bright. Way too bright.

She comes to the foot of his bed.

CUT TO

PAUL, groggy from being drugged, tries to clear the cobwebs.

> ANNIE
> *(in a soft voice)*
> Paul, I know you've been out.

> PAUL
> What?

> ANNIE
> You've been out of your room.

PAUL

No, I haven't

ANNIE

Paul, my little ceramic penguin in the study always faces due south.

PAUL

I don't know what you're talking about.

PAUL looks up at her—he is totally honest and sincere. As he talks, his hand surreptitiously begins moving toward the mattress edge.

CUT TO

ANNIE, as she brings the fat-handled knife out of her skirt pocket.

ANNIE

Is this what you're looking for? I know you've been out twice, Paul. At first, I couldn't figure out how you did it, but last night I found your key. *(She holds up the bobby pin.)* I know I left my scrap book out, and I can imagine what you might be thinking of me. But you see, Paul, it's all okay.

CUT TO

ANNIE, as she walks slowly back to the foot of the bed.

And now a THUMP comes from the foot of the bed. Something is out of sight.

CUT TO

PAUL, staring at her; waiting.

ANNIE

Last night it came so clear. I realize you just need more time. Eventually, you'll come to accept the idea of being here. Paul, do you know about the early days at the Kimberly Diamond Mine? Do you know what they did to the native workers who stole diamonds? Don't worry, they didn't kill them. That would be like junking a Mercedes just because it had a broken spring—no, if they caught them they had to make sure they could go on working, but they also had to make sure they could never run away. The operation was called hobbling.

And with that, she reaches down out of sight and comes up holding a 16-inch piece of 4 x 4 wood.

PAUL

Annie, whatever you're thinking about, don't do it.

CUT TO

ANNIE. She wedges the 4 x 4 firmly between his legs, just above the ankles, secures it and adjusts his feet.

ANNIE

Now don't fuss, Paul.

PAUL

Why would I run away? I'm a writer, Annie—it's all I am—and I've never written this well—even you said that this is my best, didn't you?

ANNIE picks up a sledgehammer.

PAUL

Didn't you? Why would I leave a place where I'm doing my best work? It doesn't make any sense.

CUT TO

ANNIE, positioning herself to the side of his right ankle.

ANNIE

Shh, darling, trust me—*(taking aim at his ankle)* It's for the best.

She takes the sledgehammer back.

PAUL

Annie, for God's sake, please.

As ANNIE swings, the sledgehammer makes contact with the ankle. It breaks with a sharp CRACK.

CUT TO

PAUL: CLOSE UP, shrieking.

CUT TO

ANNIE, moving to the other side of the bed.

ANNIE

Almost done, just one more.

And as she breaks the other ankle, PAUL shrieks ever louder.

CUT TO

ANNIE: CLOSE UP.

ANNIE

God, I love you...

CUT TO

PAUL'S FACE. He is beyond agony.

FADE TO BLACK.

For a long moment, nothing.

Then...a FAINT SOUND. After a moment, it begins to become more intrusive and we can tell what it is: a car horn HONKING.

FADE IN ON

SILVER CREEK and ANNIE in her Cherokee, HONKING for another car to get a move on.

CUT TO

A HAND AND A COIN MOVING ACROSS IT, from finger to finger.

PULL BACK TO REVEAL

BUSTER, sitting by the front window of his office, reading The Rocky Mountain Gazette.

He watches idly as ANNIE yells out the window to the car in front of her. THE DRIVER of the car yells back. Annie yells louder. The Driver guns off, and Annie pulls into the parking space next to the General Store.

CUT TO

ANNIE, getting out, shaking a fist after the other car, calling out, "You poop!" She enters the store.

CUT TO

BUSTER, staring straight ahead. Something is gnawing at him.

CUT TO

VIRGINIA, in his office, tidying the desk. BUSTER enters, looks angry.

BUSTER

Just leave it, all right?

VIRGINIA

Oh, I like that tone.

BUSTER

How many times do I have to tell you—I have a system here. *(rooting through a pile of papers)* Where the hell is that thing?

> ### VIRGINIA
> What thing?

> ### BUSTER
> That thing. *(finding what he's looking for, a 3 x 5 card)* Here it is. Right where it's supposed to be.

> ### VIRGINIA
> What is it?

> ### BUSTER
> I'm not sure. Maybe nothing.

> ### VIRGINIA
> It's good you found it.

> ### BUSTER
> There's that spice again.

As BUSTER leaves, VIRGINIA goes back to tidying his desk.

CUT TO

A LARGE LIBRARY as Buster leaves his car, hurries inside and

CUT TO

LIBRARY STACKS.

BUSTER, wearing bifocals, sits poring over bound volumes of The Rocky Mountain Gazette.

CUT TO

BUSTER, frustrated, puts one set of volumes down, picks up another, starts through it, as we

CUT TO

THE ROCKY MOUNTAIN GAZETTE, *as the pages turn.*

—only now they stop turning.

CUT TO

BUSTER, tense, adjusting his bifocals.

CUT TO

A SERIES OF HEADLINES pertaining to Annie Wilkes' murder trial.

CUT TO

A HEADLINE *which reads,* "DRAGON LADY CLAIMS INNOCENCE."

Under a PICTURE OF ANNIE *on the courthouse steps, we see a* CAPTION: *"Wilkes told reporters on the courthouse steps, 'There is a higher justice than that of man; I will be judged by Him.' "*

CUT TO

BUSTER. *He takes the 3 x 5 card out of his pocket.*

CUT TO

The CARD—*on it is printed the exact quote we just saw in the paper.*

CUT TO

BUSTER, *sitting there, staring at the quote.*

BUSTER
Interesting.

HOLD ON HIS FACE, *then—*

CUT TO

PAUL, *staring absently out the window. Both his ankles are set in splints.*

CUT TO

ANNIE, *carrying a bag of feed, followed by* MISERY, *the sow, comes into view. She slows, smiles, waves—*

ANNIE
Hi, Punkin.

CUT TO

PAUL, *staring out at her.*

ANNIE
Give us a smile? *(Paul gives her the finger. She laughs.)* Such a kidder. *(as she exits our view—)*

CUT TO

PAUL, *lifting the typewriter and repeatedly raising it over his head, this time without any difficulty.*

CUT TO

THE GENERAL STORE IN SILVER CREEK. EARLY AFTERNOON.

BUSTER enters. The place is empty. It's one of those wonderful spots that stocks pretty much everything in what seems like complete disarray. Buster goes to the coffee urn behind the counter, helps himself. He speaks to the guy who sits behind the counter nearby; these two have known each other forever.

> **BUSTER**
>
> Hey, Pete.

> **PETE**
>
> Buster.

> **BUSTER**
>
> Answer me a couple things?

> **PETE**
>
> If I can.

> **BUSTER**
>
> Do you have any of those new Paul Sheldon books?

> **PETE**
>
> We had a batch. Sold 'em all in three days.

> **BUSTER**
>
> You wouldn't happen to remember if Miz Wilkes bought one, would you?

> **PETE**
>
> Are you kidding? Every time that fella writes a book, she makes me set aside the first copy.

BUSTER opens the cash register, drops his coffee money inside, closes the register.

> **BUSTER**
>
> Has she been buying any odd things lately?

> **PETE**
>
> Miz Wilkes? Same old stuff. *(beat)* —Lest you call paper odd.

> **BUSTER**
>
> Newspapers?

> **PETE**
> *(mimes typing)*
>
> No, the typing kind.

CUT TO

BUSTER: CLOSE UP.

> **BUSTER**
> Oh. That kind. Nothing odd about that. (*He cannot hide his excitement now as we—*)

CUT TO

ANNIE, *entering Paul's room. He lies back in the wheelchair, eyes closed. Liberace music playing in the background. From the start,* PAUL'S TONE *is different—strong, he's in control.*

> **ANNIE**
> Paul, don't you think it's time for you to start writing again? It's been over a week.

> **PAUL**
> I don't know, it's weird, but a couple of broken bones hasn't done a whole lot for my creative juices. Get the fuck out of here.

> **ANNIE**
> Don't talk like that to me.

> **PAUL**
> (*staring at her now*)
> Why, what are you going to do? (*spreading his arms wide*) Kill me? Take your best shot.

> **ANNIE**
> (*taken aback*)
> Why are you so mean, Mister you'd-be-dead-in-the-snow-if-it-wasn't-for-me?

> **PAUL**
> Oh, no reason, you keep me prisoner, you make me burn my book, you drive a sledgehammer into my ankles...

> **ANNIE**
> I'll drive a sledgehammer into your man gland if you're not nicer—

> **PAUL**
> (*He spreads his legs.*)
> Be my guest.

> **ANNIE**
> (*after a beat*)
> That's disgusting.

As she exits,

CUT TO

A ROAD. *Empty. Hold for a moment—now a car appears around a curve.*

CUT TO

The car. BUSTER *is driving fast.*

CUT TO

PAUL *in his room. He sits as before, by the window. He doesn't move. Now he closes his eyes, stretches, sighs as we*

CUT TO

THE KITCHEN.

ANNIE, *busily making cocoa.*

CUT TO

BUSTER IN HIS CAR. *He stops at a mailbox. The name on the box is* WILKES. *Buster turns his car slowly into the driveway by the mailbox.*

CUT TO

PAUL. *He yawns, opens his eyes briefly. Closes them. In the distance now, growing more and more visible is Buster's car—*

—and now PAUL'S EYES *go open wide, and he's staring out the window at the car as it keeps on coming, closer, closer and*

CUT TO

BUSTER, *looking around. He's driving very slowly, carefully.*

CUT TO

PAUL. *Fixating on the window and now it's all going to be all right, everything's going to be all right—*

—and then ANNIE *is on him, hypodermic needle in hand, jabbing it into the arm. He desperately tries to fight her off, but the drug starts to take hold. He tries to grab her by the neck, but she fights him off as she wheels him out of the room, down the hall and towards the cellar door.*

> **ANNIE**
>
> I don't think I'll ever understand you. I cook your meals, I tend to you practically twenty-four hours a day, and you continue to fight me. When are we going to develop a sense of trust?

ANNIE opens the cellar door. PAUL is all but limp by now. As she picks him up and start. to carry him down the steps—

CUT TO

BUSTER pulling up in front of the house. As he gets out of his car—

CUT TO

ANNIE placing Paul on the cellar floor and heading up the stairs. PAUL is out.

CUT TO

BUSTER heading up the steps to the front door.

CUT TO

ANNIE stashing the wheelchair in the hall closet. She crosses to the front door, opens it, revealing BUSTER.

> **ANNIE**
> *(gasping)*
>
> Oh, my!

> **BUSTER**
>
> Sorry, didn't mean to startle you. You didn't give me a chance to knock.

> **ANNIE**
> *(all charm)*
>
> I guess you can tell from my reaction, I'm not all that used to visitors out here. What can I do for you?

> **BUSTER**
>
> I was just wondering if you happen to know anything about Paul Sheldon.

> **ANNIE**
> *(stammering)*
>
> What do you want to know?

> **BUSTER**
>
> Anything you can tell me might help.

CUT TO

ANNIE. The words pour out—

ANNIE
Well, he was born in Worcester, Massachusetts, forty-two years ago, the only child of Franklin and Helene Sheldon, mediocre student, majored in history...

CUT TO

BUSTER, watching her, surprised.

BUSTER
(cutting in)
Excuse me, that's not exactly the kind of information I was after. You see, he's been missing for quite some time now, and...

ANNIE
I know. It's so upsetting. I'm his number-one fan...I've got all his books, every sentence he ever put down. I'm so proud of my Paul Sheldon collection...*(stops suddenly, almost embarrassed)*...here I am, prattling on and my manners have just flown away. I haven't invited you in. Please.

BUSTER
Thank you.

ANNIE lets BUSTER in, closes the door. They linger in front of Paul's door. Buster idly checks out the hallway.

ANNIE
'Course you must know about that horrible accident.

BUSTER nods and wanders into the living room. ANNIE follows. He crosses into the study and checks out a bookcase that contains the complete works of Paul Sheldon. One shelf below contains Annie's infamous scrapbook.

ANNIE
Almost killed me, too. I prayed when I heard the news. I got down on my knees and begged for it not to be true.

CUT TO

ANNIE. She's so moved. Buster wanders into the kitchen.

ANNIE
You're going to laugh at what I'm about to say, but go ahead, I don't care...*(beat)*...when I was praying, God told me to get ready.

CUT TO

BUSTER, *watching her. This isn't at all what he expected.*

BUSTER

Get ready for what?

CUT TO

PAUL, *trying to fight the drug; just his eyes flutter.*

CUT TO

ANNIE *and* BUSTER *heading back down the hallway toward Paul's room.*

ANNIE

To try and be his replacement—he gave so much pleasure to so many people and there's a shortage of pleasure on this planet these days, in case you hadn't noticed.

BUSTER *enters Paul's room.* ANNIE *follows.*

ANNIE

God told me, since I was his number-one fan, that I should make up new stories as if I was Paul Sheldon. So, I went to town. And I bought a type-writer. And paper to type on. The same kind Paul Sheldon used. And I turned the guest bedroom into a writing studio. Would you like to see it?

BUSTER

Sure.

ANNIE

It's right this way.

BUSTER *takes a look in the bathroom.* ANNIE *waits for him.*

ANNIE

It's right here. I knew how he wrote, the kinds of words he used, the wonderful stories he told—*(moved)*—I've spent the last four weeks trying to write like Paul Sheldon. *(sad shake of the head)* But I can't do it right. I try and I try and I know all the words—*(eyes closed in despair)*—but it's just not the same.

CUT TO

BUSTER. *He just stands there, watches her.*

BUSTER

Well...*(long pause)*...maybe it takes time to get the hang of it.

ANNIE
(holding up pages from the manuscript)
I could give you a couple of hundred pages of mine, and you could tell me what you think.

BUSTER
I'm not much of a critic.

ANNIE
Well, I just thought—oh, look at me. You'd think I'd never had a house-guest before. Would you like something to drink?

BUSTER
Sure.

ANNIE
How does a nice hot cup of cocoa sound?

BUSTER
Sounds good.

As she exits into the kitchen.

ANNIE
There's some already made.

BUSTER *lingers in Paul's room for a beat, then goes into the hallway.*

BUSTER
Must get lonely, living out here all by yourself.

ANNIE (off-screen)
I always say if you can't enjoy your own company, you're not fit company for anyone else.

BUSTER
You got a point there...

As Buster moves up the stairs—

CUT TO

PAUL, *still fighting the drug. His arm twitches almost involuntarily, grazing the barbe-cue.*

CUT TO

BUSTER *opening the door to Annie's room. He looks around and just as he is about to turn to leave—*

CUT TO

ANNIE, *standing right in front of him.*

> **ANNIE**
> Here you are.

BUSTER *heads down the stairs,* ANNIE *follows.*

> **BUSTER**
> Thanks, Miz Wilkes, but I don't want to take up any more of your time.
> I best be going.

> **ANNIE**
> But you didn't even taste your cocoa.

They cross to the front door.

> **BUSTER**
> I'm sure it's wonderful, but I really should be getting back.

BUSTER *opens the door.*

CUT TO

PAUL *stirring.*

CUT TO

BUSTER *and* ANNIE *at the door.*

> **BUSTER**
> If you don't mind, perhaps I could pay you another visit some time.

> **ANNIE**
> I'd be delighted. Now that you know the way...

With that, she closes the door. We stay with BUSTER. *He stands on the front porch for a beat, thinking, then starts heading down the porch steps. Just as he reaches about halfway down, we HEAR a LOUD CRASH coming from inside the house.*

CUT TO

PAUL—*he has managed to partially fight his way through the drug, and in waking has accidentally knocked over the barbecue. He fights to clear the cobwebs.*

CUT TO

> **BUSTER**
> Miz Wilkes, are you all right?

There is no answer. He quietly moves into the house.

BUSTER

Miz Wilkes?

Again, no answer.

CUT TO

PAUL, still fighting to gain complete consciousness.

PAUL
(weakly)

Here. I'm down here. Down here.

CUT TO

BUSTER. Hearing Paul's muffled call for help, he tracks the sound to the cellar door. As PAUL continues to call out, Buster looks around, sees no one, and opens the cellar door. The shaft of light from the open door pours down on Paul, who is still lying on the floor.

BUSTER

Mr. Sheldon?

But before Paul can answer, there's the sound of a LOUD EXPLOSION. *Seemingly from nowhere a hole is ripped through Buster's chest, knocking him out of frame, revealing Annie, smoking shotgun in hand, standing at the top of the cellar steps.*

ANNIE

Don't feel bad, Paul. It had to happen. I've been waiting for this sign.

ANNIE walks toward BUSTER'S BODY and very casually takes his gun out of its holster.

ANNIE

I've known for some time why I was chosen to save you. You and I were meant to be together forever. But now our time in this world must end. But don't worry, Paul. I've already prepared for what must be done. I put two bullets in my gun, one for you and one for me. Oh, darling, it will be so beautiful.

With that, ANNIE turns and exits the cellar.

Paul's mind races desperately. He looks at the barbecue again. Next to it is a messy table with a dozen jars and cans on it.

CUT TO

THE TABLE. *One of the cans is* LIGHTER FLUID.

CUT TO

PAUL. *He stares at it for a moment. An idea hits him—*

—now, PAUL *struggles and crawls over to the table. He grabs the lighter fluid in his hands, jams it into the rear of his pants and scrambles back to where* ANNIE *left him.*

CUT TO

ANNIE *returning with her .38 special and a hypodermic needle. She stops at the top of the stairs.*

> ANNIE
> Now don't be afraid. I love you. *(She starts towards him.)*

> PAUL
> I know you do. I love you too, Annie. *(This stops her.)* And you're right. We are meant to be together. And I know we must die. But it must be so that Misery can live. We have the power to give Misery eternal life. We must finish the book.

> ANNIE
> But the time is now. Soon others will come.

> PAUL
> It's almost done. By dawn we'll be able to give Misery back to the world.

ANNIE *stares at Paul. She could go either way on this. Then, without a word, she turns and goes back up the stairs.*

We stay with PAUL, *listening for sounds. Finally* ANNIE *returns with the* WHEELCHAIR. *She places it at the top of the stairs.*

> ANNIE
> Here, Paul. I'll fix you something to eat.

She exits. PAUL *hesitates for a moment, then realizes he has no choice. He starts dragging himself over* BUSTER *and up the stairs.*

CUT TO

PAUL'S ROOM. NIGHT.

PAUL *working. Typing like a madman, totally concentrated on the white paper. His lips move but he's not even aware of it.*

ANNIE *enters quietly, holding a few pages.*

ANNIE

Oh, Paul. It's beautiful.

PAUL

Three more chapters to go.

She looks at him now, enthralled.

ANNIE

The stranger staying at the Inn, is he someone from Misery's past?

PAUL

Maybe.

ANNIE

This is so exciting. It's Windthorne, her first love, right?

PAUL

Maybe. Are you ready for the next chapter?

He taunts her with it.

ANNIE
(brimming with enthusiasm)

Oh you!

She takes the pages and goes.

CUT TO

PAUL'S ROOM. LATER.

PAUL types a moment then rips out the page and starts over.

CUT TO

ANNIE, putting the coffee down for him, putting the pages back on the main pile.

ANNIE
(more excited now than the last time)

It WAS Windthorne. I knew it—what does that do to her love for Ian?—*(thinks)*—of course, if she hadn't thought Windthorne was murdered she never would have fallen in love with Ian in the first place. *(Paul glares at her, she turns to the door.)* Sorry, it's just that this is so wonderful.

PAUL

I'm glad you like it.

> ANNIE

Paul, this will be our legacy.

> PAUL

It will.

He hands her a few more pages, she starts reading as she exits.

CUT TO

PAUL'S ROOM. MUCH LATER.

PAUL rubs his eyes. For a moment, he sags, but he fights it. He puts a clean page into the typewriter.

ANNIE bursts in.

> ANNIE

Oh, Paul. I'm dying. Does she wind up with Ian or Windthorne? You have to tell me.

> PAUL

You'll know very soon. I'm starting the last chapter. And when I finish, I want everything to be perfect. I'll require three things.

> ANNIE

What things?

> PAUL

You don't know?

> ANNIE
> *(smiling)*

I was fooling, silly. *(ticking them off)* You need a cigarette, because you used to smoke but you quit except when you finish a book, and you just have one, and the match is to light it. And you need one glass of champagne. *(thinks)* Dome Pear-igg-non.

> PAUL

Dome Pear-igg-non it is.

As ANNIE exits.

CUT TO

THE WINDOW.

The first light of morning is starting to break through.

CUT TO

PAUL, *stretching. He makes sure everything is set.*

> **PAUL**
> *(calling out)*

Annie! Annie!

With that, she enters.

> **ANNIE**

Yes, Paul.

> **PAUL**

I'm almost done.

> **ANNIE**

Oh, Paul, this is so romantic. Ian and Windthorne dueling for the right to Misery's hand. Does Ian win? Oh, don't tell me. It's Windthorne, right?

> **PAUL**

You'll know everything in a minute. Get the champagne.

> **ANNIE**
> *(dying from the suspense)*

Ahh!!!

She exits; PAUL *adjusts the manuscript on the table and then types the last line.*

CUT TO

ANNIE IN THE KITCHEN. *She takes the bottle of Dom Perignon out of the icebox, places it on a tray with two glasses—opens a drawer—takes out the gun—places it in her pocket—then takes out the hypodermic needle and places it on the tray.*

CUT TO

PAUL'S ROOM.

ANNIE *enters with the tray. She sets it down on the table.*

> **ANNIE**

Did I do good?

> **PAUL**

You did perfect. Except for one thing. This time we need two glasses.

He takes the last page out of the typewriter.

                    ANNIE
    Oh, Paul.

As soon as she exits, PAUL drops the manuscript to the floor, pulls the lighter fluid from his pants, and starts dousing the manuscript with lighter fluid. He grabs the last chapter and twists the last few pages together torch style. He douses it with the fluid and holds the match out of sight.

He smiles as we

CUT TO

ANNIE entering with the second glass...

                    PAUL
    It's all right here, Annie. Remember how for all those years no one ever knew who Misery's real father was, or if they'd ever be reunited? It's all right here. Will Misery finally lead her countrymen to freedom? Does she finally marry Ian or will it be Windthorne? It's all right here.

CUT TO

THE MATCH, *as he strikes it and*

CUT TO

ANNIE screaming—

                    ANNIE
    Paul, you can't. *(and as her hands fly out beseechingly)*

CUT TO

THE CHAMPAGNE BOTTLE—*it falls to the floor, explodes like a torpedo, shards of glass all over, curds of foam everywhere—*

                    PAUL
    Why not? I learned it from you...*(and on that—)*

CUT TO

THE LAST CHAPTER *as Paul brings the match close to it and it bursts into flame. And Paul, holding it like the torch it is. Annie starts moving forward now.*

                    ANNIE
    No, no, NOT MISERY—NOT MY MISERY...!

He drops the last chapter into the soaked manuscript and

CUT TO

THE *MANUSCRIPT, as* KA BOOM!, *it bursts into flame and—*

CUT TO

ANNIE, *transfixed by the sight for a moment,*

—AND THEN SHE CHARGES.

CUT TO

THE FIRE *as* ANNIE *rushes to the book, stoops down, grabs it with both hands, brings the burning mass up to her body, both arms across it, trying to smother the flames—*

CUT TO

PAUL, *grabbing the typewriter, raising it high above his head, then throwing it down on her with all his power and*

CUT TO

THE TYPEWRITER, *crashing into the back of her head.*

CUT TO

ANNIE, *screaming, driven to the floor by the blow, the book beneath her, and the flames fly up, her sweater is starting to burn and she's covered with shards of glass from the shattered bottle of champagne and some of the manuscript is hissing from the liquid, but she is able to struggle to her knees—*

ANNIE

I'm going to kill you, you lying cock-sucker...

As she struggles to her feet, she pulls out the gun and shoots at Paul, hitting him in the shoulder. Just as she's about to shoot again, Paul quickly wheels the chair up to her, throws himself out of the chair, and tackles her. The gun flies out of her hand and lands in the hallway, going off as it lands. They wrestle on the floor.

Flames still around them, PAUL *gets on top of her, grabs some burning pages, stuffs them into her mouth, shouting—*

PAUL

Here. Here. You want it? You want it? You can eat it—eat it—eat it till you fucking CHOKE—you sick, twisted fuck.

And as he forces more paper into her mouth—

CUT TO

ANNIE, *and she's hideous—blistered, her hands claw at her throat. She makes horrible sounds, spitting the charred chunks of manuscript out of her mouth. Shards of glass are in her hair. Now a shriek and a tremendous jerk of her body and*

CUT TO

PAUL, *falling away—*

CUT TO

ANNIE, *still making the sounds as she gets to her feet, and*

CUT TO

PAUL, *trying to crawl away after her.*

CUT TO

ANNIE—*heading for the door, she takes a step away from Paul, then another, then*

CUT TO

PAUL, *suddenly kicking out with his shattered leg, screaming in pain as it crashes into her ankle and*

CUT TO

ANNIE, *trying to keep her balance, not doing well, her arms windmilling as she fights for balance one last moment, fights and loses, and now, as she topples over—*

CUT TO

THE TYPEWRITER *as she falls and her head slams into it, collides with the sharp metal and a great wound opens in her head. There is one final cry. Blood pours. It's over. All over. We are looking at a dead body.*

CUT TO

PAUL, *exhausted, panting, lying there, trying to gather his energy. He starts to crawl for the door. Just as he reaches the door jam, an arm grabs his leg, and*

CUT TO

PAUL, *shrieking, and*

CUT TO

ANNIE, *pulling herself up his body and*

CUT TO

PAUL, *trying to buck her off, but he can't and*

CUT TO

ANNIE, *the stronger, relentless, moving up on him, and*

CUT TO

PAUL, *his grip broken as he turns and*

CUT TO

ANNIE, *all-powerful, looming over him and*

CUT TO

PAUL, *hitting up at her and*

CUT TO

ANNIE, *swelling, and the blood pours down and if she feels his blows she doesn't show it and*

CUT TO

PAUL, *whatever energy he has left he uses now, trying to twist and strike and as his body moves—*

CUT TO

A METAL BASED FLOOR LAMP *and*

CUT TO

PAUL, *grabbing the thing, suddenly bringing it across his body, clobbering Annie in the face and*

CUT TO

ANNIE, *startled by the power of the blow and for a moment she is stopped and*

CUT TO

PAUL, *as with everything he has left, he crunches her forehead with the sharp heavy metal base, just creams her as the air is forced out of her—*

CUT TO

ANNIE. *Her eyes roll up into her head. For a moment all we see are the whites—*

—then she collapses on PAUL, *a motionless mountain of slack flesh.*

CUT TO

PAUL, *scrambling free, pushing her off him, crawling for the door—*

CUT TO

—*outside the door, as* PAUL *crawls into view, makes it to the corridor, reaches back, closes the door, locks it.*

Safe, he collapses, exhausted against the wall opposite the door.

DISSOLVE TO

PAUL. HOURS LATER. *It is dawn. He is awakened by a loud smashing at the front door. After a couple of heart-stopping pounds,*

CUT TO

THE FRONT DOOR *smashed open, revealing two cops with guns drawn.*

THE POLICEMEN, *hurrying to* PAUL. *The* YOUNGER COP *kneels beside Paul.*

> ### YOUNGER COP
> It's the writer—the dead one—

> ### PAUL
> *(trying to keep himself together)*
> —right! I'm the dead one—

> ### OLDER COP
> Where's Sheriff McCain?

> ### PAUL
> He's in the cellar. She killed him.

> ### OLDER COP
> Annie Wilkes?

> ### PAUL
> Yeah. She's in there.

CUT TO

The OLDER COP, *taking the key to the room, unlocks the door, throws it open, and as he steps inside—*

CUT TO

INSIDE THE BEDROOM.